Getting (more out of) Graphics

Data graphics are used extensively to present information. Understanding graphics is a lot about understanding the data represented by the graphics, having a feel not just for the numbers themselves, the reliability and uncertainty associated with them, but also for what they mean. This book presents a practical approach to data visualisation with real applications front and centre.

The first part of the book is a series of case studies, each describing a graphical analysis of a real dataset. The second part pulls together ideas from the case studies and provides an overview of the main factors affecting understanding graphics.

Key Features:

- Explains how to get insights from graphics.
- Emphasises the value of drawing many graphics.
- Underlines the importance for analysis of background knowledge and context.

Readers may be data scientists, statisticians or people who want to become more visually literate. A knowledge of Statistics is not required, just an interest in data graphics and some experience of working with data. It will help if the reader knows something of basic graphic forms such as barcharts, histograms, and scatterplots.

Antony Unwin was the first Professor of Computer-oriented Statistics and Data Analysis at the University of Augsburg in Germany. He is a fellow of the American Statistical Society, author of *Graphical Data Analysis with R*, co-author of *Graphics of Large Datasets*, and co-editor of the *Handbook of Data Visualization*.

CHAPMAN & HALL/CRC DATA SCIENCE SERIES

Reflecting the interdisciplinary nature of the field, this book series brings together researchers, practitioners, and instructors from statistics, computer science, machine learning, and analytics. The series will publish cutting-edge research, industry applications, and textbooks in data science.

The inclusion of concrete examples, applications, and methods is highly encouraged. The scope of the series includes titles in the areas of machine learning, pattern recognition, predictive analytics, business analytics, Big Data, visualization, programming, software, learning analytics, data wrangling, interactive graphics, and reproducible research.

Recently Published Titles

Data Science for Water Utilities
Data as a Source of Value
Peter Prevos

Practitioner's Guide to Data Science
Hui Lin and Ming Li

Natural Language Processing in the Real World
Text Processing, Analytics, and Classification
Jyotika Singh

Telling Stories with Data
With Applications in R
Rohan Alexander

Big Data Analytics
A Guide to Data Science Practitioners Making the Transition to Big Data
Ulrich Matter

Data Science for Sensory and Consumer Scientists
Thierry Worch, Julien Delarue, Vanessa Rios De Souza and John Ennis

Data Science in Practice
Tom Alby

Introduction to NFL Analytics with R
Bradley J. Congelio

Soccer Analytics
An Introduction Using R
Clive Beggs

Spatial Statistics for Data Science
Theory and Practice with R
Paula Moraga

Research Software Engineering
A Guide to the Open Source Ecosystem
Matthias Bannert

The Data Preparation Journey
Finding Your Way With R
Martin Hugh Monkman

Getting (more out of) Graphics
Practice and Principles of Data Visualisation
Antony Unwin

For more information about this series, please visit: https://www.routledge.com/Chapman--HallCRC-Data-Science-Series/book-series/CHDSS

Getting (more out of) Graphics
Practice and Principles of Data Visualisation

Antony Unwin

CRC Press
Taylor & Francis Group
Boca Raton London New York

CRC Press is an imprint of the
Taylor & Francis Group, an **informa** business

A CHAPMAN & HALL BOOK

Designed cover image: © Antony Unwin

First edition published 2024
by CRC Press
2385 NW Executive Center Drive, Suite 320, Boca Raton FL 33431

and by CRC Press
4 Park Square, Milton Park, Abingdon, Oxon, OX14 4RN

CRC Press is an imprint of Taylor & Francis Group, LLC

© 2024 Antony Unwin

Library of Congress Cataloging-in-Publication Data
Names: Unwin, Antony, author.
Title: Getting (more out of) graphics : practice and principles of data
visualisation / Antony Unwin.
Description: First edition. | Boca Raton, FL : CRC Press, 2024. | Series:
Chapman & Hall/CRC data science series | Includes bibliographical
references and index.
Identifiers: LCCN 2023056155 (print) | LCCN 2023056156 (ebook) | ISBN
9780367674007 (hbk) | ISBN 9780367673994 (pbk) | ISBN 9781003131212
(ebk)
Subjects: LCSH: Information visualization. | Visual analytics. | Data
mining--Graphic methods.
Classification: LCC QA76.9.I52 U589 2024 (print) | LCC QA76.9.I52 (ebook)
| DDC 001.4/226--dc23/eng/20240417
LC record available at https://lccn.loc.gov/2023056155
LC ebook record available at https://lccn.loc.gov/2023056156

ISBN: 978-0-367-67400-7 (hbk)
ISBN: 978-0-367-67399-4 (pbk)
ISBN: 978-1-003-13121-2 (ebk)

DOI: 10.1201/9781003131212

Typeset in Latin Modern font
by KnowledgeWorks Global Ltd.

Publisher's note: This book has been prepared from camera-ready copy provided by the authors.

Contents

Preface

Have no fear of perfection; you'll never reach it. — Marie Curie

Data graphics are used extensively to present information. They can also be used to uncover information. We need to 'get' graphics, to understand them and to learn from them. This will only work if the graphics are good in the first place. It is possible to learn from bad graphics, but it may be hard work and you may learn things that are unhelpful. This book concentrates on 'getting' good graphics.

Becoming familiar with graphics and how to get the most from them is one goal. The other is the design and drawing of good graphics. 'Getting' good graphics in the sense of producing good graphics and getting to good graphics is important. Principles that help in drawing good graphics are also a help in interpreting graphics.

Why not 'great' graphics? This is a practical book written with real applications in mind. Everyone may aspire to design and draw 'great' graphics, but it will be sufficient to draw good graphics and be satisfied with that. 'Great' graphics like Minard's display of Napoleon's Russian campaign of 1812 and more modern examples from sources such as the New York Times are excellent. It is not necessary to reach that standard every time to carry out valuable work.

Readers may be data scientists, statisticians, or people who want to become more visually literate. A knowledge of Statistics is not required, just an interest in data graphics and some experience of working with data. It will help if you know something of basic graphic forms such as barcharts, histograms, and scatterplots. It will also be a help if you have software you know well for drawing graphics. Trying ideas out is much more effective than just reading about them.

Understanding graphics is a lot about understanding the data represented by the graphics, having a feel not just for the numbers themselves, the reliability and uncertainty associated with them, but also for what they mean. Looking at graphics to learn from them involves looking into the data underlying the graphics and knowing the context.

The quality of reproduction of graphics has improved enormously. Better computer representations of graphics have changed what can be seen and done.

Drawing and redrawing have become simpler, faster, and more flexible. It is easy to draw lots of graphics, getting many different views of data. Graphics can be varied, adjusted, and rearranged quickly to best advantage. All this has to be taken more into consideration in discussing graphics.

There is a range of different software systems for drawing graphics and everyone has to decide for themselves which one(s) they want to use. Getting details right may be easy with one software and difficult with another. New software releases may provide new options and sometimes substantial improvements. How exactly the graphics are drawn is not important, what the graphics look like and whether they achieve the aims they are intended to is. This book is primarily about how to interpret graphics, not so much about how to draw them.

The graphics in this book have all been drawn with R. Other software could be used to draw the same or similar graphics; in some cases, it might be easier, in others harder. Use the software that suits you best.

There are many data displays in this book and a great deal can be learned from studying them. Even more can be learned by looking closely at the graphics around you—in newspapers and other publications, on the web, on television. Developing skills in graphics requires experience and that can only be gained through practice. Look at graphics and talk about what can be seen in them. Imagine trying to explain to someone who cannot see the graphic what information might be in it and why that is so. Consider ways of checking the information by other means, be it finding out more about the data, drawing other graphics, carrying out additional calculations, or collecting further data.

The book can be read from beginning to end—if you really want to. Hopefully, it is also a book you can open at any page and get something out of it. The case studies are intended to be self-contained and instructive in their own right.

Different graphics books emphasise different aspects of graphics. "Getting (more out of) Graphics" emphasises the importance of background knowledge and context in any application, the need to be concerned with the origins and quality of underlying data, the value of drawing many graphics, the necessity of checking any conclusions drawn (with more data, more graphics, statistics, and context), and the value of having statistical nous, a sense of how to interpret graphical features and numbers, especially in making comparisons. Visualisations can show more than words, as the book's title illustrates. The main message is 'Getting Graphics', while the secondary message is that more can be seen if we look more closely at the smaller details.

Acknowledgements

Thanks are due for help, discussion, and suggestions for improvement to Bill Venables, Nick Cox, Andreas Krause, Heike Hofmann, Isabel Meirelles, Peter Dirschedl, Christina Sanchez, Friedrich Pukelsheim, Pedro Valero, Sylvia Zimmer, Anatol Sargin, Matthias Reiss, Harry Unwin, Stephen Stigler, Kim Kleinman, Svetlana Komarova, Torsten Hothorn, Thomas Yee, Martijn Tennekes, Rob Hyndman, Roger Bivand, Tim Sands, Robert Erber, David Unwin, Simon Urbanek, and James Curley. Thanks also to the publisher's anonymous reviewers who made a number of constructive suggestions. It was a pleasure to work with Lara Spieker of CRC Press, who took over the book after John Kimmel retired. Both have been a great help. Last but not least, it is essential to thank the developers and maintainers of R and its packages, in particular Hadley Wickham and Yihui Xie. All of these people contributed positively to the book in one way or another in one place or another at one time or another. Any remaining flaws and errors are mine and mine alone.

1

Introduction

It is better to be looked over than overlooked. — Mae West

Graphics are important: they influence people's opinions and they are memorable. Where do people learn how to interpret and draw graphics? There are many books, there is a lot on the web, and there are many examples in the media. Unlike most of the books on graphics, this one is about interpreting graphics rather than about drawing them. It is also more about exploratory graphics than presentation graphics.

Presentation graphics, those in published material, in reports, and, of course, in presentations, are for conveying known information, attracting, impressing, and influencing viewers. A single presentation graphic, particularly if it appears on television, may be seen by millions of viewers. These graphics should be carefully designed and reproduced and should convey their message clearly and crisply. Viewers expect to see something immediately in a presentation graphic.

Exploratory graphics are drawn to support investigations, find out information, and gain understanding. They require work, time, and effort, to ensure the information in them is uncovered. They may only be seen by one person or by a small group of people. Exploratory graphics are rarely published. Books, articles, reports, and software emphasise single presentation graphics. Very many exploratory graphics may be drawn to explore data and find out what information is there. There is strength in numbers of exploratory graphics.

Whereas presentation graphics may be closed, designed around one message (or a limited set of messages), exploratory graphics should be open and flexible, helping to identify details that may or may not be important. These could be minor features hinting at some local irregularities or issues of data quality, or they could be evidence of something substantial. Presentation graphics should smooth over unimportant variation and not distract with irrelevant details. Exploratory graphics should, at least initially, bring details to light, suggesting possible ideas to check. And checking is the key word. Ideas are generated by exploratory work, but many will be discarded after thorough checking. Perhaps the lack of a theory of graphics, the effort involved in examining graphics, and the feeling that graphics are a matter of common sense have all led to emphasising presentation graphics over exploratory graphics. Graphics are not just common sense: there is much more to them than that—even if we could agree on what common sense might be.

The approach taken in this work is to start with graphics in action, case studies illustrating what features can be seen and what they might imply. The data used are neither raw nor fully cleaned. Even after some correcting, their likely quality has to be kept in mind. Many graphics are drawn to investigate various aspects of the data and to understand them in context. Each single graphic is part of a larger analysis. There are no explicit exercises, but there is plenty to check and try for yourself, and there are many open questions.

The second part of the book discusses the principles underlying graphical analysis. A central theme is that it is too optimistic to think there might be a single 'optimal' display. It is better to look for a collection of displays that together reveal what information there is in the data. This book recommends considering many displays and many different displays, both variations of plots and distinct alternatives. Additional viewpoints provide additional insights. Nowadays, it is easy to draw informative graphics quickly and to vary them flexibly. Powerful modern software supports the exploration of multiple graphics. There is no need to be restricted to a single, mythical, 'optimal' graphic.

The emphasis is on using several graphics displays together and is more on general principles than on specific graphics. It is not about new graphic forms, more about making the best use of known forms. It is about what features can be seen in graphics and how they might be interpreted, not so much about how to draw the graphics, more about what can be got out of them. A major principle is that any interpretations have to be checked, assessed, and evaluated. This is unlike p-hacking or data dredging. There is no stopping when possible results are found—all must be carefully examined and reviewed. There are many ways of checking ideas arising out of graphical analyses and all should be pursued (cf. §32.3). Jumping to conclusions is ill-advised, cautious scepticism is better.

The case studies use larger datasets than are commonly found in books on graphics, larger in terms of numbers of observations and numbers of variables. Consequently, analysis includes more data wrangling, cleaning, and reorganising data. It is misleading to talk of single datasets, as most analyses involve more than one. Sometimes several subsets or transformations of original datasets are analysed, and sometimes associated data are added, enlarging the original dataset. The datasets are all real, not invented or simulated but based on data collected in practice.

The case studies cover a range of topics and have been chosen to hopefully ensure that there is something of interest for everyone. There are two on politics (Chapters 4 and 26), several on sports (Chapters 6, 8, 15, 16, 20, and 21), three on birds (Chapters 14, 18, and 23), two on cars (Chapters 13 and 17), and there are others, including ones on facial recognition (Chapter 22), demographics (Chapter 2), and the movies (Chapter 3).

(Almost) all the datasets can be readily found in R, one of its packages or on the web, another reason for selecting them. Some of the datasets are made available in the R package **GmooG** that accompanies the book. Anyone interested in trying out the ideas discussed here for themselves or in experimenting with alternative graphics is encouraged to do so. Reading advice may be helpful, trying to apply it is definitely helpful.

1.1   What are good graphics?

Whether someone thinks a graphic is good or not is usually a matter of taste. It is easier to agree on graphics that are not good, even if people may disagree about why they are not good. Good graphics convey information clearly in a structured way.

Sometimes it is fairly obvious that a graphic could be improved: the display might be too small or too large, too thin or too broad; the labelling might be inadequate, confusing, or overdone; the colours might be garish or indistinct; lines might be too thin or too thick; another type of graphic might display the information more effectively. The intention behind the graphic may be sensible, but the implementation may be weak.

Misleading graphics are a much more serious problem, and these are the ones that are really not good. They distract from information in the data or hide information, inhibit relevant comparisons, and direct attention to unimportant features. So it is more a matter of how and why than good and bad. You can see why a good graphic has been drawn because of the way it has been drawn.

Several criteria have been suggested for assessing the quality of graphics including accuracy in reading off numbers, clarity of message, speed in recognising information, engagement, and memorability. None are ideal and most are not relevant to exploratory graphics. A good exploratory graphic is one from which much information can be derived relatively easily, and in which features and patterns can be readily recognised and informatively interpreted in the context of the dataset. Many studies have been carried out evaluating how well viewers can assess numerical values from graphics. Graphics are not good for this; they are better for revealing and displaying information. It is the conclusions that can be drawn, not the numbers that matter. Exploratory graphics should be evaluated as to what information they provide and how well they do it. Much depends on the knowledge and experience of the analysts.

Assessing graphics, particularly complicated ones or collections of them, is not easy. Hoare's remark on software design could be adapted for graphics: "I conclude that there are two ways of constructing a software design: One way is to make it so simple that there are obviously no deficiencies, and the other way is make it so complicated that there are no obvious deficiencies." (Hoare (1981))

1.2 Graphics examples

It is easy to find examples of bad graphics. Some graphics texts and courses use bad graphics as examples to illustrate what you should not do—before explaining what you should do. This is not a common approach to teaching and will not be followed here. Musicians learn by listening to the best, artists learn by examining famous works, and footballers study how well the game can be played, not how badly. Not everyone will think all the graphics in this book are good, but there are none that have been selected because they are especially bad.

The graphics are primarily intended for data exploration and have been drawn accordingly, somewhat better than default graphics and not as polished as presentation graphics. If they were designed for presentation, then fuller captions could be helpful, some labels could be made more user-friendly (although they all should be legible and understandable), and additional formatting could be improved, especially the colour choices. Some formatting details require much more effort than others, especially when smaller versions of originally larger graphics are used to refer to earlier examples, as in the second half of the book. Graphics in this book should not be judged individually in isolation but as part of a larger analysis. Accompanying text and associated graphics contribute to the overall picture. To study features in graphics, it is useful not to be distracted by too much text and annotation. It can be like watching films with subtitles: so much effort may be directed to reading the subtitles that you do not see much of the film.

1.3   Writing about graphics

Graphics need explanation. The data they are based on and their background must be described and explained. It is essential to know where the data come from, why they were collected, and how they were collected. The more knowledge a viewer has of what the data represent, the easier it is for them to see what the graphics drawn from them show (cf. Chapter 27).

Viewers of graphics need to know what the aims were in drawing them, and they should get guidance on what can be seen in the graphics. They have to check for themselves that any conclusions make sense in terms of both the context and the data. Checking information derived from graphics is a crucial part of working with graphics and should be discussed a lot more (cf. §32.3).

Outlining how a graphic has been drawn—the variables selected, the graphic form chosen, the format specified, the overall layout design—provides additional insights. These details describe the process taken to achieve the aims, offering supporting clarification.

1.4   Reading about graphics

1.4.1   Books and articles on data graphics

There are many good sources on how to draw graphics and what principles and guidelines should be followed. Despite the plethora of good advice available, it is not always taken, judging by the graphics that are published. More relevantly for this book, there is far less advice on how to interpret graphics. It is often surprising to find graphics that have been beautifully drawn with a great deal of effort that are then barely discussed at all. When looking at graphics in a book or on a website, check whether there is text accompanying them that explains what information the authors believe their graphics convey.

Classics of graphics literature include books by Tufte (Tufte (1990), Tufte (1997), Tufte (2001)) and Cleveland (Cleveland (1993), Cleveland (1994)). Going back further, some of Playfair's work has been republished (Playfair (2005)), and Minard's work across the later part of the nineteenth century has been gathered together attractively in Rendgen (2019). There is a useful overview of the history of graphics in Friendly (2008), and this is covered in more detail in his book with Wainer (Friendly and Wainer (2021)). The book

"Design for Information" (Meirelles (2013)) includes many fine historical and modern graphics in a structured approach to visualisation for design students.

Graphics advice has always tended to be just advice without theory. Two important exceptions are Bertin (1973), an English translation is available, Bertin (2010), and Wilkinson (2005). Wilkinson's work has proved especially influential through Wickham's implementation in the R package **ggplot2**, described in Wickham (2016) and Wickham (2023) and on the web. Unwin (2015) concentrated on applications of this implementation and the graphical theory behind it using real datasets.

The graphics in this book are part of what is nowadays referred to as Data Visualisation, and are only a part of the wider field of visualisation. There is much work in Scientific Visualisation and Information Visualisation that overlaps with what is covered here. The Computer Science approach to visualisation is discussed well in Munzner (2014), and there is an extensive technical literature that is too broad to discuss here. Cairo has written popular books, deriving from his journalistic experience (Cairo (2012), Cairo (2016), Cairo (2019)), and these include some attractive examples.

Kirk's book (Kirk (2016)) offers a range of different graphics and concentrates on project flow more than traditional books do, discussing design, development, and cooperating with clients. Wilke's book (Wilke (2019)) is more about graphics for scientific reports and publications, looking at graphics from a practitioner's point of view. He recommends that every graphic has a title, good advice for presentation graphics, not so relevant for exploratory graphics where the message is not yet known. Healy's well-written book (Healy (2018)) includes some real applications, and also some invented ones. None of these books include much on what can be seen in their graphics, yet the authors have a lot of experience and there is doubtless more they could have written. Assuming readers see what you can see may flatter them, but does not assist them. "How Charts Work" (Smith (2022)) is on working with data graphics to present your ideas, mainly using examples from the Financial Times where Smith works. Chang's book (Chang (2018)) goes into the details of drawing graphics in R and has excellent complementary web pages. Murrell's book (Murrell (2018)) provides a clear overview of the technical structure underlying R graphics. Another approach to writing about graphics using R is provided by Rahlf (2017). The book is built around 111 examples of publication-worthy graphics and in each case the R code needed to draw the graphic is provided. As little advantage is taken of packages for R, the code is often lengthy, but it demonstrates how even the most elaborate (and often attractive) plot designs can be reproduced using base R. Again there is little discussion of what each graphic shows.

Much interesting and attractive work has been carried out on producing special individual graphics developed using sketching. Two prime examples of books describing this process are Posavec and Lupi (2016) and Bremer and Wu (2021). Both present striking and attention-grabbing graphics.

Kandogan and Lee (2016) describes research associated with designing automatic visualisation systems and claims that the authors found around 550 guidelines in their literature review. In a related vein, Wood, Kachkaev, and Dykes (2018) introduces literate visualisation, a scheme for integrating the process of writing data visualisation code with a description of the design choices that led to the implementation. The authors have developed a literate visualisation software environment, **litvis**, for carrying this out.

It is impossible to cover all the literature, but it would be a pity to omit mention of some of the more unconventional contributions. "Tidying Up Art" (Wehrli (2004)) demonstrates a novel way of deconstructing complex works of art into summarising statistical forms. The book "Info We Trust" (Andrews (2019)) discusses ideas about information and graphics in an amiable and personal way, using the author's own drawings.

Statistics textbooks have traditionally had a chapter on graphics, usually just describing which common graphics are available rather than explaining anything more substantial. Yet data graphics complement statistical analyses and statistical models are one of the ways that can be used to assess results found from graphics. There are some excellent books on statistics. If you need more detail on a statistical topic, look for it in one of the books you personally like.

1.4.2   Websites and other media

There are numerous websites discussing data visualisation, some more active than others, and several of the books mentioned have supporting websites. For a number of years, Kirk's website (Kirk (2023)) included monthly digests of what he considered the best of data visualisation on the web. The old selections are still worth a look.

Most printed news media, indeed all kinds of organisations, offer graphical content on the web. They provide many excellent examples—along with some not-so-excellent ones—and they are a valuable source of material for studying graphics.

1.5   Software

The R code for the book can be found in the gitbook version on the web. You will need to have some knowledge and experience of working with R (R Core Team (2023)) and the group of R packages known as the tidyverse (Wickham (2019)). Some users prefer base R for drawing their graphics and may use packages such as **lattice** and **vcd**.

There are too many books and resources on R to do justice to them here. R is a language, not a collection of software commands, and using R is like using any language: there are many alternative ways of carrying out the same tasks, and some may be better than others. There is no claim that the R code accompanying the book is to be recommended, but it may be helpful.

Software alternatives for drawing graphics include using languages like Python, statistical software such as SPSS, SAS, or Stata, business graphics software such as Tableau or Microsoft Power BI, popular workhorse software like Excel, and sophisticated graphics software like Adobe Illustrator: the list just goes on and on.

1.6   Structure of the book

There is an old adage: "In theory it works in practice, in practice it doesn't". It might also be said that there is theoretical clarity and practical ambiguity. The applications in case studies come first in the book and the theory in the form of general advice arising from the case studies follows. The case studies can be read in any order, depending on what topics and graphics attract and interest. The second part pulls together ideas from the first part and offers an overview of the main factors affecting understanding graphics. If only the advice is of interest, just stick to the second part. (Ideally that will send readers back to the examples in the first part.) There are also brief summaries at the end of each chapter, listing some of the points made. The graphics are important and need as much attention or more as the text. Switching between studying graphics and reading text disrupts a smooth reading flow but is worth the effort. This is a book that can be flicked through and dipped into.

The terms graphic, plot, and display all refer to graphic displays of data. Figure, chart, and graph also arise. Sometimes one seems to fit better than another, and there is no intention to suggest different meanings. The vocabulary of graphics is like the theory of graphics, flexible rather than rigid. This is also why much of the book's advice is expressed in cautionary fashion. Words like 'may', 'might', 'could', 'possibly', 'sometimes' qualify what is said. Readers who are looking for clear-cut, straightforward rules may (!) be surprised. Exploring graphics in practice should convince them of the value of an open approach.

The layout of individual pages of the book has been strongly influenced by the need to ensure that the discussion of a graphic is always on the same or facing page as the graphic itself. This required minor adjustments to the size of graphics, to the text, and to the order of text and graphics. Some sections have been expanded a little and some cut back a bit. A few pages are shorter than others, where it was thought better to leave space.

1.6.1   Part I Graphics in Action

Graphics are an integral part of all of Data Analysis: they are not just for presenting results. Looking at individual graphics on their own is like testing your eyesight by identifying individual letters or testing your hearing by recognising individual words. It is valuable for assessing your knowledge of the graphics, but not the same as looking at them as a group in context. Your mind can work out what words you are seeing without identifying each letter and can work out the meaning of what is being said to you without hearing every word clearly. The same holds for groups of related graphics. It is like having a conversation with the data.

Graphics are part of data exploration and of the quality control of data. Reporting a case study ignoring these important activities would be misleading, while reporting false trails and repeated analyses would be confusing and irritating. So the reporting of case studies here tries to follow a middle path. If the order seems surprising, such as only correcting some bad data late on, this is because sometimes this is the way analyses proceed. With large datasets new data problems may continually emerge. Not every variable is checked initially, they are investigated as they are needed. New details become apparent, sometimes relevant, sometimes not. Details can enlighten and enliven, shedding new light and awakening interest. Documenting case studies as if they consisted of steady progress from beginning to end, culminating in impressive conclusions, would be unrealistic. Case studies are not like mathematical proofs. Most of the case studies suggest further work and not all have as substantial conclusions as might have been hoped for initially.

1.6.2   Part II Advice on Graphics

The chapters in this part cover general topics on graphics taking examples from the case studies to demonstrate the ideas. The illustrations are sometimes smaller versions of the graphics used in the case studies to make a particular point. They are cross-referenced so that it is easy to check the original versions. There are chapters on provenance and quality (investigating the sources of data and what has been done with the data); wrangling (cleaning, organising, and restructuring data); colour; setting the scene (layout and formatting); ordering, sorting, and arranging; interpretation (paying attention, understanding, checking); varieties of plots and developing plots. This part could be read first to see what factors the book regards as important and to get a summary of the book's advice, but readers would miss out on getting the experience of graphics in action.

In a nutshell (tl;dr)

For readers who have had enough already, here is the short summary.

- Get insights from looking into graphics
- Draw many graphics
- Look for patterns and interpretations
- Vary all graphics in all sorts of ways
- Know the context and the data
- Check, check, check

Part I

Graphics in Action

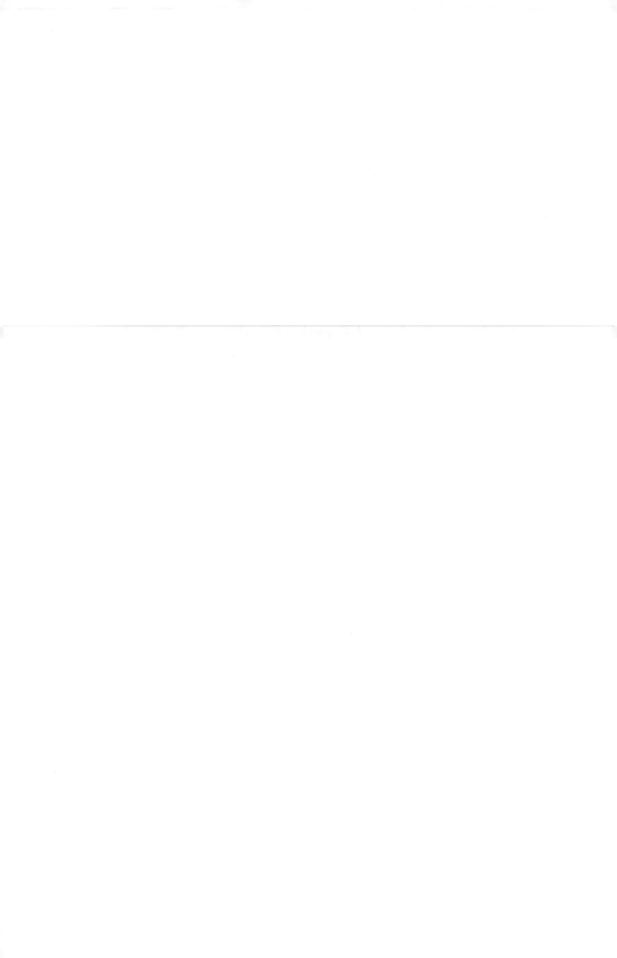

2

Graphics and Gapminder

The world cannot be understood without numbers. But the world cannot be understood with numbers alone.

— Hans Rosling

Background Hans Rosling and his Gapminder team have done excellent work in collecting and presenting data on developments in world health, country by country, over many years.

Questions How has life expectancy changed over time? How do the patterns differ by countries? How good are the data?

Sources Gapminder website (Rosling (2013))

Structure Life expectancy estimates for 187 countries from 1800 to 2016. There are also forecasts up to 2100 giving 301 data points per country in all.

2.1   Gapminder and Hans Rosling

The Gapminder Foundation that Hans Rosling and colleagues set up continues to collect and monitor global patterns of health. Anyone who has seen a film of one of Rosling's talks (Rosling (2009)), or was lucky enough to attend one, will remember his scatterplots animated over time. One he used was of life expectancy at birth plotted against fertility rate. The main patterns he described are clear and informative, emphasising the overall increases in life expectancy across all countries. If life expectancy is examined over time on its own, there are additional features that Rosling did not have time to discuss, including some dramatic sharp drops and rises.

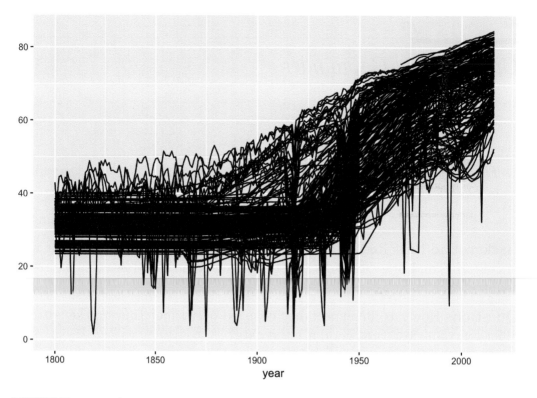

FIGURE 2.1: Life expectancy at birth in years for 187 countries over the years 1800 to 2016

The life expectancy data for each country has been plotted against time in Figure 2.1. This is a default plot and could be improved in many ways. Nevertheless much can be seen in it. Two striking features were not mentioned in Rosling's talks: the sharp falls and rises just mentioned, and the unchanging levels (horizontal lines) during the nineteenth century. Figure 2.2 picks out these two features.

The plot above picks out some of the falls and rises. For certain countries in certain years it is well known that there were population disasters: the famine in Ukraine in 1932-33 and the Irish potato famine in the second half of the 1840s. The Gapminder researchers endeavoured to estimate data for these and other catastrophic years using modelling techniques described in a paper published on their website (Lindgren (2014)). It is impressive that they went to so much trouble to deal with this issue, although, as they write themselves, they can only provide guesstimates. It is important that they draw attention to catastrophes, it would be wrong to simply ignore them. Europeans readers may have heard of the Ukrainian famine in 1932-33 and the Irish famine in the late 1840s, but few will know of the plague in Tunisia in 1891 or of the measles epidemic in Fiji in 1875.

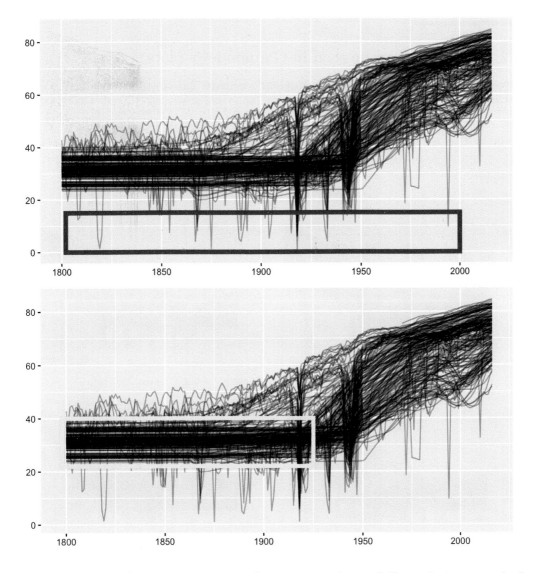

FIGURE 2.2: Life expectancy graphics: some sharp falls and rises marked (above), straight lines marked (below)

The straight lines highlighted in the lower plot imply that life expectancies for many countries were constant over the period. That is highly unlikely! What has happened is that a single value was estimated to cover many years, where no other information was available. Although Rosling did not talk about this, the information is available in the Gapminder display under a button labelled "Data Doubts" at the foot of the plot to the right.

2.2   What else can be seen in Gapminder's plots?

Several further features can be noticed. Figure 2.3 highlights them. Which countries had higher life expectancy in the 19th century (upper left)? Which countries had the most dramatic falls most recently (upper right)? Which country had consistently lower levels in the first half of the 20th century (lower left)? Which country's data began or continued after a gap around 1970 (lower right)?

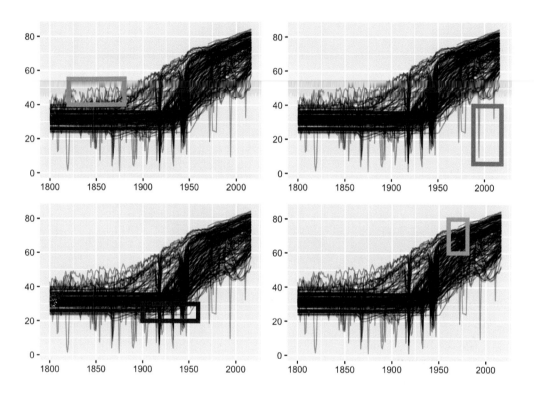

FIGURE 2.3: Further features in the life expectancy graphic

Countries with highest values in the nineteenth century can be found by looking at the maximum values by year. Norway had the highest value for 68 of the hundred years and Sweden came second with the highest value for 11 years. Norway and Sweden were in a political union for most of the nineteenth century, but they kept their own institutions and presumably reported their own statistics. At the very beginning of the century Norway was in a union with Denmark. Figure 2.4 shows the life expectancy time series of the three countries and they are very similar. The only noticeable differences are that Denmark was less affected by Spanish Flu at the end of World War I and consistently reported slightly lower levels more recently.

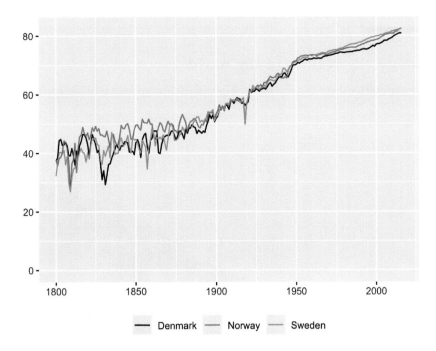

FIGURE 2.4: Life expectancy for Denmark, Norway, and Sweden

The two countries with recent serious falls (the upper right graphic in Figure 2.3) were Rwanda in 1994 (the civil war) and Haiti in 2010 (an earthquake). They can be identified by selecting countries with life expectancies less than 40 after 1990.

The country with lower levels of life expectancy in the first half of the 20th century (the lower left graphic in Figure 2.3) can be found by looking at the data for 1950, when it had the lowest value of all countries, just before it started to improve. This was Yemen, a country whose recent history of civil war will have made conditions worse again.

The country whose data appear to begin around 1970 (the lower right plot in Figure 2.3) can be found from having the highest life expectancy in 1975. This was Andorra, one of three small countries with values reported only from 1970 on that were excluded from further analyses in this chapter. Another ten small countries with little data, e.g., the Holy See (Vatican City State), were excluded as well.

Not all features are equally important and individual ones may be of more interest to some people than to others. There is much to be seen in graphics and looking closely will prove rewarding.

2.3   Analysis by regions of the world

Colouring countries by Gapminder's classification of the world into four regions gives Figure 2.5.

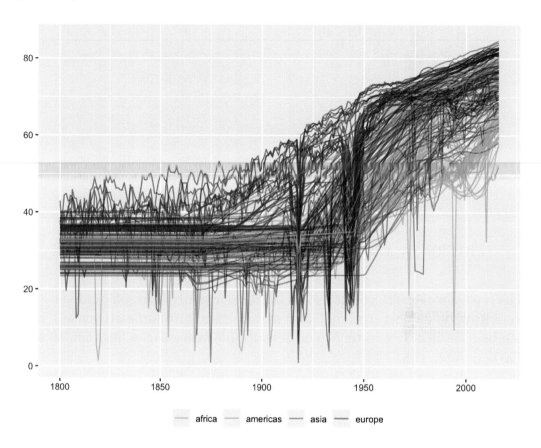

FIGURE 2.5: Life expectancy time series coloured by the four regions classification

European countries have had the highest life expectancies over the last two hundred years and African countries have had most of the lowest in recent years. There were two sharp falls for European countries in the first half of the 20th century. The first was due to a combination of World War I and the Spanish flu, while the second was due to World War II.

It is difficult to see much more and any colour scheme would have problems with overplotting. A better approach with so many series is to use faceting, splitting the data into subsets and plotting them in a grid. Figure 2.6 shows the same series by each region separately.

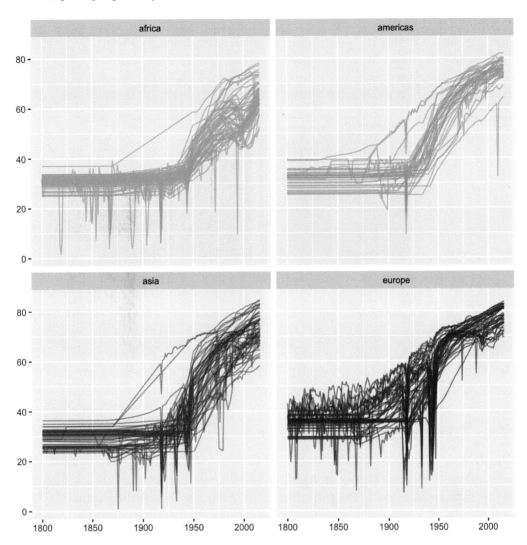

FIGURE 2.6: Life expectancy time series drawn separately for the four regions classification

Features now stand out that were not visible before. A few countries in all three regions other than Europe had much higher life expectancies between 1880 and 1950 than most countries in their regions. There is a country in Europe that had lower values from 1950 to 1990 than other European countries.

Finding the countries with the top values in each of the three other regions in 1900 picks out Australia and New Zealand in Asia (so it is not surprising that they have very different patterns), Seychelles in Africa, and, again unsurprisingly, the USA and Canada in the Americas. The European country with lowest values for many years after 1950 was Turkey.

It would be useful to know how big and comparable the regions are. The numbers of countries in each region in 2016 are shown in Figure 2.7.

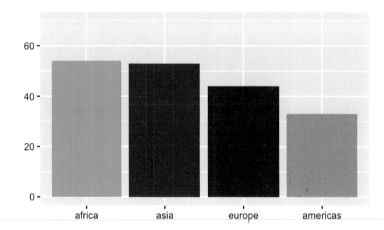

FIGURE 2.7: Numbers of countries in each of the four regions, ordered by the numbers

The numbers are not too far apart, but population data would provide more information on size. This is covered next.

2.3.1   Taking account of country size

Population data are also available from the Gapminder website and these have been downloaded and merged with the life expectancy data. The sizes of the four regions by total population in 2016 are shown in Figure 2.8. The regions are ordered by population. This paints a different picture. Asia had more population in 2016 than the other three regions combined.

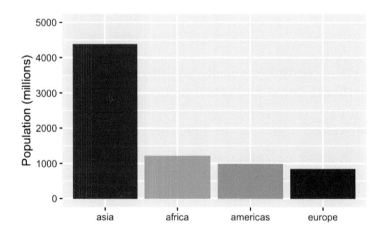

FIGURE 2.8: Total populations for each of the four regions

Up till now the time series graphics in this chapter have treated each country displayed equally. Gapminder itself (Rosling (2013)) makes much use of bubble charts to additionally show the sizes of countries in its scatterplots. That would not work well for time series, which is why Gapminder uses animation. Two other approaches are possible. Countries could be selected by population size or the data could be aggregated across regions using population data by year as weights.

The first approach is shown in Figure 2.9. Life expectancies for the six countries with a population of over 200 million in 2016 are shown.

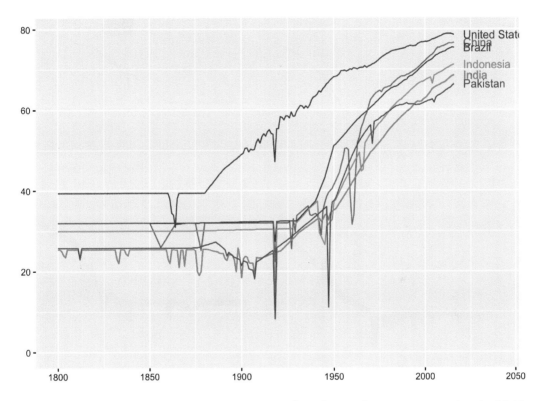

FIGURE 2.9: Life expectancy time series for the six biggest countries in 2016

As with earlier graphics, the overall trend of rising life expectancies can be seen, mainly during the second half of the 20th century, and the effects of wars and other disasters on individual countries. These would be more visible if each series was drawn separately. That has the further advantage of being able to use the width of the line to represent the population in 2016 (Figure 2.10).

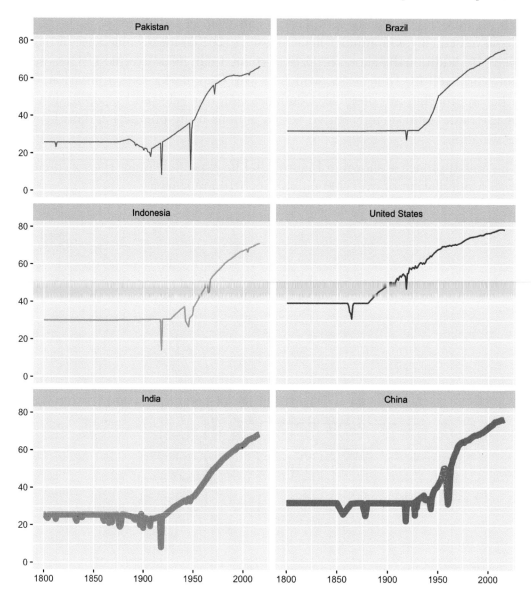

FIGURE 2.10: Life expectancies for the six biggest countries with line widths scaled by their 2016 populations

There is a disadvantage in incorporating population size. China and India are so much bigger that the finer details of their series are lost, although six major falls in Chinese life expectancy stand out. All six countries suffered from the Spanish flu in 1918, Brazil least of all. Pakistan suffered dramatically in 1947 after they gained independence from Britain. Their border conflict with India after partition had a much greater relative effect on them than on India.

These six countries actually accounted for 50.2% of the total world population in 2016. It is interesting to see how that changed over time, cf. Figure 2.11.

If the nineteenth century population figures for China are to be believed, if indeed any of the population figures from that period are to be believed, China used to be relatively far bigger!

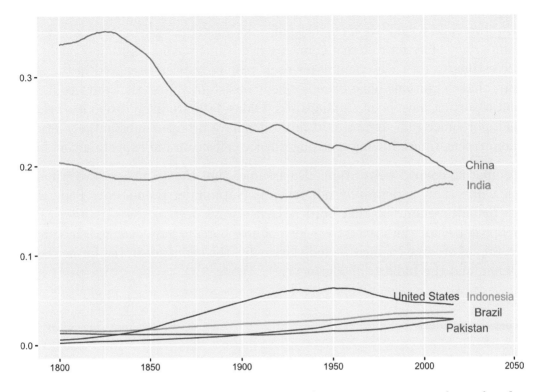

FIGURE 2.11: Proportion of the world population over time made up by the six biggest countries in 2016

2.4   Checking what is in the data

The life expectancy at birth data are provided by Gapminder for 187 countries for the years 1810 to 2016. UN forecasts for the years 2017 to 2100 are also included. Gapminder offers a separate file of countries by regions with groupings into 4, 6 or 8 regions. Merging the two files reveals that there are 11 countries in the region file with no corresponding life expectancy data. 10 of these are small areas (including the Holy See and Tuvalu) and one is Macedonia FYR. It turned out this is called North Macedonia in the life expectancy file and the name North Macedonia has been used. Checking for completeness of the data showed that three further small countries (Andorra, Dominica, Marshall Islands) had some life expectancy data, but not for the years 1800 to 1969 and they were excluded from most of the plots.

2.5   The importance of data definitions

Gapminder defines life expectancy at birth as the average number of years a newborn child would live if current mortality patterns were to stay the same. In comparing values for different countries over time, the assumption is made that the estimates for each country for each year have been prepared in the same way, that definitions have been applied consistently, and that data collection and reporting have been standardised. Older data are likely to be less reliable and more uncertain. Infant mortality rates have dropped substantially, even in more recent times, having a strong positive effect on life expectancy at birth.

Comparing countries over time also assumes that the countries have remained the same. This is definitely not true, as Gapminder points out. They make the default assumption that borders have always been as they are now. (Their webpage includes an instructive video of how borders have changed since 1800.) Examples of large changes include Germany, the countries in the former Soviet Union, and the Indian subcontinent.

2.6   Discussion

Gapminder offers a lot more data than has been studied here. Graphics help bring the information out and help present it to others. The time series plots in this chapter have analysed just one variable, life expectancy at birth. If scatterplots are drawn, as Hans Rosling often did, and all the options available in the Gapminder software are used, two or more variables can be displayed. Analyses can quickly get very complicated, which just shows that graphics can be more difficult to work with than might be expected.

In a study reported by Tonnessen (2020), eighteen-year old schoolchildren were observed using Gapminder to carry out tasks set by their teacher. The researcher noticed several difficulties the participants faced, mostly because they did not have enough knowledge and experience of the software or with that kind of graphical display. The assumption that graphics are easy to understand is an easy, if mistaken, one to make.

Answers Life expectancy has improved dramatically, with some interruptions, over the last one hundred years, particularly for Western nations. Other countries have caught up a lot, but still lag behind. Data for the 19th century is incomplete and suspiciously constant.

Further questions Life expectancy is one of hundreds of indicators available from Gapminder, covering not only health, but education, environment and many other areas. There is an unlimited number of investigations that could be carried out.

Graphical takeaways

- One graphic is not enough. Different versions of the same graphic provide more information. (Figures 2.1 and 2.6)
- Graphics show information directly that analytic methods cannot find. (Figures 2.2 and 2.3)
- Faceting picks out differences within groups. (Figure 2.6)
- Unpolished graphics can still reveal important information. (Figure 2.1)

3

Looking at the movies

The stuff that dreams are made of

> — Humphrey Bogart as Sam Spade, in 'The Maltese Falcon'

Background The Internet Movie Database (IMDb) collects information on a huge number of films and TV shows including ratings provided by users.

Questions How long are film runtimes? What ratings do films get? How many users rate them? How have the numbers of films of different genres developed?

Sources IMDb website (IMDb (2022))

Structure
Two datasets were merged. One contained basic information on each film or show and the other supplied average user ratings and the numbers of ratings.

3.1   Trailer

Many people use IMDb ratings to help them decide what they would like to watch. The ratings are contributed by users of the site. This chapter studies the data on films for which ratings are available. There is a dataset of 58,788 films scraped from IMDb several years ago that is available in the R package **ggplot2movies**. Nowadays, IMDb makes regularly updated datasets available for download from their website. The one used here was downloaded in July 2022. There were 9,033,256 items and 1,251,317 had user ratings or votes. Excluding items labelled TV or video and restricting the data to movies and shorts that had more than 100 ratings left 124,667 films.

FIGURE 3.1: Movie runtimes in weeks

The film runtimes are shown in Figure 3.1 in a boxplot—or rather a few outliers are visible. The film lasting over 5 weeks (over 50,000 minutes), is called "Logistics" and records in reverse the journey of a pedometer from its production in China to its sale in Sweden. To look at runtimes in more detail, the 682 films longer than 3 hours were excluded. Figure 3.2 shows a histogram drawn with a binwidth of 1 minute, the level of resolution of the data.

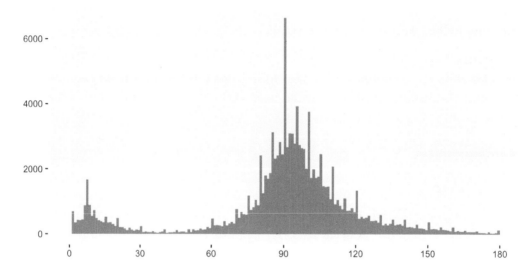

FIGURE 3.2: Distribution of movie runtimes in minutes for films of 3 hours or under

Many films are recorded as having runtimes of 90 minutes and others runtimes of values of multiples of 10 or, to a lesser extent, 5, a form of data heaping. The most common runtime for short films is 7 minutes. IMDb provides information on technical specifications of the various releases of films. The famous Japanese film "The Seven Samurai" is reported as having eight different runtimes ranging from 150 minutes to 207 minutes. The highest value was the one supplied in the dataset.

3.2 Movies in IMDb over the years

Figure 3.3 looks at whether movie runtimes changed over time. Alpha transparency has been used to reduce the effect of overplotting and to show where there is a lot of data.

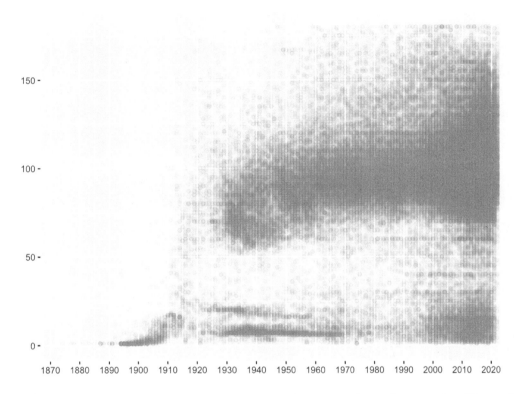

FIGURE 3.3: Movie runtimes in minutes by year of production for films of 3 hours or under using alpha = 0.05

Early movies were short and later on there was a mixture of films and shorts. The distribution of runtimes each year and the number of films each year are only hinted at in this scatterplot. The following graphics use boxplots and a histogram to provide more informative views.

Figure 3.4 displays boxplots by year with a histogram of the number of movies in each year below. The runtime distribution has been fairly constant for over 50 years. The slight rise recently may reflect incomplete recording, as the lower plot shows fewer films produced in the latest three years included overall. This is obvious for 2022, for which only the first six months could be covered. The numbers for 2020 and 2021 suggest that it may take time for all films for a year to be added to the database.

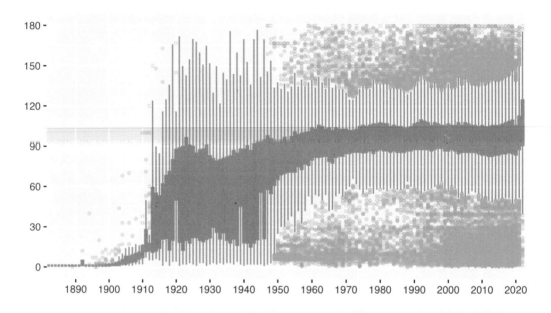

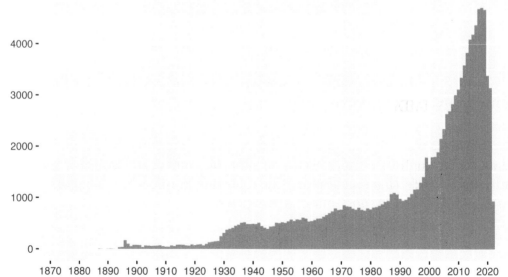

FIGURE 3.4: Movie runtimes in minutes (above), number of movies by year (below) for films of 3 hours or under

3.3   What might IMDb code numbers mean?

Every film has been given a code by IMDb, so merging their datasets is straightforward. As the codes are all of the form 'tt' followed by a number, those numbers were plotted against year to see if there were any patterns. The resulting scatterplot is shown in Figure 3.5.

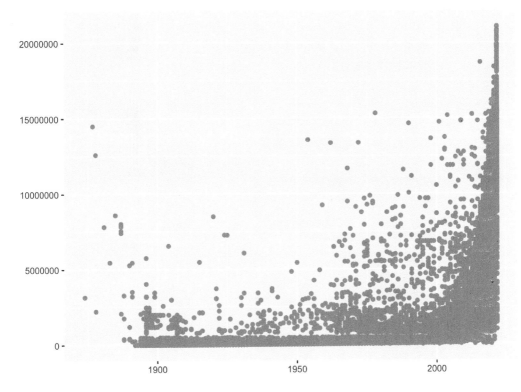

FIGURE 3.5: IMDb code numbers by year for films and shorts with over 100 votes

It looks as though most numbers were allocated in order of production year, but that some films were added to the database later. This is particularly true of the very early films. People might have thought that the Lumière brothers' films of 1895 were the first, but there are 67 recorded earlier, and it appears, judging by the numbering, these were initially not in the database. The earliest film listed is "Passage de Venus" (Transit of Venus) from 1874, a few seconds recorded using a photographic revolver. Several early films are by the extraordinary Eadweard Muybridge, the man who showed that all four hooves of a galloping horse are off the ground at the same time.

As Figure 3.5 only includes films and shorts that received at least 100 votes, it may be misleading. The same plot was drawn for the over 1.25 million items with any ratings at all. This suggested that there might be informative features for low code numbers. Figure 3.6 limits code numbers to less than 1,000,000 and facets by type of item. The scatterplots imply that a set of code numbers between 500,000 and 750,000 was reserved for TV episodes. The TV categories predominantly start in the 1950s and the video category in the 1960s. Quite why the major categories appear to have a tail to the left is unclear. All this may have little importance but is an example of what graphics may uncover that would be difficult to find in other ways. There is an advantage in having something to talk about with domain experts, and it may lead to other, more pertinent, information emerging.

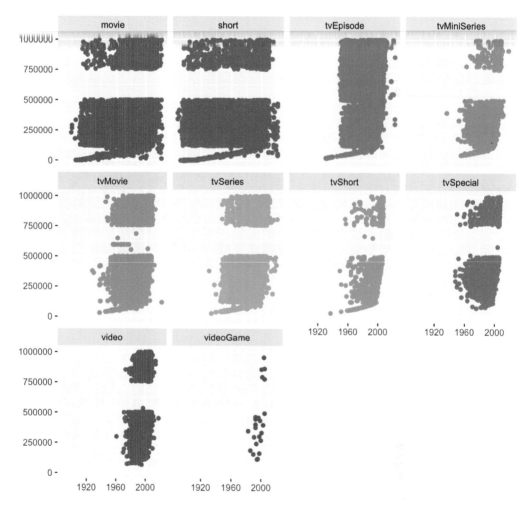

FIGURE 3.6: IMDb code numbers by year for all items with ratings and with code numbers less than 1,000,000

3.4 What ratings do people give films?

Users can give films a rating from 1 to 10. IMDb applies an unpublished algorithm to calculate a weighted average rating for every film. The distribution of average ratings for films is shown in Figure 3.7.

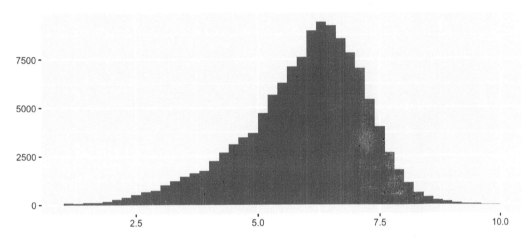

FIGURE 3.7: Average user ratings for movies with over 100 ratings

These average user ratings are based on anything from 101 votes to over two and a half million. Average ratings tend to be higher rather than lower.

The distribution of the number of ratings is skewed to the right, meaning that most films do not get many ratings and a few get a large number of ratings. After taking logs to see more, the distribution is still skew, albeit less so, as is shown in Figure 3.8.

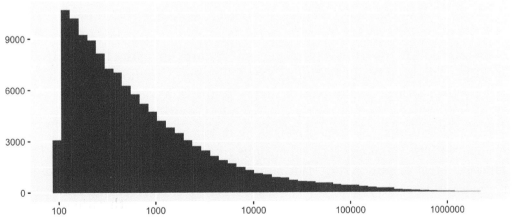

FIGURE 3.8: Numbers of votes for each movie on a log base 10 scale

Figure 3.9 shows how the average rating for films relates to the number of
ratings submitted. This is a plot of 124,667 films, so many of the points to the
left represent a large number of films. The points have been drawn relatively
large and with no use of alpha transparency to ensure that high and outlying
values can be seen. As an example of the density of points with low numbers
of ratings, there are 2621 films that were rated between 100 and 500 times and
have an average rating of 6.3. The plot has an unusual form, like a lower case
r, with several features that are marked by boxes in Figure 3.10.

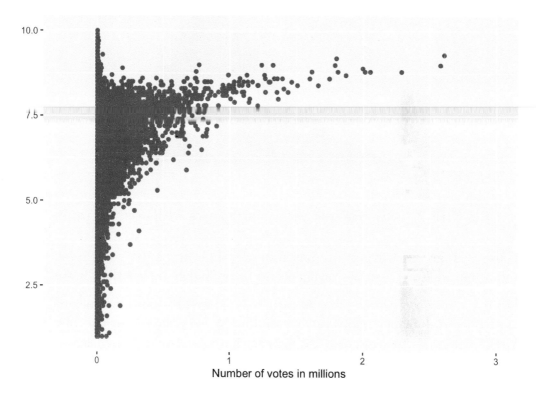

FIGURE 3.9: Average user rating by number of votes

There are no films with a low rating and many votes (the first plot of Figure 3.10). The relatively few films rated by over a million users all have a
high average rating (second plot of Figure 3.10). However, the highest average
ratings are achieved by films with much fewer votes (third plot of Figure 3.10)—
possibly the support of family, friends, and colleagues? A few films have low
average ratings compared with other films receiving the same number of votes
(fourth plot of Figure 3.10). "Batman & Robin" (over 250,000 votes and an
average rating of 3.7) and "Fifty Shades of Grey" (over 300,000 and 4.1) are
two examples.

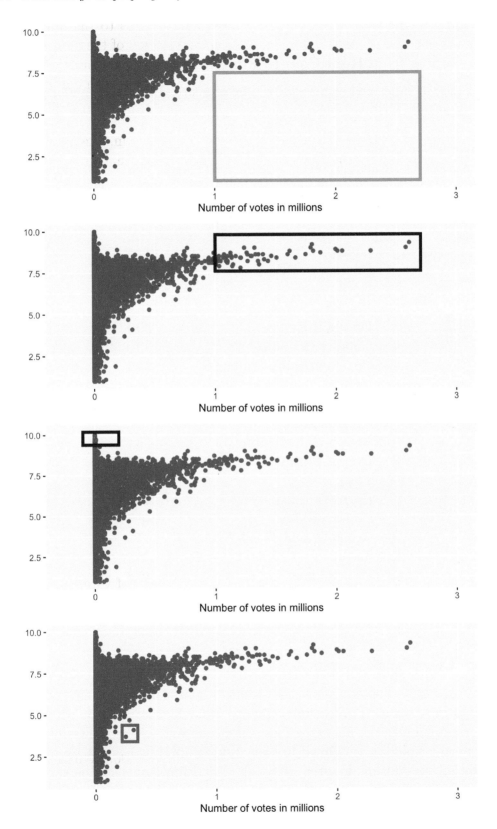

FIGURE 3.10: User ratings by number of votes with features marked by boxes

3.5   Genres from Rom-Com to Film Noir

Films may be described as being of a type or genre. There is no uniform way of doing this and IMDb uses descriptions of up to three genres for each film. When there is more than one genre listed for a film, they are listed alphabetically. In this dataset of films with more than 100 ratings there are almost 1250 different descriptions, i.e., combinations of up to three genres. The top 20 combinations of up to three genre descriptors with cumulative percentages were

genres	cumPerc
Drama	11.9
Comedy	18.8
Documentary	22.8
Comedy,Drama	26.7
Drama,Romance	30.1
Comedy,Romance	32.4
Comedy,Drama,Romance	34.7
Horror	36.9
Animation,Comedy,Family	38.6
Crime,Drama	40.0
Action,Crime,Drama	41.3
Drama,Thriller	42.6
Thriller	43.9
Horror,Thriller	45.0
Comedy,Short	46.1
Crime,Drama,Thriller	47.2
Short	48.1
Drama,Short	49.1
Western	50.1
Documentary,Short	51.0

Figure 3.11 shows the corresponding cumulative distribution.

There were 22 individual genre descriptors that are each mentioned over 3,000 times in the dataset. This excludes films with no description, Adult films, Film Noir, and four other minor categories. Film Noir is a well-known term referring to cynical crime dramas filmed in black and white, but has not been used by IMDb for any film made after 1958. The last Film Noir listed is the famous Orson Welles film "Touch of Evil".

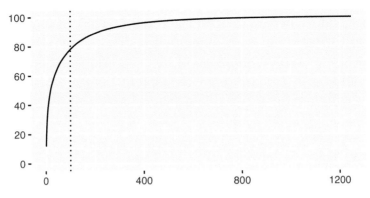

FIGURE 3.11: Percentage of films by number of combinations of genres, almost 80% of films are covered by the first 100 combinations (dotted line)

Another version of the dataset has been constructed with up to 3 records per film, listing the genres separately in the same column. This allows grouping by genre, but means that some films may appear in up to 3 groups. Figure 3.12 plots time series of the percentages of films for which three particular genre descriptors were used. In the silent era the descriptor Comedy was used a lot, but there were far fewer films and they were shorter. Romance had a peak when sound came in. Drama has been used the most for many years. As on average around two descriptors were used for each film, the percentages for all would add up to about 200.

FIGURE 3.12: Percentages of films using the genre descriptors Drama, Comedy, Romance

Instead of calculating percentages on the total numbers of films, it could have been done on the total numbers of genre descriptors used. As an alternative to percentages, the absolute numbers of films for which particular descriptors were used could be plotted, and this is done in Figure 3.13 for the 22 main genres by year from 1901 to 2019. The genres have been put into groups with roughly the same maximum number of films in a year. Each group is plotted on a separate row with its own vertical scale, so that the top row has a range over ten times that of the bottom row. Otherwise the Drama genre would determine the scale and the development over time of the other genres would hardly be visible.

Drama is the genre listed most often, whether alone or as one of two or one of three descriptors, and its number increased steadily until around the year 2000, when the increase became much more rapid. The Comedy genre followed a related pattern, but with a slower increase since 2000. Of the four genres in the second row, Action and Thriller rose earlier, and Horror even fell in the 1990s, while Documentary only took off after 2000. All four are at about the same annual level in 2019. In the third row, the peak in Romance films after sound films began stands out. A related feature can be seen in the fourth row, where both the Family and Animation genres had peaks across the 1930s and 1940s. The numbers for the genres in the fifth and final row are lower. There were more musicals made shortly after sound was introduced than at any time afterwards. War films peaked in World War II and Westerns had their last peak in the 1960s.

The increasing number of films in more recent years is probably due to the development of film industries in countries like India. Lower numbers in earlier years may reflect the restriction to films having more than 100 ratings. Comparing the old dataset referred to in §3.1 with the new one, numbers of ratings have increased. This is likely to have favoured newer films. IMDb first moved to the web in 1993 and is relatively young compared to the film industry itself. This doubtless also favours new films over old in terms of whether they are rated by someone.

There are a large number of genres and combinations of genres. The accuracy or otherwise of the classifications of films may be debatable, but, if nothing else, these kinds of graphics offer much opportunity for entertaining discussion. Experts in film may be able to offer explanations for some of the features on view. As always, good graphics can stimulate more involvement with the data than tables or text alone.

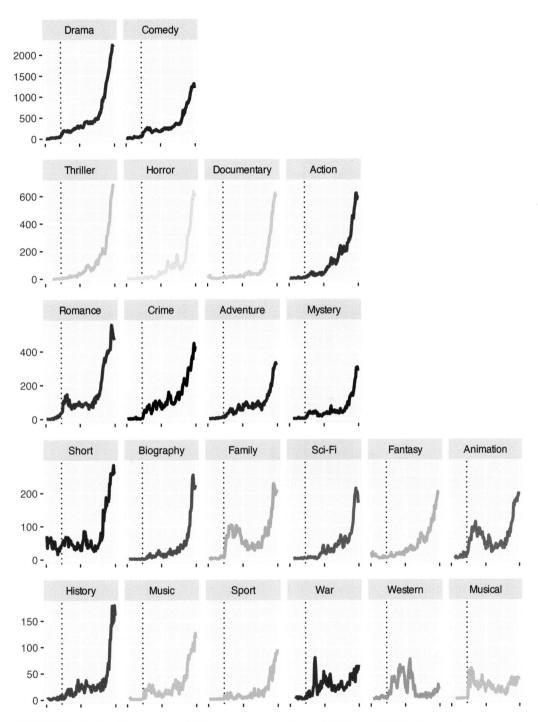

FIGURE 3.13: Number of films by year from 1901 to 2019, faceted by genre in order of highest number per year, a dotted line marks the introduction of sound in 1927 and vertical scales are different for each row

3.6   Comparing Raging Bull with Jane Austen

Every IMDb webpage for a film includes a barchart of individual ratings received by a film and average ratings and numbers of votes by sex and four age groups. Around 30% of users do not report their own sex and age It is not known how reliable the information from the other 70% might be.

Two films were chosen that would have different user responses, "Raging Bull", the Robert De Niro boxing picture about Jake LaMotta, and "Sense and Sensibility", the Emma Thompson version of Jane Austen's novel. Figure 3.14 shows barcharts of the rating distributions. The vertical scales are quite different, as there were around 115,000 ratings of "Sense and Sensibility" and just over three times as many of "Raging Bull". The patterns are fairly similar, very few poor ratings and the most popular rating being 8 out of 10.

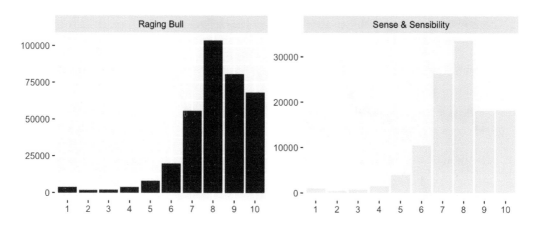

FIGURE 3.14: User ratings of two films

Only average ratings are available for the demographic groups, but the number of users in each group is given. Of the 348115 who rated Raging Bull, 69.3% reported their sex and the corresponding figure for Sense and Sensibility was 70.2%. Figure 3.15 uses a bubble chart to show the results.

Few rating these films reported their age as under 18, so this age group has been left out. A lot more men (around 230,000) than women (about 21,600) rated "Raging Bull" and the men rated the film more highly than the women on average. More women (over 45,000) than men (about 38,800) rated "Sense and Sensibility". This is unusual on IMDb, as usually more men rate a film. The women rated "Sense and Sensibility" more highly than the men on average.

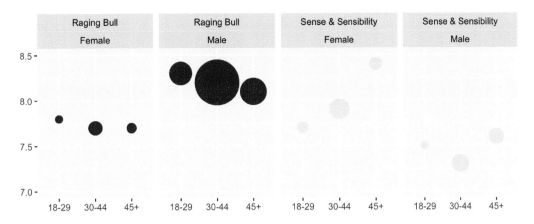

FIGURE 3.15: Average ratings of two films by user age and sex with point size proportional to number of ratings

Answers There are a very few extraordinarily long films, but most are less than 3 hours. Many have rounded runtimes, especially 90 minutes. Runtimes have not changed much over the last 50 years.

Most films get an average rating of between 5 and 7.5 out of 10. Apart from a few films that are relatively rarely rated, the top-rated films have an average of just over 9. Some of the most highly rated films have been rated over 1,000,000 times.

The number of films produced in the last 20 years has increased sharply for most genres, at least for the films in the IMDb database. War films, Westerns, and Musicals have not.

Further questions
How do ratings and numbers of votes change over time? How do ratings vary by age and sex? Are films from different countries rated differently?

Graphical takeaways

- Data heaping is visible in histograms when the binwidth is equal to the data resolution. (Figure 3.2)
- Alpha transparency shows where the data are in scatterplots. (Figure 3.3)
- Faceting emphasises distinctive features of groups. (Figures 3.6 and 3.13)
- Scatterplots can display many different kinds of information. (Figure 3.9)

4

Voting 46 times to choose a Presidential candidate

Don't write so that you can be understood; write so that you can't be misunderstood.

— William H. Taft (U.S. President 1909-1913)

Background In 1912 the battle for the Democratic Presidential nomination was particularly fierce. Woodrow Wilson finally won on the 46th ballot.

Questions How did the support for the various candidates change during the voting? When were the crucial moments?

Sources Woodson (1912)

Structure The number of votes received by each candidate from each state in each ballot (3839 observations of 4 variables).

4.1 A first look at the 1912 Democratic Convention

American political conventions are an important part of the four-year election cycle, when the parties' presidential candidates are nominated. For many years the winning candidates have been known before the conventions started. That was not always the case. In 1912 Woodrow Wilson was only selected on the 46th ballot.

Wilson is known for his participation at the Paris Peace Conference after World War I and the fourteen points for peace he propounded. His regressive policy on racial segregation is not so well-known and was not apparent before his election as President either. W. E. B. Du Bois, the famous black sociologist known for his maps and charts, campaigned for Wilson, but must have been very disappointed by Wilson's actions afterwards.

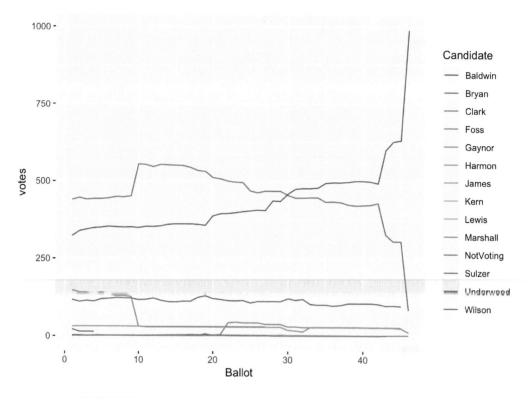

FIGURE 4.1: Votes for the candidates over the 46 ballots

Figure 4.1 shows the development of delegate support for the candidates during the convention. There were two main contenders, Wilson and Clark, with Clark initially ahead and then going even further ahead before Wilson gradually caught up with him and edged in front. The convention finally turned for Wilson in the last few ballots.

While the default plot in Figure 4.1 tells the main story, there is other information in the data too.

4.2 The USA in 1912 and 2020

The USA in 1912 was not the same as the USA in 2020. There were only 48 states. Arizona and New Mexico achieved statehood in the early part of 1912, while Alaska and Hawaii did not join the Union until 1959. These territories had delegates at the Convention as did Washington DC and Puerto Rico. The numbers of delegates in 1912 were far fewer in total than at the Democratic Convention in 2020. There were 1088 in 1912 whereas there were 3979 pledged delegates in 2020. (There were other kinds of delegate in 2020, but the most relevant by state were the pledged delegates.) Figure 4.2 compares the numbers of delegates per area for the two Conventions. The states have been ordered by number of delegates in 1912 and coloured by the four main regions used by the Census Bureau. California and Florida stand out as having substantially bigger shares of delegates. Iowa (which had the same number of delegates as California in 1912) and Missouri are amongst the losers.

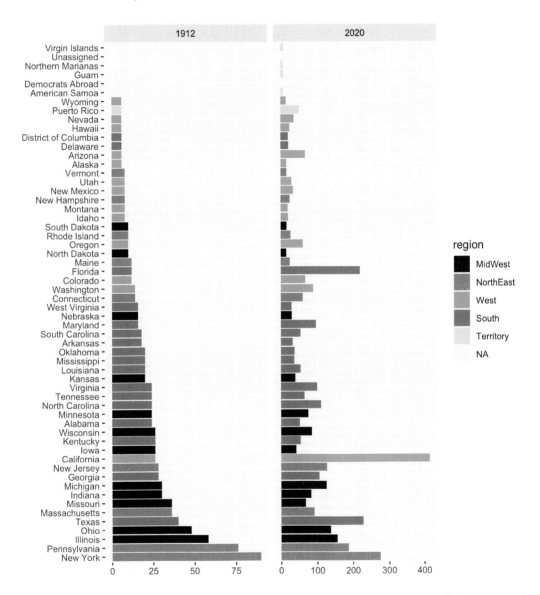

FIGURE 4.2: Numbers of delegates by state and territory at the 1912 and 2020 Democratic conventions (different horizontal scales)

As the total numbers of delegates have increased almost fourfold, the percentage shares of delegates by state were compared. Figure 4.3 is a scatterplot of those shares in 2020 against the shares in 1912. The points are coloured by region again and the point areas are proportional to the numbers of delegates in 2020. The five states with the most delegates in 2020 have been labelled. The big increases for California and Florida stand out again and in this plot Texas does too. It is interesting to see that California had a bigger share of delegates in 2020 than New York had in 1912. Puerto Rico, which had relatively few delegates at both conventions, has been left out, as it counts as a territory and is not in one of the four regions.

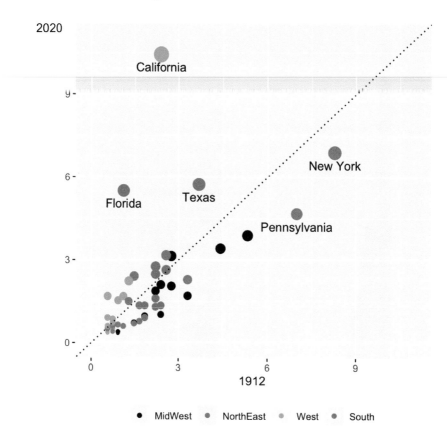

FIGURE 4.3: Percentage state shares of delegates at the 1912 and 2020 Democratic conventions (point sizes are proportional to the number of delegates in 2020)

What happened in the different regions can be more easily assessed using facets. Figure 4.4 shows the scatterplot of Figure 4.3 faceted by region. Most of the Western states, but not all, increased their share like California, but by smaller amounts. Only one MidWest state out of 12 increased its share, albeit slightly. That turned out to be Michigan. States in the NorthEast also lost share.

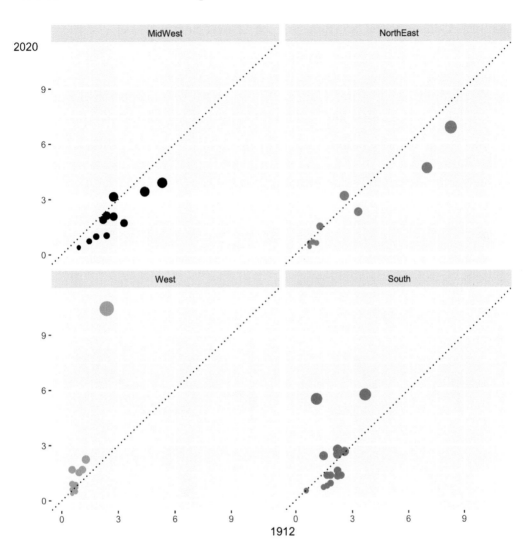

FIGURE 4.4: Percentage state shares of delegates by region

There is a further distribution of votes per state to consider, their votes in the Electoral College that actually elects the President. Figure 4.5 shows scatterplots of the number of delegates per state v. the number of Electoral College votes in 1912 and 2020. Alaska, Hawaii, Puerto Rico are excluded for 1912 (they had no Electoral College votes then), as is D.C. which first got Electoral College votes in 1964. Many smaller states had the same number of Electoral College votes, so there is a lot of overplotting.

There is a simple linear relationship, shown by the dotted line, that the number of delegates a state had at the Democratic Convention in 1912 was twice the state's number of Electoral College Votes—with one exception down to the bottom left: New Mexico had 8 delegates, but only 3 Electoral College Votes.

The picture in 2020 was more varied. In this plot the dotted line is a regression on the data with a slope of 7.7. New York and Pennsylvania had more delegates per electoral vote and Texas fewer.

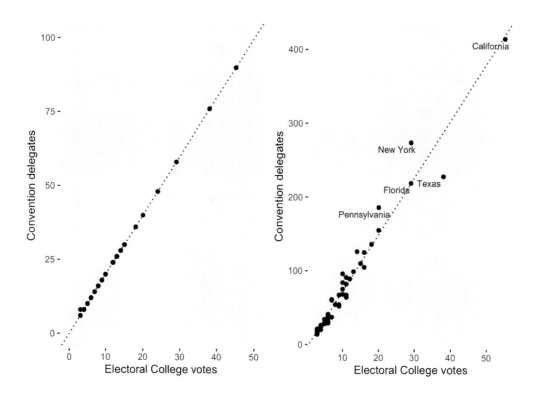

FIGURE 4.5: Delegates and Electoral College votes by state in 1912 (left) and 2020 (right)

4.3 How the nomination contest unfolded

In 1912 the Republicans held their convention first and the party was torn apart by the dispute between the supporters of a previous President, Theodore Roosevelt, and the then President, William Howard Taft. Roosevelt started a new party after the convention and it was expected that splitting the Republican vote would lead to the Democrats' winning the election. The Republicans and former Republicans together got 7.6 million votes in the election, while the Democrats won only 6.3 million votes, but they won 40 of the 48 states and swept the Electoral College.

There is a good chapter on the 1912 Democratic convention in the first volume of Link's biography of Woodrow Wilson (Link (1947)). The main source for the analysis here is the official report on the convention (Woodson (1912)) that includes all the counts in detail.

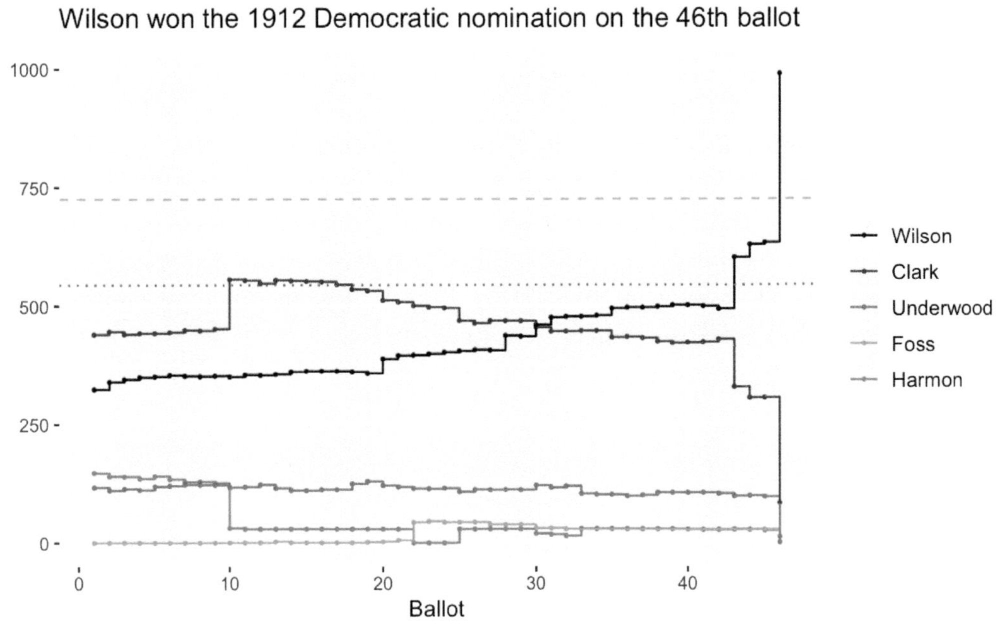

Wilson won the 1912 Democratic nomination on the 46th ballot

FIGURE 4.6: Votes for the main candidates over the 46 ballots

Figure 4.6 is a revised version of Figure 4.1 restricted to the more important candidates. A horizontal dashed line marking the level of two-thirds support that was needed to win the nomination has been added, as has a horizontal dotted line marking 50% support. Here are the key developments.

4.3.1   Developments

1. On the 10th ballot, New York, with 90 delegates, the largest number of any state, switched allegiance from Harmon to Clark, the front runner. This gave Clark an overall majority and it might have been expected that other states would follow. The supporters of Wilson and Underwood—a third candidate with hopes of being selected if Clark and Wilson deadlocked—held firm. They were strengthened by a speech by the three-time Democratic candidate for the Presidency, William Jennings Bryan, just before the 14th ballot. Bryan criticised Tammany Hall, the corrupt Democratic political machine in New York, and rallied the progressive wing of the party.

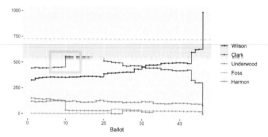

2. During the steady decline in Clark's support there was a gradual increase for Wilson, with minor jumps in support on the 20th ballot (when the 20 delegates of Kansas moved from Clark to Wilson) and on the 28th ballot (when Marshall of Indiana dropped out and 29 of the state's 30 votes went to Wilson. Marshall went on to be chosen as the party's Vice-Presidential candidate.)

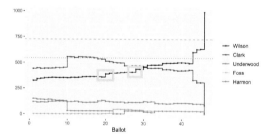

3. The introduction of Foss on the 22nd ballot and the reintroduction of Harmon on the 25th ballot were attempts to find a compromise candidate. Neither gained ground.

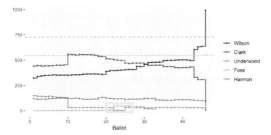

4. Wilson's breakthrough came on the 43rd ballot, when Illinois with 58 delegates went from Clark to Wilson. This was the first point at which Wilson had the support of more than half of the delegates.

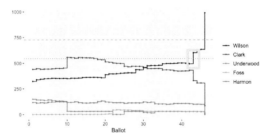

5. Before the 46th ballot began, Underwood (with 97 delegates) withdrew without a recommendation to his supporters and it was clear that Wilson would win. Missouri, long-time supporters of Clark, insisted on a final ballot. Their spokesman said: "We are going to cast our vote for Clark on the last ballot. We have got to go back to Missouri."

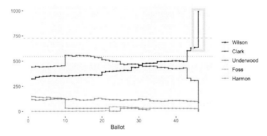

Some of these features, possibly the second and definitely the third, would be difficult to identify just from the graphic and without background information. Graphical analysis benefits from an understanding of what is being represented. Dramatic features are easy to spot, but still have to be interpreted. Descriptions of what took place indicate additional places to look in the graphic. Both approaches are valuable and they complement one another. Good graphics can provide summarising overviews, while reports flesh out the details. Neither alone is enough.

4.4   When did the ballots actually take place?

Using the ballot number as a measure of time is an approximation of what actually happened. The first ballot took place on the morning of Friday, 28 June, and the last ballot took place on the afternoon of Tuesday, 2 July. The official report of the convention (Woodson (1912)) does not record when exactly ballots were taken, but does record to the minute when the convention was adjourned and when it restarted. Making the assumption that each ballot took about the same time, and adding extra time for special polling of individual states and speeches, gives Figure 4.7.

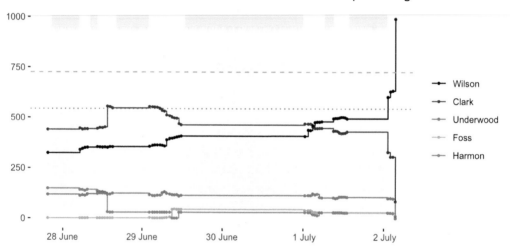

FIGURE 4.7: Convention voting using estimated ballot times with the date labels at midday and adjournment periods shaded grey

This picture makes a different impression. Instead of a string of equally spaced events, there are bunches of ballots, separated by a number of breaks in the proceedings, especially that from midnight on the Saturday to 11am on the Monday. There were no official meetings on the Sunday. The crucial breakthrough for Wilson took place after the overnight break between Monday and Tuesday. Discussions must have been taking place all through the convention. Sometimes more than one plot is necessary to get the full picture.

Answers Many ballots took place without any change in support for the various candidates. There were up to six critical points that determined the result.

Further questions Which states voted as one during the convention? In which other years were there many ballots to select a candidate?

Graphical takeaways

- Guidelines support reading of graphics. (Figures 4.3 to 4.7)
- Time series with discrete jumps should be represented with steps. (Figure 4.6)
- Precise time scales are better than using equal intervals between data points. (Figure 4.7)
- Interpretation requires domain knowledge. (Figures 4.6 and 4.7)

5

Measuring the speed of light

Time flies. You can't. They fly too fast. (Children's word puzzle)

Background The speed of light is a central physical constant. Several complex experiments were carried out in the second half of the 19th century to measure it, including Michelson's 100 measurements made in the summer of 1879 (Michelson (1880)), and Newcomb's measurements from 1882 (Newcomb (1891)).

Questions Are the estimates close to today's value? How did Michelson's and Newcomb's estimates compare? Can the results be treated as independent random samples?

Sources Michelson's report of 1880 for the U.S. Nautical Almanac Office and Newcomb's paper of 1891.

Structure Michelson's results of 100 experiments from 1879 included date, time of day, temperature, and estimate of the speed of light. Newcomb's 66 experiments of 1882 included date, weights grading the observation quality, observer's name, and estimate of the speed of light. Some experimental settings and intermediate measurements listed in the original sources have not been included.

5.1 Michelson, the Master of Light, and his data

Stigler (1977) used Michelson's 1879 data in a study of robust estimators. For reasons of convenience he split the data into five sets of 20 measurements each. Several researchers have since assumed that that was how the experiments were carried out, but Michelson's report makes clear it was not. Researchers have displayed the data as time series, using the order of the experiments as an equally spaced time index. Again, the original paper provides dates and there were some days with no observations and four which had as many as 10. Michelson's detailed description includes a number of factors which varied between his experiments. To treat all the experiments as independent and identically distributed is a useful first approximation, but not an accurate reflection of what took place. MacKay and Oldford (2000) uses the dataset as a central example for their article on scientific and statistical method. They do respect the order and timing of the data and provide a complete copy of Michelson's table of experimental results.

Figure 5.1 shows Michelson's estimates of the speed of light in air by date and time. Measurements were made on 18 separate days starting on 5 June 1879 and ending on 2 July 1879. Experiments on the same day have been assumed to start at 9 in the morning with one hour gaps in between if recorded as A.M., and at 3 in the afternoon with one hour gaps in between if recorded as P.M. This was done to separate them. The five artificial groupings introduced by Stigler have been coloured, and red dotted lines drawn as boundaries between them.

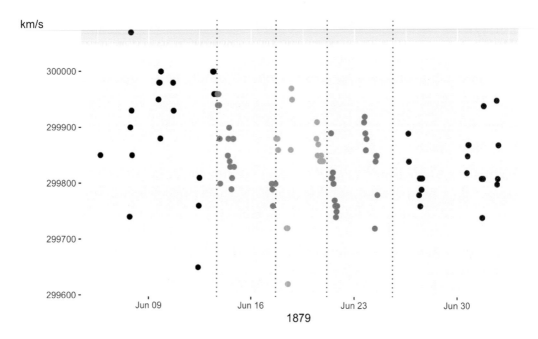

FIGURE 5.1: Measurements of the speed of light in air by Michelson by date and time with dotted lines drawn to separate Stigler's artificial groupings. There is a limited amount of overplotting due to exact equality of measurements close together in time.

Michelson adjusted for temperature and refraction to convert his average estimate of the speed of light in air to the speed of light in a vacuum. Today the speed of light in a vacuum is given as 299792.5 km/s. Converting this to a speed in air using the inverse of Michelson's conversion gives a value close to 299700 km/s. All but 2 of Michelson's 100 results are higher than this.

The temperature for each experiment varied from just under 60° Fahrenheit, around 14.5° Celsius, in the morning to as high as 90° Fahrenheit or 32.2° Celsius in the afternoon. Figure 5.2 shows the estimates of speed of light in air vs. temperature. The very first reading was taken at night under electric light, marked black in the figure, but it was regarded by Michelson as unsatisfactory. There is little sign of any effect and this matches the magnitude of Michelson's correction for temperature that amounted to just over 1 km/s for each additional degree Fahrenheit.

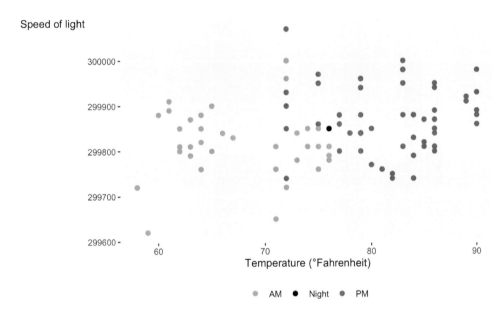

FIGURE 5.2: Michelson's estimates of the speed of light in air by temperature, coloured by time of day

5.2 Newcomb, self-educated polymath, and his data

Simon Newcomb carried out three series of experiments from 1880 to 1882 and the results are all in his report (Newcomb (1891)). His conclusion there on p. 201 is that "The preceding investigations and discussions seem to show that our results should depend entirely on the measures of 1882 [i.e. the third series]."

The results from Newcomb's third series of experiments from 1882 have also been used many times, sometimes in the order of the experiments, sometimes not. As the experimental setup and conditions changed over time, it is worth respecting the order and, where possible, the actual dates and times.

There were 66 measurements made of the time taken in millionths of a second for light to travel a distance of 7.44242 kilometres in air. Stigler suggested in his article that the 'true' value would have been 24.83302 millionths of a second after taking account of Newcomb's adjustments for mirror curvature and refraction.

Figure 5.3 shows a histogram of the data suggesting that there are two suspicious values, one at over 300,600 km/s that is far away from the rest of the data and one at over 300,100 km/s that is moderately away from the rest. Stigler writes that Newcomb excluded the higher of these two, but not the other one.

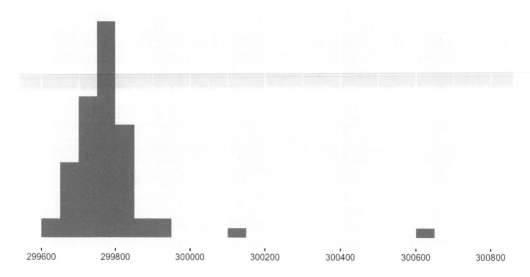

FIGURE 5.3: Histogram of measurements of the speed of light by Newcomb

Looking at data in simple graphics directly is an effective way of spotting obvious problems (like the case over 300600) and potential problems (like the case over 300100). Some statisticians may prefer to use a statistical test to see if there are outlying points, but there is not general agreement on which test or tests would be best. A boxplot is one possibility, as in Figure 5.4. This suggests that both cases are outliers.

FIGURE 5.4: Boxplot of measurements of the speed of light by Newcomb

Figure 5.5 shows a further alternative, a kernel density estimate of the data, excluding the most extreme case. It does look as if the other outlier should be dropped as well.

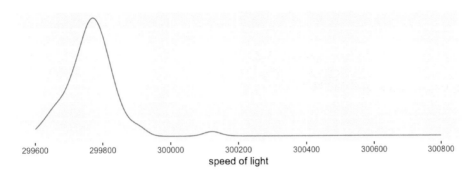

FIGURE 5.5: Density estimate of measurements of the speed of light by Newcomb excluding an outlier

Newcomb's paper provides details of each experiment and this information can be used too. Figure 5.6 plots the data in the order given in the paper. Stigler (1977) uses Newcomb's order (not all republishers of the dataset do).

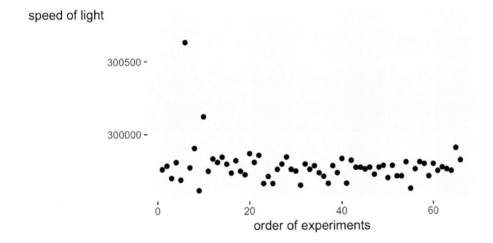

FIGURE 5.6: Measurements of the speed of light by Newcomb displayed in the order the experiments were carried out

Viewing the data this way does make the potential outlier with the value of over 300100 look out of sync with the main part of the dataset. However, there is more information in Newcomb's paper. There are the actual dates and order of the experiments and the names of the observers on those days. More than half of the observations in this series were made by Ensign Holcombe of the U.S. Navy, who joined Newcomb after Michelson became Professor in Cleveland in September 1880.

Figure 5.7 displays the estimates by the date they were made and coloured by who made them.

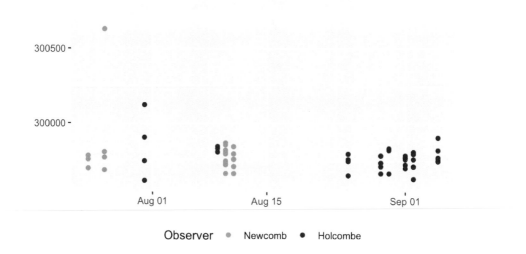

FIGURE 5.7: Measurements of the speed of light by Newcomb in 1882 displayed by date, coloured by observer

The second outlier of over 300100 does not look so outlying in the context of the four experiments by Holcomb on 31 July (the four dark blue dots in a vertical line to the left of 1 August). It is notable that the lowest data value was also amongst the four observations that day.

Analyses of these data generally assume that the observations can be treated as if they were independent and (mostly) identically distributed. The detailed descriptions in Newcomb's paper of problems with individual experiments and of adjustments to experimental settings as they proceeded suggest this assumption should be looked at more closely. Newcomb attempted to assess the quality of the observations. He reported three weights for them, two for the quality of the images and one overall weight to be given to an observation (p. 170, Newcomb (1891)). Figure 5.8 gives the distribution of overall weights.

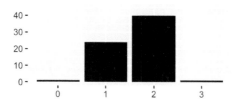

FIGURE 5.8: Weights assigned to each observation by Newcomb.

Only one case was assigned a weight of 0 (the extreme outlier) and only one the top weight of 3, the last measurement by Holcombe on 31st July, the second lowest value of the four observations that day. The weights for image quality bear little relationship to the overall weight. Newcomb wrote "Only a small range is assigned to the weights, because from the very nature of the case it is impossible to determine them with actual precision."

5.3 Comparing the data of Michelson and Newcomb

Both researchers made measurements of the speed of light in air, averaged their results, and only then converted their final estimate to one for the speed of light in a vacuum. This meant adding 92 km/s for Michelson (Michelson (1880) p. 141) and 94 km/s for Newcomb (Newcomb (1891) p. 201). The main adjustment was to multiply the speed in air by the index of refraction of air at the temperature of the experiments. The technical details (and much more) are in their papers. Given the adjustments are so similar the estimates for the speed in air can be compared. The extreme outlier in the Newcomb data has been excluded for this comparison, so the horizontal scale is different from the scale of the earlier plots.

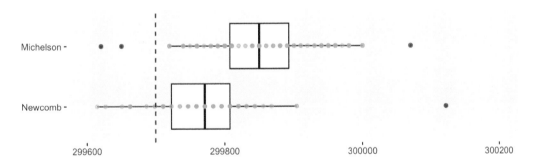

FIGURE 5.9: Boxplots and dotplots of estimates of the speed of light in air by Michelson in 1879 and by Newcomb in 1882 with the transformed value of today marked by a dashed blue line

Michelson's estimates were higher than Newcomb's and further away from the 'true' value. In 1924, some forty years later, using similar, but improved techniques, Michelson estimated the speed of light in vacuo to be 299,796 km/s (Michelson (1927)), very close to-day's 299,792.458 km/s.

No intervals for the estimates have been given here. As Youden pointed out over 50 years ago (Youden (1972)), reported intervals for estimates of the values of physical constants included random error but not systematic error and that was typically larger.

Answers Newcomb's estimates were closer to today's value than Michelson's. The individual experiments of each of the two researchers can only approximately be treated as independent random samples.

Further questions How have experiments to estimate the speed of light changed since Newcomb's time? How have the estimates themselves changed?

Graphical takeaways

- Going back to original sources can reveal relevant information. (Figures 5.1 and 5.7)
- Graphics are useful for identifying outliers. (Figures 5.3 and 5.4)
- There is no one best display: different graphics offer alternative views. (Figures 5.3 to 5.7)

6

The modern Olympic Games in numbers

Faster, Higher, Stronger — (former) Olympic motto

Background The modern Olympic Games have taken place every four years for over 120 years—barring the years of the two World Wars. They started small in 1896 in Athens and have expanded enormously to become one of the biggest global events.

Questions How many Olympic events have there been? Which events have taken place at many Games and which rarely? How have performances improved over the years? How have the numbers of countries and participants developed?

Sources Two datasets scraped from websites reporting Olympic results, one from a private source and one from Kaggle (Griffin (2019)).

Structure One dataset included 108789 competitors, reporting whether they won medals or not and, where available, their performance, just for Summer Olympics. The other dataset included all 222522 competitors with medals, age, height, weight and sex, but not performance data, and covered Summer and Winter Olympics.

6.1 How good are the data?

There is much data on the changing events at the Olympic Games (IOC (2022)), the new countries taking part, and especially on the improved performances of the participants over the years. Two datasets are studied for the Summer Olympics, one with performance data and one with no performance data but a more complete list of competitors.

The performance dataset for the Summer Olympics from 1896 to 2016 was scraped from the web in advance of the 2020 games that took place in 2021 because of the Covid pandemic. The data were used for commenting on the shape of the trend in improvement and not for any detailed analysis and were made available on request. A closer look uncovered a number of problems and illustrates how graphics can be used to support checking, editing, and restructuring data, as well as for exploring and displaying results.

The performance dataset had almost 110,000 entries. A barchart of the over 1100 events reported there (Figure 6.1) reveals a long list with numbers of participants ranging from 1 to 2644. Some events only took place at one Olympic Games and there were various alternative spellings and misspellings of events, which is why there appear to be so many.

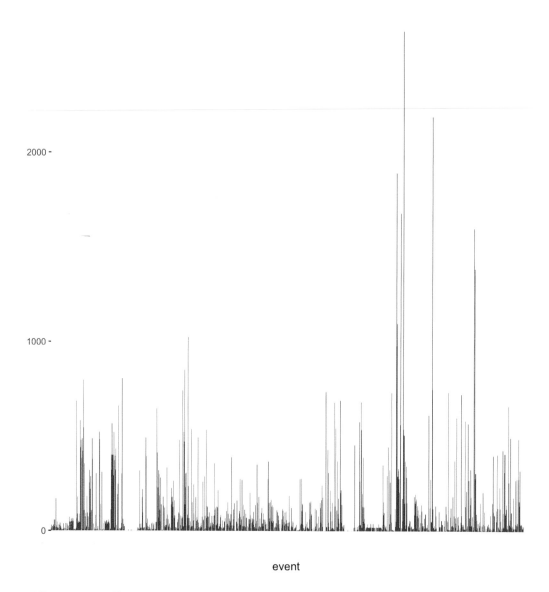

FIGURE 6.1: Summer Olympic events by total numbers of participants in the Games of 1896 to 2016, ordered lexicographically (the default), based on the first dataset

Events are grouped in sporting disciplines and looking at those instead also gives a surprisingly long list, ranging from athletics and swimming to cricket and basque-pelota. The top two disciplines in terms of participants, athletics and swimming, include many different events, as do some of the other disciplines.

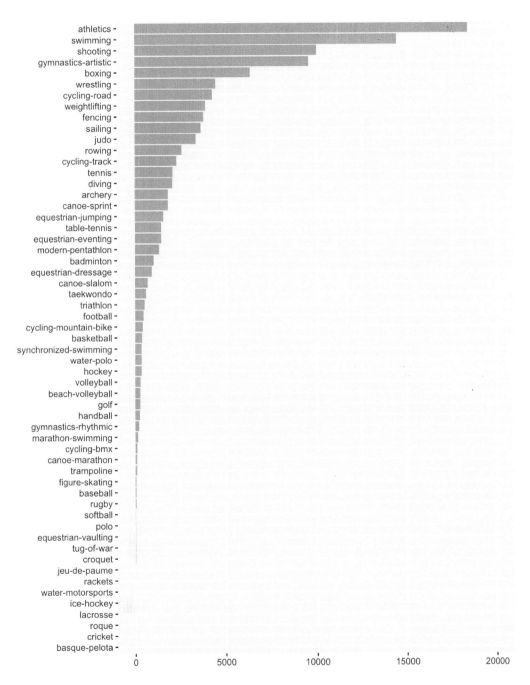

FIGURE 6.2: Summer Olympics sporting disciplines by total numbers of participants in the Games of 1896 to 2016, based on the first dataset

There are events for men and for women, and there are mixed and open events. Concentrating on the two most frequent disciplines, athletics and swimming, excluding mixed and open events, and restricting the dataset to gold medal winners gave Figure 6.3 showing the numbers of events at each Olympic Games. The patterns for the two disciplines are very different. After initial peaks before and just after the first World War, the number of athletics events for men barely changed. The number of athletics events for women increased steadily from a very low start in 1928. In swimming, the numbers of events for men and women followed similar paths from 1924 on.

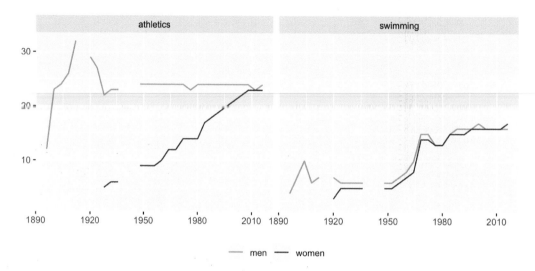

FIGURE 6.3: Numbers of athletics and swimming events for men and women at the Summer Olympics from 1896 to 2016

Figure 6.4 has more detail, showing which events took place for men and for women at which games. It was drawn to investigate why there appeared to be so many events listed. Despite the small print, two problems can readily be seen. The long line of dots to the right of each plot and the matching gaps above suggest that there was an issue with how athletics and swimming events were named at Beijing in 2008. The data source for Beijing used "-metres", where the sources for other Olympics used "m". The straggly lines to the left of the two plots for men show that some events only took place at early games (e.g. long-jump-standing and underwater-swimming). A minor issue is that there are individual gaps that will need to be investigated further.

Comparing the top two displays for athletic events, it is clear that women did not take part until much later than men. Athletic events for women began at the 1928 Olympics. Comparing the two displays on the right shows that swimming events for women began earlier, at the 1912 Olympics. Why were women allowed to swim before they could run?

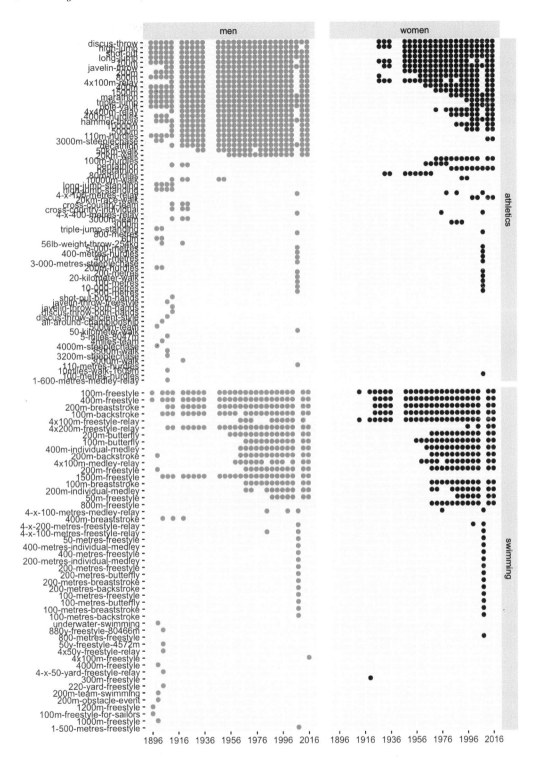

FIGURE 6.4: Athletics and swimming events for men and women for which gold medals were awarded by Olympic year, ordered by numbers of gold medals awarded

After fixing the event names for the Beijing Olympics and setting aside the early events, displays were drawn separately for athletics and swimming (Figures 6.5 and 6.6). The correcting code was applied to the whole dataset and some of the corrections for Beijing fixed other minor issues. The ordering of the events is a little different from that in Figure 6.4 because the corrections have changed the total numbers of gold medals awarded for events.

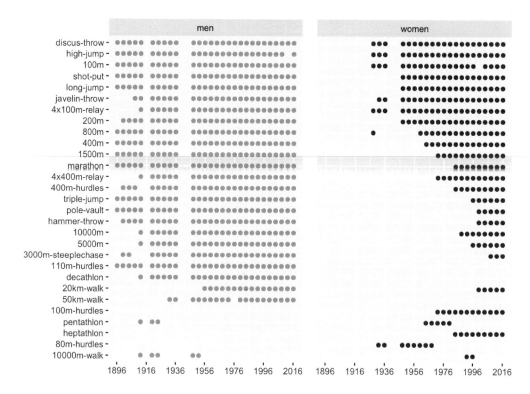

FIGURE 6.5: Athletic events by Olympic year after amendments

Some events were only for men and some only for women. Men compete in the decathlon of ten events, whereas women compete in the heptathlon of seven events (and in earlier Games only in the pentathlon of five events). Men run the 110 m hurdles, while women run the 100 m hurdles (and formerly the 80 m hurdles). The women's pentathlon and the women's 80 m hurdles were excluded from further analysis. Other events that have taken place rarely (defined here as less than six times for men or women) were also excluded. There were gaps due to events not taking place or medals not being awarded. The men's 50 km walk took place at all Games from 1932 to 2016 except for 1976. The winner of the men's high jump in 2012 was later disqualified for doping offences and the other medals promoted in 2021. That had not been done at the time the dataset was scraped and so there was no gold medal winner and no data point in Figure 6.5. For a number of reasons related to doping, no gold medal was awarded for the women's 100 m in 2000.

The 800 m for women stands out as first taking place at the Amsterdam Games of 1928 and then not again until the Olympics in Rome in 1960. The men in charge of the Olympic Games decided that the event was too strenuous for women and were supported by some highly dubious reporting in the newspapers (English (2015)). According to Robinson (2012), Harold Abrahams, the famous English runner, Olympic official, and journalist, said "The sensational descriptions are much exaggerated I can assure you." Others must have held other opinions.

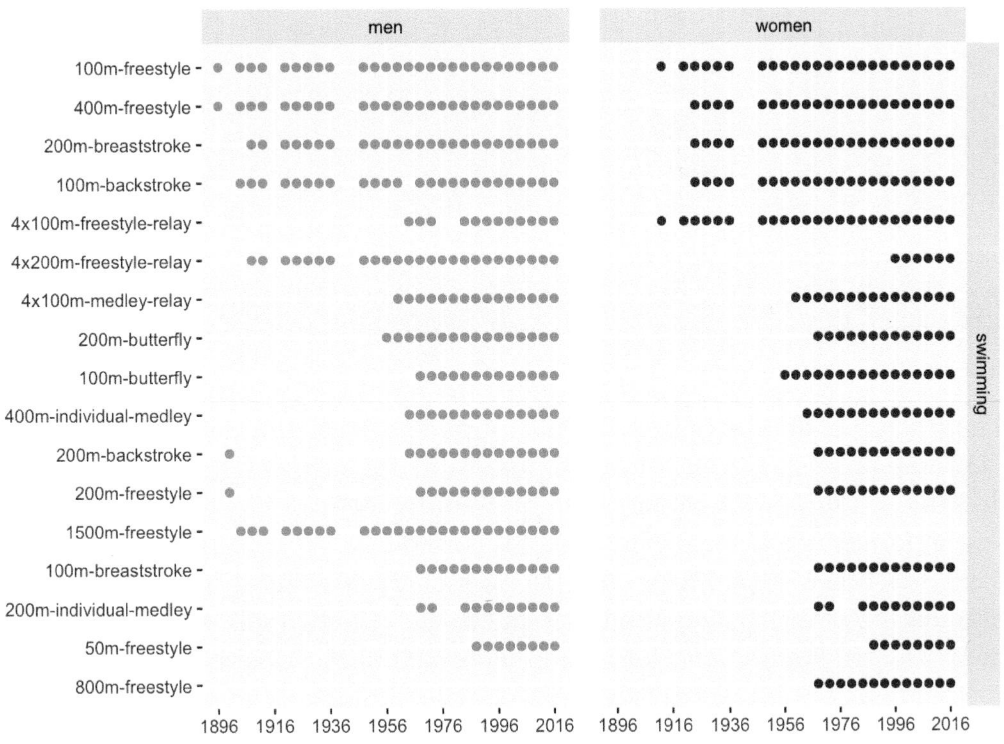

FIGURE 6.6: Swimming events by Olympic year after amendments

Since 1996 women have swum the same events as men, with one exception. The men's longest freestyle event was 1500 m, while the women's was 800 m. Interestingly, for the first time at the Tokyo Olympics of 2021, both races are now swum by both sexes.

Two striking gaps are apparent in men's swimming events. Both the 200 m backstroke and freestyle were raced in 1900 in Paris and not again until 1964 (backstroke) and 1968 (freestyle). Results are missing for the men's 400 m freestyle relay in 1976 and 1980, presumably a scraping problem. Results are not included for either men or women for the 200 m individual medley in 1976 and 1980, because the events did not take place at those Games.

6.2   How much have performances improved?

Performances in a few disciplines, such as in swimming and athletics, can be directly compared, although the continual improvements in technique, equipment, training, and support of all kinds, as well as the growing population of athletes have to be borne in mind. Rule changes can also have significant effects. Most other disciplines such as boxing, gymnastics or sailing are even harder to compare over time.

Gold Medal performances are sometimes world records, more often not. The best performance in one Olympics may not be as good as the best performances in earlier Olympics. Athletes may miss out because of injury or ill health or because their country boycotts a Games (as happened for various reasons at the Games of 1976, 1980, 1984). In the early years travel time and costs limited participation. So Olympic performances are not ideal for studying developments over time. Nevertheless, the Olympic Games offer regular simultaneous checks on performance changes in many sporting events and that has its advantages too.

There were a number of additional problems with the data. Some values were missing (e.g., several for the pole vault for men). The heptathlon and decathlon results were reported on quite different scales in different years. A few performances at some games were reported with a 'w' at the end signifying wind assistance. This means that there was a tail wind of more than 2 m/s, invalidating record attempts but not the result. It only applies to certain sprint races, the triple jump and long jump. Four 100 m races were affected and one complete long jump competition. Three triple jump gold medal performances were marked as wind-assisted. For jumps, it made no difference once the 'w' was removed. For 100 m races the times were in seconds instead of thousandths of seconds. This included times in Jesse Owens' 100 m final at the 1936 Olympics in Berlin. There were other issues that had to be resolved. Only events that had taken place at least six Olympics were included.

In the analysis carried out by the scrapers of the dataset the gold medal performances were standardised by calculating how much better or worse they were in percentage terms than the average of the gold medal winners over all the Games at which the event took place. For events that have been included in the Games a long time the overall average then tended to reflect a poorer performance than if results were only included from more recent games. The solution adopted here is to compare results with the average over the Olympics from 1996 to 2016.

Figure 6.7 shows data for individual athletics events grouped by sex and whether they are a field event like the shot put (higher numbers are better) or a track event like the 100 m (faster times are better). The percentage differences between the gold medal performances at each Games and the averages of gold performances over the six Games from 1996 to 2016 are plotted against years to show the overall trends.

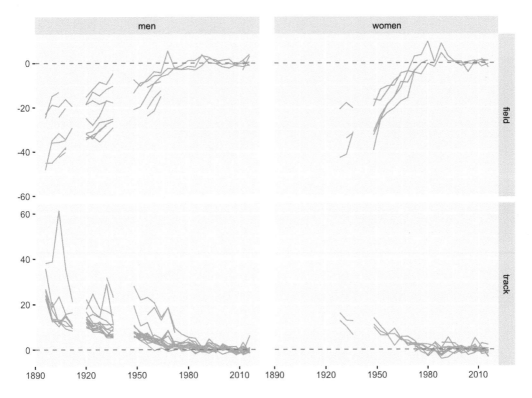

FIGURE 6.7: Percentage differences in gold medal performances in athletics events compared with averages over the last six Games

Scales are primarily determined by relatively weak performances at early Games and mostly there is a general improvement. Studying the graphics closely, other features are apparent. There are no early data for women, because female athletics events were first held at the 1928 Games in Amsterdam. Some events were introduced later than others. There are some odd peaks and some surprising gaps (in addition to the gaps for the two World Wars). There are many missing data points for the field events, where there should be 8 events for the men and 6 for the women for these data. The averages were calculated ignoring missings, so for three events only one value contributed to the average and for five events only two. A more refined analysis would be more reassuring, but is unlikely to make much difference to the overall impression.

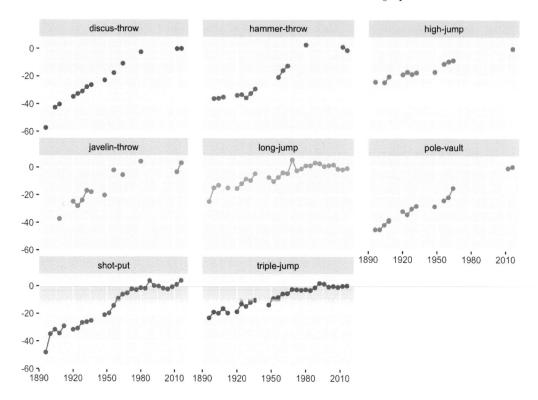

FIGURE 6.8: Field events for men: percentage differences in gold medal performances compared with averages over the last six Games

The four graphics were separately faceted by event for more details. Figures 6.8 and 6.9 show men's track and field events. The graphics for women's events showed similar issues, but fewer and less dramatic ones. For field events a lot of data is missing, for the pole vault and high jump in particular. These problems must have been due to failed data scraping. Early low values dominate, but the values higher than the recent averages are also worth studying. Bob Beamon's famous long jump at Mexico City 1968 is still the Olympic record and the second longest jump of all time. The discus, hammer throw, and javelin could all be checked in more detail.

The time for the 1904 marathon race in Figure 6.9 is clearly out of line. According to Abbott (2012), "the 1904 marathon was less showstopper than sideshow, a freakish spectacle" and "The outcome was so scandalous that the event was nearly abolished for good." The time for the 3000 m steeplechase in 1932 also looks wrong. Due to an error in lap counting, the runners had to run an extra lap of the track.

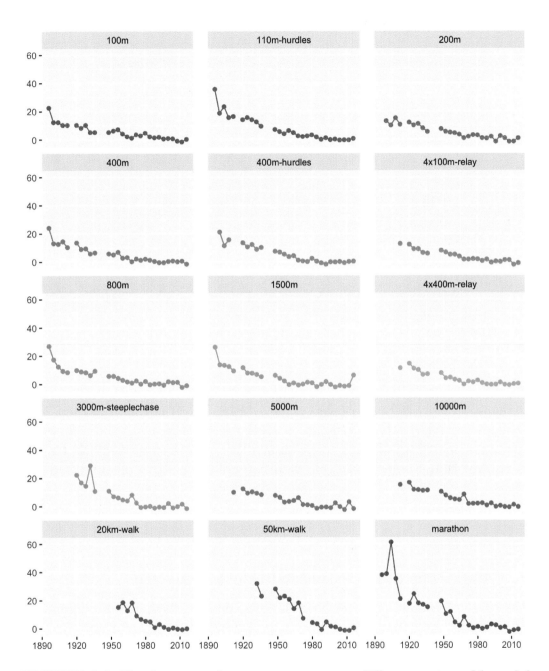

FIGURE 6.9: Track events for men: percentage differences in gold medal performances compared with averages over the last six Games, events are ordered by distance

Sometimes particular events stand out. Looking at the swimming results, most have similar patterns for men and women, but one stands out in each case, interestingly the same event, the 100 m freestyle, as Figure 6.10 shows:

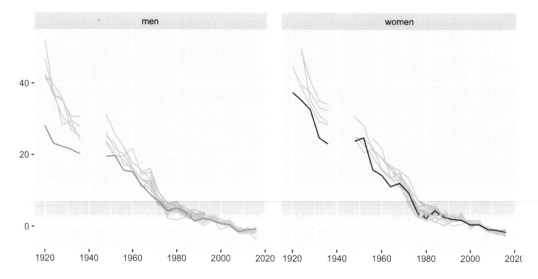

FIGURE 6.10: Percentage differences in gold medal performances in swimming events for men and women compared with averages over the last six Games since 1920 with the 100 m freestyle highlighted

Perhaps strong performances were achieved earlier for the 100 m or there have been greater relative improvements in other events. The men's 100 m freestyle champion in 1924 and 1928 was Johnny Weissmuller who went on to play Tarzan in Hollywood movies. He won five gold medals in all (and had five wives).

6.3   How many countries and individuals competed?

The second Olympics dataset covering both Winter and Summer Olympics is available from Kaggle (Griffin (2019)). This has also been scraped from the web and aimed to include all participants from the modern Olympic Games, not just finalists, as in the first dataset. It also includes the 1906 Intercalated Games, then considered Olympic Games, but not now and not included here. Medals, if any, are reported, but not the performances. The events are named differently in various ways in the two datasets, which makes it difficult to merge them. For example, in the first dataset there is the cycling event "team-pursuit-4000m-men" and in the second one it is called "Men's Team Pursuit, 4,000 metres". More surprisingly—and unexpectedly—the second dataset includes the participants in the Arts Competitions that were held in the Games of 1912 to 1948. This is how the famous painters Max Liebermann and Sir John Lavery were both able to participate in the 1928 Games.

The numbers of countries sending teams for men and women to the Summer Games are shown separately in Figure 6.11.

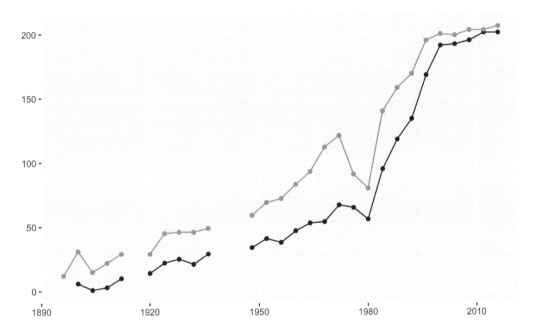

FIGURE 6.11: Numbers of countries competing at the Olympic Games over the years (male numbers in green above, female in purple below)

The number of countries has steadily increased with the exception of the 1976 Montreal Games (when 29 countries, mainly African, did not take part because New Zealand had played South Africa at rugby and had not been banned from the Olympics as a consequence) and the 1980 Moscow Games (when over 60 countries did not take part because of the Soviet invasion of Afghanistan). There was also a boycott in 1984 at Los Angeles when 14 countries led by the Soviet Union did not take part. Since the 2000 Games in Sydney the numbers of countries with female teams is almost equal to the number of countries with male teams. (An elegant and more detailed visualisation of the numbers of countries taking part can be found at Nicault (2021).)

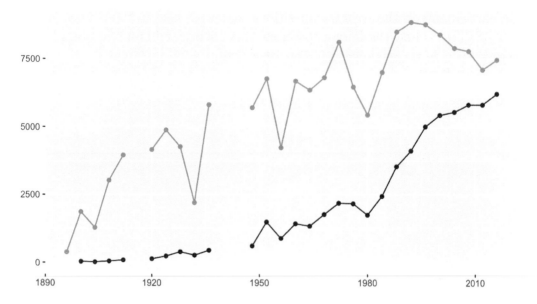

FIGURE 6.12: Numbers competing at the Olympic Games over the years

More males compete as can be seen from Figure 6.12 showing the numbers of participants by sex. While the number of female participants has risen relatively steadily, the numbers of male participants declined at Los Angeles in 1932 (because of the Depression), at Melbourne in 1956 (possibly because the Games were held in November and December, the Australian summer), and at Moscow in 1980 (because many countries did not take part). There was also something of a reduction in numbers of male participants between the peak of 8772 in 1996 at Atlanta and the low of 7105 at London in 2012.

Looking at the time series for individual countries picks out a feature that is obvious with hindsight (Figure 6.13), there are more participants from a country when it is the host. The early peaks of 1900 for France, 1904 for USA, 1908 for Great Britain, 1912 for Sweden, and 1920 for Belgium are unmistakable. Travel time and costs would have influenced the participation of other nations then. Also obvious are the peaks of 1968 for Mexico, 1976 for Germany, 2004 for Greece, 2008 for China, and 2016 for Brazil. Less obvious are 1896 for Greece, 1924 for France, 1936 for Germany, 1948 for Great Britain, 1952 for Finland, 1956 and 2000 for Australia, 1964 for Japan, 1988 for Korea, and 1992 for Spain. Other peaks may be due to (relative) geographic nearness, such as numbers of Korean and Australian participants at Tokyo in 1964.

The figures for Russia are for Imperial Russia before 1914, for the Soviet Union till 1988, for the Unified team of 12 of the former 15 Soviet Union republics in 1992, and for Russia since 1996. In 1924 no Soviet Union team took part, but three competitors in the Arts Competitions called themselves Russian. Figures for Germany include those from both East and West between 1968 and 1988.

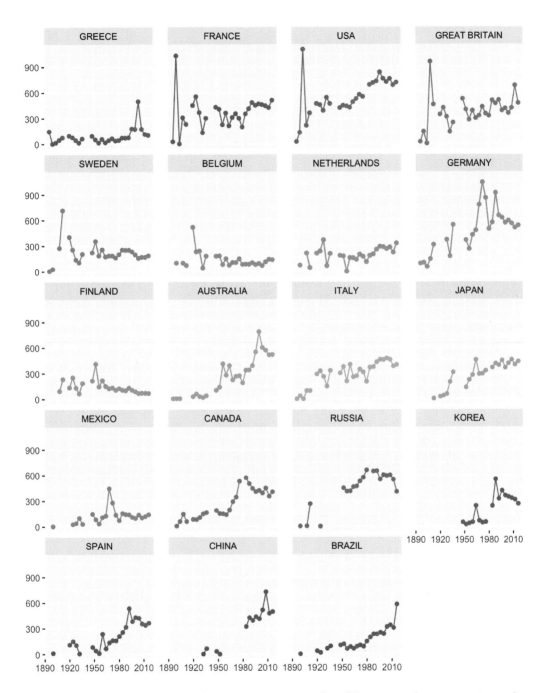

FIGURE 6.13: Numbers of participants at the Olympics for countries who have hosted the Games (in order of first hosting)

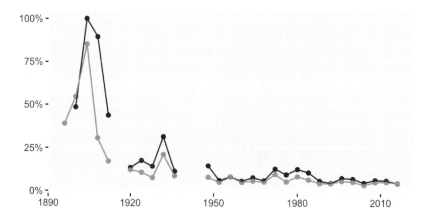

FIGURE 6.14: Percentages of host country participants at the Olympic Games over the years for women (purple) and men (green)

Host country dominance at the early Olympics is shown in Figure 6.14 for both women and men. In 1904 at St Louis, only 16 women took part and they were all American. 85% of the participants at the 1904 Olympics were American.

Answers The dataset including performance data needed a lot of editing, but included much interesting information. Gold medal performances have improved since the early Games, but not so much lately. More and more countries take part in the Olympic Games and the number of competitors has increased as well. Individual countries have had their highest number of participants when they have been host nation.

Further questions How do changes in performance over time look when logarithms of results are used instead of actual results? Might it be useful to compare results to world records over time? Is there evidence of possible use of doping in earlier Games before more stringent controls were introduced?

Graphical takeaways

- Good orderings make patterns visible. (Figure 6.4)
- After fixing errors and excluding unusual cases, redrawn graphics reveal more information. (Figures 6.5 and 6.6)
- When time series overlap, use faceting to pick out patterns in individual series. (Figures 6.8 and 6.9)
- Regular time series should be plotted so that it is clear where data are missing. Plotting both points and lines helps. (Figures 6.11 to 6.14)

7

Re-viewing Bertin's main example

How can you govern a country which has two hundred and forty-six varieties of cheese?
— Charles de Gaulle

Background The famous Semiology of Graphics book (Bertin (2010)) includes analysis of a dataset on the structure of the French workforce by administrative region (département) in 1954.

Questions How were the workers distributed across the departments? Which sector of the workforce employed the most? Were there geographic patterns?

Sources The table in Bertin's book for the data, areas of the departments from the **Guerry** package and Wikipedia, and the Institut Géographique National for the map.

Structure Numbers of workers in three sectors for each of the then 89 departments of France and Paris.

7.1 Bertin's classic book

The book `Semiology of Graphics` (Bertin (2010)) is deservedly a classic amongst texts on statistical graphics. Wainer has written that "For technical details [it] is without peer" (Wainer (1997)) and that it "laid the groundwork for modern research in graphics" (Wainer (2004)). Lee Wilkinson has stated (Wilkinson (2005)) : "It has taken me ten years of programming graphics to understand and appreciate the details in Bertin." Bertin's work is important because he wrote about general principles for drawing graphics and introduced theoretical structure.

The book includes a whole chapter of 39 pages devoted to the workforce dataset (Part One Chapter III A). As a section heading on its first page says, "A hundred different graphics for the same information". Most of the data are printed out at the beginning of the chapter: the numbers of people working in the three sectors of Agriculture, Industry, and Commerce in each department, given in thousands. An original source for the data is not given and there are no details on how the sectors were defined. There are minor inconsistencies in the totals, some, but not all, doubtless due to rounding. Paris is included as a separate entity and Corsica is excluded.

Bertin also draws graphics for numbers of workers per square kilometre, based on the areas of the departments. To calculate these here, most department areas were taken from a dataset of France in the 1830s provided in the R package *Guerry*. For the few newer French departments the data were taken from Wikipedia.

A shapefile map of the current French departments is available on the website of the Institut Géographique National. Details are given in a French article on cartography with R (Coulmont (2010)). The map does not have the five overseas departments, which are not relevant for Bertin's dataset, but it does include the two Corsican departments and the six new departments created in 1967 by splitting up Seine and Seine-et-Oise. To adjust for 1954, the year of Bertin's data, the map was amended accordingly.

Dedicated Geographic Information System (GIS) software includes ways of dealing with enclaves, parts of one area completely enclosed by another. This was not expected to be an issue, but surprisingly it turned out that five departments have enclaves, amongst them, most notably, the Enclaves des Papes in Drôme, which is actually part of the department of Vaucluse. Discovering such tidbits of information is one of the serendipitous pleasures of Exploratory Data Analysis: you end up learning more than just about the data to hand.

7.1.1   A first map: agricultural workers

Figure 7.1 shows the 90 departments of France in 1954 with the 40 highlighted in which agricultural workers made up at least 40% of the workforce. There is a fairly clear division into East and West, something that is described in French texts under the heading of the Le Havre-Marseille line. The line may have declined in importance over the last thirty years, but in 1954 it was still relevant.

Given the large number of maps that Bertin included, you would expect several geographic patterns to be identified and discussed. It is a puzzling omission.

7.2   Bertin's many graphics of the French workforce data

There are just over 100 graphics in the chapter, all giving views of the same dataset. The exact number depends on how sets of multiple graphics and

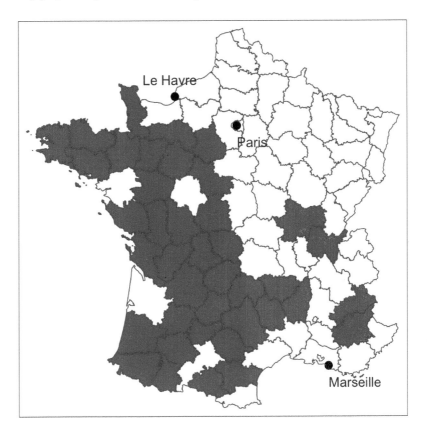

FIGURE 7.1: Departments in France in 1954 where agricultural workers made up at least 40% of the workforce.

intermediate graphics illustrating how graphics were constructed are counted. About two-thirds of the graphics are maps of France, the rest are barcharts, scatterplots, histograms, and other graphic forms. Many of the graphics are drawn to show that they do not work well, as these remarks in the book show:

- In no case does the image yield useful information. [Referring to Figures 1, 2, and 3] (p. 103)

- It is difficult to draw a useful conclusion from this group of images. (p. 105)

- Note that the resemblances among the sectors are hardly visible and, in fact, are overwhelmed by the striking differences in total working population per department. (p. 121)

- In no case, however, can the notion of quantitative value be obtained from these images. (p. 124)

- This solution reduces considerably the information transmitted and opens the door to unjustifiable interpretations. (p. 126)

- Different value steps, applied to absolute quantities, result in completely erroneous images. (p. 130)

Comments in a similar vein can be found on pages 109, 119, 122, 131, and 135. The first edition of Bertin's book was published in French in 1967. Perhaps he wanted to emphasise that not all of many different graphics are equally good. Judging by some of what is published today, this advice is still relevant.

Interestingly, the main (and pretty well only) conclusion that Bertin draws from all his graphics is that the data for two of the sectors are related. This conclusion is drawn by him from each of the groups of displays on pages 106, 107, 108, 109, 111, 112, 113, 115, 129, 135, and 137. He likes the final four maps on p. 137 best and writes: "The correlation between sectors II [Industry], III [Commerce] and the total population suggested by the earlier diagrams, is particularly striking here." Bertin is referring to the total working population, the sum of the data for the three sectors. Since the two biggest sectors are highly positively correlated, it is obvious that the total will be positively correlated with them as well. Curiously this is not mentioned.

7.3   Viewing the data today

Bertin was a cartographer and geographer concerned with the individual values for the departments. The first eleven maps on p. 116-117 are maps of France for each of the four variables (the three sectors and totals) in terms of the absolute values, the densities per unit area, and the sector percentages, with the department boundaries marked and the values written in. Presenting individual department values is important, especially as French readers would want to know the value for their own department, but it does not show us how those individual values stand in relation to the distributions of all values. For instance, Gironde had 115000 working in Agriculture, 107000 working in Industry, and 170000 working in Commerce. It was 6th biggest in Agriculture with 70% of the highest value, 16th biggest in Industry with 19% of the highest value, and 8th biggest in Commerce with 18% of the highest value.

The sorted barcharts drawn by Bertin provide some distributional information in terms of rankings, although histograms are better for studying distributions and that is what statisticians would draw, as in Figure 7.2. The three plots have been drawn with common scales to make them directly comparable.

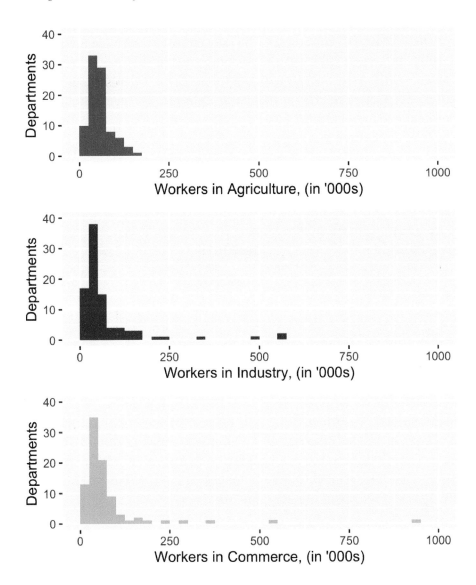

FIGURE 7.2: Histograms of the numbers working in the three sectors in 1954

The total numbers of workers in the three sectors are of the same order (Commerce 6.9 million, Industry 6.7 million, Agriculture 5.2 million). The distributions for both Industry and Commerce are highly skewed due to a handful of big values in both, primarily Paris and Seine. The distribution of agricultural workers is less skewed. No department has more than the 164000 agricultural workers of Finistère in the furthest North West of France.

Histograms of percentage shares of the sectors by department or of logged
values of the sectors (to counteract the skewness) can provide some additional
information, but scatterplots are more informative. Figure 7.3 shows scatterplots for the three pairs of sector variables. Each variable has been scaled
individually. In particular, the agricultural numbers are much smaller than the
numbers in the other sectors.

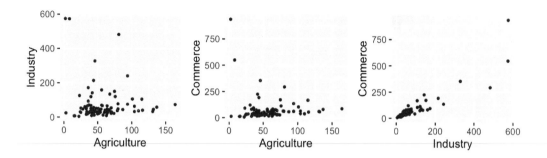

FIGURE 7.3: Pairwise scatterplots of the numbers in thousands working in
the three sectors in France in 1954

Bertin's conclusion that Industry and Commerce values are strongly related
is immediately clear, as is the lack of relationship between Agriculture and
the other two sectors. Identifying the highest values reveals that Paris has
most workers in both Industry and Commerce and is out of line with the
general Industry/Commerce relationship, having relatively more workers in
Commerce. One department, Nord, manages to have a high value for Industry
and a relatively high value for Agriculture.

There may be a little more information in the data alone, but what makes this
dataset interesting is its geographic basis. That is surely why Bertin drew so
many maps of the French workforce data.

7.4   Are there other geographic patterns?

There are a number of possible geographic patterns that might be found in
mapped data, for example local clusters of related values, trends from North
to South, similarities along coasts or borders. This means that any pattern
identified should be treated with caution, as it is almost certain that something
will be found. Nevertheless, geographic patterns discovered in the data may
be useful in summarising information and in suggesting new ideas. It may be
possible to find supporting evidence elsewhere, once it is known what should
be looked for.

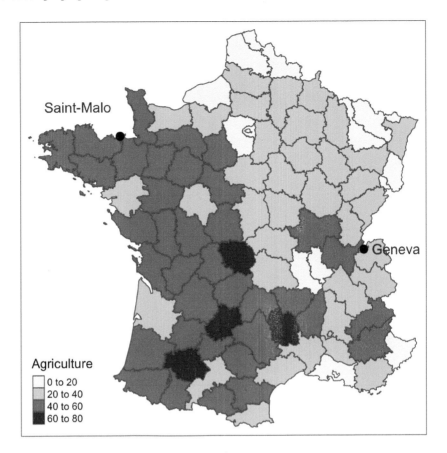

FIGURE 7.4: Choropleth map of percentage of agricultural workers in France in 1954

In Friendly's revisiting of Guerry's work (Friendly (2007)), he refers to a line across France from Saint-Malo in the North-West to the Swiss border at Geneva in the South-East, which divided France into 'France obscure' (the uneducated South-West) and 'France eclairee' (the educated North-East). This is a famous line in French historical geography, first suggested by Dupin in 1828. Judging by the results of a recent Google query, it still attracts attention, although for different reasons. Looking at Figure 7.4, there seems to be some evidence for a similar geographic division in the 1950s.

Apparently, there is a further region called the Blue Banana, a European corridor of urbanisation, running from Northern Italy through Switzerland, Germany, the North Eastern departments of France, Belgium and Holland, finishing in a broad path across the South East and Midlands of England (Wikipedia (2020c)). That would imply lower levels of agricultural workers as in the plot.

As the areas with the highest workforces in and around Paris can barely be seen in the maps, a cartogram might be drawn. A cartogram redraws regions to match population size or another quantitative measure instead of geographic area. The regions are drawn to minimise distortion, but this is difficult, especially when regions of large area have small populations and vice versa. A number of algorithms have been proposed. Figure 7.5 has been drawn using a rubber sheet distortion algorithm and is based on the total working population for each department.

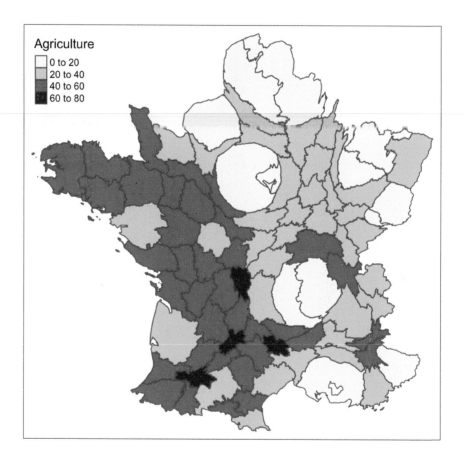

FIGURE 7.5: Cartogram of working population size shaded by the percentage of agricultural workers in France in 1954

The major industrial and commercial areas, where there is little agriculture, dominate the eastern half of the country. The Rhône and Loire departments almost touch the departments around Paris. Many different cartograms might be drawn, but they will all convey roughly the same message.

7.5   Density of the workforce by area

Bertin included four maps of the density of the workforce by area, thousands per square kilometre, on p.117 of his book. Every department has the relevant value written in, apart from Seine (covering Paris as well) for which the value is written at the top of each map, as the corresponding area is so small. He does not discuss what might be seen in the data although there are some unusual features. Choropleth maps for densities of the total working population, both including Paris and Seine and excluding them, are shown in Figure 7.6.

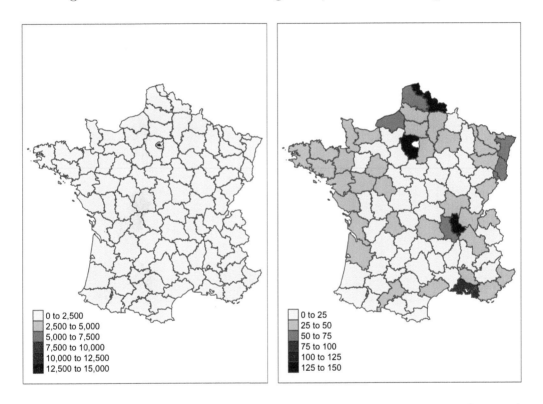

FIGURE 7.6: Maps of the density of the total working population in thousands per square kilometre in France in 1954, all departments (left), excluding Seine and Paris (right)

The values for Paris and Seine for total density are so high that no differences can be seen amongst the other departments in the first map. Looking closely it is just about possible to see that Paris is coloured dark red. The map on the right has a completely different scale (by a factor of 100) and shows that some of the departments with the otherwise highest densities were on the western edge of Seine. Despite the dramatic change in scale, many of the departments are still in the lowest grouping.

An alternative that avoids excluding departments is to use natural logarithms of population density. Figure 7.7 shows two versions, one using a default colour scale and one using a more detailed one. The first puts most of France in the same group, emphasising the three departments with lowest density in the South and Southeast and the few high density departments. The second suggests a difference in population density between the West and the Centre, apart from the departments with very high or low levels.

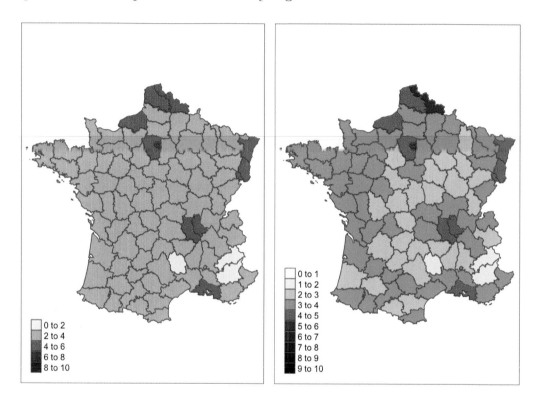

FIGURE 7.7: Maps of the log of population density of the total working population in thousands per square kilometre in France in 1954, default scale (left), more detailed scale (right)

7.6   Comments on Bertin (with hindsight)

Bertin's "Semiology of Graphics" contains many important ideas and was an attempt to develop a theory of graphics that could be built on and extended. Reviewing the dataset he considers in most detail does not reflect this. There are too many unsatisfactory graphics and there are few conclusions drawn from the data. The emphasis is more on presenting the available data in a broad range of different graphics than on deriving information from the data using graphics. Given the amount of work that was necessary to produce the graphics—some are beautifully drawn—this is disappointing. As Bertin himself says on p. 419 "Graphics has two objectives: 1. Data processing to understand the data and derive information from them. 2. Communication of this information."

Bertin is worthy of serious study and applying his ideas to new datasets may be more effective than studying his examples. There are no reproductions of Bertin's graphics here, hopefully encouraging readers to look at "Semiology of Graphics" for themselves.

Answers Each of the three sectors employed between 5 and 7 million. There were relatively more agricultural workers in the West of France. Numbers working in Industry and Commerce were positively related.

Further questions How have the numbers changed since 1954? Are there other sectors which have become important?

Graphical takeaways

- Graphics are for showing structure more than for providing exact individual values. (Figures 7.1 to 7.6)
- Scatterplots show associations between two variables. (Figure 7.3)
- Drawing graphics without outliers or extreme values creates space for showing the main structure of the data. (Figure 7.6)

8

Comparing chess players across the board

A strong memory, concentration, imagination, and a strong will is required to become a great chess player.

— Bobby Fischer

Background FIDE (the International Chess Federation) has used an Elo system since 1970 to rate the relative strengths of chess players based on the results of all official individual games.

Questions What is the distribution of ratings? How does rating change with age? How do the ratings of men and women compare? Which countries have the players with the highest ratings?

Sources FIDE (the International Chess Federation) publishes rating lists of players every month (FIDE (2020)). Country population data for 2019 was taken from the World Bank website (Worldbank (2020)).

Structure The FIDE dataset for December 2020 includes 362502 players with their name, country, rating, and year of birth.

8.1 FIDE ratings of chess players

FIDE (the International Chess Federation) publishes ratings of chess players regularly and these are the ratings that will be discussed here. Like many sporting organisations they use a system based on Elo's ideas (Elo (1978)). The main assumption is that the performance of a player is normally distributed the player's current strength. A further assumption is that players' performances in a game are independent of one another. Ratings are updated based on game results. Ratings in the December 2020 dataset range from 1001 to 2862 (the then world champion, Magnus Carlsen).

Figure 8.1 gives one view of the distribution of player ratings.

FIGURE 8.1: Histogram of ratings of all chess players rated by FIDE in December 2020

There is certainly no sign of a normal distribution, but then that would not be expected. There is a sharp lower boundary, presumably because lower ratings are not included. The very best players are not visible, as the histogram bars where they would appear are too small. There is a suggestion of a one-sided peak at 2000. Perhaps players who reach this level stop playing to avoid the risk of falling below 2000. Making the binwidth of the chess ratings histogram narrower (10 rating points instead of the 25 points used in Figure 8.1), there are weak hints of one-sided peaks at 1250 and 1500, similar to the one at 2000.

The best performing players are of interest and they are not visible in Figure 8.1. A boxplot of the ratings data is shown in Figure 8.2 and now the best players stand out (individual outliers drawn in red). It is clear that there were some exceptional players with ratings over 2750. Going back to the data shows that there were 18 of them.

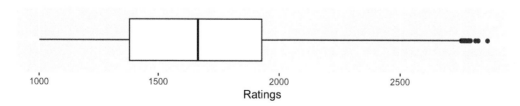

FIGURE 8.2: Boxplot of ratings of all FIDE rated chess players in December 2020

8.2 Comparing chess players by age and sex

Further information in the dataset includes the sex of the players, their year of birth, and whether they are "active" or not. An inactive player is one who has not played a rated game in the past 12 months (temporarily extended by FIDE to 24 months because of Covid). Gary Kasparov, the former world champion, retired in 2005 and has kept his then rating of 2812. He is recorded as inactive. Comparing the distributions of the active and inactive players gives Figure 8.3. The one-sided peak at 2000 is pretty much all due to the inactive players, as suspected.

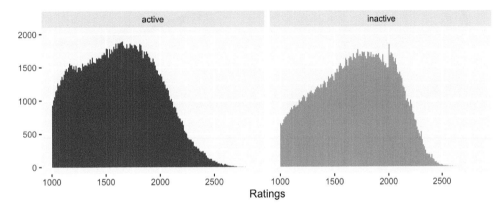

FIGURE 8.3: Histograms of ratings for active and inactive players

There are relatively fewer inactive players with low ratings. This can be better seen by superposing density estimates for the two groups, as in Figure 8.4.

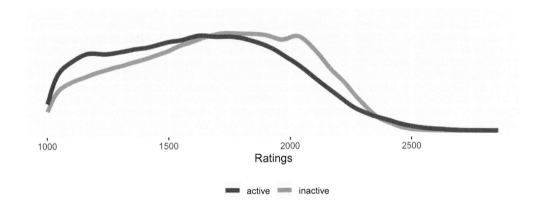

FIGURE 8.4: Density estimates of distributions of ratings for active and inactive players

Many players take up the game when they are young and do not have high ratings initially. Chess is an extremely strenuous activity at higher levels and there are many reasons why players may stop playing as they get older. The year of birth for a little under 98% of the players is given in the dataset. Plotting density estimates of the distributions of the players' ages for the inactive and active groups gives Figure 8.5. There is a high proportion of active players who are young, peaking in the early teens.

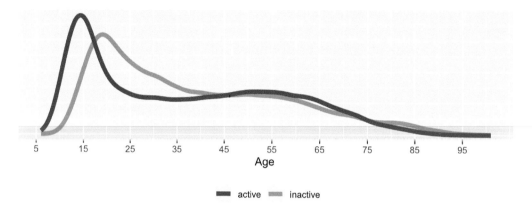

FIGURE 8.5: Density estimates of age distributions for active and inactive players

Far fewer women play chess than men. In December 2020 women comprised 10.5% of players with a rating. This dropped to 10.1% amongst active players. Figure 8.6 compares the rating distributions for active male and female players.

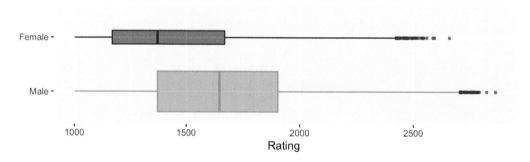

FIGURE 8.6: Boxplots of ratings for active players by sex (boxplot widths are proportional to the square roots of group sizes and outliers are drawn in red)

The female ratings are lower than the male ratings, mainly because far fewer females play. This was analysed in Bilalic et al. (2009) using only German ratings from 2008. The authors concluded that the difference in numbers playing explained about 96% of the rating differences between the sexes for the top 100 players of each sex.

Figure 8.7 shows the data for the December 2020 FIDE ratings for the top 1000 active players of each sex. The male ratings are higher. At the very top the differences are smaller and then they get steadily bigger.

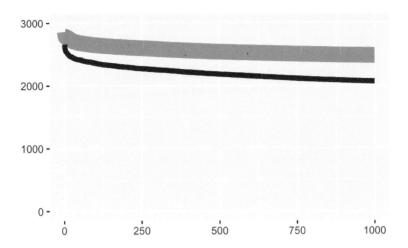

FIGURE 8.7: Ratings of the top 1000 male and top 1000 female players in December 2020 with line widths proportional to group sizes

The increasing differences can be seen directly in Figure 8.8. This agrees with what Bilalic et al. (2009) found with their data and also with the theoretical expected values they calculated assuming underlying normal distributions of ratings. The FIDE ratings are not normally distributed, but the increasing differences between male and female ratings at these top levels is likely to be true in general for order statistics for groups of such different sizes.

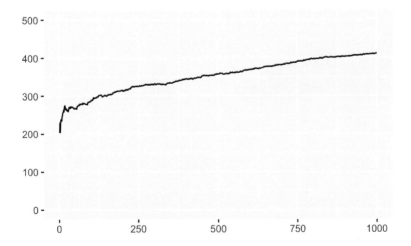

FIGURE 8.8: Differences between the ratings of the top 1000 male and top 1000 female players in December 2020

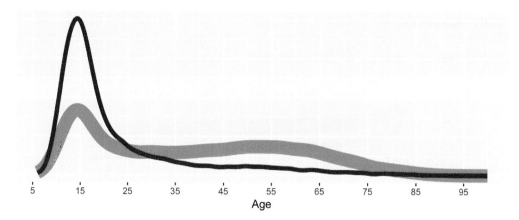

FIGURE 8.9: Density estimates of age distributions of active players (females in purple, line widths proportional to group sizes)

Age also has an effect as Figure 8.9 suggests. Many teenagers of both sexes play, but the proportion of the young amongst female chess players is much higher than the proportion of the young amongst male chess players. Many young players will give up the game before reaching their full potential. Overall there are about nine times as many male players as female players. Looking at the data in another way, Figure 8.10 shows the absolute numbers of active players by age and sex in December 2020.

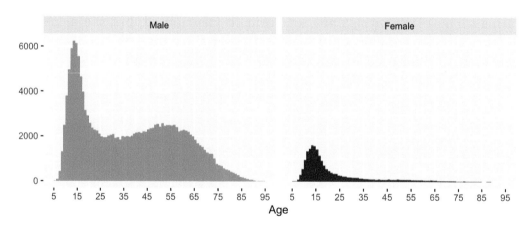

FIGURE 8.10: Age distributions of active players (females in purple)

The much higher number of male players is obvious, as is the sharp decline in participation by both sexes. What is also clear is that far more older men are still playing. What is not clear is whether the distributional shape is due to there being many more young female players now than there were in the past.

8.3 Which nations have the best chess players?

For much of the twentieth century, the USSR was the strongest chess nation. Over the last thirty years the game has become popular in other nations and it is surprising, which were the largest chess playing nations in December 2020, measured by the number of active rated players. Figure 8.11 shows the 30 chess federations with the highest numbers. The rest are combined into the group 'Other'. Countries are coloured by region, using the classification and colours of the World Bank (Worldbank (2020)).

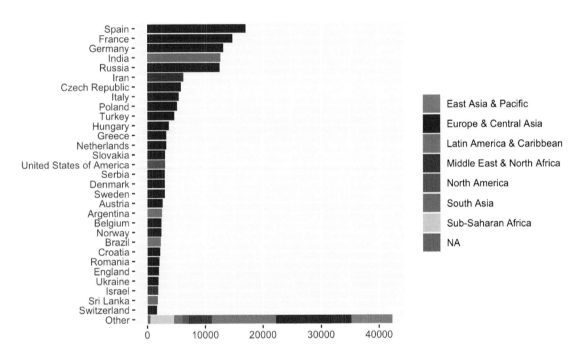

FIGURE 8.11: Numbers of active rated players by country

Not only is Russia not the country with the most active rated players, there are four other countries with more: Spain, France, Germany, and India. The increased popularity of chess in India is surely due to Anand being undisputed World Chess Champion from 2007 to 2013. The United States is only 15th in the list and most of the top 30 countries are European. Iran stands out in 6th position. The fact that the 'Other' group is so large underlines the spread of the game across the world.

Countries are of very different population sizes and other ways of looking at chess-playing strength include the number of active rated players per million population and the number of active grandmasters per million population.

These statistics tend to pick out countries with small populations. Instead we can look at how the number of Grandmasters is related to the number of players. Figure 8.12 plots both with bubbles drawn for each country proportional to their population sizes. Only countries with a population of at least one million are included. Russia is the country at the top with far more Grandmasters than any other. The other four countries to the right are India (large in blue), Germany, France, and Spain. China and the USA are the big countries to the left with many grandmasters and relatively few rated players.

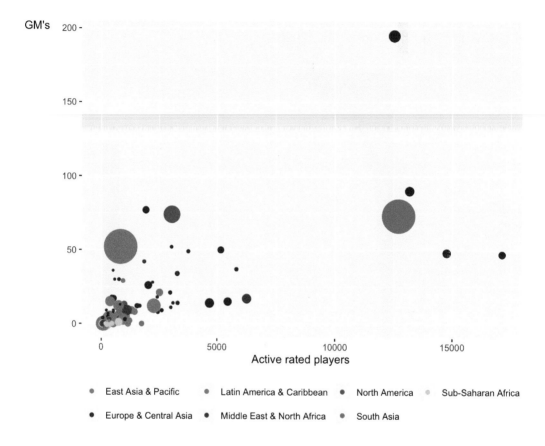

FIGURE 8.12: Grandmasters and active rated players per million population, where circle areas are proportional to country population sizes

Another approach is to look at rating distributions for individual countries. Figure 8.13 shows boxplots of ratings for all countries with more than 3000 active players ordered by their medians. Boxplot widths have been drawn related to numbers of players and the countries coloured again by region.

Serbia and the Netherlands have the highest median values and also some low outliers implying they have fewer players with low ratings. Perhaps different countries have different policies concerning registering players with official

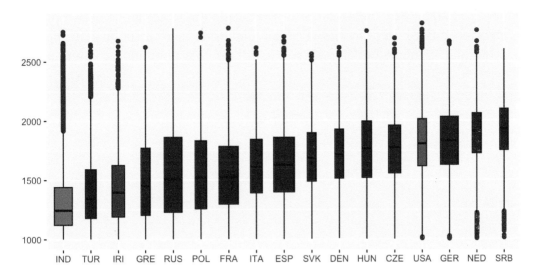

FIGURE 8.13: Chess ratings of active players for countries with over 3000 active

ratings. As in Figure 8.11, you can see that Spain, France, Germany, India, and Russia have the most active players and the German players look stronger in general. India has many players, but is the weakest of the big nations, possibly because chess has developed in popularity only recently there. The US has the highest rated player in this display, even though they are one of the smaller countries in terms of the number of active registered players. Norway, the home of the World's top player, Magnus Carlsen, does not have enough registered players to appear in this chart.

8.4 Ratings change over time

FIDE's website used to offer datasets going back to January 2001. Currently it offers almost 8 years of monthly ratings datasets and also ratings charts for individual players going back 20 years. The ratings in December 2020 were unusual because tournaments had not taken place due to the Covid pandemic. The December 2015 ratings were chosen for comparison.

The January 2001 dataset only includes players with a rating of over 2000 and has just 36979 players, slightly over a tenth of the number for December 2020. The December 2015 list has no rating restriction, but only 227960 players, so there were about 59% more at the end of 2020, five years later. The proportion of players flagged as inactive has also gone up from 42% to 47% and that explains part of the difference in overall numbers.

Figure 8.14 compares the densities of the rating distributions of active players in December 2015 and December 2020. The difference in the distributions is striking and it might be that there was a higher proportion of young active players in 2020.

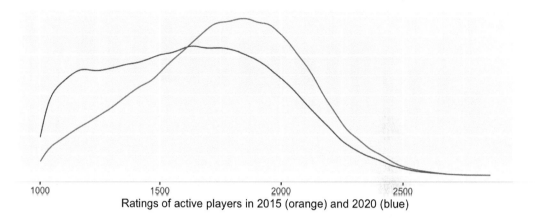

Ratings of active players in 2015 (orange) and 2020 (blue)

FIGURE 8.14: Density estimates of distributions of ratings in December 2015 and December 2020

Figure 8.15 compares density estimates of players' ages and confirms that there was a higher proportion of younger active players in 2020.

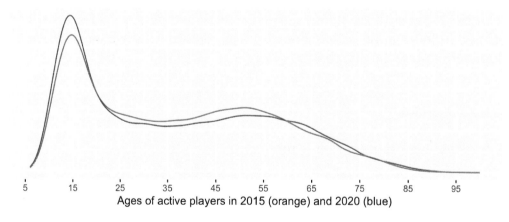

Ages of active players in 2015 (orange) and 2020 (blue)

FIGURE 8.15: Density estimates of active players' ages in 2015 and 2020

Ratings can be plotted against age in a scatterplot to study how they depend on age. Usually statisticians want more data than they have, so that they can study their data in greater depth. With the chess ratings there is almost too much data! Figure 8.16 illustrates the problem for the December 2015 data. 132489 points have been plotted and there are many overlapping points. An alpha value of 0.05 means that only locations where there are 20 or more points

are completely black. This alpha value is too high where there is a lot of data
(the very young) and too low where there is little data (the top rated players).
Nevertheless we can see that there are no very young high-rated players and
that there are relatively few low-rated players aged over 20 or so. There is a
decline in the numbers of the very top-rated players with increasing age.

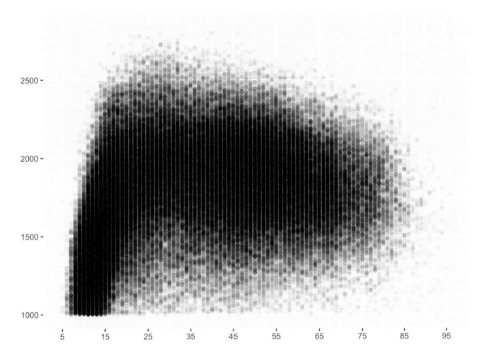

FIGURE 8.16: Rating by age for active players in 2015 (an alpha value of 0.05
has been used)

The bulk of the players form a shape like a short-necked bird with a long head,
perhaps a brent goose. The discreteness of the age data is noticeable due to
the striping effect of the gaps. It would not arise with exact ages. The points
could be made bigger, but then there would just be one big black blob.

One approach would be a form of two-dimensional density estimation or
hexagonal binning (Carr et al. (1987)), possibly including jittering of the age
values. Since the dataset is a December one it can be safely assumed that
almost all players are at least the calculated age, so that if jittering is carried
out it should be by adding a jitter term from [0,1).

A way to both show the densest parts of the data and pick out the top-rated players would be to colour the points for those top players and use different alpha values for the two groups. Figure 8.17 uses an alpha of 0.01 for most of the data and an alpha of 1 for the 44 players coloured red with ratings over 2700.

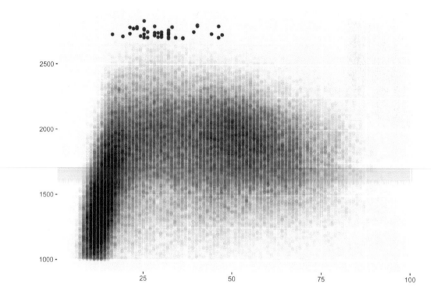

FIGURE 8.17: Rating by age for active players in 2015 (players with ratings over 2700 are coloured red and an alpha value of 0.01 has been used for the others)

Simplest would be to take a random sample and this has been done in Figure 8.18 using a 10% sample and alpha = 0.1. The advantage of sampling from a large dataset is that even a much smaller sample than this 10% one would give an excellent estimate of the overall structure and it is not necessary to draw so many points for that purpose. To be on the safe side a second or even a third sample could be taken to check any results. The disadvantage is that anything rare, such as outliers or unusual cases, may not be included in the samples.

Another alternative, using the enforced discreteness of the age variable, would be to draw boxplots for each age (Figure 8.19). The 38 players over 90 have been excluded as have the 2889 players whose year of birth is not known. The medians of the boxplots show the same pattern as the smooth in Figure 8.18, as do the upper and lower hinges of the boxplots, and the display gives a clear picture of where the middle 50% of the data lie at each age. The upper outliers are players who are exceptional for their age and the lower outliers are players who still compete although they are weak. The first lower outlier appears at age 23, perhaps an indication that many weaker players have given up by then.

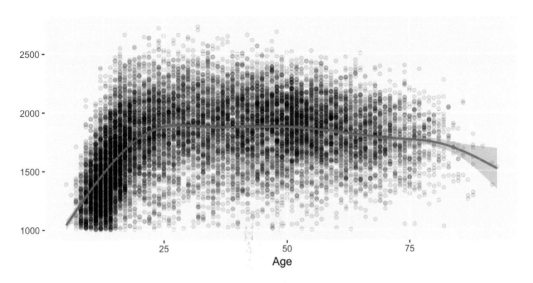

FIGURE 8.18: Rating by age for a 10% sample of active players in 2015 with a nonlinear smooth and confidence band

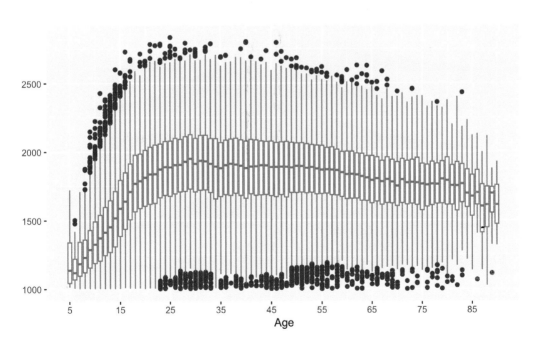

FIGURE 8.19: Boxplots of ratings by age for active players in 2015

The disadvantage of using boxplots is that they cannot show multimodality, if it exists. To check for multimodality, consider ridge plots, as in Figure 8.20. Most of the ridges look close to unimodal, symmetric distributions. Ridges have only been drawn here for ages at every 5 years for the main part of the dataset from ages 15 to 65. While ridges are good for the central bulk of distributions they are not so good at the extremes where they may imply higher or lower values than are reasonable. As no players can have ratings less than 1000, an option has been chosen to set a boundary there. Similarly, the upper tails of the distributions have been bounded. Using ridgeplots and boxplots in combination is a promising solution.

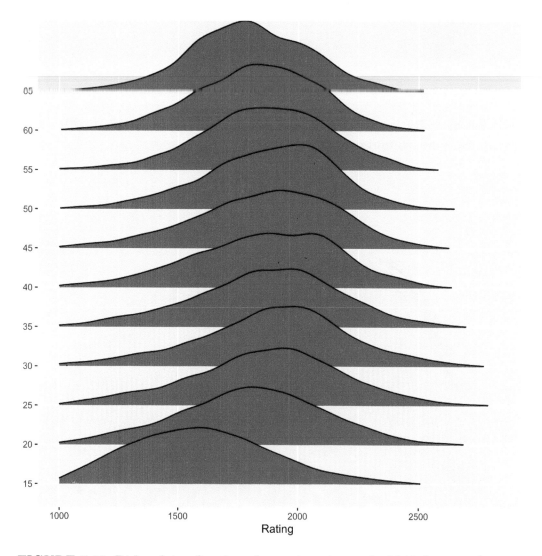

FIGURE 8.20: Ridgeplots of ratings for active players in 2015 for ages from 15 to 65 in 5 year jumps

Returning to comparing the rating datasets in December 2015 and 2020, Figure 8.21 shows two scatterplots of rating by age, one for the active players in the December 2015 dataset and one for the active players in the December 2020 dataset. Smooths have been drawn to show how rating varies with age.

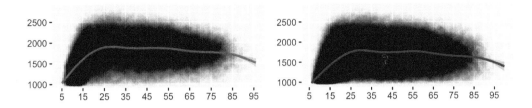

FIGURE 8.21: Rating by age for active players in 2015 and 2020

The scatterplots look fairly similar in form. A direct comparison of the smooths is shown in Figure 8.22.

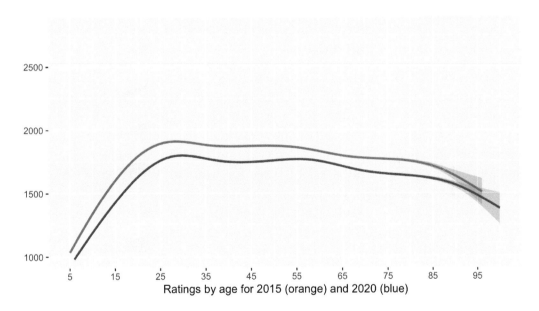

Ratings by age for 2015 (orange) and 2020 (blue)

FIGURE 8.22: Smooths for ratings by age for active players in 2015 and 2020

Smoothed ratings by age for active players were uniformly lower in 2020 than in 2015. This is likely because there were many more active players in 2020 than in 2015. It is curious that the smooth for 2020 starts at a higher age than the one for 2015. Exploring the data showed that there were fewer very young rated players in 2020. The data reveal that there were 0 five-year-olds in the 2020 dataset and only 12 six-year-olds (in 2015 the corresponding numbers were 10 and 52). This was probably due to the pandemic leading to few tournaments being played, so that the very youngest players could not get started.

8.4.1   Individual players

The changes between December 2015 and December 2020 could be explored further by looking at the three populations of players involved: those who appear in both lists, those who were present in 2015 but not in 2020, and the new ones.

Merging the two data files by player ID number reveals that 226450 players appear in both lists, 1510 players are on the 2015 list, but not on the 2020 list, and 136052 players are only on the 2020 list. It seems to be much harder to leave the ratings list than to join it!

Rather than studying population changes between two particular time points, it would be more informative to create a longitudinal dataset by combining all the rating datasets and studying players' career paths over the months and years.

8.5   Grandmasters and Masters

There are four titles for chess players: candidate master (CM), FIDE master (FM), international master (IM) and grandmaster (GM). The history of the introduction of titles for players is not fully clear. The GM title started to be used informally just before the first World War and official international regulations for the award of the titles GM and IM were introduced by FIDE in 1950. There are a parallel set of titles for women (WCM to WGM), but the strongest women opt for the open titles. Titles are awarded based on performance as well as rating, and the regulations are relatively complex. In the December 2020 ratings there were 37 female grandmasters (GM's) (of whom 8 were inactive) and an additional 317 WGM's (105 inactive). By comparison there were 1686 male GM's (300 inactive).

Figure 8.23 includes a barchart of the numbers of active players with different titles and scatterplots of the ratings of those players against their ages.

There are more players in each of the open categories than in any of the female categories, although the qualification levels for those are lower. This is another effect of far fewer women playing than men. There are more FIDE masters (FMs) than any other title.

The point clouds rise as the title level rises, but there is quite a lot of overlap between titles. The highest ratings for each title drop with age, partly because players gain a higher title, partly because players' performance tends to decline with age. The levels for open titles are higher than the levels for women for

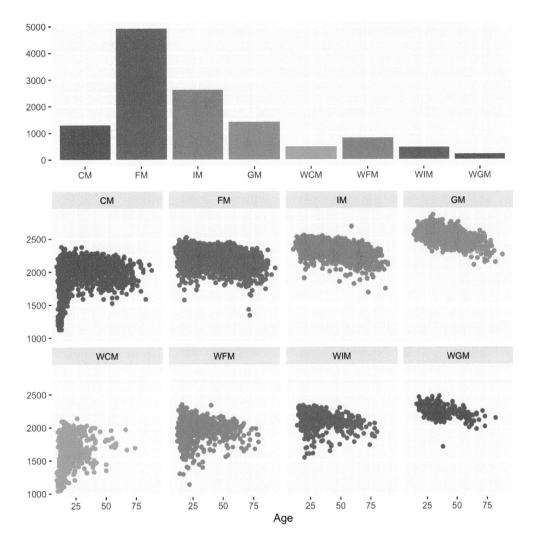

FIGURE 8.23: Numbers of active titled players and their ratings by age

each title. Some very young players with low ratings qualified as candidate masters. There are a few low outliers, presumably players who have lost form badly for one reason or another. There is a single upper outlier in the IM category, Igors Rausis, who admitted cheating and lost his grandmaster title in December 2019. As he immediately retired, he should be counted as inactive, but remained classified as active for a year under the special 2020 pandemic rule.

Answers Ratings have a skew distribution. More younger players have ratings than older players. Far fewer women play chess than men. Russia has the most grandmasters, while Spain and France had the most active rated players in 2020.

Further questions How do the ratings of individual players develop over time? How have numbers of active players by country changed over time? FIDE now publishes ratings for Rapid and Blitz chess as well as the so-called Standard ratings considered in this chapter are Standard ratings. How do the three types of rating compare for the players?

Graphical takeaways

- Boxplots are good for extreme outliers in large populations. (Figures 8.2, 8.6, and 8.19)
- Density estimates are effective for comparing distributions. (Figures 8.4, 8.5, 8.14, and 8.15)
- Line widths proportional to group sizes work well when the sizes are very different. (Figures 8.7 and 8.9)
- Smooths summarise scatterplot relationships in large datasets. (Figures 8.22 and 8.21)

9

Results from surveys on gay rights

Surveys show that surveys never lie. — Natalie Angier

Background Attitudes to same-sex marriage have been surveyed over a number of years. The survey discussed here was part of Annenberg's 2004 election year survey in the United States.

Questions How did people's opinions on same-sex marriage vary with age? How did the opinions vary across the country? Were there differences between people's opinions on a law at state level and their opinions on a Constitutional Amendment at federal level?

Sources The Annenberg Public Policy Center of the University of Pennsylvania

Structure There were 81422 people surveyed and 84 variables.

9.1 Survey results by age, sex, and race

Annenberg carried out rolling cross-section surveys for the US presidential elections of 2000, 2004, and 2008. The interviews for the 2004 National Annenberg Election survey were carried out between October 2003 and November 2004. Questions were asked on a range of topics and the dataset includes responses to many, but not all. Only a few questions are studied here. A third of respondents were asked if they would favour or oppose a law allowing same-sex marriage in their state, while all respondents were asked if they were in favour of or opposed to introducing a Constitutional Amendment making same-sex marriage illegal.

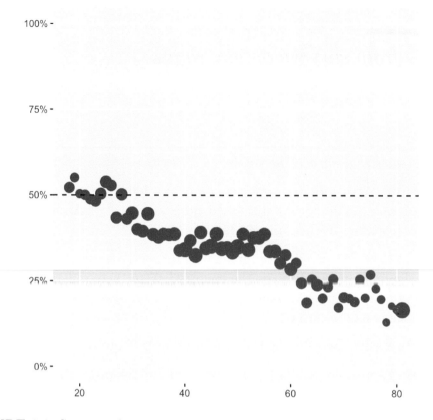

FIGURE 9.1: Support for same-sex marriage at state level by respondent age. A red dotted line marks 50% support. Cases with any values missing have been excluded and data for ages over 80 combined into one value at 81. Point areas are proportional to the number of respondents of that age.

There is a fairly steady decline in support by age, starting with a few young ages with majority support for same-sex marriage (amongst those expressing an opinion, those responding "Don't know" or refusing to answer have been treated as missing). With increasing age it looks like a step function with about the same level of support between ages 40 and 55 and similarly between ages 62 and 77. This was discussed in Gelman, Hill, and Vehtari (2020) where they suggested and compared several nonlinear models.

The dataset is large enough to look at opinions by age and sex together. Figure 9.2 shows that females are more in favour than males at almost every age. The effect on these opinions of sex and race together can also be investigated. Figure 9.3 shows a doubledecker plot for this. The patterns of support by race are the same for males and females, with female rates being higher. Rates for blacks are lowest.

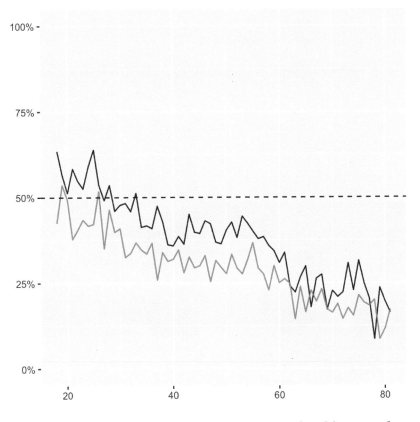

FIGURE 9.2: Support for same-sex marriage at state level by age of respondent for females (purple) and males (green)

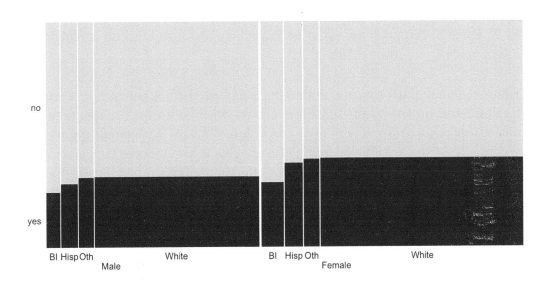

FIGURE 9.3: Support for same-sex marriage at state level by sex and race

9.2   Mapping the survey results

It is possible to look at how rates of support vary by state and, unsurprisingly, there are substantial differences. Figure 9.4 is a choropleth map of the support for a state law permitting same-sex marriage in each state. (Except that there is no information for Alaska and Hawaii as the survey was restricted to the 48 continental states and Washington D.C.)

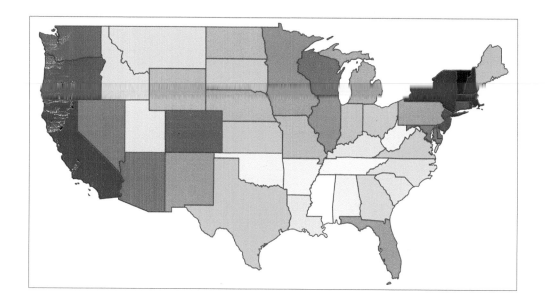

FIGURE 9.4: Support for same-sex marriage at state level on a continuous colour scale from 10% to 70%

Some regional patterns are apparent, such as the higher support in New England and on the West Coast. As always with choropleth maps, area does not reflect population. There are several larger states with small populations and smaller states with larger populations. This is also reflected in the numbers asked in each state. Figure 9.5 shows the estimates of proportions supporting a same-sex marriage law with 95% confidence intervals. The longest interval is for Washington, DC, with only 31 asked and the shortest interval is for California with 1891 asked. The states have been grouped by Census Bureau regions and ordered within region by percentage in favour. The NorthEast states split into two groups with Pennsylvania and Maine having much lower levels of support. The South also splits into two groups with Florida and the three small most northerly states having higher levels of support. The MidWest states have fairly similar values. Overall, very few states show a majority for same-sex marriage.

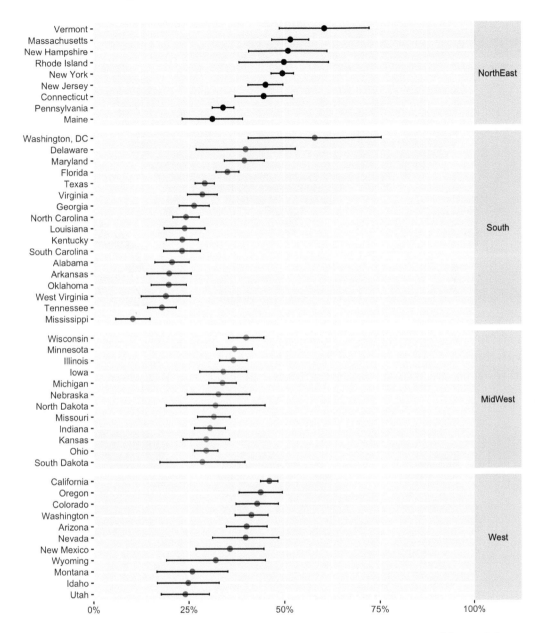

FIGURE 9.5: Support for same-sex marriage by state with 95% confidence intervals, states grouped by region and ordered within region by estimated population proportion in favour

Figure 9.6 shows a map of the regions.

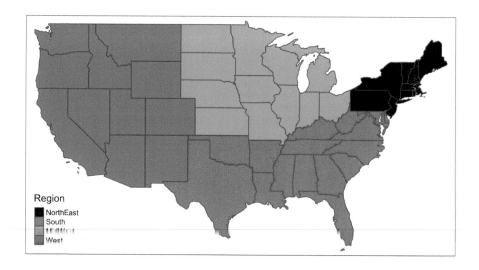

FIGURE 9.6: The four US regions defined by the Census Bureau

Cartograms can be effective in getting round the population issue. Figure 9.7
uses numbers of respondents as a substitute for state populations. It suggests
states separate into three main groups, the East, the West, and the centre.

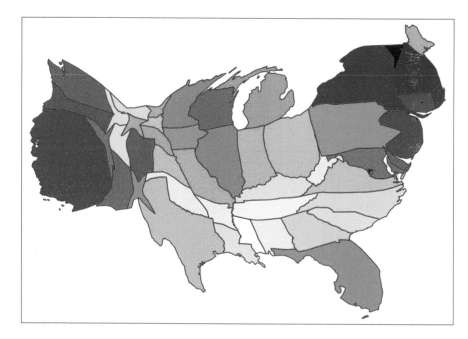

FIGURE 9.7: Support for same-sex marriage at state level using a population
cartogram

9.3 Comparing responses to related, but different questions

Another question about same-sex marriage was whether respondents were in favour of or opposed to introducing a Constitutional Amendment making same-sex marriage illegal. All respondents were asked and the support shows a quite different pattern with age to that of Figure 9.1, as can be seen in Figure 9.8.

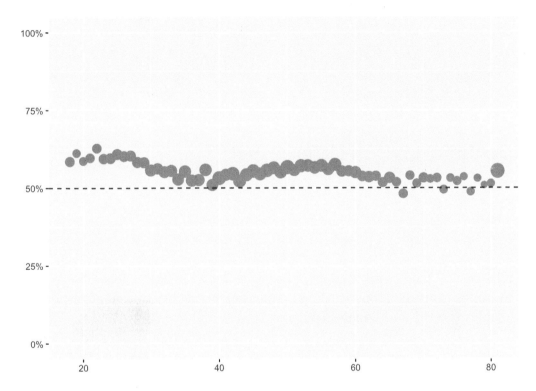

FIGURE 9.8: Scatterplot of opposition to a Constitutional Amendment making same-sex marriage illegal by age of respondent. Cases with any values missing have been excluded and data for ages above 80 have been combined into one value at 81. Point areas are proportional to the number of respondents of that age.

While there was a majority against same-sex marriage at state level for most ages except the youngest, there is a majority against a Constitutional Amendment at almost every age. There is also little difference in opinion across the ages concerning a Constitutional Amendment.

Including the influence of sex and drawing the graphics for the two questions beside one another helps making comparisons. Opposition to a Constitutional Amendment is higher for females than males at every age. The greater variability in the left graphic on state law is because only a third of the survey population was asked this question.

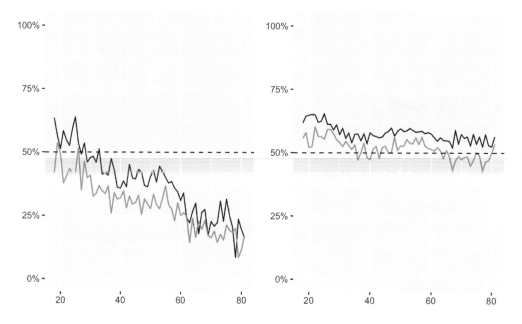

FIGURE 9.9: Line plots of support for same-sex marriage at federal level (left) and opposition to a Constitutional Amendment (right) by age of respondent by males (green) and females (purple)

The differences between the graphics depend on the exact form of the questions asked. Annenberg provide access to the full survey information on request. There were two versions of the state question asked at different times in the 2004 survey and five versions of the federal question. The differences within each group were slight, but there were major differences between the two groups. For the state question, "in favour" meant in favour of same-sex marriage. For the federal question, "in favour" meant in favour of a Constitutional Amendment banning same-sex marriage. Respondents to this question were offered an additional possible answer of "Neither favour nor oppose".

Figure 9.10 shows barcharts for the full sets of responses on both questions, excluding respondents who were not asked. Most people with opinions on the issues have strong opinions. The different framings of the two questions were important.

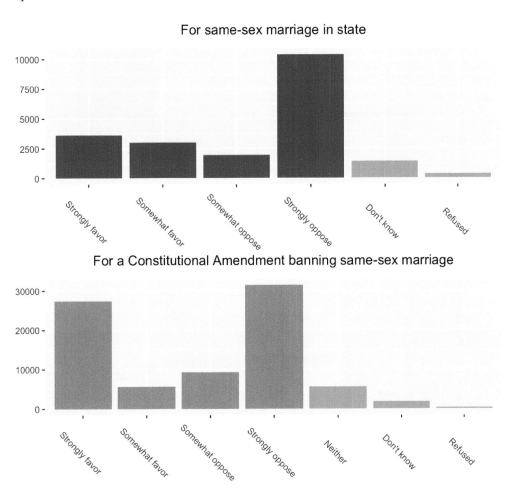

FIGURE 9.10: Barcharts of the full responses to the two questions

There were small numbers of "Don't know" and "Refused", as well as some who were neither for nor against the Constitutional Amendment question. Those who did not express opinions one way or the other have been coloured grey. The vertical scales are quite different, as only one third were asked the state question.

Figure 9.11 studies how those responded who gave their opinions on both questions, either strongly or just somewhat. Comparing answers of individuals is more informative than comparing distributions of aggregated answers.

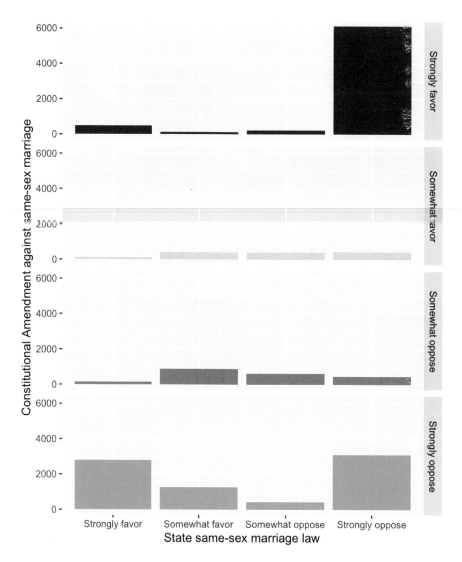

FIGURE 9.11: Multiple barcharts of the responses to supporting same-sex marriage at state level by the responses to supporting a Constitutional Amendment banning it

The most interesting feature is the combination of strongly opposing a same-sex marriage law for your own state while also strongly opposing a Constitutional Amendment banning same-sex marriage (bar lower right). This group is the main reason for the difference between the two graphics in Figure 9.9.

Responses to the two questions across the states can be compared by looking at the proportions who responded in favour of a state law for same-sex marriage and those who opposed a Constitutional Amendment making same-sex marriage illegal. Figure 9.12 shows the result, with circle sizes proportional to numbers giving an opinion on the Constitutional Amendment question.

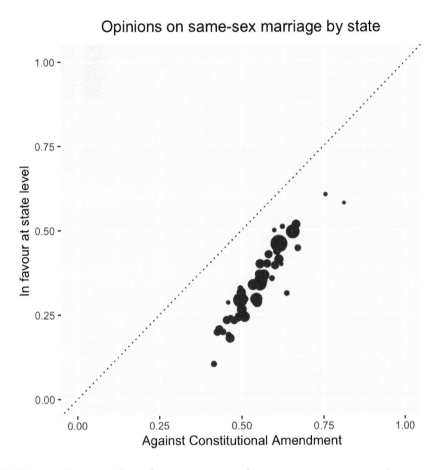

FIGURE 9.12: Scatterplot of responses to the two same-sex marriage questions by state (point areas are proportional to the number of respondents in that state)

Opposition to the Constitutional Amendment making same-sex marriage illegal was much stronger than support for a state law permitting same-sex marriage in all states. The two responses were highly correlated across the states with a slope greater than one, so as the federal variable rate increased, the state rate increased more. Opinions on gay rights are a complicated matter and there were several other related questions asked in the Annenberg survey. Much more analysis could be done. That survey was carried out almost twenty years ago and more recent surveys suggest that the US population has become more favourably disposed towards same-sex marriage.

Answers Older people were more against a same-sex marriage law in their state. Women were more in favour than men at all ages. There was a majority at all ages against a Constitutional Amendment banning same-sex marriage.

Further questions Respondents were asked additional related questions: How did their responses to those relate to their responses on same-sex marriage? What results do more recent surveys show? How do people's opinions vary on other contentious issues in the survey?

Graphical takeaways

- Bubble charts show how much evidence underlies a particular point. (Figures 9.1, 9.8, and 9.12)
- Doubledecker plots show both group rates and group sizes. (Figure 9.3)
- For large numbers of categories it is helpful to sort them into groups first and then order them by value. (Figure 9.5)

10

Who went up in space for how long?

The sky's the limit. (Idiom)

Background Human space travel has captured the world's attention since the first spaceflight by Yuri Gagarin in April 1961.

Questions How many men and women have gone up in space? How long were they in space? Which countries did they come from?

Sources rfordatascience (2020a)

Structure 1277 records each of 24 variables

10.1 What human spaceflights have there been?

The Tidytuesday project includes a collection of interesting datasets, adding a new one each week (rfordatascience (2020b)). The one uploaded in July 2020 (rfordatascience (2020a)) contained information on manned spaceflights up to the end of 2019. Each flight by each person is a separate record, making 1277 in all. Several flew more than once and there are 565 different people in the dataset. Two Americans, Jerry Ross and Franklin Chiang-Diaz, each flew seven times. There is demographic information on the individuals (sex, year of birth, nationality) and some information on the missions (title, year, spacecraft used, length of mission).

Human spaceflight may be defined as a human reaching outer space by going beyond 100 kms from the earth. The Challenger mission of 1986 that ended in disaster did not get that far, but is included in the dataset. The non-fatal Soyuz mission of September 1983 when the launch vehicle caught fire before launching is not included.

The number of people each year is shown in Figure 10.1. There are sharp drops in numbers after the Soyuz 1 crash in 1967, after the Challenger disaster in 1986 and after the Columbia disaster in 2003. The deaths in Soyuz 11 in 1971 do not seem to have had such an effect, but may have curtailed existing plans of the time.

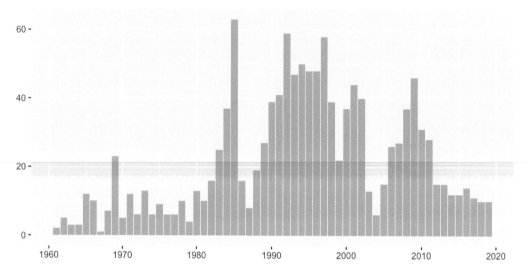

FIGURE 10.1: Numbers of people by year of flight

Early on, the participants were male and younger than later on. There have been fewer females and they were on average younger than the males. Figure 10.2 is a scatterplot of age by year of mission with smooths plotted separately for males and females. Age has been calculated as the difference between year of mission and year of birth, so is not exact. The vertical scale is extended beyond most of the data because of the high outlier, John Glenn's third spaceflight at the age of 77 in 1998. The males have been drawn first and the females on top to emphasise the females.

Scatterplots with many points do not convey actual numbers in groups well. In this dataset there are 11 participants aged 41 who went up in space in 1997, 9 men and two women, including three who went up twice. All these 14 points are represented by the same single point in Figure 10.2, coloured female (because of the order of plotting), although they all contribute equally to their respective smoothed fit. Figure 10.3 shows barcharts for males and females across the decades. There have been far fewer females and, in particular, the bar for the only female in the 1960s, Valentina Tereshkova, is barely visible. More went into space in the 1990s than in any other decade.

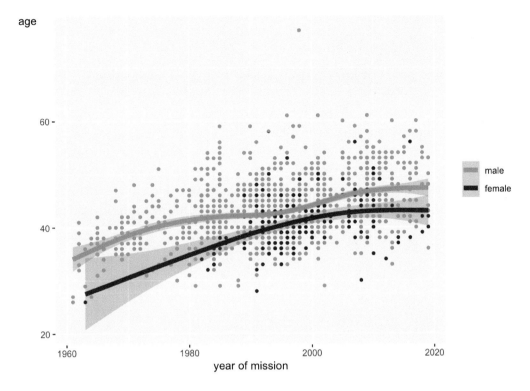

FIGURE 10.2: Scatterplot of age by year of flight coloured by sex, with smooths and their confidence intervals

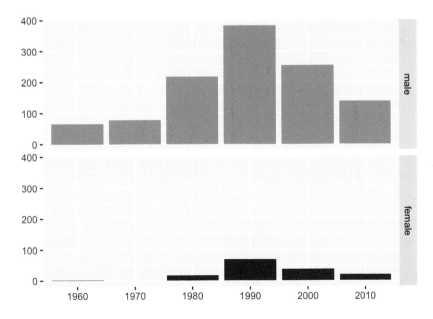

FIGURE 10.3: Numbers of participants by decade and by sex

10.2   Mission times in space

One important piece of information is the length of each mission, the time
from launch until return to earth. Figure 10.4 shows a scatterplot of this time
against flight year. Most flights were relatively short, especially in the 1960s
and later on there were still many short flights of up to a few weeks, but also
a group of longer ones, closer to six months, and a few very long ones of up to
a year or more. Missions with more than one person are only plotted once if
all those on the mission are recorded as having the same time, so this is not a
plot of individual mission times. Missions with differing individual times are
discussed later.

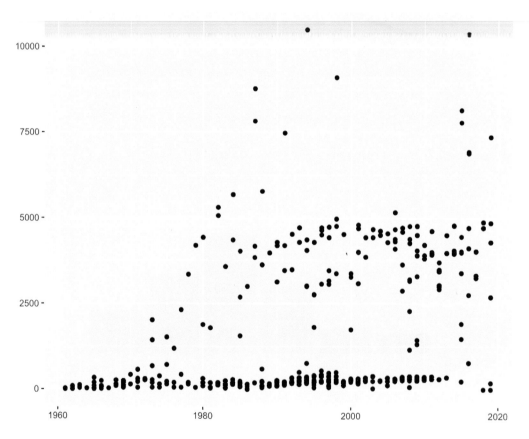

FIGURE 10.4: Scatterplot of mission time in hours by year of flight

There is some information that might explain why flights are either short or
longer, in particular whether the mission involved a visit to a space station.
That is the reason as can be seen in Figure 10.5. A new variable has been
created that records if a space station was visited and which programme it

was part of: the initial U.S.S.R. Salyut programme, the US Skylab programme, the intermediate U.S.S.R. Mir programme or the ISS (International Space Station) programme. All the long flights are part of space station missions. The flight in 1980 marked as "none" was in fact a space station flight by the Cuban Arnaldo Mèndez. This is a curious error as his mission time was also incorrectly reported, multiplied by 10 in the dataset. The case only stands out because both errors were made, otherwise it would not have been noticed.

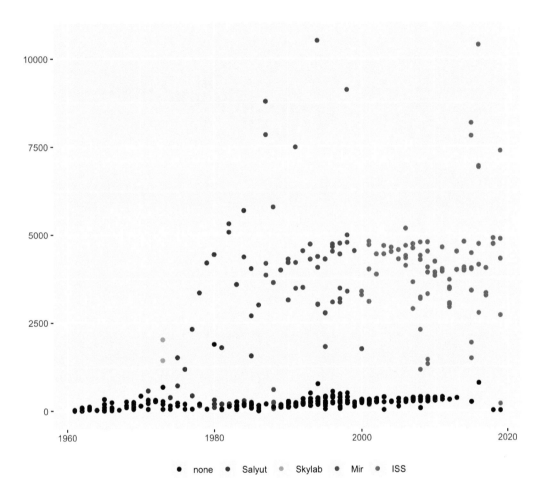

FIGURE 10.5: Mission time in hours by year of flight coloured by space station programme

The code for this plot converted two values of the variable `in_orbit` to "Salyut", those with "Salyut" in them and those with the misspelling "Saluyt". Minor typos like this can be irritating or seriously misleading. The problem was discovered when colouring the display.

10.2.1 Logging mission times

As there are so many short mission times that cannot be distinguished, logarithms of the times could be used. Figure 10.6 shows the result. The vertical scale has been manually constructed to offer interpretable tickmarks.

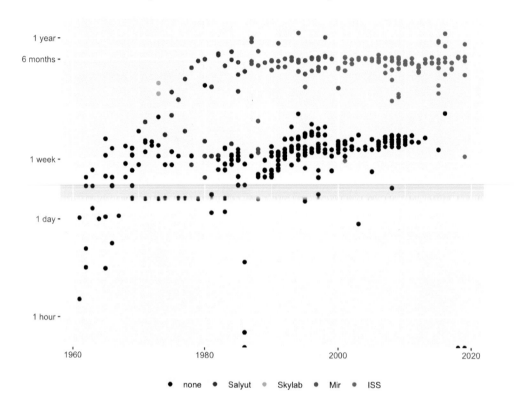

FIGURE 10.6: Scatterplot of log mission time by year of flight coloured by space station programme

There are several striking features. The two groups of short and long missions look less variable than in Figure 10.4 and the number of shorter missions declines after 2010. The latter is a useful piece of information, as an earlier analysis concluded that mission times had increased in recent years without explaining why. The average time certainly increased, but the reason was the decline in flights that did not visit a space station.

There are a few unexpected half points at the foot of the plot. These are mission times recorded as zero and hence logarithms of $-\infty$. Rather than just offering a warning message that they cannot be plotted (which **ggplot2** does in other circumstances), the semi-circles are drawn. The 1986 value is from the Challenger disaster and the 2018 and 2019 values are for the two on an aborted 2018 mission. For one of them, Ovchinin, the year of mission is incorrectly recorded as 2019.

There are some low outliers. The lowest one in 1986, just above one of the semi-circles, can be found by ordering the dataset in ascending order of times. It turns out that four of the seven people who died in the Challenger disaster were given times of 0 and the other three times of about 35 minutes. It seems particularly unfortunate when the data for such tragedies are inconsistent.

Sadly, Challenger was not the only disaster. The Space Shuttle Columbia disintegrated on re-entering the atmosphere in early 2003. The dataset ascribes (almost) the same time to the seven on board, but the variable in_orbit is recorded as "Exploded" for only three of them.

The other lowish value in 1986 was for Bill Nelson, who was on Columbia's STS-61-C mission. He was given a time of 6.03 hours, whereas five other crew members were given times of 146 hours, and one of 74 hours. Bill Nelson's Wikipedia page (Wikipedia (2020a)) said he was in space for 6d 02h 03m, so perhaps the error was a result of inaccurate webscraping. There are also three lowish values in 2005 and 2008. These were the first Chinese flights. Wikipedia records the first as having taken place in 2003.

Nationality is another factor to consider. Forty nationalities are included in all, but U.S. and U.S.S.R./Russia nationalities account for 88% of participants, so a new variable has been created for these two with the rest categorised as 'Other'. Plotting all the cases coloured by the new variable leads to some overplotting, so faceting has been used in Figure 10.7. The whole dataset has been plotted first in grey and the groups coloured and plotted on top (ghostplotting). The Russians were first with longer flights, while the Americans took part in many more shorter flights in the 1980s and 1990s. Other nationalities flew for the first time at the tail end of the 1970s and had more short flights.

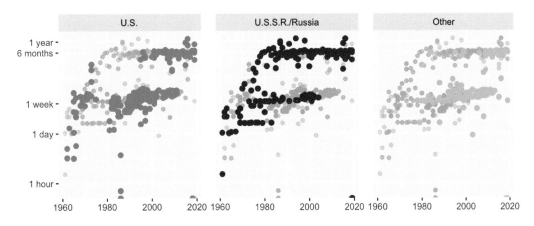

FIGURE 10.7: Scatterplots of log mission time by year of flight by nationality

10.3   Checking the data with graphics

Checking whether other missions had differing times for their crews in the dataset uncovered a number of inconsistencies. It was not enough to use the mission title, as sometimes these included multiple flights, so the dataset was grouped by the variables `mission_title`, `ascend_shuttle`, `in_orbit`, `descend_shuttle`, `year_of_mission`. This grouped together many correctly, but failed to group all missions properly as occasionally different codings (upper/lower case, hyphens or not) were used and there were errors. A boxplot of the biggest differences in mission times for the 538 groups found is displayed in Figure 10.8. There are four gross differences and plenty of smaller ones. The biggest difference concerns the American/Russian trio who went to the ISS in 2001. The time for Susan Helms is, correctly, over 160 days, while the time for James Voss is 163 hours. Yuri Usachyov gets a similar time to Susan Helms but is not in the same group, as the dataset reports he returned on a different spacecraft.

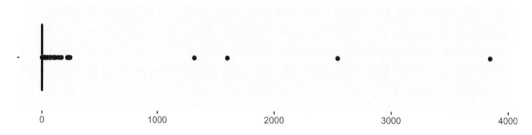

FIGURE 10.8: Boxplot of biggest differences in times for (possibly) the same missions

Ideally, all typos and errors should be corrected. The very first line of the dataset raises concern. Yuri Gagarin, who went up in space in April 1961, cannot have gone up in Vostock 1, been in orbit in Vostock 2, and come down in Vostock 3! It is said of John Hartigan, that when he discussed datasets at Yale seminars, he might take 20 minutes to examine the first line. This dataset is an example of why that approach can be valuable.

It would be informative to use exact flight dates, not just the years, and the dates are available on the Wikipedia page for human spaceflights (Wikipedia (2020b)). The dataset illustrates some of the issues that can arise with datasets that are made publicly available and how graphics can help to identify and deal with them. It also shows that even when there may be individual data problems, a dataset can still reveal much interesting information.

Answers Many more men than women have gone up in space and the men have been older. Initial flights were short. Since the space station programmes began, people have stayed much longer in space. Most of them have been Russians or Americans, but this is changing.

Further questions How many spaceflights have individuals made? Are there differences between the groups of U.S.S.R./Russians and Americans?

Graphical takeaways

- Graphics uncover problems in datasets, be they typos, errors or more serious issues. (§10.2 and §10.3)
- Scatterplots are excellent, but it is well to check for duplicate pairs of values and draw additional complementary plots. (Figure 10.2)
- Colours should be used consistently for the same categories. Different palettes should be used for other groupings to avoid confusion. (Figures 10.2 and 10.3 v. Figure 10.5 or Figure 10.7)
- Log (or other) transformations are effective for skewed distributions, especially with interpretable scaling. (Figure 10.6)
- Faceting disentangles overlapping groups in scatterplots. (Figure 10.7)

11

Data in the sky at night

The proportions and relations of things are just as much facts as the things themselves.

— Dorothy L. Sayers

Background The *diamonds* dataset from the R package **ggplot2** provides data on each of almost 54000 round diamonds that were offered for sale.

Questions Do the data need cleaning? How are the individual variables distributed? Are there any special features?

Sources The data were originally scraped from the web in 2007 by Hadley Wickham (Wickham (2007)) and he made them available in his R package **ggplot2**.. Many of the results in this chapter were found and written up by him then in an article that was rejected by a journal that should have known better.

Structure The dataset covers 53940 round diamonds with information on price, dimensions, and quality.

11.1   Data on diamonds for sale

Experts talk of the four c's of diamonds: carat, cut, colour, and clarity. These are the first four variables in the dataset. Carat is the weight of the stone (1 carat is 200 mg), while the other three c's are ordered grades with 5, 7, and 8 levels respectively (in this dataset). Three measurements are included: length (x), width (y), and depth (z). Confusingly there is another variable actually called `depth` that is defined as total depth percentage and will be referred to as `depthp` here.

Diamonds may have one of ten shapes, either round or one of the nine fancy shapes. Only round diamonds are considered here.

A histogram of the lengths is shown in Figure 11.1. The green circle is to indicate that with a sharp eye a bar might be seen at zero. Histograms of large datasets like this are not good at representing bars with only a few points. There must be at least one point with a length much above 9 too. Boxplots, as in Figure 11.2, are better for displaying possible outliers. The default scaling of a histogram is to include enough of the axis to include all the data, so whether a bar at zero was visible or not, there had to be data somewhere out to the left (and to the right) and the boxplot shows where.

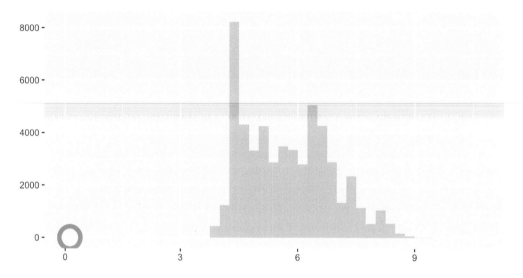

FIGURE 11.1: Histogram of diamond lengths (the bar at zero has been circled in green)

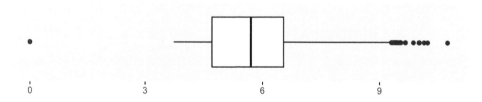

FIGURE 11.2: Boxplot of diamond lengths (outliers coloured red)

The lowest length values were checked and there were 8 diamonds of zero length. There were also some zero values reported for width and depth. The simplest solution was to remove these diamonds (unless the original data source could have been checked to find out the actual values). The scale of the vertical axis in Figure 11.1 goes up to over 8000, so a bar of height 8 will have a very small height in the plot, perhaps too small to be shown, depending on how big or small the plot is drawn.

Boxplots can be good for identifying possible outliers. Histograms are good for showing distributional shape—provided that informative binwidths are chosen. Redrawing Figure 11.1 after removing the diamonds of zero length and choosing a binwidth of 0.05 gives Figure 11.3.

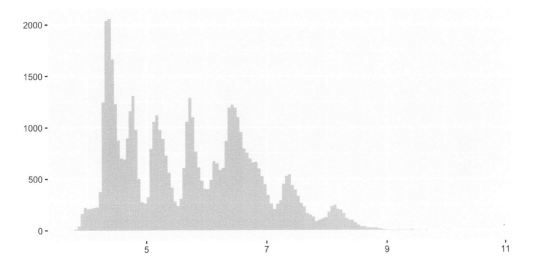

FIGURE 11.3: Histogram of diamond lengths (without zero-length diamonds)

It looks as if there is a mixture of groups of diamonds. Similar patterns can be found for the widths and depths while a related, but different, pattern is apparent for the distribution of carats. The one-sided peaks in the display suggest that far more diamonds of a rounded number of carats are offered for sale than diamonds of just under a rounded number. Two round diamonds of the same number of carats will have similar lengths, widths, and depths and this is likely to be the explanation for the shapes of their distributions.

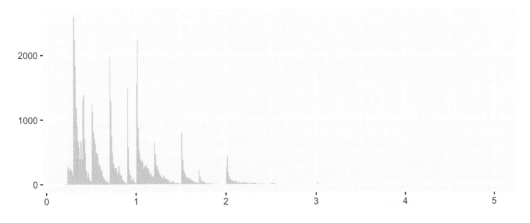

FIGURE 11.4: Histogram of diamond carats

The histogram binwidth was chosen to be the smallest possible, i.e. the same as the resolution of the data. If there is any pattern to be found in a large dataset, it will be shown at this level—provided the plot is big enough for the bars to be seen. This just about works for `price` in Figure 11.5, and there is enough detail to see something else, an unexpected gap around $1500.

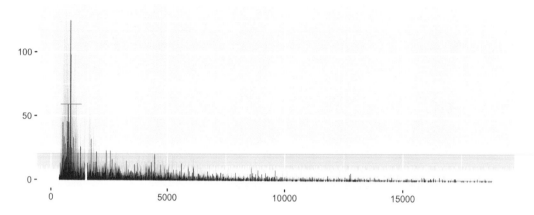

FIGURE 11.5: Histogram of diamond prices

Apparently there was a problem with scraping the data from the web that was not noticed early enough. There are no prices between $1455 and $1545, inclusive, in the dataset. The adjective 'unexpected' is important when talking about the gap. Features stand out that surprise us and they surprise us because they do not match expectations. You have to have expectations to be surprised.

11.2   Checking for outliers and unusual values

In all there are 20 diamonds with zero values for length, width or depth. All have zero depth, 8 have zero length, and of those 8, there are 6 with zero width. No other diamonds have zero width. These 20 cases must be errors and might be identified as outliers. Outlier detection methods tend not to find them when the whole dataset is used to look for them, because they are not far enough away from the rest of the data in multivariate space. After removing the 20 zero cases there are still three extreme outliers, two cases with extremely high values of width and one with an extremely high value of depth.

After removing the outliers, a scatterplot matrix of carats and the three dimensions, length, width, and depth identifies other possible outliers. The scatterplots with carat are curved, as it is really a volume measurement, so the cube root of carat was used to get linear plots.

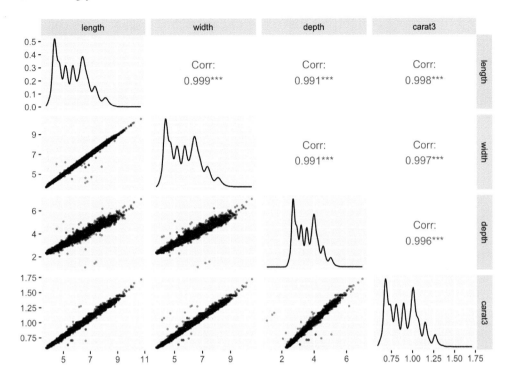

FIGURE 11.6: A scatterplot matrix of length, width, depth, and carats to the power one third for the dataset after removing the zero cases and three extreme high outliers

The correlations are all very high, despite the apparent variability. The reason is the size of the dataset. Most of the data are linearly related and hidden by overplotting. Several two-dimensional outliers are visible. The three lowest values of depth have middling values of length and width, so the problem is the depth measurement. There are a few other cases that seem too far away from the main body of the data. If a point is a two-dimensional outlier and not an outlier on either of the variables separately, then it could be an error on one or both of the variables or an unusual case. Outliers on individual dimensions are a problem for graphics because they distort the axes and shrink the space available for the main part of the data. This affects one-dimensional plots like histograms, but also higher dimensional displays like scatterplots and parallel coordinate plots.

Figure 11.7 shows a scatterplot matrix of `carat` with the other three continuous variables. An extreme outlier on the variable `table` has been excluded for the reason just mentioned. A few more cases appear to be outliers. The density estimate for `table` looks odd. Checking the frequencies of observed values in Figure 11.8 shows that most are integers.

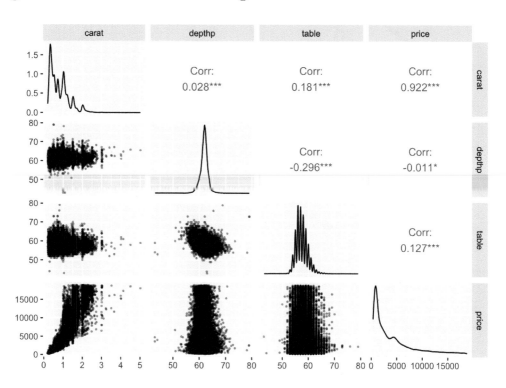

FIGURE 11.7: A scatterplot matrix of carat, percentage depth, table, and price for the dataset after removing the zero cases and four extreme outliers

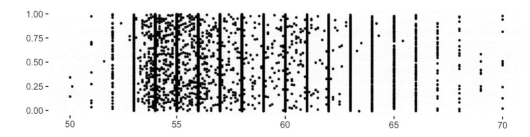

FIGURE 11.8: A vertically jittered dotplot of diamond table, excluding 12 outlying values, showing heaping at integer values

Figure 11.7 shows a few extreme values of percentage depth. According to the R help file for the dataset, percentage depth is calculated from the variables, length, width, and depth. Carrying out the calculation and plotting the reported percentage depth (depthp) against the newly calculated one (Depthp) gives Figure 11.9.

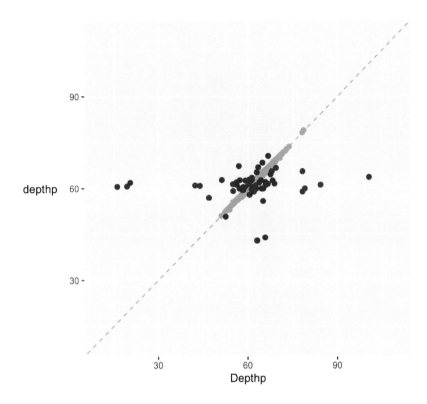

FIGURE 11.9: A scatterplot of reported percentage depth (depthp) and percentage depth calculated from the data (after removing the zero cases and three extreme outliers). Cases where the difference is bigger than 1 have been coloured red and drawn last.

There are 69 cases where the reported depth percentage and the calculated depth percentage differ by more than 1 and more detailed investigation of the four variables involved would be necessary to determine which cases to keep and/or correct.

11.3   Intriguing features

The scatterplots of `price` in Figure 11.7 look as if they have been flattened or bounded at the top. Figure 11.10 shows an enlarged version of the price-carat scatterplot with the implied boundary line added.

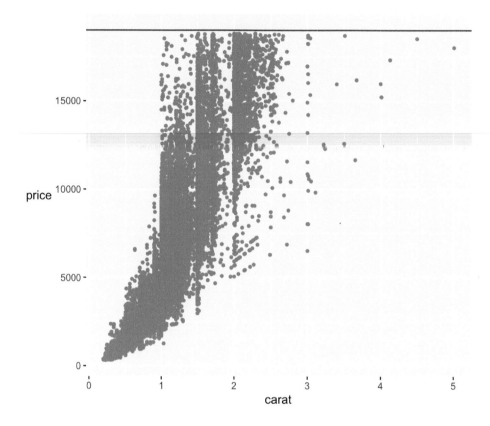

FIGURE 11.10: A scatterplot of price against carat with a red line at $19000, just above the maximum reported price.

Given that the data were scraped from a website selling diamonds, it could be that the scraping of the dataset was in the order of carat size and was stopped at some point. It seems more likely that very expensive gems were just not included. Those kinds of diamonds are probably sold in personal transactions. One of the effects of the boundary is that there are few larger diamonds in the dataset, as can be seen in Figure 11.10. Smaller diamonds of very high quality are doubtless not included either. This kind of bias should be taken into account when modelling the data.

Until now the three categorical variables in the dataset, `cut`, `color`, and `clarity` have been ignored. It is worth looking at their association with `carat` (i.e., the size of the diamond). Figure 11.11 suggests that there is a decline in the median carat size as clarity improves and an increase in the median carat size as colour quality decreases. The colour classification refers to how colourless a diamond is on a scale from D (best) down to Z. There are no examples of the poorer categories in the dataset.

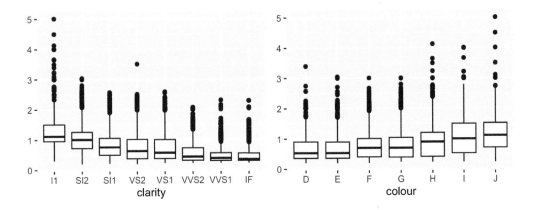

FIGURE 11.11: Boxplots of carat by clarity and by colour

One part of the explanation could be that bigger diamonds can be sold with poorer clarity or poorer colour. Another could be the effect of the price boundary so that bigger diamonds with better clarity or better colour would be too expensive to be included in the dataset. A similar effect, if not so strong, can be seen plotting `carat` by `cut`.

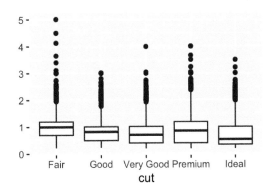

FIGURE 11.12: Boxplots of carat by cut

Answers There are a number of data cleaning issues such as impossible zero values, outliers, and missing price data. The distribution of carat values with one-sided peaks at rounded numbers is an unusual feature. The apparent upper limit on price will affect modelling.

Further questions What are the distributions of colour, cut and clarity? What influence do colour and cut have on price?

Graphical takeaways

- For large datasets choosing the narrowest histogram binwidth can reveal otherwise hidden information. (Figures 11.4 and 11.5)
- Individual outliers on one dimension affect higher dimensional plots as well. It is worth drawing new plots without them. (Figures 11.6, 11.7, and 11.9)
- Surprising plot shapes usually mean there is structure to be uncovered in the data. (Figure 11.7)
- Parallel boxplots are a quick and informative way of comparing groups. (Figure 11.11)

12

Psoriasis and the Quality of Life

The most important practical lesson that can be given to nurses is to teach them what to observe.

— Florence Nightingale

Background Psoriasis is an unpleasant skin condition and there is no known cure. The research data discussed here come from a phase 3 clinical trial of a possible treatment.

Questions Is the treatment better than the placebo? Does it show better results on all criteria?

Sources PSI (2021b)

Structure Each of the 450 patients involved has two records, one for their quality of life assessment at the beginning of the study and one for the same assessment at the end of the study.

12.1 Comparing treatment and placebo groups

As part of their Wonderful Wednesdays project (PSI (2021a)), the Statisticians in the Pharmaceutical Industry group made available a dataset of a treatment for psoriasis (PSI (2021b)). There was a treatment group of 300 patients and a placebo group of 150. The PASI score (Psoriasis Area and Severity Index) was assessed for each person at the start of the study. The DLQI questionnaire (Dermatology Life Quality Index) was administered to every patient at the start and to almost all patients after 16 weeks—a few must have dropped out. The questionnaire has ten questions, each to be answered on a discrete scale of 0, 1, 2, 3, with 0 meaning no impact on quality of life and 3 meaning maximum impact. Figure 12.1 is a display of three plots summarising the study.

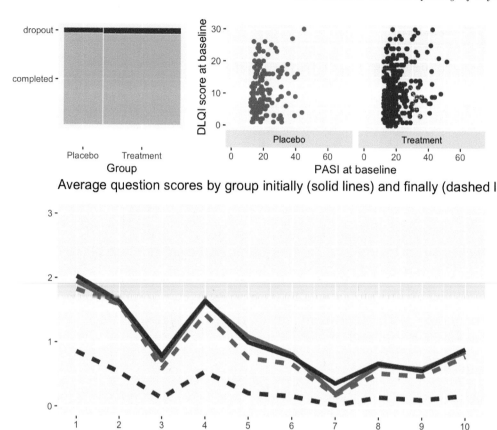

Average question scores by group initially (solid lines) and finally (dashed l

FIGURE 12.1: The spineplot top left shows the treatment group was much bigger than the placebo group and the dropout rate was small for both groups. The scatterplots of PASI and DLQI scores at the start of the study top right show the two groups had similar initial distributions. The bottom plot shows that average initial scores on the 10 questions were similar for the groups (solid lines) and mostly slightly lower for the placebo group after 16 weeks (blue dashed line). For the treatment group average scores were substantially less on all questions after 16 weeks (dark orange dashed line).

To be included in the study patients had to have a PASI score of at least some level. In the dataset the minimum was 12. Only one participant had a score over 50; the scale goes up to 72. Some of the DLQI questions had higher averages than others, with questions 1 (how itchy, painful), 2 (how embarrassed), and 4 (influenced clothes worn) having initial averages of over 1.5. Other questions had initial averages less than 1 or slightly over (question 5: affected social, leisure activity).

12.2 Examining responses to individual questions

Treatment led to improvements in the averages for all the individual questions. Averaging ordered categorical data is an approximation, so it is worthwhile looking at the separate questions in more detail. Figure 12.2 shows the barcharts of responses to question 1 (how itchy, painful, sore or stinging the patient's skin was over the previous week) for the two groups at the end of the trial, and compares them with how they were at the start. The placebo group distributions look pretty much identical, whereas the treatment group distribution moved from right to left over the trial, showing improvement for almost all patients.

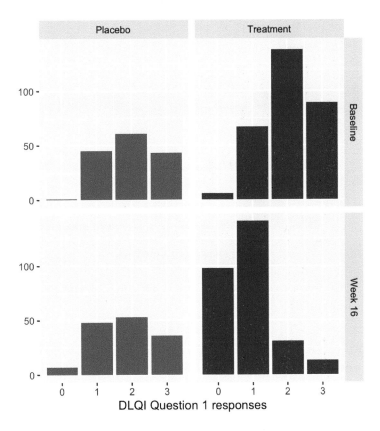

FIGURE 12.2: Distributions of answers to question 1 at the start of the trial (top) and at the end (bottom): quality of life declines to the right

Of course, Figure 12.2 does not show the changes for individual participants, just the changes in the group distributions. Figure 12.3 does show the individual changes.

The bottom row of shows how respondents who answered 3 to question 1 initially responded to the same question at the end of the trial. Most of the treatment group answered 1 or 0, evidence of a lot of improvement. Most of the placebo group answered 3 or 2, evidence of little or no improvement. The biggest bars for each of the initial responses of 1, 2, or 3 in the placebo group are the no change bars, supporting evidence that there was little effect in the placebo group.

Figures 12.2 and 12.3 have a similar form but a different meaning, so they have to be interpreted with care.

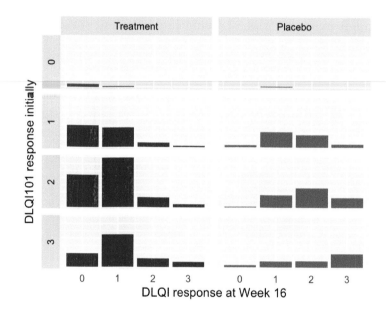

FIGURE 12.3: Answers to question 1 at the start of the trial (rows) and at the end (columns within the groups).

Answers The treatment group reported better quality of life on all criteria on average. Deeper analysis of question 1 showed that most individuals reported improvements in their quality of life.

Further questions Do the answers to the other questions display similar patterns to the answers to question 1?

Graphical takeaways

- Ensembles of graphics can summarise the main features of a study succinctly. (Figure 12.1)
- Plotting individual scores is more informative than plotting totals. (Figure 12.1)

13

Charging electric cars

We all make mistakes, and it is better to make them before we begin.

— Nikola Tesla

Background A study was carried out in 2014-15 of how electric car drivers used charging facilities provided by a firm participating in the U.S. Department of Energy workplace charging challenge.

Questions How often did users charge their cars? When did they charge them? How long did they charge them for? Which charging stations were used most? Which incentives work in controlling use of charging stations?

Sources Asensio et al. (2021a) and Asensio et al. (2021b)

Structure 3395 charging sessions with 24 variables were reported, including user, location, time, charge, and cost.

13.1 How was the study organised?

The hierarchical structure of the study was that there were four types of company facility, each with a number of different locations, and that there were different numbers of identical charging stations at the various locations. Distances driven and use of other charging options for the drivers were not recorded. Financial and other incentives were employed to reduce congestion and waiting. There is no information on what congestion and waiting may have occurred.

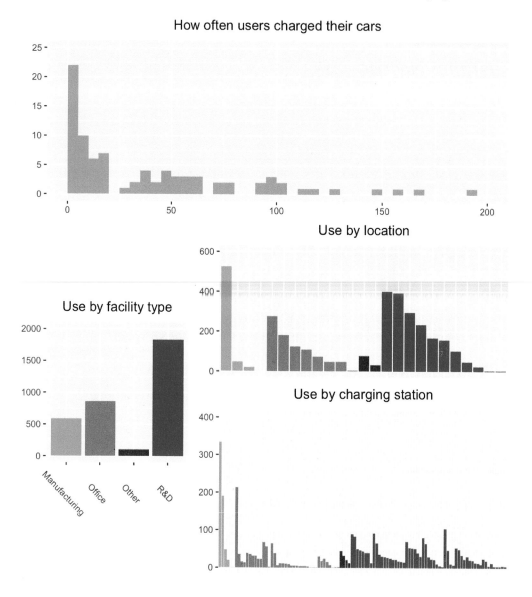

FIGURE 13.1: Number of chargings carried out by user, by facility type, by location, and by charging station (locations and charging stations are coloured by the type of facility where they were located)

Figure 13.1 is an ensemble of plots summarising some of the data. A few users charged their cars many times. Around half charged their cars hardly at all. There were four types of facility where the stations were installed. Most locations were at R&D facilities as were most stations. One Manufacturing location was used more than any other location. One of the Office charging stations was used far more often than any of the other office charging stations. Some charging stations and even a few locations were hardly used.

Figure 13.2 shows the 25 locations by type of facility and the number of charging stations at each location. The locations have been sorted by facility type and within facility types by numbers of stations.

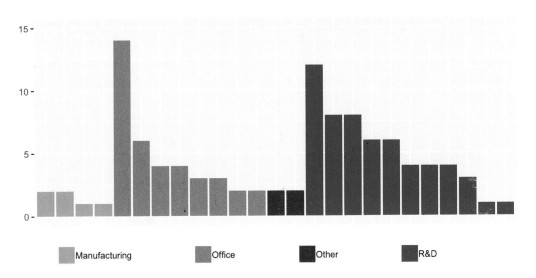

FIGURE 13.2: Numbers of charging stations by facility type and location

That there are different numbers of locations at the types of facilities may say something about the geographic spread and business of the company. The different numbers of stations at the locations may reflect the numbers of staff.

The numbers of charges over the period of the study are shown in Figure 13.3. The sharp dips are probably at weekends (as confirmed by Figure 13.11 later).

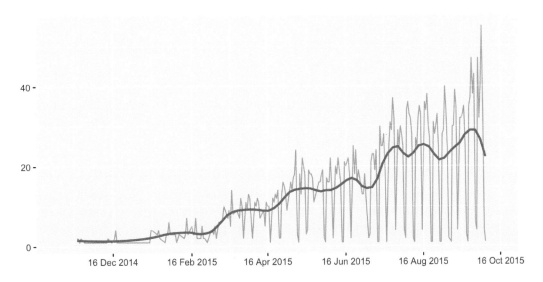

FIGURE 13.3: Numbers of charges per day with smooth added

The study lasted for a year from mid-November 2014 to early October 2015. The researchers state in their article (Asensio et al. (2021a)) that the first three months were a testing period and that the remaining nine months were the analysis period. Their code (which they provide on the web along with their dataset) shows that the testing period began on 18 November 2014, when the first charging was recorded, and ended on 18 February 2015. Charging facilities were introduced at different locations over time ("The charging stations were installed at a rate of approximately 2 per week"), so not all could be used over the full analysis period. Figure 13.4 displays the cumulative number of charging stations available for each facility type based on the date of first use.

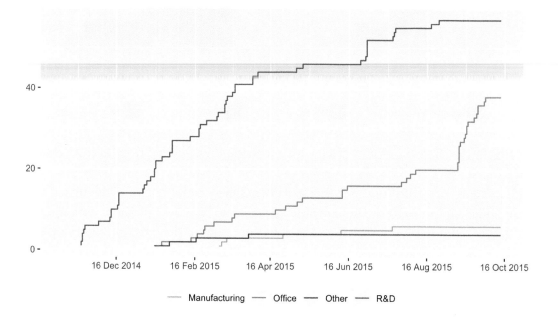

FIGURE 13.4: Numbers of charging stations by FacilityType over the study

Throughout the study there were always more charging stations available at R&D facilities than elsewhere, mostly a lot more. (This assumes that charging stations were first used immediately after they were installed). Several of the stations at Office locations were only added late on in the study.

Figure 13.5 shows when charging stations were used. This default plot shows little use early on, some charging stations that were used very little (e.g., the two at the top), and a group of chargers that were only used late on in the study (presumably after they were first installed).

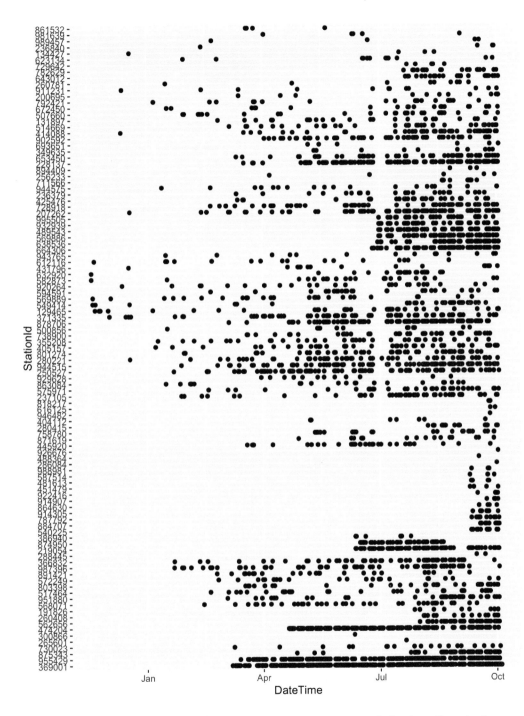

FIGURE 13.5: When charging stations were used during the study

Patterns of user use are can be seen in Figure 13.6. Most heavy users charge their cars occasionally first and then more regularly.

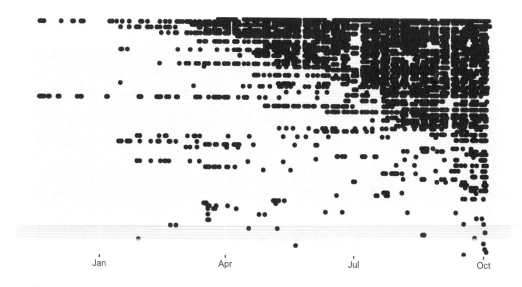

FIGURE 13.6: When users charged their cars, sorted by number of charges

Figure 13.7 shows an amended version of Figure 13.5. Charging stations are grouped by location. Locations are ordered by first use, as are stations within location. Points are coloured by facility type. Axis labels and individual station labels have been dropped, while location labels have been included. Dates have been made more precise. The time when the test period ended and the analysis period started has been marked in red. The aspect ratio has been increased to make more space for drawing the points for each of the charging stations.

In addition to what could be seen in before, there is now information on locations. Some had few stations and were barely used. Of the two Manufacturing locations, introduced in March after the testing period was over, each with two charging stations, one was heavily used and the other hardly at all. A further Manufacturing location was only used once. The first charging stations were installed at R&D facilities and two of the R&D locations that were introduced later were hardly used. At one Office location one station was little used and two were used more often until one stopped being used. It would be informative to know why some locations and charging stations were much more popular than others.

The analysis period appears to be only seven and a half months, not the nine months reported in the paper. Overall, the lack of balance in the study is surprising. The study environment developed as the study evolved and would have been an influence on drivers' behaviour. They may have made use of other opportunities to charge their cars, say at home.

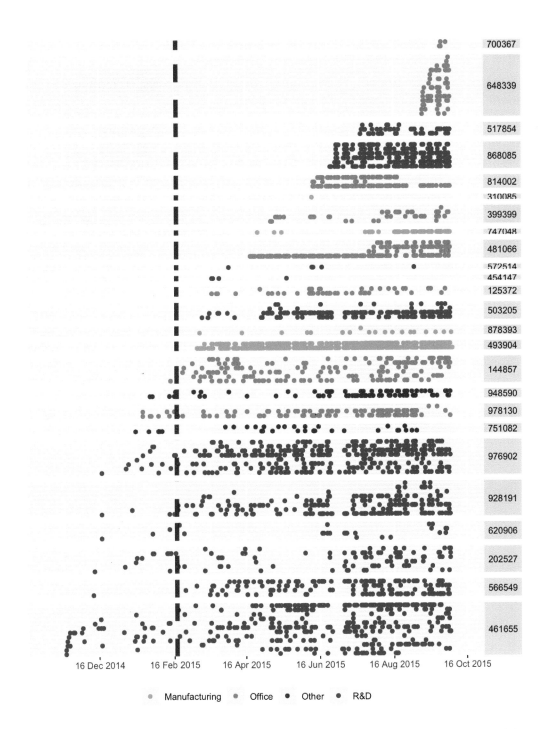

FIGURE 13.7: Use of charging stations, coloured by facility type, grouped by location, ordered by first installation at location and by first date of use, with the end of testing marked in red

13.2   How long does charging cars take?

Charging electric cars can take a long time. Charging was free for up to four hours, after that there was a \$1 per hour fee. It was also recommended to staff that they try not to connect for more than two hours at a time. Figure 13.8 shows the distribution of charging times with the two hour and four hour limits marked with dotted red guidelines. One outlying charging time of over 55 hours has been excluded as have 55 sessions with a total charge of zero. Either cars were fully charged within 4 hours or many people did not want to pay any fee. There appears to be no drop at 2 hours. There are a few very short times.

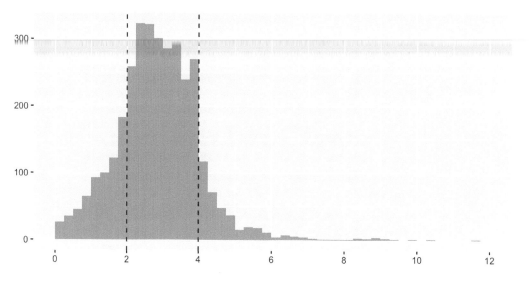

FIGURE 13.8: Distribution of charging time in hours

Plotting charge against charging time produces a surprising graphic, Figure 13.9. An alpha value of 0.2 has been used (i.e., a point is coloured black where there are at least 5 cases). For a lot of the data there is a rising linear pattern from 0 to 2 hours, which then flattens off. There are plenty of individual values, some where charging has been more effective, some where charging has been less effective, even some where it seems to have barely worked at all. The apparent horizontal boundary across the plot from 2 hours on could be due to cars being completely charged but not having been disconnected from the charger. There are a few cases of high charges in a very short period that might be errors. All but one of the cases above 10 kWh are due to 6 of 85 users, as can be seen in Figure 13.10. Possibly they had bigger cars.

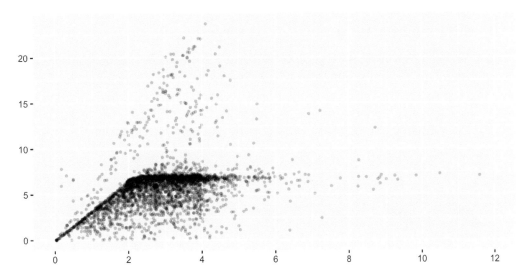

FIGURE 13.9: Energy charge in kilowatt-hours by charging time in hours

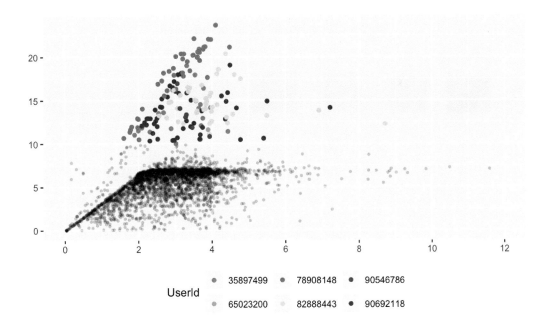

FIGURE 13.10: Energy charge in kilowatt-hours by charging time in hours, where charges higher than 10 kwh have been coloured by the user ID (charges less than 10 kwh for those users have not been coloured)

13.3   Charging patterns through the week

Figure 13.11 shows how scatterplots of total kilowatt charge by charge times
vary by day of the week and type of facility, excluding longer charge times of
over six hours and the few sessions at the two 'Other' locations.

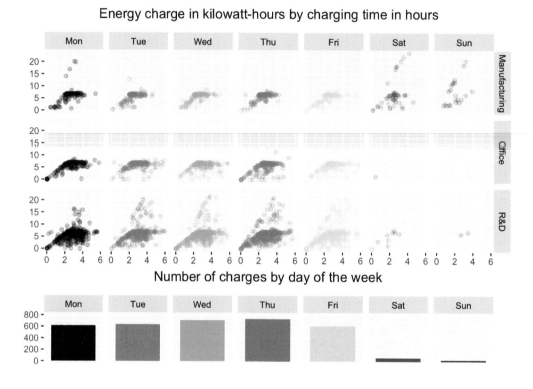

FIGURE 13.11: Energy charge in kilowatt-hours by charging time in hours,
grouped by day of the week and type of facility, excluding charging times over
six hours. The barchart shows the number of charges by day.

There were few charging sessions at the weekends. As Figure 13.1 showed, there
were more sessions at the R&D locations than elsewhere. The scatterplots
suggest some kind of limit at around 7 kWh and the sessions at R&D included
a few bigger charges during the week. There seems to be a lower boundary
that at least a certain amount of time is needed for a particular charge. The
authors of the study omitted 55 charging sessions when no charging took place,
even though charge times were not negligible. They did include sessions with
very small charges.

Answers About half the users in the study charged their cars rarely, if at all. Cars were seldom charged at weekends. Some charging locations were not used much at all. Users generally charged for less than 4 hours, at which point they had to start paying a fee.

Further questions Do charging patterns change over time? When did users start and stop using chargers during the day? What percentage of time had stations got cars connected to them?

Graphical takeaways

- Initial exploratory graphics suggest questions to be followed up. (Figures 13.1 to 13.5)
- Colour, separating space, and (nested) ordering are valuable for distinguishing groups. (Figure 13.7)
- Ensembles of graphics are effective at pulling information together. (Figures 13.1 and 13.11)

14

Darwin's Finches

It is always advisable to perceive clearly our ignorance.

— Charles Darwin

Background Darwin's finches are species that live on the Galápagos Islands. They are an important example in the Theory of Evolution.

Questions How do the species differ? Are there differences between the same species on different islands? Are there differences between the sexes?

Sources Dryad Digital Repository (Snodgrass and Heller (2008)) for the data and https://biogeo.ucdavis.edu for the map.

Structure 549 birds and 20 variables

14.1 How do Darwin's finches differ?

Darwin visited the Galápagos Islands in 1835 as part of his voyage on HMS Beagle. He collected many specimens, including birds he described as species of finches. Later researchers decided they are passerine birds belonging to the tanager family. Although Darwin collected finches, he only decided how important they might be a few years later. There is much written on Darwin's finches and anyone with a deeper interest should read the book by Peter and Rosemary Grant (Grant and Grant (2014)), describing their forty years of detailed investigations on one small island. There is also an earlier populist book about the Grants' work (Weiner (1994)).

The Galápagos Islands are fairly isolated from the rest of the world and relatively similar to one another, so Darwin was surprised at the numbers of different species of finch he identified. Classifying the species and investigating how they evolved is still part of ongoing research. A crucial feature is the size and shape of the beaks of the birds. Several datasets of measurements are available from the Dryad Digital Repository. Some have more information, some less. In this chapter morphological data from the Snodgrass and Heller Stanford expedition of 1898-99 to the Galápagos Islands are investigated (Snodgrass and Heller (1904), and Snodgrass and Heller (2008) for the data), as more features were measured and there were fewer missing values. The dataset is in the R package **hypervolume** (Blonder (2019)) called *morphSnodgrassHeller*.

The first few plots display finches from the biggest island, Isabela, showing only species of the genus *Geospiza* with at least 10 birds (four species are excluded). Only birds with complete sets of measurements are included (so sixteen are not). Figure 14.1 shows the numbers of the five species in the subset. There are more specimens of *Fuliginosa parvula* than of the other four species combined.

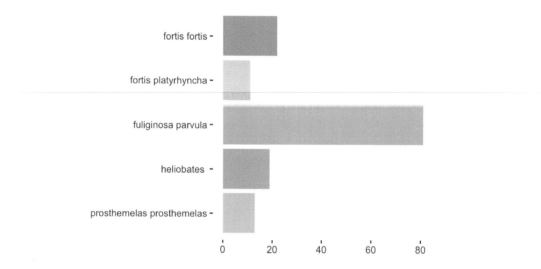

FIGURE 14.1: Numbers of finch species from Isabela Island with at least ten birds and complete data

One way of comparing species measurements is to use boxplots. Figure 14.2 shows an example for body and wing lengths of the finches. The patterns are consistent. Two species are generally shorter than the others, two are in the middle, and one is bigger. The low numbers in each of the groups and the overlaps make firm conclusions based on Figure 14.2 difficult. Displaying the two variables together in a scatterplot might show if the variables separate the groups. The two variables together appear to separate some of the species pairs, but there is clearly some overplotting, so caution is necessary. A check confirms that 17.1% of the pairs of values are duplicates.

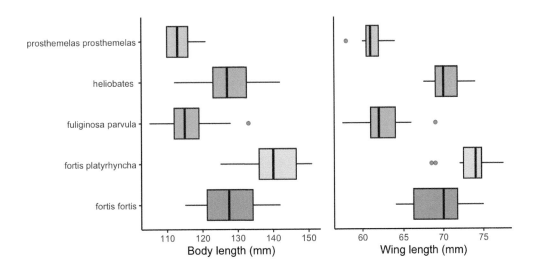

FIGURE 14.2: Body and wing lengths for the five species from Isabela Island

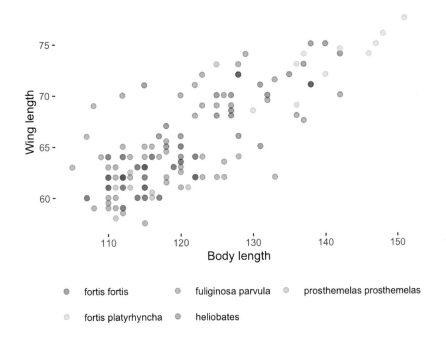

FIGURE 14.3: Scatterplot of wing length and body length for the five species from Isabela Island

Other variables could be more discriminatory. The parallel coordinate plot in Figure 14.4 uses all nine measurements available.

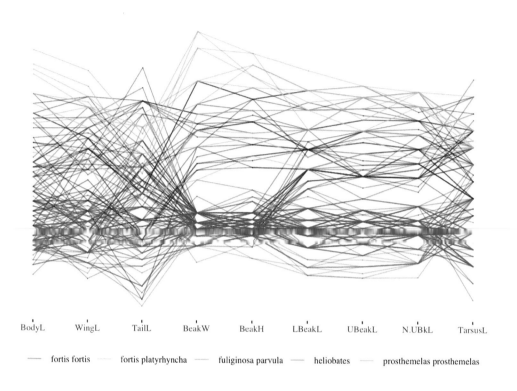

FIGURE 14.4: Parallel coordinate plot of nine measurements of five Galápagos finch species from Isabela Island

The first two beak measurements of width and height (BeakW and BeakH) separate the two bigger species from the other three. The following three variables (LBeakL, UBeakL, and N.UBkL, also beak measurements, the last being the distance from nose to upper beak) separate the smaller species from one another. The two bigger species might be separated using a multivariate technique, but these two species are considered to be related subspecies, so demonstrable differences are unlikely. Having all the beak measurements together in their order in the dataset turns out to be informative. Alphabetic order or a random order of the nine variables would not be so effective.

What about the other four species on Isabela? Drawing separate parallel coordinate plots for all nine species and including all 195 birds in Figure 14.5 reveals that three of the extra species are distinct in some way from the other eight. In each plot the rest of the dataset is drawn in a transparent black in the background, ghostplotting. The species *Crassirostris* has longer body and tarsus lengths than the other species, *Olivacea olivacea* has the shortest wings, *Scandens rothschildi* has the longest upper and lower beak measurements.

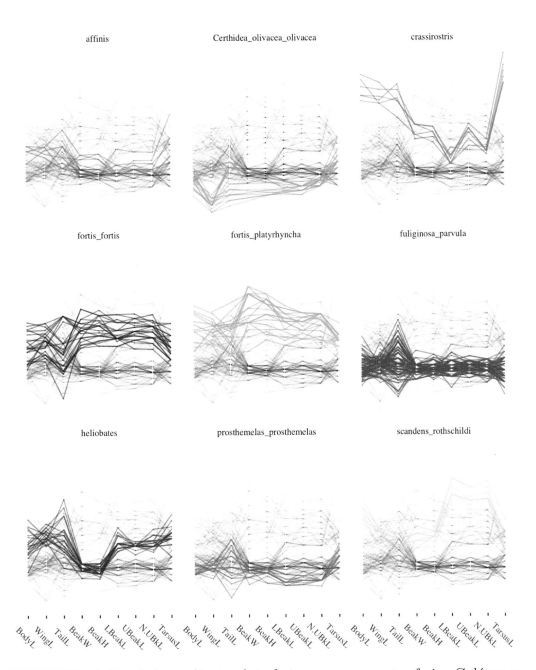

FIGURE 14.5: Parallel coordinate plot of nine measurements of nine Galápagos finch species from Isabela Island

14.2 Do species vary across the Galápagos islands?

Isabela is the biggest of the Galápagos islands and the equator crosses it to the North. Figure 14.6 gives a map of the islands, which lie about 900 km west of Ecuador. The distance between Española to the South and Darwin to the North is 220 km.

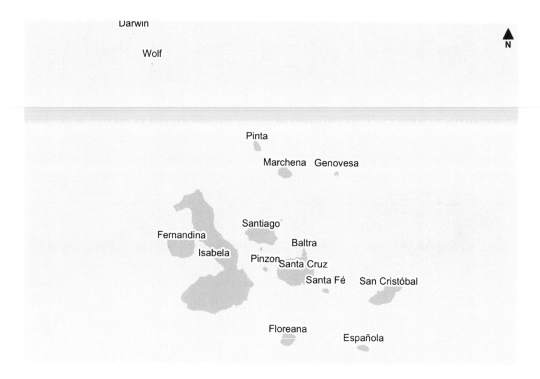

FIGURE 14.6: Map of the Galápagos Islands

The Daphne islands, where the Grants did a lot of their work (Grant and Grant (2014)), are a little to the North of Santa Cruz and too small to appear here. Daphne Major, the bigger of the two, is less than half a square kilometre in size.

Several species live on more than one island. Snodgrass and Heller's dataset covering 15 islands ranges from Isabela with 195 birds from 9 species to Santa Cruz with 9 birds from 2 species. Looking at the data the other way round, they reported 32 species in all, ranging from the 15 they found each only on 1 island to *Fulginosa parvula* which they found on 9 islands. These data refer to the numbers of birds they collected and measured; there must have been many more.

The species *Fuliginosa parvula* may be used for comparing one species living on different islands. Figure 14.7 displays parallel coordinate plots with ghostplotting for *Fuliginosa parvula* on four islands where at least 9 birds were recorded. The full dataset for all four islands is drawn in the background in each plot.

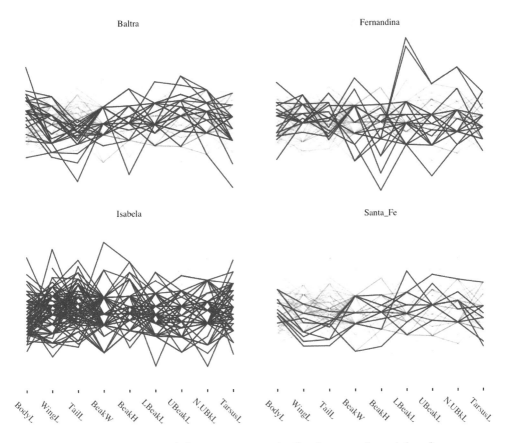

FIGURE 14.7: *fuliginosa parvula* finches on four islands

On average there do not appear to be distinct differences between *Fuliginosa parvula* finches on the four islands. Some birds have unusual measurements, such as the two with long lower beaks on Fernandina and the one with a particularly short tarsus on Baltra.

It is frequently the case that males of a species are generally bigger than the females. This is to some extent true here, for instance for the wing length measurements compared in Figure 14.8. Four species for which there were data for at least ten examples of each sex are shown.

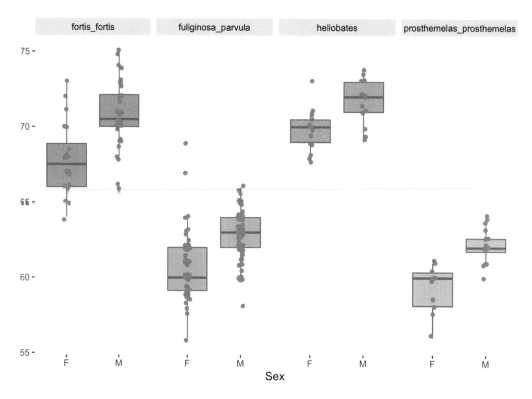

FIGURE 14.8: Boxplots of wing lengths by sex for 4 different species with jittered dotplots drawn on top. Species colours are the same as used earlier. There are not enough specimens of *fortis-platyrhyncha* for the species to be included.

Two species, *Fortis fortis* and *Heliobates*, have longer wing lengths than the other two species. It is curious that for the species with most birds, *Fulginosa parvula* with 62 females and 99 males, the birds with the two longest wing lengths are both females.

Twice as many males as females were measured by Snodgrass and Heller. The research by the Grants (Weiner (1994)) revealed that weather variation over the years can have dramatic effects on the sex ratio of the finches, with droughts leading to more females dying, particularly the smaller ones. Perhaps 1898-99 was shortly after such a period.

Answers The nine species on Isabela can almost all be distinguished from one other with the measurements provided. Species do not appear to differ between islands. Males are generally bigger than females of the same species.

Further questions Are the different bird measurements correlated with each other? How do the data on the finches of the Galápagos Islands collected by other researchers compare with the data studied here?

Graphical takeaways

- Colour consistency across displays helps readers. (Figures 14.1 to 14.5 and 14.8)
- The orderings of variables and categories in parallel coordinate plots makes a big difference to what can be seen. (Figure 14.5)
- Faceted parallel coordinate plots distinguish species better when the complete dataset is plotted in the background (ghostplotting). (Figures 14.5 and 14.7)

15

Home or away: where do soccer players play?

Milan or Madrid, as long as it's Italy.

— Andy Möller, then of Dortmund

Background The European Football Championship takes place every four years. It has gradually gained in importance since the first competition took place in 1960 when the finals involved only four teams.

Questions Do European international football players play their league football in their own country? How has this changed over the years?

Sources Abel (2021)

Structure There are 4012 players included with 21 variables.

15.1 The European Football Championship since 1960

The UEFA European Championship has grown considerably over the years. There were 17 entries for the first competition in 1960 with 4 qualifying to compete in the finals. The size of the finals was expanded to 8 teams in 1980, to 16 in 1996 and to 24 in 2016. In 2020 there were 55 entries in the qualifying stages competing for 24 places in the finals. Wikipedia says that there are 51 independent European states. However, there were four separate teams from the United Kingdom (England, Scotland, Wales, Northern Ireland) and one from the British Overseas Territory of Gibraltar. The Faroe Islands, an autonomous territory of Denmark entered, as did Israel, although it is neither fully European nor transcontinental (such as Russia and Turkey). The only European states not to take part, other than the UK, were Monaco and Vatican City.

The squad sizes increased over time too, beginning with 17 and rising to 26. Bigger tournaments need more players.

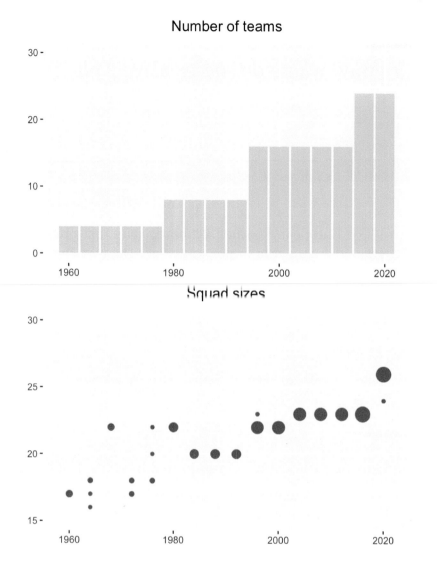

FIGURE 15.1: Numbers of teams (above) and squad sizes (below) over the 16 European Championships. A point's area in the lower plot is proportional to the number of countries with that value (and the vertical scale starts at 15).

There may have been no regulations concerning squad sizes in the early competitions and that would explain the variation in 1964 and 1976. Since then, there must have been a fixed limit that all teams followed with two exceptions. In 1996 Germany had several injured players and were allowed to call up an extra player, Jens Todt, before the final, although he did not actually play. In the 2020 competition the Spanish manager called up only 24 of the 26 players permitted, not wanting to work with a large squad, when several would not be needed in the tournament.

At the first competition in 1960 just 4 teams took part and they only used players from their own national leagues. As the competition expanded, the squads got bigger and more teams from smaller countries took part. Their best players often played for richer clubs in bigger countries. The steady downward progression in the average percentage of players coming from a nation's own league can be seen in Figure 15.2.

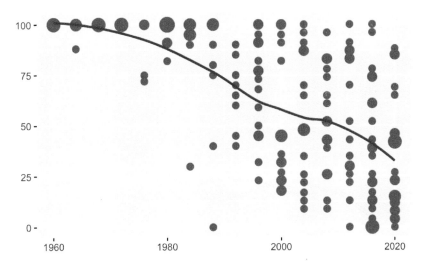

FIGURE 15.2: Percentage of a nation's players who played in their own country's league for each of the 16 European Championships. Circle area is proportional to the number of countries with that percentage. A loess smooth has been added.

The first team to have players from another league was Spain in 1964, who included two players based in Italy. The first team with no players from their own country's league was the Republic of Ireland in 1988. This was partly because their best players played elsewhere, but also because of "the grandparent rule", whereby players could play for the country of any of their parents or grandparents. The Ireland manager at the time, Jack Charlton–who was English, used this a lot. He sought players out with Irish ancestry who would not be selected for the country of their own nationality and encouraged them to experience international football by playing for Ireland. In 2016 there was only one team with all players playing in its own country (England), and four teams with no players playing in their own country.

15.2   Which leagues do international players play in?

Four of the biggest European leagues are those of England, Germany, Italy, and Spain. Figure 15.5 shows how many players there were from those leagues in the EUROs from 1992 on. Until 2008 the numbers were fairly equal. Since then the English league has become much more important and numbers from Spain have remained static.

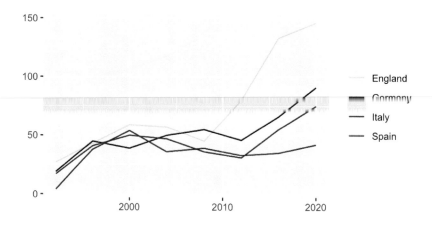

FIGURE 15.3: Numbers of players from four major leagues

The 2020 competition was delayed until 2021 because of the Covid pandemic. Abel (2021) constructed a website of all the players who ever took part and drew chord diagrams to show the relationships between the nationalities of the players and the countries they played in at club level. Here barcharts are drawn to display the data for Euro 2020.

Bars have mostly been coloured by the main shirt colour of that country. Several teams use white, so England has been given light blue, Germany black, and Russia red. Countries whose leagues provided less than 5 players have been grouped together into a final 'Other' category, including five nations who took part in the competition. Of the 622 players, just under a quarter, 152, played in England.

A few players played in leagues outside of Europe. For those playing in Europe, Figure 15.5 shows the numbers playing in the different national leagues, including Turkey and Russia in Europe, and combining the numbers for the English and Scottish leagues.

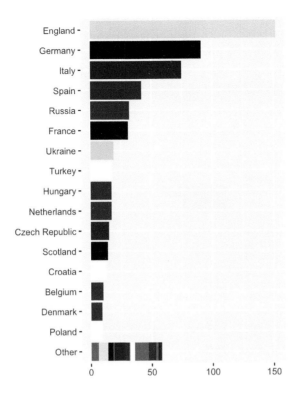

FIGURE 15.4: Numbers of Euro 2020 players playing in the different European leagues

FIGURE 15.5: Numbers of Euro 2020 players playing in various European national leagues

To show which players play where, barcharts are drawn, one for the national team of each participating country. Figure 15.6 shows the chart for Finland. The individual bars show where Finland's players play their club football. The bars have been ordered by the total number of players from that league playing in Euro 2020. Countries with less than 9 players in the competition have been grouped into "Other". The first bar represents the number of Finnish players currently playing in England.

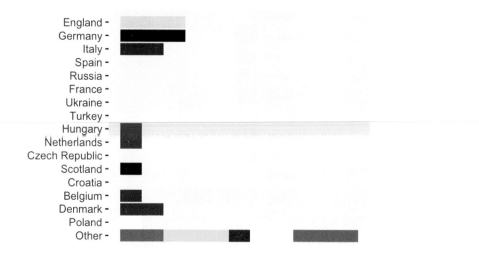

FIGURE 15.6: Where Finland's Euro 2020 players play

Figure 15.7 has 24 barcharts, one for each competing team. The team charts have been ordered by the percentage of players playing in their own national league, so the chart for England comes first, as most of the English squad were playing in England. Every country's team includes players from at least three different countries. For some of the big teams (England, Italy, Russia), almost all the players come from their own league. Germany's team includes several players playing in England and a few elsewhere. Spain has as many players playing in England as in Spain. France has about the same number of players playing in England, Germany, Spain, and France itself. Most of the other countries have players playing in many leagues, the exceptions being Ukraine, where most play there, Austria whose team play mostly in Germany, Wales whose players play in the English league (even though a few of the teams are based in Wales), and Scotland whose players almost all play in England or Scotland. Finland boasted the most distributed players. Their squad of 26 played in 16 different national leagues. Curiously, the country that had no team at the Euros but the most club players taking part was Cyprus with 8 (3 playing for North Macedonia, 2 for Finland, 2 for Slovakia, and 1 for Hungary). Only Russia of the 24 competing countries had no players playing in England.

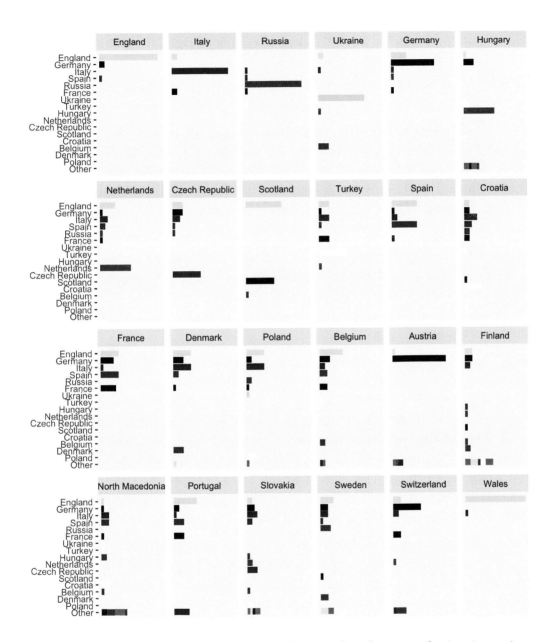

FIGURE 15.7: Numbers of Euro 2020 players of each team playing in various countries' leagues

15.3   How have countries changed?

Over sixty years much has changed in Europe. Countries have split up (like the Soviet Union and Yugoslavia) or combined (like the two Germanies). Other complications are that the four countries in the United Kingdom each have their own national team and all have reached the Euro finals at one time or another.

The dataset has four country variables: the squad name, the name of the national team (these two only differ for the Soviet Union/USSR); the name of the country of the player's club, and an amended version (differing for the Soviet Union/USSR, Yugoslavia, and for clubs based in Wales that play in the English leagues). Three players had no club contract while playing in one of the competitions and their club details were recorded as missing.

Making the strong assumptions that the Soviet Union in the early competitions is the same as Russia in the later competitions and that Germany is the same country as West Germany before unification, the percentages of home players in the teams have been plotted for the countries that qualified for at least 8 of the Euro finals in Figure 15.8.

There is an interesting variety of patterns. The rate for Germany, who have played most often despite not entering the first two competitions, shows a slight decline over time. The exception was 1992 when 8 of their 20 players were playing in Italy. The finals in 1992 were also different for Russia, when 12 of their players were playing abroad, a big change from the Soviet Union days. Since 2004 they are back to a high percentage of home players, like Italy and England. Both the French and Dutch rates dropped a lot in 2000. In that competition Spain only used home players, but their rate has declined to less than 50% in the most recent competition.

There was no information included on results. One possibility to make Figure 15.2 more comparable across the years would be to restrict it to the four semi-finalists in each competition. The information was added to the dataset and the graphic drawn, but the main conclusion did not change.

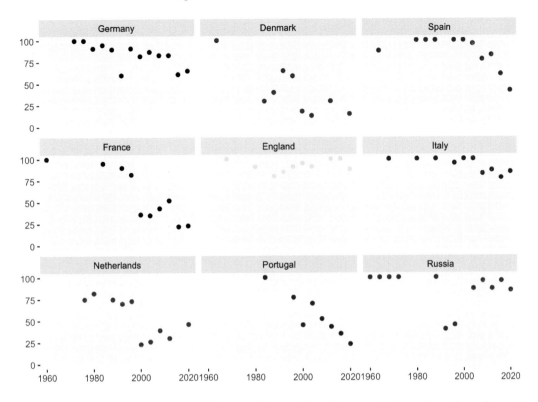

FIGURE 15.8: Percentages of home players for the countries who played most often in the 16 European Championship finals

Answers More and more international players play their football abroad. Just over half of the players of the 24 teams at Euro 2020 played in England, Germany, or Italy.

Further questions Which team had the biggest variability of home player percentage across the years? Are their similar patterns for teams competing in the World Cup? Is there data available on the composition of club teams by nationality?

Graphical takeaways

- Alignment of identical axes supports viewing ensembles of graphics. (Figure 15.1)
- Smooths are effective for discrete datasets too. (Figure 15.2)
- Faceting works for plots with many groups. (Figure 15.7)

16

Watching soccer—the English leagues

Football: it's a funny old game. — Jimmy Greaves

Background The English soccer league is the oldest in the world, the first season being 1888-89.

Questions Are there more draws now than before? Has home advantage always been the same? Do teams score fewer goals now? Can we display the histories of teams over the years? How do teams perform over a season?

Sources The **engsoccerdata** package contains results for all English soccer games in the top four tiers from the 1888-89 season to the 2021-22 season (Curley (2022))

Structure Results of 203956 games summarised in 12 variables

16.1 History of the English football leagues since 1888

The English league started out with one division of 12 teams in 1888 and quickly added another in 1892. After the First World War a third division started and this was doubled and split into North and South divisions one year later. In 1958 the two third divisions were combined and split into national third and fourth divisions. In 1992 the old first division became the Premier League and the other divisions also changed their names (and again later). For simplicity's sake this report, like the dataset, refers to the different levels as the four tiers. Seasons are denoted by the year they began, so 2021-22 is referred to as 2021.

Much information on the intricate details of football history can be found on the Wikipedia sites for individual league seasons. These have been very helpful for explaining how the league developed and for understanding various initially surprising features. The maintainer of the package, James Curley, has published several insightful articles on the 538 website using the dataset (Curley (2016)).

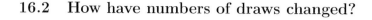

16.2   How have numbers of draws changed?

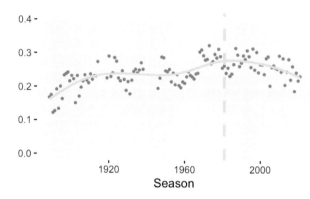

FIGURE 10.1: Rate of draws over the years in the English league's top tier with a gam (general additive model) smooth

The proportion of drawn games in the top tier climbed until the First World War. Afterwards it remained relatively constant until the 1960s, when it rose again. After the introduction of three points for a win in 1981 (the vertical dashed line) it dropped slightly again. There was a lot of variability by season.

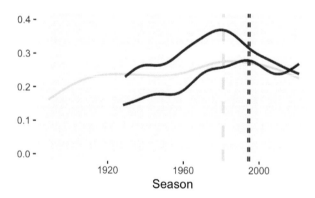

FIGURE 16.2: Smooths of the rates of draws for the top tiers in Italy (dark blue), England (light blue), and Spain (red)

The rates of draws in other countries were sometimes quite different as Figure 16.2 shows. The corresponding dotted lines show when the 3 points for a win rules were introduced. Italy had a higher rate of draws, particularly in the 1970s and 1980s, but this was declining before the new rule came in. The rate in Spain was lower, rose briefly above the English rate, then fell again. For the most recent data considered here, the rates of draws for Italy and England are about equal and Spain's rate is the highest of the three leagues for the first time.

16.3 How big is home advantage?

Home advantage is a common feature of team sports (Gómez-Ruano, Pollard, and Lago-Peñas (2022)). One way to measure it is to consider the proportion of a team's points won at home. As the number of points awarded for a win was increased in 1981 from 2 to 3, the proportions before and after 1981 would not be comparable. Figure 16.3 assumes that a win was always worth 3 points.

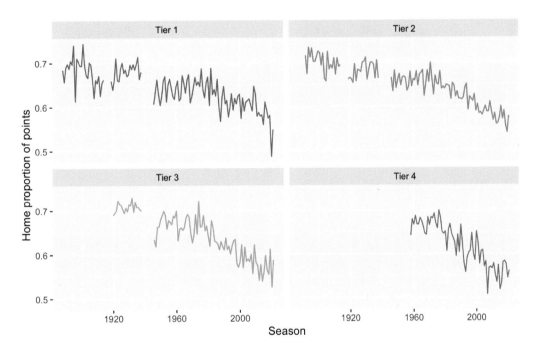

FIGURE 16.3: Proportions of points won at home over time in the various tiers of the English league

The two striking features are the relatively steady decline since 1980 for the lower three tiers and the dramatic drop to below 50% in the Premier League in season 2020-21. Most of the 2020-21 Premier League games were played without fans because of Covid, so an important factor in home advantage disappeared. The sharp drops in levels in tiers 1 and 3 when the leagues restarted after the Second World War are a little surprising: why would that have happened? There is quite a lot of variability over the years and some relatively extreme values.

The home and away records for individual teams can also be calculated and Figure 16.4 shows the results for the four tiers separately (the gaps are the First and Second World Wars).

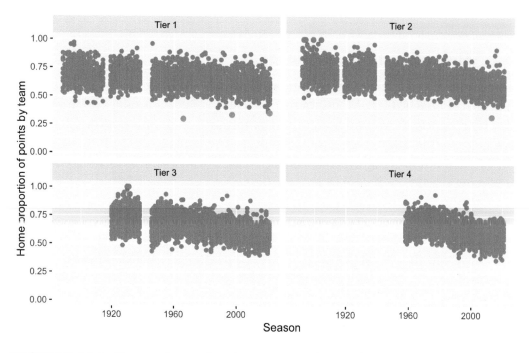

FIGURE 16.4: Proportions of points won at home for every team for every season

The overall trend is the same as in Figure 16.3 (but the vertical scales are different as these are rates for individual teams not for averages). There are some striking individual outliers. The four outliers in the early days of the second division with a home proportion of 1 (they got no points away from home), and the two from the third division later on, have been drawn bigger and coloured orange. They were:

	Season	tier	team	away	home	HomeProportion
1	1893	Tier 2	Northwich Victoria	0	12	1
2	1894	Tier 2	Crewe Alexandra	0	13	1
3	1899	Tier 2	Loughborough	0	9	1
4	1904	Tier 2	Doncaster Rovers	0	11	1
5	1930	Tier 3	Nelson	0	25	1
6	1931	Tier 3	Wigan Borough	0	10	1

They all finished last except for Wigan Borough in 1931, who folded. In the first season after the Second World War Leeds United drew one away game and lost the other 20 in the first division (the top tier), although they managed six wins and five draws at home. (And yes, they finished last as well.)

The teams with the worst relative home record (proportions less than 0.35) have been drawn bigger and coloured green. They were:

	Season	tier	team	away	home	HomeProportion
1	1966	Tier 1	Blackpool	19	8	0.296
2	1997	Tier 1	Crystal Palace	22	11	0.333
3	2013	Tier 2	Birmingham City	30	14	0.318
4	2021	Tier 1	Watford	15	8	0.348

All were relegated bar Birmingham, who survived on goal difference.

16.4 Have the numbers of goals scored gone down?

The number of goals scored per game in the first few years of the league was a lot higher than now, but it declined quickly. In 1925 the offside law was changed and that led to a short-term dramatic increase. After the Second World War levels rose again to peak around 1960. There was then a steady decline until 1970 and since then goal scoring has remained fairly constant, close to 2.5 goals a game. This is all shown in Figure 16.5.

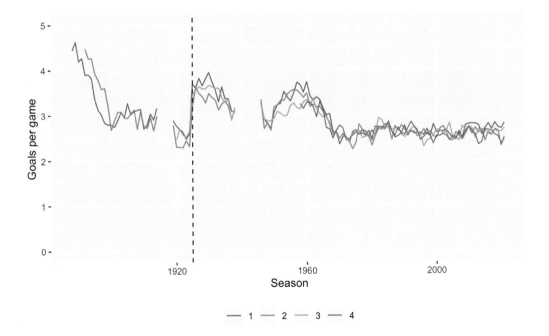

FIGURE 16.5: The numbers of goals per game for the four tiers of the English league (the change in the offside law is marked with a red dashed line)

16.5   How well have teams performed over the years?

Everyone interested in football has their own favourite team and remembers the times their team was strongest. There is also a lot of interest in local rivalries. The following graphics use league tables for every division and give teams an overall ranking for each season. The top teams come from the first tier, the next ones from the second tier, and so on. For the period when there were two third tiers, the Third Divisions North and South, the tables for the two have been interwoven and the rankings estimated accordingly.

Until 1976 teams equal on points were ranked on the ratio of the number of goals they scored to the number their opponents scored. This was called, misleadingly, goal average. From 1976 on, goal difference was used. The rankings used here reflect these rules. Goal average was introduced in 1894. Before that there was no official way of ranking teams with equal points. These tables use goal average for those years. You would think it might have been an issue as in the very first season with 12 clubs, there were three pairs on equal points. What are the chances of that? Two teams finished at the foot of the table on equal points, Notts County and Stoke City. Notts County had the better goal average and Stoke City the better goal difference. It did not matter, both—and the two teams above them—had to apply for re-election. A more dramatic example arose in 1923. Huddersfield Town won on goal average from Cardiff City who would have won on goal difference (although only because they scored one more goal, the goal differences were the same). It would have been the only occasion a team based outside England won the English League Championship.

There was one further problem. In season 2019-20 not all games were completed in the bottom two tiers because of the disruption caused by Covid. The teams did not all play the same number of games and final league positions were decided by the ratio of points won per game and then goal difference.

The rankings of all teams are plotted in light grey in the background and the selected teams are plotted in colour in the foreground, ghostplotting. (Specifying colours to match team colours and keep the teams distinct is easier for some groups of teams than for others.) The lowest level of each tier is marked with a black line.

Of the three South Coast teams, Portsmouth was the most successful for a long time (including two league titles). Southampton was mostly best from the 1960s on. They briefly dropped to the third tier in 2009 from which they bounced straight back, just as Portsmouth were going up and down in the

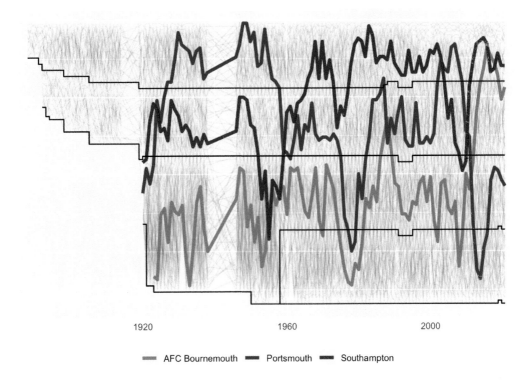

AFC Bournemouth Portsmouth Southampton

FIGURE 16.6: Comparing the three South Coast teams: Bournemouth, Portsmouth, and Southampton

opposite direction. Bournemouth have pretty well always been below the other two until the last few years.

There is an unusual pattern in the line dividing the top and second tiers around 1990, shortly before the Premier League, replacing the old First Division, was introduced. The First Division had 22 members in 1986-87, 21 in 1987-88, and 20 in 1988-89, returning to 22 teams in its last season, 1991-92. The Premier League began in season 1992-93 with 22 members, but dropped to 20 members after four seasons. These changes were doubtless part of the ongoing negotiations at the time about the distribution of television money to the clubs. The minor bump in the lines dividing the bottom two divisions in 2019 is because Bury were expelled for insolvency in August 2019 before they had played any games.

Plots of historical trajectories of team performance can be found on various Wikipedia sites for individual teams.

Linear ranks mean that the difference between first and second at the top gets the same weight as any difference between consecutive rankings. To emphasise differences at the top more, the scale can be stretched using a square root function as in Figure 16.7. It is now clearer that Southampton did not ever win the league (they finished second in 1983).

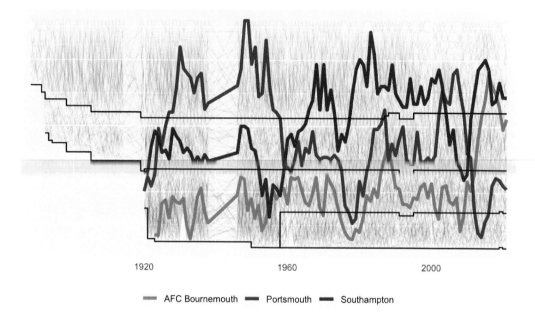

FIGURE 16.7: Comparing Bournemouth, Portsmouth, and Southampton on a square root scale

16.6   Wormcharts show league progress over a season

League tables give a snapshot of the current positions in a league competition. Wormcharts show how the positions of the teams changed over time and, if drawn for a full season, show the paths by which the top and bottom teams reached their final positions. The wormcharts drawn here use the number of games played as the time axis. An alternative would be to use the actual dates games were played. The advantage would be historical accuracy. The disadvantage would be making it harder to standardise over time, as teams have often played slightly different numbers of games by different stages of a season. The vertical axis measures the difference between the number of points a team has achieved in that number of games and the average number of points across all teams.

16.6.1 Leicester City are Champions for the first time!

Figure 16.8 shows the how teams fared in the Premier League in season 2015-2016. The winners, to everyone's surprise, were Leicester City. It was the first time they had won the league title since they were elected to the Football League in 1894 and they were the first new team to win the top division since Nottingham Forest in 1977-78.

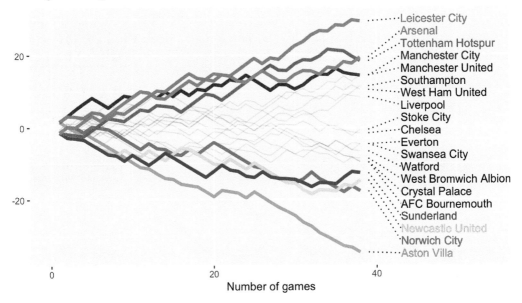

FIGURE 16.8: Team performances in points above/below average in 2015-16

The chart shows that Leicester finished well clear at the end, ten points in front of second-placed Arsenal, and they led from the front for the last third of the season. At the other end of the table there was an even larger gap, with Aston Villa finishing bottom on 17 points, another 17 points behind the next team Norwich City.

For each round of games of a season (in the Premier League there are currently 20 teams and hence 38 rounds) the cumulative points up to then are recorded. The mean number of cumulative points across the teams is subtracted from each team's total. A line of the chart shows a team's cumulative performance relative to the average performance. If some kind of adjustment like this (the median could have been used) is not done, all the teams' lines increase in steps, making a fanned-out diagonal up the page. A lot of plotting space is then not used and comparisons are more difficult. The assumption is made that all games of a round take place at the same time, which is not always true in the Premier League.

Only the four teams finishing at the top of the table and the four finishing at the foot of the table are coloured to make the display more readable. These numbers can, of course, be changed. In principle the line colours should match the colours of the teams. That would not work so well if, say, four teams playing in blue were all at the top—or bottom.

16.6.2 The 1982-83 season had a few surprises

The main story was that Liverpool won the league easily. What can also be seen in Figure 16.9 is that they did very poorly in their last seven games, losing five and drawing two. When the league has already been won, the final games do not matter as much.

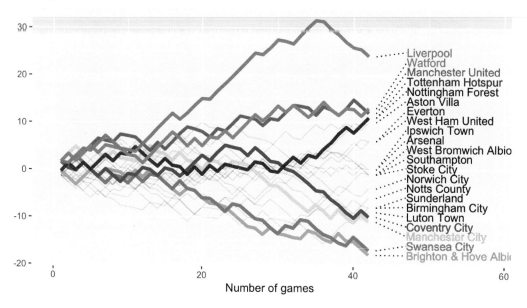

FIGURE 16.9: Team performances in points above/below the average in season 1982-83). There were 22 teams and each played 42 games.

Other stories include Coventry City's disastrous run for the last third of the season. Checking the results reveals that they had one win, three draws, and eleven losses. One of the draws was with Liverpool after they were certain of winning the league. If you follow each of the eight teams picked out, then the performance of Manchester City, who were relegated, is unusual. They won their first three games and were top of the league at that stage. Almost halfway through the season, after 20 games, none of the three sides who were relegated at the end of the season were in the bottom three.

16.6.3   The most equal and unequal seasons

Individual default scales have been used for the vertical axes in Figures 16.8 and 16.9. To draw scales suitable for all years in which 22 teams competed for the Championship with two points for a win, the scale would have to cover from +26 (i.e. 68 points, Liverpool in 1978-79) down to −24 (i.e. 18 points, Leeds United in 1946-47 and Queens Park Rangers in 1968-69). Curiously, Leeds United won the league in 1968-69 with 67 points, so they were involved in both of the low point seasons, albeit at different ends of the table.

It is interesting to look at how much of a common scale might be used in different seasons. The biggest range was 49 points in 1968-69, from QPR with 18 to Leeds with 67. The smallest range was 16 points in 1927-28 (from Middlesborough with 37 to Everton with 53) and in 1937-38 (from West Bromwich Albion and Manchester City with 36 to Arsenal with 52). Season 1937-38 had other unusual features. Manchester City scored 80 goals, more than any other team, and had been Champions the year before. All teams in 1937-38 won more points than the bottom four teams in 1968-69 and less points than the top four teams in 1968-69.

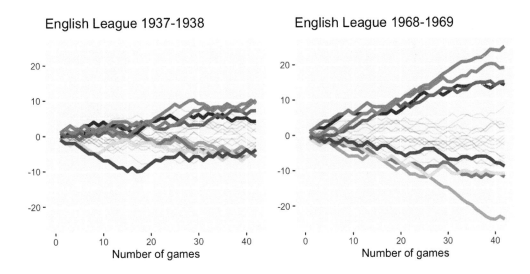

FIGURE 16.10: Wormcharts for the two seasons with extreme point ranges for the English 1st Division Championship with 22 teams and two points for a win between 1919-20 and 1980-81

Answers The proportion of drawn games has increased from the low initial rates, but not changed much on average over the past 40 years. Home advantage has declined, particularly for the lower tiers of the league. The numbers of goals scored has remained steady for the last 50 years. Wormcharts give an overview of how teams' league positions change over a season.

Further questions Would using goal difference rather than goal average before 1976 ever have made a difference (and vice versa)? Which teams have spent the longest in each tier? Which teams have moved between tiers most often?

Graphical takeaways

- Graphics of time series should mark when the rules or context changes. Guidelines help. (Figures 16.1, 16.2, and 16.5)
- Drawing cases of interest bigger, in colour, and on top of other points makes for effective highlighting. (Figure 16.4)
- Transformations can be used to emphasise different parts of a scale. (Figure 16.7)
- Wormcharts are an illuminating way of displaying how a league progresses over a season. (Figures 16.8 to 16.10)

17

Fuel efficiency of cars in the USA

It's ugly, but it gets you there.

— Volkswagen advertisement 1969 at the time of the first moon landing

Background Fuel economy data for individual models of cars and trucks is made available by the US Department of Energy.

Questions Are cars more fuel efficient than in the past? Which cars use the most fuel and which the least? How have the available models changed over time? How has fuel efficiency changed over time for particular models?

Sources Environmental Protection Agency (2021)

Structure A dataset with 43516 cases and 83 variables covering vehicles introduced in the years from 1984 to 2021.

17.1 How efficient are different types of car?

The dataset includes vehicles over many model years. The numbers refer to the numbers of models evaluated, not the numbers of vehicles on the road, so one Rolls Royce counts the same as one Toyota Corolla. Only cars are considered here, also excluding cases with missing values and some specialist small groups. There is information on the individual cars, the fuels used, fuel consumption under different conditions, and car emissions. Only estimated average mpg (miles per gallon) figures have been used in this chapter, but the dataset contains much more detailed information.

The various types of 4-Wheel and All-Wheel Drive cars have been combined in the All-Wheel category.

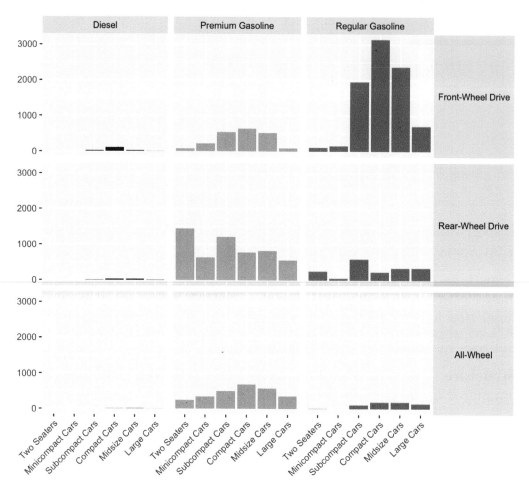

FIGURE 17.1: Numbers of car models tested by the U.S. Environmental Protection Agency by fuel, drive type, and class

There were relatively few diesel cars (280 out of 21443 cars in this display). Front-Wheel Drive cars used mainly regular gasoline. Rear-Wheel and All-Wheel Drive cars used mainly premium gasoline.

Americans (and the British) measure fuel efficiency in mpg (miles per gallon). Europeans would use an inverse measure, litres per 100 kilometres. The dataset provides two estimates of fuel efficiency, one for city driving and one for highway driving, and these are combined in an overall figure that assumes 55% of driving distance is in city conditions. There is an R package, **fueleconomy**, that makes the data available but only up to 2015. Figure 17.2 uses boxplots to summarise mpg data for the two gasolines. There were some high outliers amongst the Regular Gasoline cars with Front-Wheel Drive, i.e., they use far more fuel than other models in their class.

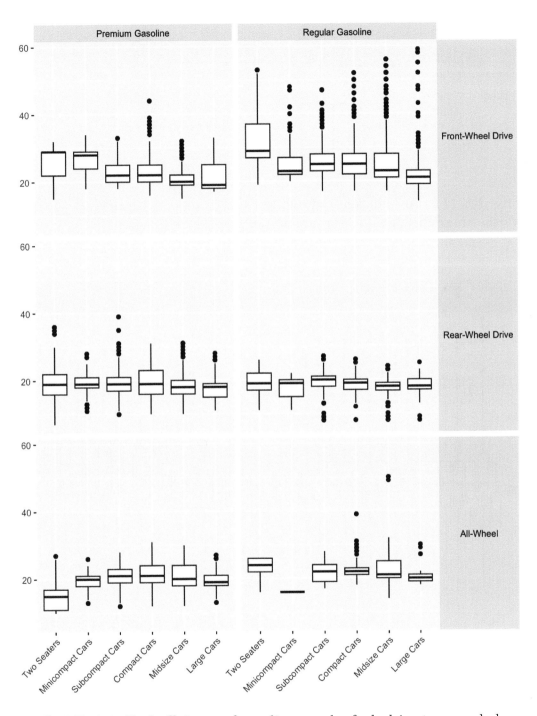

FIGURE 17.2: Fuel efficiency of gasoline cars by fuel, drive type, and class

Figure 17.3 shows that these were mainly hybrid cars (including plug-in hybrids) and Figure 17.4 suggests a few more were cars of model year 1998 or earlier.

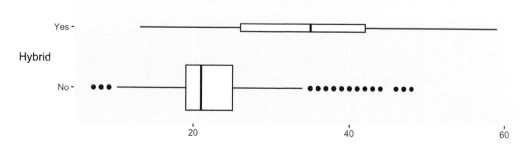

FIGURE 17.3: Fuel efficiency of hybrid cars compared with the rest (boxplot widths are proportional to the square roots of the group sizes)

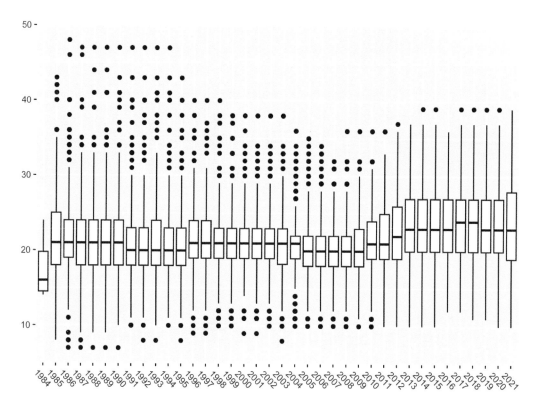

FIGURE 17.4: Fuel efficiency of non-hybrid cars over the years

Figure 17.4 also shows that the worst mpg values were recorded over 15 years ago or more. Testing procedures have changed over time and so like may not be being compared with like over such a long period.

17.2 Small (?) luxury cars

In Figure 17.2 there were some low outliers for Rear-Wheel Drive cars, especially surprising for Minicompact and Subcompact Cars. Ordering the dataset in ascending order of mpg uncovers some unexpected classifications. Who would have thought that Rolls-Royces, Aston Martins, and Ferraris would be classified that way?

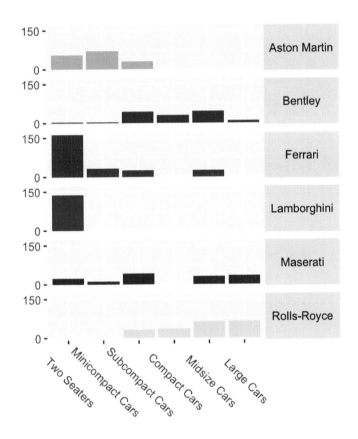

FIGURE 17.5: Numbers of cars by class for six car manufacturers

Lamborghini have only Two Seaters in the dataset and Ferrari mainly do. Minicompact, Subcompact, and Compact models were relatively commonly produced by all of the six luxury manufacturers barring Lamborghini.

According to the website maintainers: "The EPA classifies cars based on interior volume which is a combination of the passenger volume and luggage volume. The exterior dimensions or vehicle weight are not considered. The system has been in place since the mid-1970s and sometimes those classifications produce unexpected results."

17.3 How many car models have been evaluated over the years?

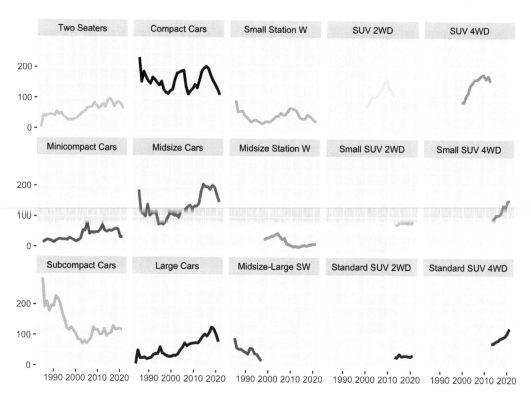

FIGURE 17.6: Numbers of models per year

Figure 17.6 shows a sharp decline in the number of Subcompact Cars, and an increase in the number of Large Cars. The patterns amongst Station Wagons and Sport Utility Vehicles (SUVs) need a closer look.

17.3.1 Station wagons and SUVs

There are three categories for station wagons and six for SUVs. Nobody talks much about station wagons these days and the term SUV is relatively new. Figure 17.7 displays barcharts of the numbers of each type for each year.

The patterns are clear. The 'Large' in the category Midsize-Large Station Wagons was dropped after 1998. SUV classifications were introduced in 1999 and further split in 2013. The numbers of station wagon models were declining before SUVs were introduced. After 2007 it appears that mainly small station wagons were produced. Numbers of SUV models for 2WD (two-wheel-drive) and 4WD (four-wheel-drive) followed similar patterns initially. After the split into Small and Standard SUVs, only the number of 4WD ones increased.

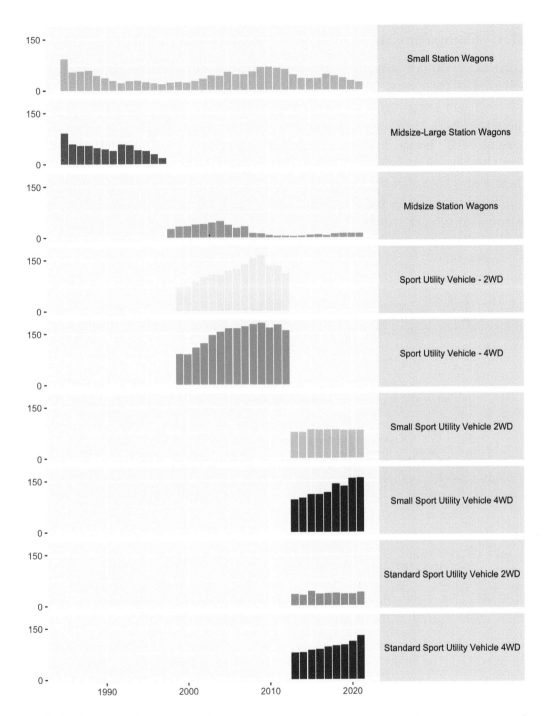

FIGURE 17.7: Numbers of station wagon and SUV models by year with categories arranged by station wagons and SUVs and within those groupings by year and size

17.4   Comparing fuel efficiency of individual models over time

Car models do not stay the same for long. Manufacturers continually develop and change their cars. By grouping on the characteristics of each model in the dataset, including number of gears and displacement (engine size in litres), those that have been tested in most years can be selected. Two have been chosen here in both manual and automatic versions, the Toyota Corolla (1993-2016) and the Mazda MX-5 (2006-2021). They are two very successful models in their respective classes. Figure 17.8 shows the estimated city, highway, and combined mpg figures for the Toyota. Note that the estimates are only reported in rounded integer values. Unrounded values for all models are provided from 2011 on but have not been used here.

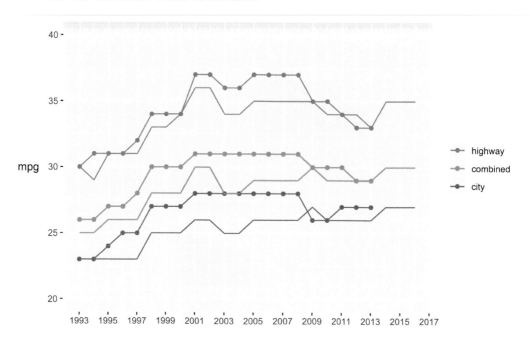

FIGURE 17.8: Fuel efficiency of Toyota Corolla models for manual transmission (lines with points) and automatic (lines) transmission

As expected, the highway mpg figures are better than the city figures. Manual transmission is generally slightly more efficient than automatic transmission. There were improvements in the first few years, then a level performance and then, surprisingly, a decline. Perhaps the cars became heavier. Unfortunately there is no information on car weights in the dataset. Unsurprisingly, there is some variability in the EPA's estimates. The introduction of new model versions in 1995, 2000, 2006, 2012 does not appear to have had immediate effects. Additional changes may have been introduced in other years.

The estimates for the Mazda MX-5 are shown in Figure 17.9.

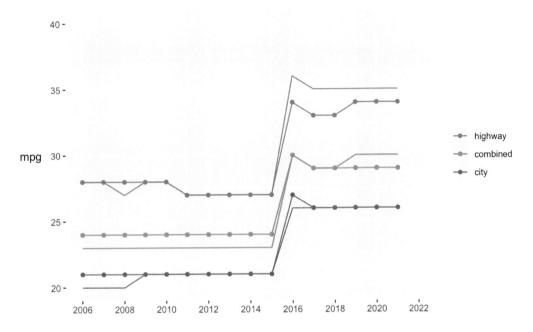

FIGURE 17.9: Fuel efficiency of Mazda MX-5 models for manual transmission (lines with points) and automatic (lines) transmission

The MX-5 estimates are less variable than the Corolla ones. The large jump in 2016 was due to the introduction of a new model. The manual and automatic transmission models appear to achieve very similar fuel efficiency.

Answers Small cars get higher mileage in general. Hybrids and newer cars get better mileage than other cars. Sector classifications give some surprising results for luxury cars. SUVs have mostly replaced station wagons.

Further questions How does fuel efficiency vary between city and highway driving? How does displacement influence fuel efficiency?

Graphical takeaways

- There are many different orderings in faceted displays. Look for informative ones. (Figures 17.1, 17.2, and 17.7)
- Small numbers of boxplots are better horizontally. (Figure 17.3)
- Drawing (longer) labels at an angle improves readability. (Figures 17.1, 17.2, 17.4, and 17.5)

18

Differences amongst the Palmer penguins

One can't be angry when one looks at a penguin.

— John Ruskin

Background The Long Term Ecological Research Network (LTER) (National Science Foundation (2022)) carries out research at Palmer station, Antarctica. Their work includes studying different species of penguins on islands in the Palmer Archipelago.

Questions How do the species differ? How do the penguin populations on the three islands studied differ?

Sources Horst, Hill, and Gorman (2020)

Structure One raw dataset of 344 penguins with 17 variables and one cleaned dataset with 8 variables.

18.1 Getting an overview of the penguin data

A good example of the LTER research can be found in Gorman, Williams, and Fraser (2014). Some of the data have been made available in the **palmerpenguins** R package, primarily size measurements and isotopic signature information for three species of penguin: Adélie, Chinstrap, and Gentoo. Colour information is not included, but Gentoo penguins have a distinctive orange bill and white marking above the eyes, while Chinstrap penguins have a narrow black chinstrap. Attractive drawings of the three species are shown on the **palmerpenguins** package webpage.

The Palmer Archipelago lies to the West of the Antarctic Peninsula, where warming linked to climate change has occurred very fast. According to Fountain (2022) this is bad for Adélie penguins that do better to the East in the Weddell Sea where it is still cold. Gentoo penguins are not so affected.

Figure 18.1 shows four plots of the dataset. There are barcharts for the three species and the three islands, a histogram of penguin body mass, and a scatterplot of flipper length against body mass.

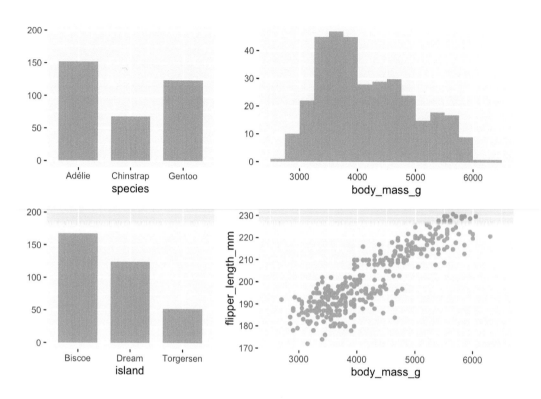

FIGURE 18.1: Four plots of the Palmer penguin dataset

There are fewer Chinstrap penguins and fewer penguins from Torgersen Island. The distribution of body mass may have that skewed shape because it is a mixture of the body mass distributions of three separate species. Flipper length and body mass are highly positively correlated.

Different subsets can be selected and highlighted to look for patterns. Figures 18.2 and 18.3 show examples of selecting a species or an island across these plots. Gentoo penguins were only sampled on Biscoe Island, and they are generally heavier with longer flippers than the other two species. Dream Island has all the Chinstrap penguins and some Adélie penguins. The penguins on Dream Island have smaller body mass and flipper length.

The penguins in this dataset were nesting pairs that had at least one egg. The sampling procedure is described in Gorman, Williams, and Fraser (2014). Detailed information on estimated total penguin numbers at Antarctic sites over the years is available on the MAPPPD website described in Humphries et al. (2017).

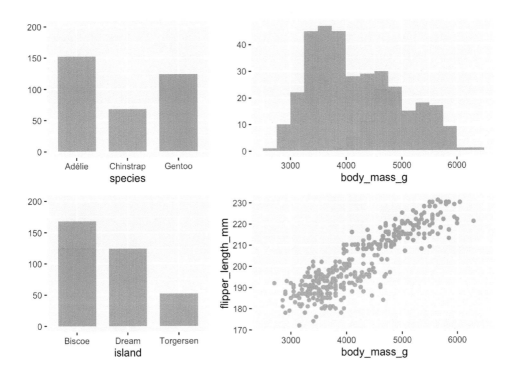

FIGURE 18.2: Gentoo penguins highlighted in all plots

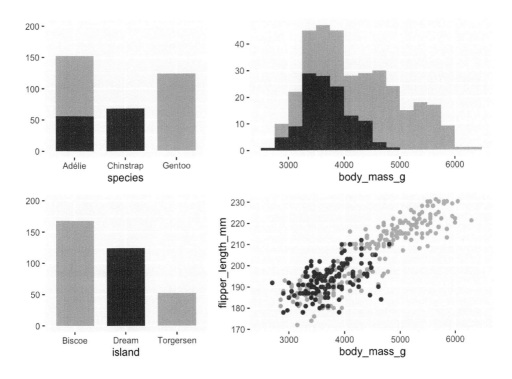

FIGURE 18.3: Dream Island penguins highlighted in all plots

Groups of cases defined in other ways could also be highlighted. Figure 18.4 highlights the penguins weighing no more than 3 kg. As was already known from Figure 18.2, the penguins are either Adélie or Chinstrap. Interestingly, there are examples of the lightest penguins on all three islands.

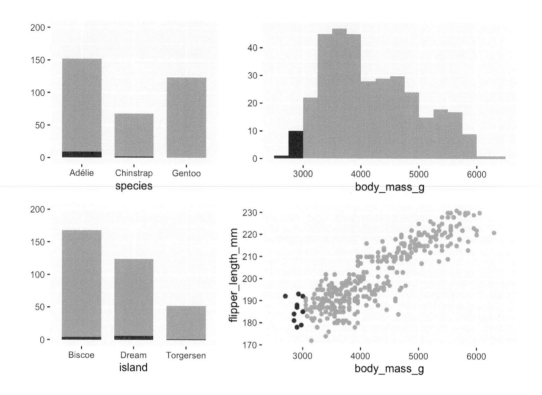

FIGURE 18.4: Penguins weighing no more than 3 kg highlighted in all plots

At this stage, it could be worth investigating what values these subsets have for other variables. This could be done by drawing the additional plots with the appropriate subset layer. Figure 18.5 shows boxplots for bill length and depth with the lightest penguins drawn in separate boxplots in brown beside boxplots for the rest of the data. With two exceptions, the light penguins have shorter bills than most other penguins. Their bill depths are about the same.

The boxplots have been drawn with widths proportional to the square roots of the numbers in the groups (331 and 11). The effect may be dramatic, but it emphasises how small the selected group is. By contrast consider boxplots of the same two bill measurements comparing Dream Island penguins to the rest. Bill lengths are about the same, while bill depths are larger.

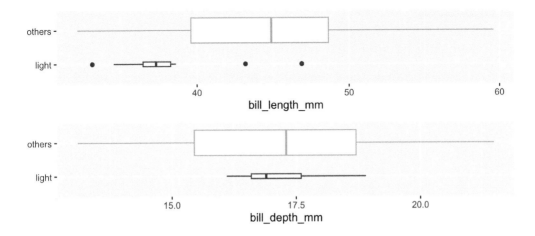

FIGURE 18.5: Penguins weighing no more than 3 kg plotted beside the rest, comparing bill lengths and bill depths

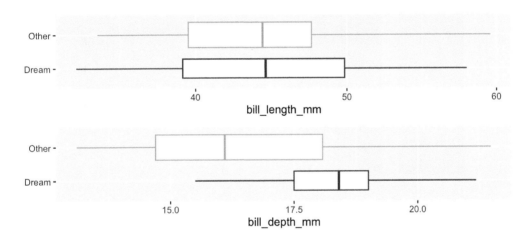

FIGURE 18.6: Dream Island penguins plotted beside the rest, comparing bill lengths and bill depths

Highlighting like this is a basic tool in interactive graphics where you select cases in one plot and they are then immediately highlighted in all other plots. Static versions, ghostplots, do not offer the same immediacy and flexibility, but can be drawn by creating a subset of just the selected cases. The plots required are drawn with the full dataset, using a muted colouring, and an additional layer is added to each plot using the subset. The selected objects are coloured more strongly, for instance in red or blue.

18.2   Looking at several variables in one plot

Examining all variables together can be helpful in determining which differentiate between the species. Figure 18.7 is a parallel coordinate plot of the data with the cases coloured by species.

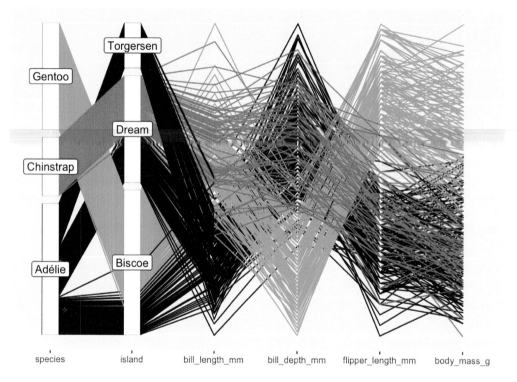

FIGURE 18.7: Parallel coordinate plot of the Palmer Penguin data

The first two axes show the information already seen in Figures 18.2 and 18.3 that Gentoo penguins are only to be found on Biscoe and Chinstrap penguins only on Dream. Other features can be seen too, such as the different patterns between bill length and bill depth for the species.

Further features may be separated out better in a parallel coordinate plot by reordering categories and variables. Chinstrap are only on Dream Island, so those categories should be at the top or bottom, and Gentoo are only on Biscoe Island, so they should be at the other end. It also seems better to place island before species. Most measurements have higher values for Gentoo penguins, but bill depth has lower values, so it could be reversed to reduce the numbers of line crossings. Finally, bill length has a different pattern to the other measurement variables and so might be moved to the far right. Figure 18.8 shows the data with the species and islands reordered, with bill depth reversed, and variables reordered.

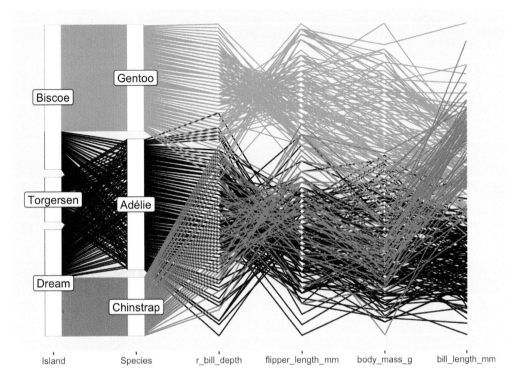

FIGURE 18.8: Reordered parallel coordinate plot of the Palmer Penguin data

In this display Chinstrap and Adélie penguins have similar measurement distributions, apart from bill length: Chinstrap penguins have longer bills. Gentoo penguins have higher values on several variables, except for bill depth—remember that this variable has been reversed in Figure 18.8. The fact that all blue (Gentoo) crossings between reversed bill depth and flipper length are above all other crossings between the two variables means that together they separate Gentoo from the other species.

There may be a more effective reordering of the categories and variables. Minimising the total number of line crossings could be a goal or, given the aim of distinguishing between the species, minimising the number of line crossings of different species, but how would a search through the myriad options be carried out? There are 6!=720 orderings of the six variables, 3!=6 orderings of the islands, 3!=6 orderings of the species, and 2^4=16 ways of mapping the variables (each one can be plotted as is or inverted). Some of these are equivalent (a reverse ordering of the variables will give the same result as an unreversed ordering), but there does not appear to be an obvious search procedure.

Bivariate associations seen in parallel coordinate plots can be examined more closely with scatterplots. Figure 18.9 confirms how bill length and bill depth combined separate the species (left) and how bill depth and flipper length combined separate Adélie penguins from the other two species (right).

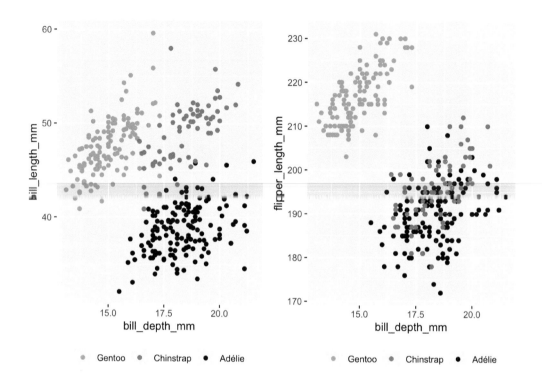

FIGURE 18.9: Scatterplots of bill depth with bill length and flipper length

Another way of exploring groups is to use facets. Figure 18.10 shows bill lengths and depths for each combination of species and island. To aid comparisons, the plot for all the penguins has been drawn in the background.

Whichever graphics or tables are drawn to investigate this dataset, it is quickly clear that the Chinstrap penguins are only found on Dream Island and that the Gentoo penguins are only found on Biscoe Island. Fig 18.10 shows that the association between bill length and depth is positive for all species on any island they are found on. It also suggests, if you look at the subplots with no highlighted cases, that the association between bill length and depth for all penguins together is negative. The calculated correlation for the whole dataset is -0.24, while the correlations for the highlighted groups in the individual facets range from 0.25 to 0.65.

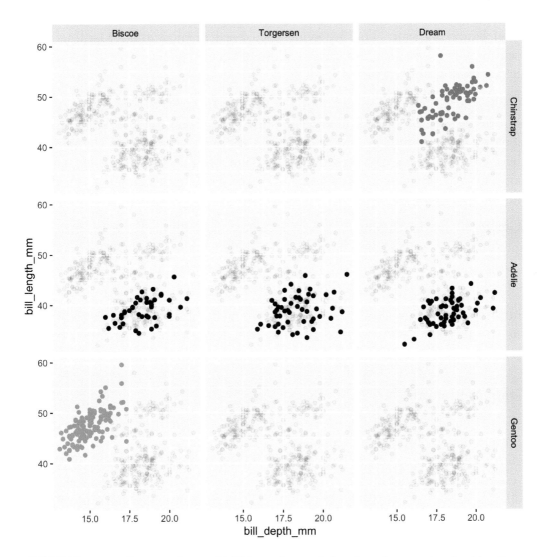

FIGURE 18.10: Scatterplots of bill lengths and depths of penguins by the three species and three islands

18.3   Using raw data to get more information

There is a second dataset with more variables in the **palmerpenguins** package called penguins_raw. This includes nesting observations and two isotope measurements. It provides enough information to compare the male and female in each nesting pair. The following set of scatterplots plots the four main measurements for the males against those of their female partners. In each plot the horizontal and vertical axes have identical scales.

As expected, the male in each pair is generally bigger than the female. One of the female Chinstrap penguins has a surprisingly long bill, possibly an error. Looking at the points as pairs combining the measurements of the male and the female from one nest, it can be seen that bill-depths, flipper lengths and body masses separate Gentoo pairs from the rest, while bill-lengths separate Adélie pairs from those of the other two species.

Answers Gentoo penguins are heavier with longer flippers and less deep bills and, of the islands studied, are only found on Biscoe Island. Adélie penguins have shorter bills. Chinstrap penguins are only found on Dream Island. Male penguins are usually bigger than their female partners.

Further questions Do the isotope measurements in the raw dataset differ for the species? The study was carried out over three years: Do results differ in any way across the years?

Graphical takeaways

- Selection and highlighting are instructive for studying groups of cases across ensembles of graphics. (Figures 18.2 to 18.4)
- Orderings of many kinds are crucial for getting the most out of parallel coordinate plots. (Figure 18.8)
- If data are paired, plotting the pairs in scatterplots provides more information. (Figure 18.11)

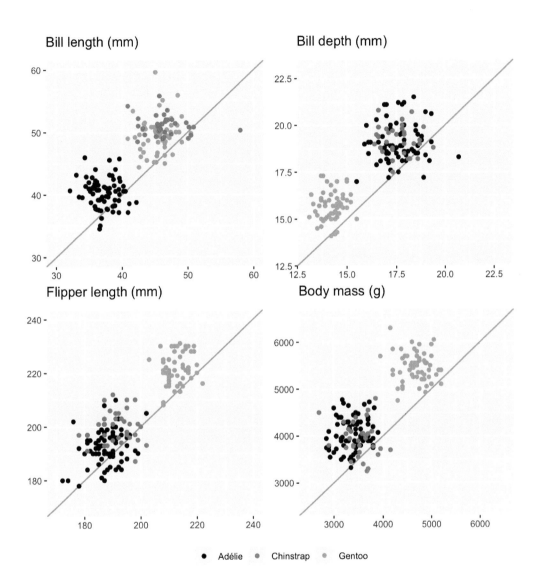

FIGURE 18.11: Measurements of four variables for the male (vertical axes) and female (horizontal axes) in each pair (green lines mark where values would be equal)

19

Comparing tests for malaria

There are more people dying of malaria than any specific cancer.

— Bill Gates

Background The data come from an investigation of a new magneto-optical method, ROMD, of testing for malaria. It could offer a swifter and cheaper approach than three other tests (PCR, RDT, LM).

Questions Do the results of the four tests agree? On which cases do they differ?

Sources Arndt, Koleala, and Orbán (2021)

Structure A dataset of 956 observations and 24 variables

19.1   How much agreement is there between the four tests?

Malaria is endemic in Papua New Guinea. The authors of Arndt, Koleala, and Orbán (2021) have made available the raw data of their study there, involving 956 individuals checked with four different tests, so that the methods could be compared. Each test uses a different measure of the disease. Eleven cases were excluded where there were missing values for two of the tests.

Figure 19.1 summarises the results for the remaining 945 cases.

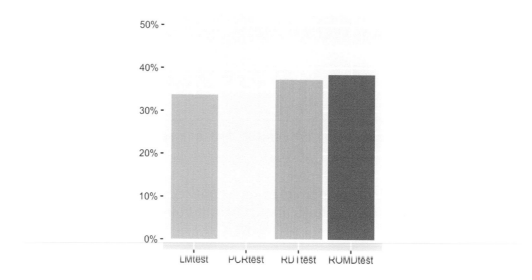

FIGURE 19.1: Percentages of positives for the four tests

The tests found between 33.7% and 38.4% positives with the new test reporting the most positives. The authors believe that the new method may detect previous as well as current infections. Figure 19.2 displays how often the different combinations of test results arose.

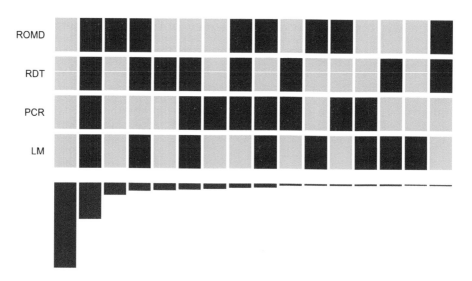

FIGURE 19.2: Combinations of individual malaria test results (red rectangles are positives)

The first column shows the cases in which all tests gave negative results for malaria (47.4%) and the second column all cases with positive results (20.3%).

The barchart at the foot of the plot shows how often each combination of test results was observed. Rules for the four tests are given in Arndt, Koleala, and Orbán (2021). There was disagreement at one level or another for 32.3% of the cases. All 16 possible combinations of results are in evidence.

The next display shows that no one test dominates another. The main diagonal elements in each subdisplay show the numbers of disagreements between those two tests. In each case there are disagreements of both kinds, positive-negative and negative-positive. Serious cases are presumably recognised by all methods. Borderline cases may be recognised by some but not by others.

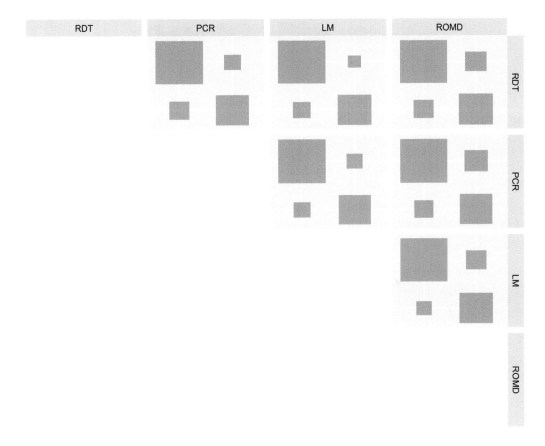

FIGURE 19.3: Paired comparisons of the results of the four tests

19.2 Additional analyses

According to the paper, the LM test is the gold standard and it can be seen how the distribution of the new ROMD measurement differs according to cases testing negatively and positively on LM in Figure 19.4.

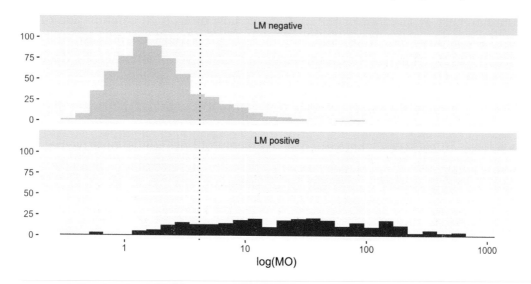

FIGURE 19.4: Magneto-optical measurements on a log10 scale grouped by the corresponding LM test result

Dashed lines have been drawn at the magneto-optical test cut-off. The log(MO) values are higher for the positive LM group, although there are some small values too. The same applies in reverse for the negative LM group. The choice of cut-off will depend on the numbers of 'errors' and on the relative importance assigned to false negatives and false positives.

Some other information was available in the dataset, including the age, weight, and sex of those tested. Figure 19.5 plots weight by age for females and males separately.

It is interesting to see how many young people were tested. In general those tested do not seem particularly heavy. There are a couple of low weights which look unusual and a few heavy younger women.

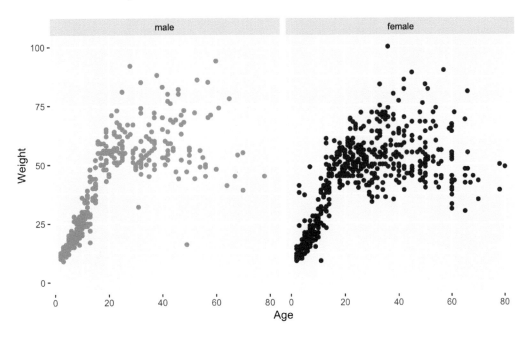

FIGURE 19.5: Weight by age and sex of the people tested for malaria

Answers The methods mostly agreed but disagreed on about one third of the cases. ROMD, the proposed new method, identified more cases as having malaria than the other three methods.

Further questions How sensitive are the results to changing the ROMD cut-off? Do any of the additional variables in the dataset provide information on the cases the methods differ on?

Graphical takeaways

- Matrix plots display multivariate categorical data, treating each variable equally. (Figure 19.2)
- If test results are quantitative, graphics show the effect of cut-off points. (Figure 19.4)
- Scatterplots summarise the association between two variables better than analytic methods. (Figure 19.5)

20

Are swimmers swimming faster?

Swimming could be taught by lecturing the student swimmers in the class-room three times a week on the various kinds of strokes and the principles of buoyancy and so forth. Some might believe that on completing such a course of study, the graduates would all eagerly run down to the pool, jump in, and swim at once. But I think it's much more likely that they would want to stay in the classroom to teach a fresh lot of students all that they had learned.

— George Box

Background Comparing swimmers' best times for different strokes and distances.

Questions Which strokes are swum fastest? How much faster are men than women? What effect did full body swimsuits have?

Sources Website of the International Swimming Federation (FINA (2021))

Structure 7685 observations of 23 variables

20.1 Best times for different strokes

The website of the International Swimming Federation (FINA (2021)) publishes results of competitions and datasets containing swimmers' best times for different strokes and distances. Spearing et al. (2021) used some of this data to compare the performances of swimmers over time and across events using a model based on extreme value theory. They also assessed which world records were most likely to be broken next. As the data are best times for individual swimmers, each swimmer can only appear once in the list for an event. The data used here include the 200 best times for men and women over each of 17 events for individuals, with fewer best times for three relay events. All times are in seconds and have been rounded to two decimal places. Only races in 50 metre pools (long course metres or LCM events) are considered here.

Figure 20.1 is a display of best times by date for an event, in this case the 100 m freestyle for men. Most of the best times have been achieved recently, partly because training methods have improved, partly because there are more swimmers, and partly because more competitions are included on the FINA website. There are a few impressive older performances. It looks like there is an upper limit of just over 22.2 seconds and this must have been the 200th best performance. The very best times were achieved after the introduction of full body swimsuits in 2008 that were permitted at the Beijing Olympics. The suits were banned from 1st January 2010 (marked by a red vertical line).

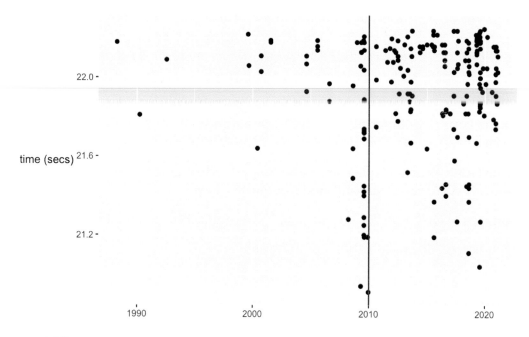

FIGURE 20.1: Best times by male swimmers for the 100 m freestyle

There are four different events over 50 m: freestyle, breaststroke, butterfly, and backstroke. Plotting the sets of 200 best times for men all in the same display presents a striking picture (Figure 20.2).

The times for the events are almost completely separated. There is a possible overlap between the fastest butterfly time and the slowest freestyle times. In fact the best time for the butterfly was 22.27 seconds and the two-hundredth best time for the freestyle was 22.25 seconds. Three of the four plots have the same patterns seen in Figure 20.1, a few fine older performances, a string of best times with full body swimsuits in 2009, and a gradual improvement over the past 10 years from the slower times recorded in 2010. There are two exceptions. One is the 50 m backstroke time of Camille Lacourt in 2010. The other is the extraordinary time of Adam Peaty in the 50 m breaststroke in 2017.

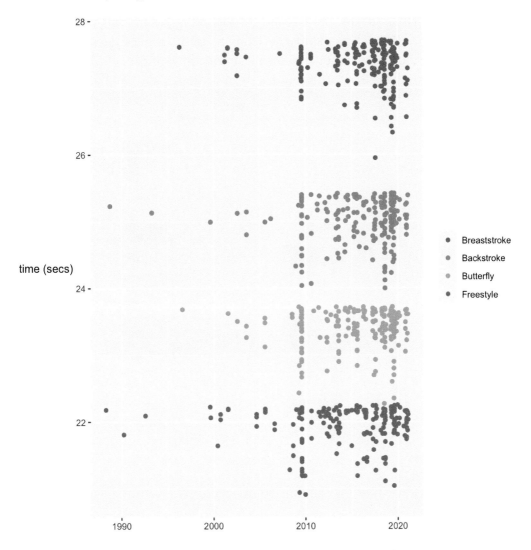

FIGURE 20.2: Best times by male swimmers for the four 50 m events

Unlike in the other events, several breaststroke swimmers have beaten the best full body swimsuit time. Was it of less benefit to breaststroke swimmers?

The ordering of the events is hardly surprising to swimmers. Backstroke swimmers start in the water, while swimmers in the other three events have the advantage of diving in and swimming briefly underwater at the start. The butterfly is a relatively new stroke in official terms. It was introduced before the Second World War and was later used by swimmers in breaststroke competitions. In the early 1950s the best breaststroke times were swum by butterfly swimmers and the butterfly was declared a separate stroke in 1953 (Oppenheim (1970)). This is why the breaststroke world record times increased then, as afterwards breaststroke swimmers had to actually swim breaststroke!

The same patterns hold for the women for the 50 m events with one notable exception. Figure 20.3 shows that the women are in general slower than the men (although the best women swimming freestyle would beat the best male breaststroke swimmers and probably the best male backstroke swimmers too).

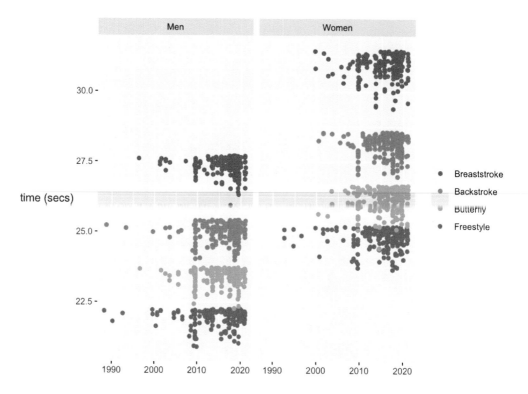

FIGURE 20.3: Best times for the four 50 m events achieved by men and women

The graphic suggests an overlap between female butterfly and freestyle swimmers that was suspected but not confirmed amongst the males. Drawing only the times for women as boxplots in Figure 20.4 provides confirmation. Sarah Sjöström swam an incredible time for the butterfly of 24.43 seconds in the 2014 Swedish Championships. The asymmetric pattern of the boxplots is to be expected, distributions of best times are skewed to the left.

Do the same patterns apply for the longer standard distances of 100 m and 200 m? It turns out that the separations between the four strokes increase for both sexes, except for backstroke and butterfly where there is increasing overlap. Figure 20.5 shows this for the 200 m events.

The 200 m LCM races include three turns and the turn rules are different for the four strokes. In particular, breaststroke and butterfly swimmers must touch the end with both hands at the same time, while freestyle and backstroke swimmers can touch the end with any part of their body. This explains at least partly why backstroke times catch up on butterfly times.

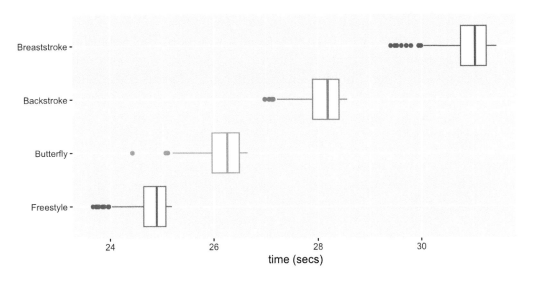

FIGURE 20.4: Boxplots of the best times by women for the four 50 m events

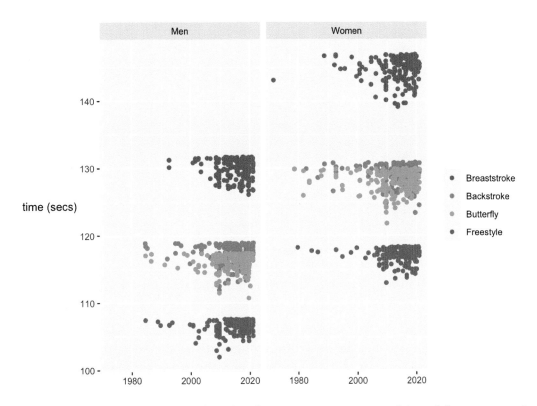

FIGURE 20.5: Best times for the four 200 m events achieved by men and women

One point stands out in Figure 20.5, the superb pre-1980 time in the women's 200 m breaststroke. Checking with the results for the 1971 6th Pan American games on the web revealed that Lynn Colella won both the 200 m breaststroke and the 200 m butterfly, but the FINA database recorded her butterfly time as a breaststroke time. Looking at the differences between the butterfly and breaststroke times overall, it is clear that there would be no traditional breaststroke swimmers in competitions any more had the butterfly not been declared a separate stroke.

The performances of men and women can be compared by plotting the time differences between the swimmers of the same rank order for an event. Figure 20.6 shows this for the four 100 m events.

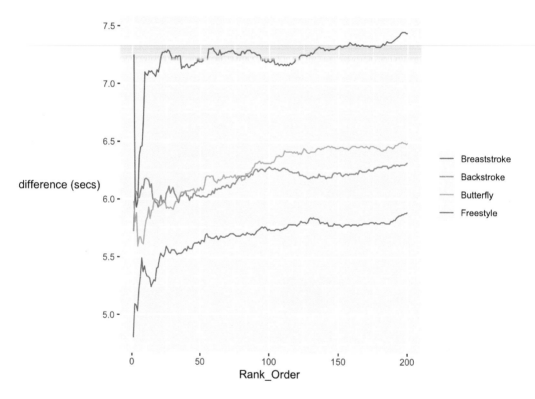

FIGURE 20.6: Time differences between men and women for the four 100 m events by rank

The display suggests that the very best women are a bit closer to the very best men in time and that the difference between the sexes increases as ranking increases. The big exception to this is the breaststroke, due to Adam Peaty's 2019 world record of 56.88 seconds. In general, differences between equal ranks increase if one group is bigger than the other.

Differences in times between events are affected by the popularity of the events amongst the swimmers. This can be seen, for instance, in the numbers of swimmers taking part in the heats for the events at the 2019 World Championships (FINA (2021)). There were 41 in the men's 4x100 m medley and 134 in the men's 50 m freestyle. The corresponding numbers for the women were 26 and 106.

20.2 How good are the best swimmers across multiple events?

A few swimmers compete at the top level in more than one event. The outstanding example in this dataset is Katinka Hosszu, whose best time is amongst the top 200 in 14 events. Figure 20.7 shows her results as purple dots on top of letter-value boxplots (Hofmann, Wickham, and Kafadar (2017)) for the 200 best times in the 17 events for women. The events have been sorted by stroke and ordered by distance. Each plot has its own time scale.

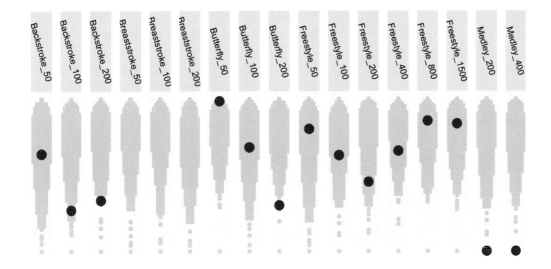

FIGURE 20.7: Katinka Hosszu's best times by event (in purple) compared with the 200 best in each event

Given that she is good at so many events, it is perhaps not surprising that she is the best overall in the two medley events. Her 'weakest' stroke is the breaststroke, the only events where she is not in the top 200.

The most versatile male swimmer in the dataset, Michael Phelps, is also strong in the two medley events, as can be seen in Figure 20.8. He is amongst the best in 10 of the 17 individual events for men.

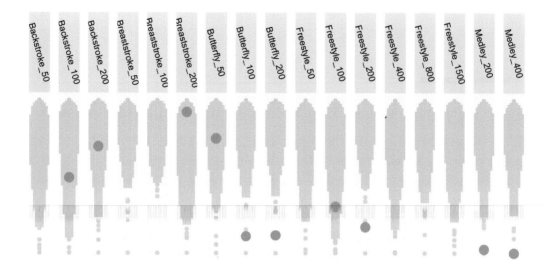

FIGURE 20.8: Michael Phelps's best times by event (in green) compared with the 200 best in each event

20.3 Comparing events graphically

Another way of comparing events is to plot the times standardised by event by rank in a parallel coordinate plot. Figure 20.9 shows this for the 34 individual events, where the 200 times for each event have been standardised on a $[0,1]$ scale.

The vertical line on the left represents the rescaled fastest times, i.e. the times of the top ranked swimmer in each event and the vertical line on the right represents the rescaled 200th time for each event. The variation to the left of the plot might be expected. Some world record performances are much faster than the second best performances. The order statistics only seem to become relatively equal near rank 200 at the right of the plot.

Possibly choosing a different common scaling and sorting the events by stroke and ordering by distance would be more informative. Sorting by the relative difference between the best two performances smooths the plot out a little, while confirming that the distribution of times for the men's 200 m breaststroke is a bit different.

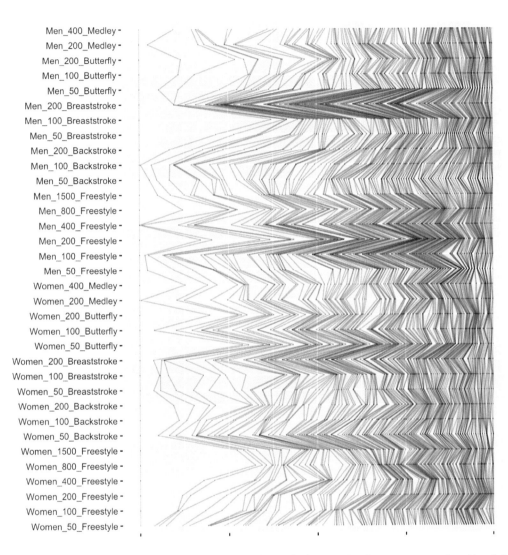

FIGURE 20.9: A parallel coordinate plot of the ranked times standardised by event across the individual events

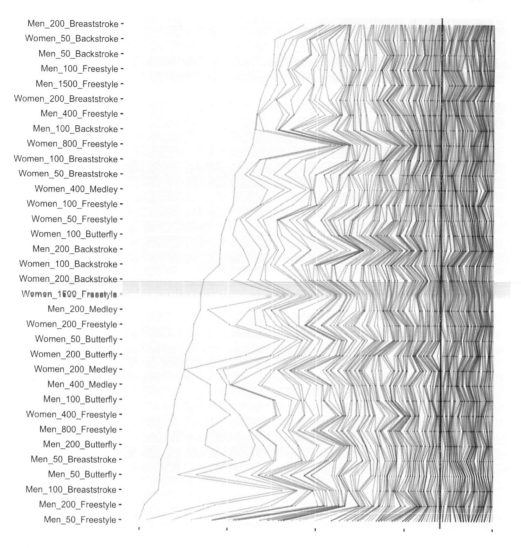

FIGURE 20.10: A parallel coordinate plot of the ranked times aligning the 100th ranks (the red line) across the individual events, sorted by relative fastest times

Another approach tried was to align the 100th rank performances for all events, scaling accordingly (the 200th rank performances remain aligned), and sorting events by the relative fastest times. This is shown in Figure 20.10. The 200 m breaststroke for men stands out as the relatively most compressed of the event time distributions. Wave-like patterns are apparent around events where the (relatively) biggest differences between the best and second-best times occur. A good example is the 100 m breaststroke for men, due to Adam Peaty's performance, the third from the bottom of the plot. It is almost as far away from the 200 m breaststroke for men as it could be.

20.4 How do relay races compare with individual races?

There are three relay events for men and women, the 4x100 m medley and the 4x100 m and 4x200 m freestyle. The very best times for the relay events are better than the very best times for the comparable individual events.

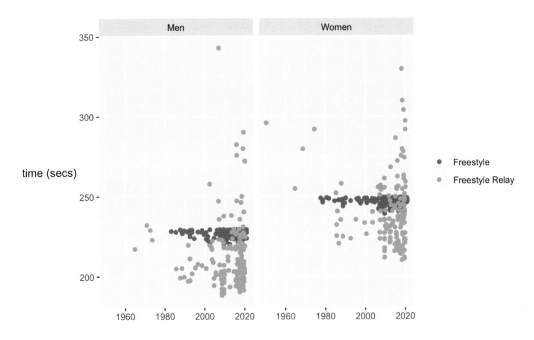

FIGURE 20.11: Best times for the 400 m freestyle events for men and women, individual (red) and relay (blue)

Best times are achieved by relay teams and not individuals over the same total distance, because each swimmer in a team swims only a quarter of the distance. In the medley event you can have a specialist for each of the four strokes. Individuals only have one diving start, but relay teams have three (in the medley) or four.

The high variability amongst relay times compared with individual times is because each country's team is treated as one competitor. There is only one best time for each country, whether it is the USA or Togo. This also means that there are not 200 best times in the 4x100 m relay, just 168 for the men and 144 for the women, the numbers of countries who have had teams in those events. Countries which no longer exist (such as Yugoslavia and Rhodesia) are included, which is why there is even a best time for the 4x100 m freestyle relay for women from 1950!

20.5   How do countries compare?

The USA is currently the strongest swimming nation and that can be measured in a variety of ways. Instead of looking at that, consider the strengths of nations across the same events for men and women. Figure 20.12 plots the number of female swimmers of a country in the top 200 for an event against the number of male swimmers of that country in the same event. The graphs are shown for the nine countries with the most swimmers in all amongst the 200 best times for the 17 events for men and women.

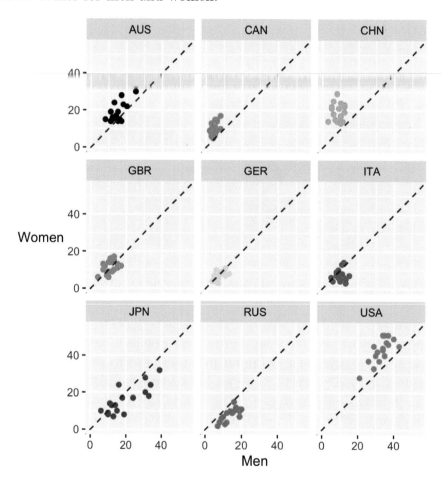

FIGURE 20.12: Numbers of female swimmers in the top 200 plotted against numbers of male swimmers in the top 200 for each of 17 events by country (the dashed lines represent equality)

The USA, Canada, and China have more female swimmers than male swimmers in the respective top 200's in all events. Russia has more men than women in the top 200 lists in all events.

Answers Freestyle is fastest, then butterfly, backstroke, breaststroke. Backstroke catches up on butterfly over longer distances. The 200th fastest man is faster than the fastest woman in all four strokes. After full body swimsuits were banned it took several years to get near to the earlier records again.

Further questions How do the performances of individual swimmers develop over time? What effect do turns have on swimming performance? Comparing times over different pool lengths could be used to study the effect.

Graphical takeaways

- Legends should be close to the data and in the same order. (Figure 20.2)
- Scatterplots and boxplots offer complementary views of the same grouped data. (Figure 20.3 right and Figure 20.4)
- Sorting, ordering, and arranging make finding information in graphics easier. (Figures 20.7 and 20.8)

21

Over 90 years running 90 km

Success supposes endeavour.

— Jane Austen

Background The Comrades Marathon in South Africa between Durban and Pietermaritzburg has been run over 90 times since 1921.

Questions How many people take part? Who takes part and how has that changed over the years? How long do the best runners take and how long do most runners take? Are men much faster than women? Is there a difference in times between the "down" runs starting in Pietermaritzburg and the "up" runs starting in Durban?

Sources Data from Stratton (2019), race profile information from 28East (2022).

Structure Information on 445129 participants' runs in 12 variables.

21.1 How many run in the Comrades (Ultra)Marathon?

The data were scraped from the Marathon's website (Comrades Marathon Association (2022)) and made available on Kaggle. More detailed data, including runners' ages and split times for the 2019 race, have been analysed elsewhere (Collier (2019)).

The race was run for the first time in 1921 from Durban to Pietermaritzburg ("down"), with 16 runners finishing. In 1922 the race was run in the other direction ("up"). Mostly the directions alternated in successive years, but on three occasions they did not.

Figure 21.1 shows the numbers of finishers and the directions in each year. The race distance was not always the same and usually a little under 90 km.

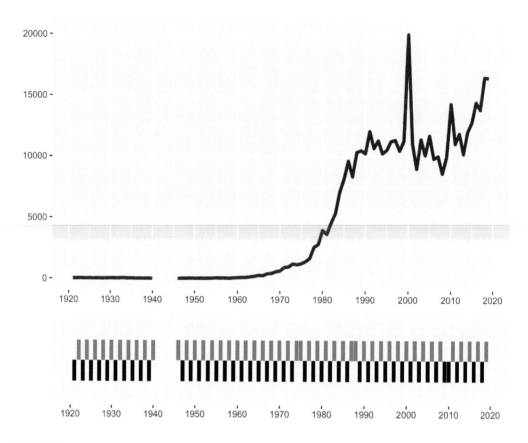

FIGURE 21.1: Numbers of finishers of the Comrades Marathon and the race direction by year (dark orange is up, black is down).

Numbers remained low until the 1960s and rose sharply in the 1970s and 1980s (Figure 21.1). No races took place from 1941 to 1945 during the Second World War. There was a sharp peak in the year 2000 when just over 20,000 finished, almost twice as many as in the surrounding years. There were two reasons. First, it was the 75th running of the race and there was much publicity, so many more entered. Second, the limit on finishing time was extended from 11 hours to 12 hours for that year. In 2019 there were 25,000 entrants (not all started) and over 16,000 finished. Detailed information can be found on the website for the race (Comrades Marathon Association (2022)) and some summary information on its Wikipedia page (Wikipedia (2022)).

21.2 Numbers by age and sex

The race was originally only open to white males. In 1975 both women and blacks were allowed to enter officially for the first time, although a woman, Frances Hayward, ran in the third race in 1923 and the first black man, Robert Mtshali, ran in 1935.

Runners have to be at least 20 to participate and are divided into separate groups by age: SENIOR (20-39), VETERANS (40-49), MASTERS (50-59), GRANDMASTERS (60+). Figure 21.2 is a plot of the numbers in each group for each sex. The four female groups are drawn with dashed lines and the four male groups with solid lines. There is an additional unlabelled brown solid line for entrants having no known birth year.

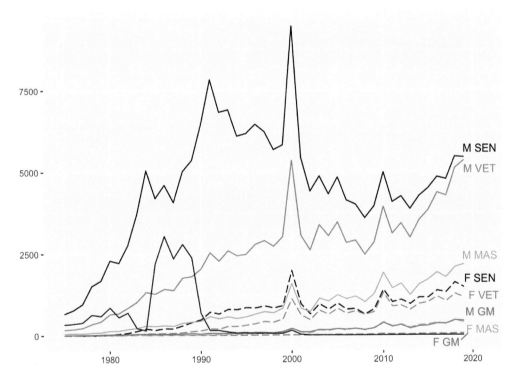

FIGURE 21.2: Numbers of finishers by age group and sex from 1975 to 2019 (the brown line is for those whose birthyear is not given)

The male seniors group dominated the race until 2000, apart from a few years in the 1980s when entrants with no birth years recorded could not be assigned to any age category. In recent years the number of male veterans has become larger and almost the same as the number of seniors. The other smaller groups follow a common pattern of a general increase with peaks in 2000 and 2010.

The first foreign entrants were a group of four top runners from England in 1962 (Wikipedia (2022)). All four finished in the top five with one of them, John Smith, winning the race. Figure 21.3 shows how the numbers of female and foreign finishers have developed since 1975.

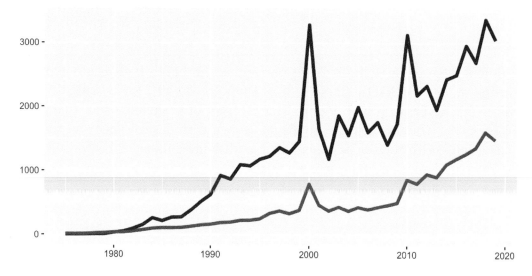

FIGURE 21.3: Numbers of female (purple) and foreign (red) finishers since 1975

Both groups have grown in numbers over the years with the numbers of foreign finishers increasing more slowly and with less variability. The number of female finishers peaked sharply in 2000 and in 2010. A new highest number for female finishers was established in 2018.

21.3   How long do runners take to finish?

The race was limited to 12 hours in the first few years until 1927. From 1928 to 2002 the limit was 11 hours, apart from the 75th race in 2000 when it was extended to 12 hours. Since 2003 the limit has been 12 hours again. In recent years qualifying as a finisher required runners to additionally reach up to six cut-off points along the way within specified times.

Detailed time comparisons across years are difficult because of the different numbers running, the different weather conditions, the different directions of the run ("down" and "up"), and the different distances run. Comrades Marathon Association (2022) gives the distances of the four Comrades Marathons from 2016 to 2019 as 89.2 km, 86.7 km, 90.2 km, and 86.8 km.

Boxplots of the times in hours for each year are displayed in Figure 21.4. The few times of over 12 hours listed in the dataset have been removed.

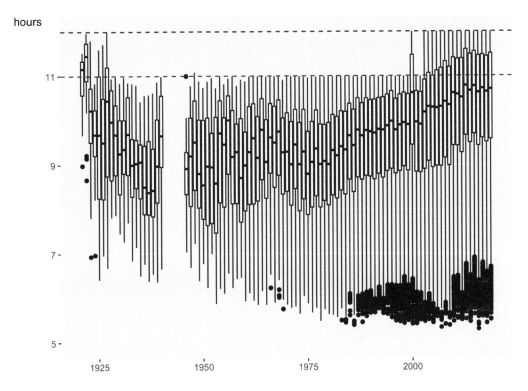

FIGURE 21.4: Distributions of finishing times in hours by year

The wartime gap when no races were run is obvious here as it was in Figure 21.1. The finishing limits of 11 and 12 hours have been marked with red dotted lines. The best times have improved since the early days, but very few runners took part then and support and conditions are undoubtedly far better nowadays. Winning margins were sometimes quite large early on, again because few runners took part. The median finishing time has increased since 1975 as more runners participated. The increased number of participants has also led to more runners being declared 'fast' outliers as the boxplot rule for defining outliers has become less stringent.

The distribution of finishing times in 2000 is quite different from the distributions of neighbouring years, having a higher median and higher box. This was due to the extended time limit and the much higher number of participants.

The median and best times in hours are plotted together with the numbers of runners in Figure 21.5.

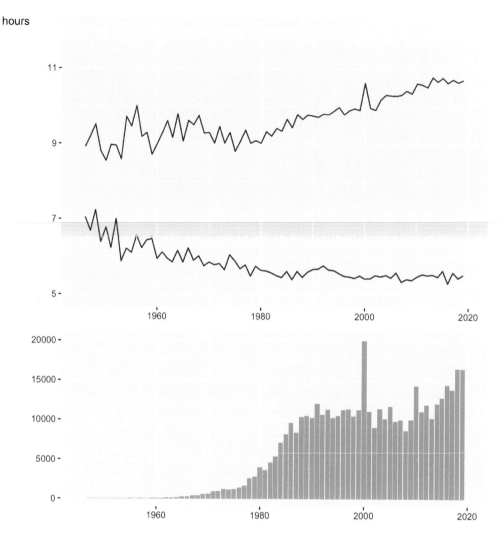

FIGURE 21.5: Median times (red), best times (blue) and numbers of finishers (barchart) from 1946 to 2019

This confirms what we know already, but emphasises the huge differences in numbers finishing. The best time has remained relatively constant for a while and the median time has increased.

21.4 Comparing times for men and women

21.4.1 Best times for men and women

Women have officially been allowed to run since 1975. At first few took part. Since 1980 over 30 women have finished each year, rising to over 3000 in 2019.

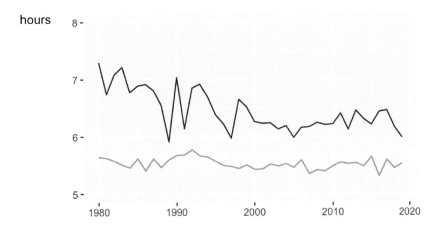

FIGURE 21.6: Best times for women (purple) and men (green) since 1980

Between 2000 and 2019 the mean best time for men has been about 5.5 hours and for women about 6.25 hours. Over this period four to five times as many men have finished each year as women. The record for women is still the 1989 time of 5:54:43 by Frith van der Merwe. Not many records last that long.

The proportion of women taking part rose fairly steadily from 1980 to 2010 and has remained at about 20% since (Figure 21.7).

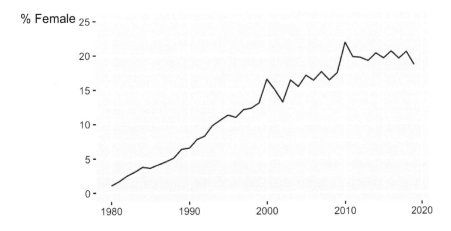

FIGURE 21.7: Percentage of women participants since 1980

21.4.2   Median times for men and women

Best times can vary quite a lot between years, whereas median times are likely to be more stable. Figure 21.8 shows the patterns of medians for men and women since 1980.

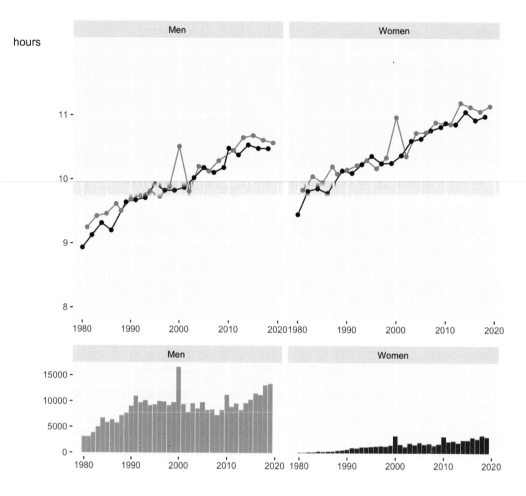

FIGURE 21.8: Median times for men and women for "up" (dark orange) and "down" (black) races since 1980 and the numbers finishing

The medians have been increasing steadily, apart from the year 2000 which has already been discussed. The graph for the "up" runs tends to be slightly higher than the graph for the "down" runs. The average difference between the male and female medians has been just over half an hour. Again, it is important to remember the much greater numbers of males running.

21.5   How many runners get medals?

Figure 21.9 displays the distributions of finishing times in the 2019 Comrades Marathon for females and males separately. It looks rather as if a set of skew distributions has been stuck together, each one ending at a particular time limit.

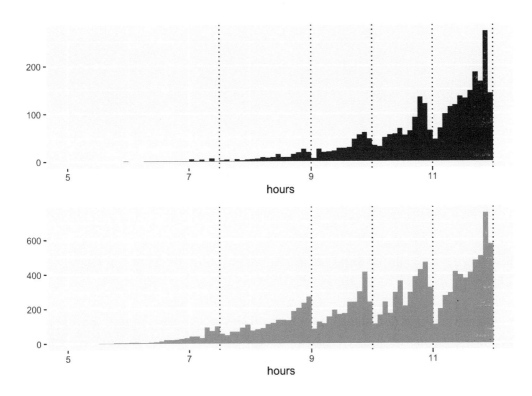

FIGURE 21.9: Finishing times in the 2019 race for females (above) and males (below), dotted lines mark limits for awarding medals other than gold

The vertical scales of the plots differ, as fewer women took part. The same intermediate boundary effects can be seen in both histograms. Some runners clearly wish to finish within certain target times. Dotted lines have been drawn to mark times governing the awarding of medals other than gold. The top 10 of each sex get gold medals. Men finishing under 6 hours but not in the top 10 get a Wally Hayward medal and women finishing under 7.5 hours but not in the top 10 get an Isavel Roche-Kelly medal. Every finisher gets a medal, and details of all the medals can be found in Wikipedia (2022).

21.6   How different are the "up" and "down" races?

As the races take place in different years over different distances in different directions, comparisons are inexact.

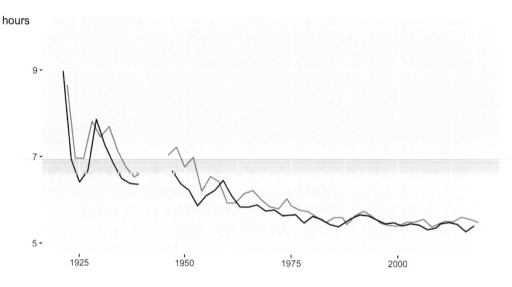

FIGURE 21.10: Comparisons of best times in hours for the "up" (dark orange) and "down" (black) races since 1921

In general the best times for the "up" races are slightly higher than the best times for the closest "down" races. Race distances for each year are given on the Marathon's webpage, so that the average pace of the races can be compared too (Figure 21.11). Speeds are faster for the "down" races than the "up" races. The "down" races are slightly longer as Figure 21.12 shows.

The "down" race is not all downhill and the "up" race is not all uphill, but overall there is a difference of around 700 m in elevation between Pietermaritzburg and Durban as the profile plot for the planned, but cancelled, 2020 Comrades Marathon shows (28East (2022)).

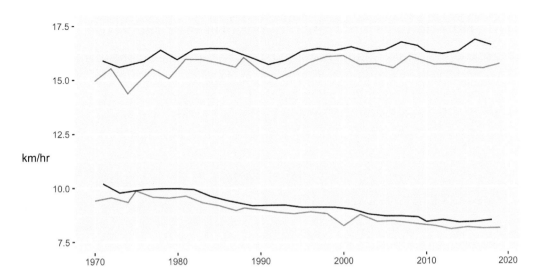

FIGURE 21.11: Average speed of the fastest runners (above) and of the median runners (below) in km/hr for the "up" (dark orange) and "down" (black) races since 1970

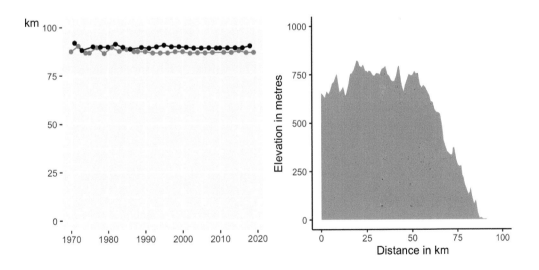

FIGURE 21.12: Distances in km for the "up" (dark orange) and "down" (black) races since 1970 and a profile plot for the down race from Pietermaritzburg to Durban that was planned for 2020

21.7   How do individual runners perform over the years?

Two of the best female runners are particularly interesting, the identical twins Elena and Olesya Nurgalieva. Elena ran every year from 2003 to 2015, while Olesya missed the 2006 and 2012 races. Their performances are compared in Figure 21.13. The plot on the left has the same vertical scale as in Figures 21.4 and 21.14, while the plot on the right has been magnified to show more detail.

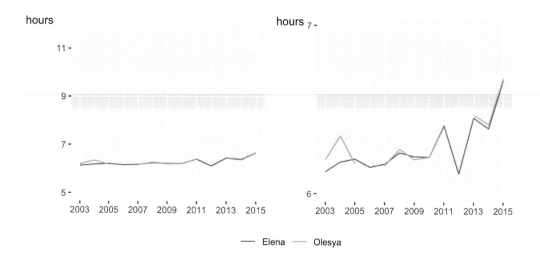

FIGURE 21.13: Performances of the Nurgalieva identical twins

The sisters ran very similar times over the years, with mostly less than two minutes between them. Elena's best performance was in 2012 when Olesya did not run. Elena had the best overall time for females eight times and Olesya twice. There are a number of good photos of the sisters in action on the web (just search for "Nurgalieva").

Some runners have participated very often and Figure 21.14 shows the times achieved by the 12 runners with more than 40 appearances. The points and lines are coloured according to the runner's age category at the time. You might expect a hockey-stick shape: an initial slower run followed by swift improvement to a best time and then a gradual decline in performance with increasing age. To some extent this is true, but with a lot of individual variation.

Some runners have isolated poor performances compared with their other results (e.g., Barry Holland in 1995, Dave Lowe in 1985). Some show more variability in performance (e.g., Vic Boston and Wietsche Van Der Westhuizen). Most show a decline in performance as they get older.

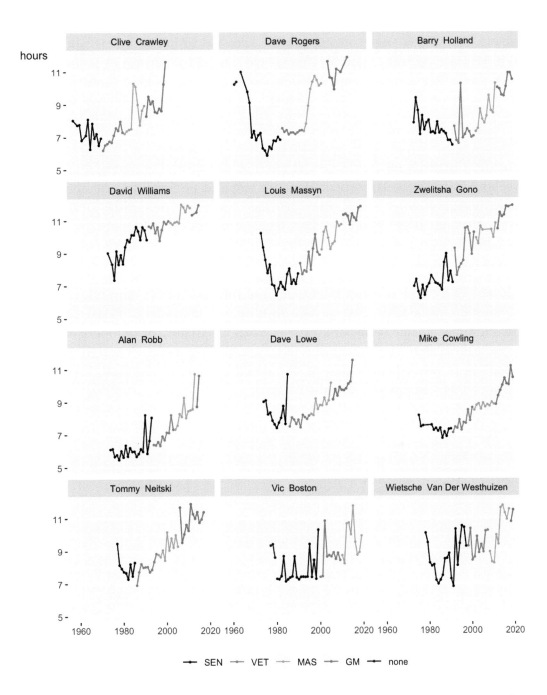

FIGURE 21.14: Runners who have finished more than 40 times, ordered by the first time they ran the race

Answers Numbers of participants have increased enormously since the early years. Since the race has been made open to all, many women now run. The proportion of older runners has increased. International participation has also grown. The fastest time to complete the race has dropped, but not noticeably so in the last 20 years. Median times have tended to increase as more runners participate. Men's best times are quicker than women's best times, but there are far more male runners. The difference is currently about 45 minutes. Overall the best times for the "up" race are generally slightly higher than the best times for the "down" race.

Further questions Birthyears of runners are available on the Marathon's website, but were not scraped. How are age and performance related? Other marathons are newer and shorter. Do the results for them differ substantially from what has been found for the Comrades Marathon?

Graphical takeaways

- Boxplots by year provide a great deal of information. (Figure 21.4)
- Scales do not always have to start at 0. (e.g., Figures 21.6, 21.11, and 21.14)
- Combining a time series of statistics with a barchart of numbers over time works well when the time scales are aligned. (Figures 21.5 and 21.8)
- Scaling of related data may vary across plots to get the most information from them. (Figures 21.9 and 21.13)

22

Comparing software for facial recognition

Here's looking at you, kid.

— Humphrey Bogart to Ingrid Bergman in 'Casablanca'

Background Buolamwini and Gebru (2018) is an important paper studying how well three facial recognition softwares performed in identifying people with different skin shades.

Questions How do the error rates vary by sex and skin colour? Are the error rates and patterns similar for the three softwares?

Sources Buolamwini and Gebru (2018)

Structure Prediction numbers for three software packages predicting for sex across 1270 individuals with six different skin shades.

22.1 How well do the softwares do?

The authors introduced a new facial analysis dataset, balanced by sex and skin type, that they used to test three commercial facial recognition software packages. The study task was to determine the sex of a person from a photograph. Results were that there was a high predictive error rate for dark-skinned females ($> 34\%$) and an almost negligible error rate for light-skinned males ($< 1\%$). The authors concluded that this unsatisfactory and uneven performance was due to the training databases the software systems used.

The summary data were reconstructed from the published paper by assuming that each percentage reported had to produce an integer number when combined with the relevant total.

Figure 22.1 is a barchart of the numbers in each of the 12 groups (6 skin tones for each sex). The patterns are similar, but there are more males overall, mainly in the second and sixth skin tone groups.

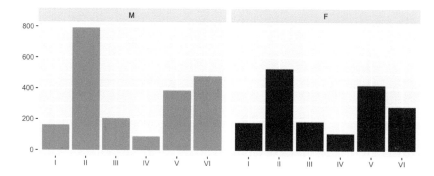

FIGURE 22.1: Numbers of different skin tones in the dataset for both sexes

Figure 22.2 shows the error rates by sex and skin shade (see article for details) for each of the three software systems tested using doubledecker plots of error rates side by side. Microsoft had mostly the lowest error rates—by quite a lot for the group where all software packages performed worst, the darker females.

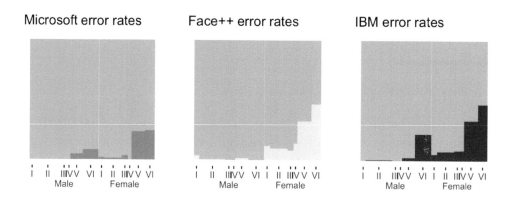

FIGURE 22.2: Error rates by sex and skin colour for three software systems drawn side by side. In each plot males are to the left, females to the right, and skin colour gets darker from left to right within sex. The width of each bar is proportional to the size of the group it represents.

Figure 22.3 draws the doubledecker plots above one another to show more detail and provide a better comparison of the distributions of error rates across sex and skin tones. The error rates were low for males and high for females, and they also increased as skin tone got darker. Microsoft mostly did better than Face++ and did better than IBM across the board. Males were put on the left, so that the error rates generally rose from left to right. The softwares were ordered from overall best to worst performing from top to bottom—although none did particularly well. The group widths are the same for each software as they are proportional to the group sizes for this criterion.

Microsoft error rates

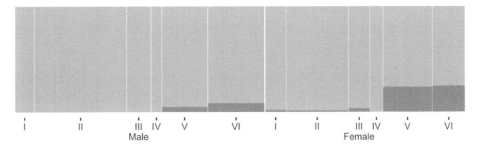

Face++ error rates

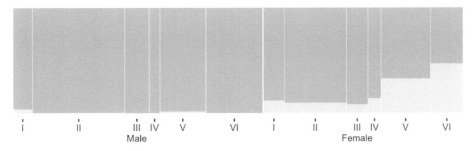

IBM error rates

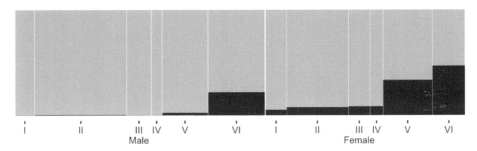

FIGURE 22.3: Error rates by sex and skin colour for three separate software systems. Males are on the left, females on the right, and skin colour gets darker from left to right within sex. The width of each bar is proportional to the size of the group it represents.

22.2   Are positive predictive values (PPV) a good criterion?

There are many different possible measures for assessing binary predictions and the paper also uses PPV (Positive Predictive Value). PPV is the number of true positives divided by the total number of positives. Ideally the predictions for each case should be compared directly, but only summary information is available.

PPV values tend to be high. The graphics can look more informative if (1-PPV) = FDR (False Discovery Rate) is plotted instead. FDRs for each combination of sex and skin shade for each software are shown in Figure 22.4. Whereas the bar widths in Figures 22.3 and 22.2 were the same for each software, being proportional to the number of cases in that group, this is no longer true here. The bar widths are proportional to the number of predictions of that group and that may be different for the different software systems.

Figure 22.4 displays low rates, as in Figure 22.3, but there are important differences. More men are predicted than there are men in the study, in particular by Face++. The FDR values are mostly higher for males than females. These two conclusions are related. If you predict more males, then you will make fewer mistakes with your predictions of females. The higher FDR rates are for skin shades V and VI, the darkest ones.

There are a number of other criteria that could be plotted and it is astonishing just how many there are, including TPR, TNR, FPR, FNR, SPC, ACC, FOR, DOR, NPV (Wikipedia (2021)). The ones shown seem quite sufficient and the error rates show clearly that the three software systems are not good enough. The analysis also shows where their weaknesses lie, with the highest error rates being for dark-skinned females.

Microsoft FDR

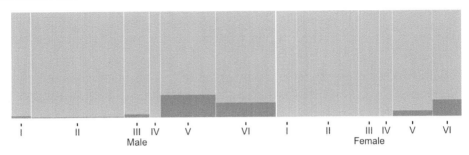

Face++ FDR

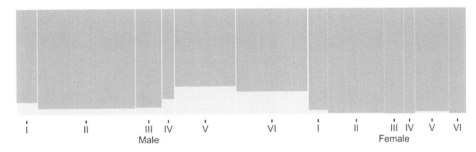

IBM FDR

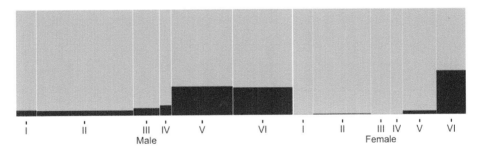

FIGURE 22.4: FDRs by sex and skin colour for three separate software systems. Males are on the left, females on the right, and skin colour gets darker from left to right within sex.

Answers All three software packages had higher error rates for females than for males and error rates rose as skin shade darkened.

Further questions If the individual data were made available, it would be informative to compare predictions across individuals and not just in summary.

Graphical takeaways

- Graphics are better than tables of percentages for displaying overall results. (Figures 22.3 and 22.2)
- Doubledecker plots underline why error rates can better be compared across softwares than Positive Predictive Values. (Figures 22.3 and 22.4)

23

Distinguishing shearwaters

There are approximately ten thousand species of birds on the planet and no single individual has seen them all.

— Bernd Brunner

Background Comparison of three species of shearwater.

Questions How could the species be distinguished? If there was no species information, what clusters might be found?

Sources *seabirds* dataset in the **CoModes** package (Marbac, Biernacki, and Vandewalle (2016))

Structure A list of two parts, a dataset of 153 birds with 5 variables and a separate classification variable.

23.1 Distinguishing shearwaters and puffins

There are five pieces of morphological information on three species of seabird, Audubon's shearwater (*Puffinus lherminieri*), Galápagos shearwater (*Puffinus subalaris*), and Tropical shearwater (*Puffinus dichrous*). In the **CoModes** package from which the dataset has been taken, the birds are described as puffins. Part of the dataset has been used in some publications to illustrate clustering methods for the first two species, e.g., Lebret et al. (2015) and Bouveyron et al. (2019). These data are available with varying variable coding labels in another three R packages, in all of which the birds are also called puffins. The Latin name of the genus is *Puffinus*, which possibly led to this error. Beautiful images of both puffins and shearwaters, illustrating how very different they are, can be found on the web (Ornithology (2022)).

23.2   Comparing two shearwater species (Audubon and Galápagos)

Figure 23.1 is an overview comparing two species on each of five variables. Numeric codes have been replaced with text labels and variable categories ordered for better interpretation. Vertical scales are the same, aiding comparison across graphics as well as within.

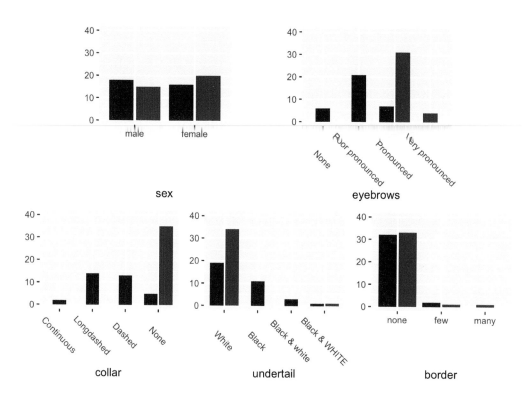

FIGURE 23.1: Barcharts of five variables comparing two species, with Audubon's shearwater in brown and Galápagos shearwater in dark blue

The data are fairly balanced on sex. eyebrows are a distinguishing feature, with Galápagos shearwater having pronounced or very pronounced eyebrows. collar is also a distinguishing feature with only a few Audubon's shearwater having no collar. undertail gives mixed results, although the single Galápagos shearwater with a Black & WHITE undertail looks suspicious. border is similar for the two species with most birds having no border.

A way of looking at several variables together is a parallel coordinate plot, as in Figure 23.2. The variable border has been left out as it does not distinguish the species. The variable undertail has been reversed to reduce line crossings between the species. The separation of Audubon and Galápagos by collar and `eyebrows` is clear. The single unusual Galápagos case is emphasised, partly because it turns out to be one of the few birds with very pronounced eyebrows.

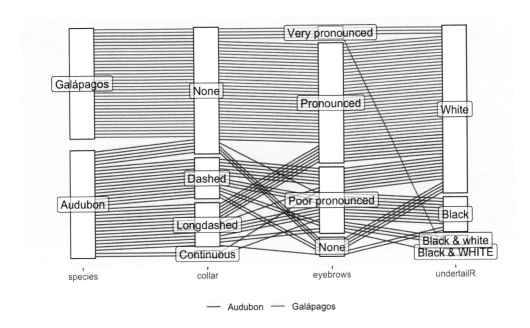

FIGURE 23.2: Parallel coordinate plot for Audubon and Galápagos shearwaters with three descriptive variables

Comparing the species using `collar` and `eyebrows` is shown in Figure 23.3. Using both variables together distinguishes the two species except for one bird, an Audubon's shearwater with no collar and pronounced eyebrows.

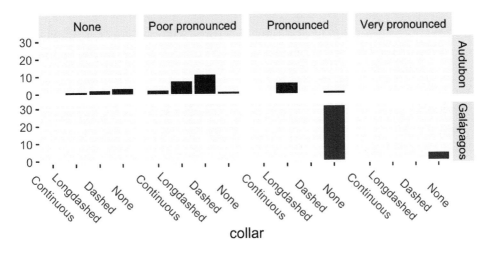

FIGURE 23.3: A comparison plot of Audubon and Galápagos shearwaters, using barcharts of `collar` faceted by `eyebrows`

23.3   Can the species be clustered?

If a clustering analysis of the data for the two species were carried out, the species information would not be used. Figure 23.4 displays all combinations of the four descriptive variables (i.e., excluding sex) by the numbers of birds for each combination. There are barcharts of collar faceted by eyebrows in the columns and by border and undertail in the rows. Six of the twelve combinations of the latter two variables do not occur for the two species, so there are only six rows.

Any clustering of these four variables would have to assign all 31 cases in the largest bar to the same cluster. These cases have pronounced eyebrows, no collar, white undertail, and no border. The case with pronounced eyebrows and a border value of many and the four cases with very pronounced eyebrows should probably be in that cluster too. Putting the remaining cases all in a second cluster gives the following comparison table for the two species.

species	clus1	clus2
Audubon	1	33
Galápagos	35	0

The single misclassified bird is then an Audubon's shearwater with pronounced eyebrows, no collar, white undertail, and no border, also remarked on in Figure 23.3. Most clustering methods should be able to separate the two species almost completely.

A parallel coordinate plot of the four variables without species information is not as effective for identifying possible clusters and is not shown here.

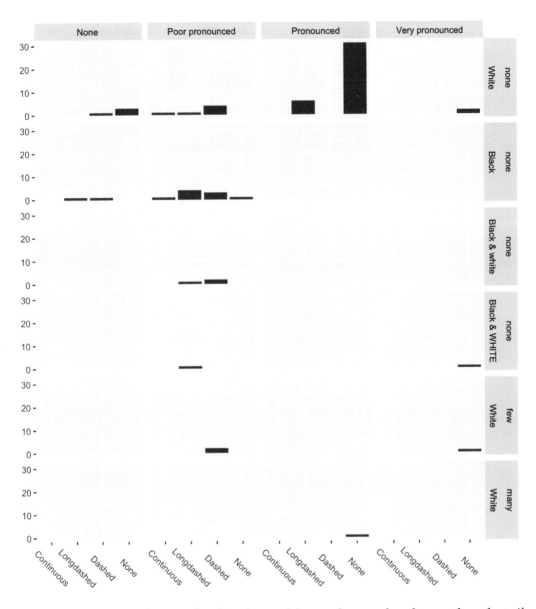

FIGURE 23.4: Barcharts of collar faceted by eyebrows, border, and undertail for the Audubon and Galápagos shearwaters

The full version of the dataset includes an additional species, 84 Tropical shearwaters. There is an extra collar category for two of the Tropical shearwaters, but with no description given. Figure 23.5 shows the data in the style of Figure 23.4, but with the bars coloured by species.

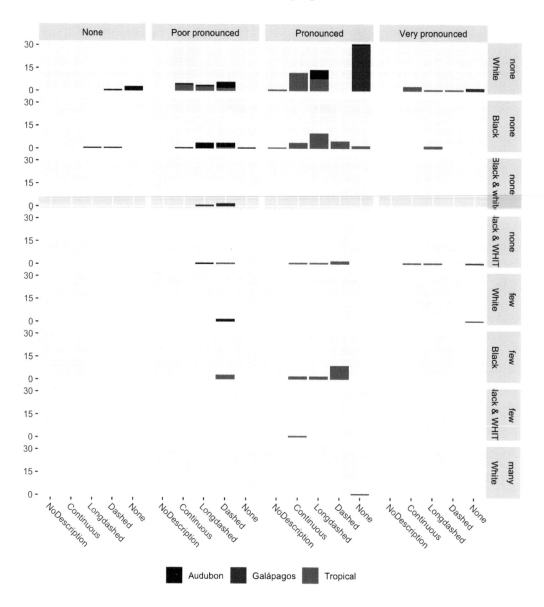

FIGURE 23.5: Barcharts of collar faceted by eyebrows, border, and undertail, coloured by species for the full dataset of three species

The Galápagos species is still partially separated from the others, but the Audubon and Tropical species overlap. A cluster analysis is unlikely to be able to group the three species.

Answers It is possible to almost completely distinguish Audubon and Galá-pagos shearwaters using two morphological variables. A faceted graphic of barcharts suggests that it should be possible to use clustering to produce groups closely matching the species. A corresponding graphic for the three species, including Tropical shearwaters, suggests distinguishing or clustering them would be more difficult.

Further questions How well can Galápagos shearwaters be distinguished from Tropical shearwaters?

Graphical takeaways

- Barcharts for the same dataset should have the same frequency scale for ease of comparison. (Figure 23.1)
- Ordering of categories in categorical variables and arrangement of faceting variables strongly influence how easy it is to read a plot. (Figures 23.3 and 23.4)
- Faceted barcharts show where cases are in multivariate categorical data. (Figures 23.4 and 23.5)

24

When do road accidents with deer happen in Bavaria?

But like other Bruegels, the painting is in part about details that hide in plain sight. If you didn't know the title, you might not notice Icarus at all.

— E. H. Gombrich writing about 'Landscape with the Fall of Icarus' (a painting formerly attributed to Bruegel)

Background In some parts of Europe vehicle accidents with deer are a serious problem.

Questions How many accidents with deer are there? Is it roughly the same across the year? At what times of day is the risk greatest?

Sources Hothorn (2020)

Structure Two data frames, each of 172596 observations, giving the numbers of vehicle accidents every half hour in Bavaria, one for accidents involving deer and one for other accidents.

24.1 Vehicle accidents involving deer

Bavarian data of the numbers of vehicle accidents involving deer over the full ten years from 2002 to 2011 have been modelled in depth in Hothorn et al. (2015). The data were also used in Hothorn (2020) and are available in the supplementary material on the publishing journal's website.

Figure 24.1 shows a smoothed version of the daily number of vehicle accidents involving deer. There was an increase of around 50% over the ten years.

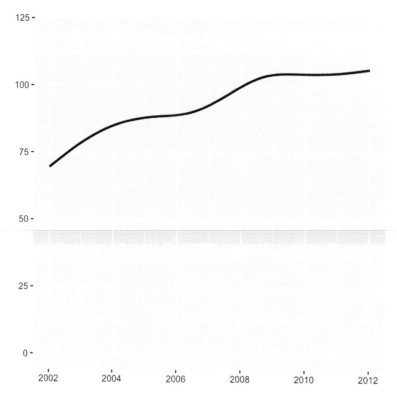

FIGURE 24.1: Smoothed numbers of deer-vehicle accidents per day in Bavaria over ten years from Jan 1st 2002 to Dec 31st 2011

In Figure 24.1, and in all the plots in this chapter, the time axis labels are placed at the start of the labelled period.

Figure 24.2 shows an initial plot to explore monthly seasonality. Each panel of the plot displays the aggregate data from that month for each year and the average for the month over the whole time series in blue. Here the data are per month, which is the why the vertical scale is so different to that in Figure 24.1.

There is an overall rise in each monthly series with some, occasionally dramatic, variation, and a possible seasonal pattern. Summarising over months is a bit of an approximation, as the months are not all the same length. An alternative is to fit another smooth across the data, rougher than the one in Figure 24.1, and overlay the resulting individual annual series. This has been done in Figure 24.3. An adaptive smooth has been used.

The plot shows a fairly regular pattern across the years with peaks in May-June and October-November and lower values in Spring and, to a lesser extent, Summer. The highest numbers are about double the lowest ones.

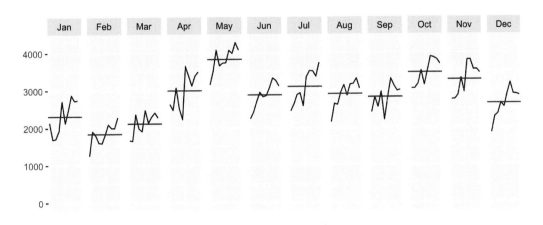

FIGURE 24.2: Monthly numbers of deer-vehicle accidents across the ten years 2002 to 2011.

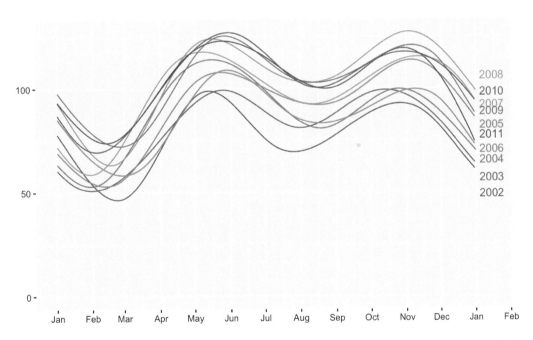

FIGURE 24.3: Numbers of deer-vehicle accidents across all ten years overlaid from Jan 1st to Dec 31st

Given the differences in vehicle traffic between weekdays and weekends and public holidays, there could well be weekly patterns as well. An initial analysis, without treating public holidays as similar to weekends is shown in Figure 24.4.

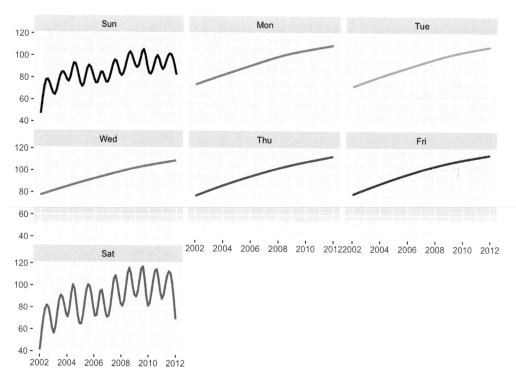

FIGURE 24.4: Day of the week patterns in numbers of deer-vehicle accidents

A few values of the smoothing parameter were tried and the rounded value leading to this display was chosen, as it suggested a clear differentiation between weekdays and weekends. The peaks in summer and the troughs in winter stand out. Presumably there is less vehicle traffic at weekends in winter and hence fewer accidents with deer then than in summer. The lack of seasonality in the weekday plots offers supporting evidence.

In the early days of time series analysis there were suggestions that time series could be decomposed into components of trend, seasonality, and noise. Sometimes this works well, sometimes it is difficult to disentangle trend and seasonality. That is to some extent the case here.

The data available are more detailed than these graphics imply. Numbers of accidents are reported for every half-hour of every day, i.e. there are 48 numbers per day. Figures 24.5 and 24.6 investigate the monthly averages of these daily data across months by year and across years by month. Unsurprisingly there are differences in the patterns by years, as the data are shifted for the individual months. This is easier to see in Figure 24.6, where the two peaks are further apart for the summer months and closer together for the winter months. According to Hothorn et al. (2015) the deer are on the move more around sunrise and after sunset, which explains these peaks and their pattern across the year. In that paper, heat maps were used to display the daily data.

Figures 24.5 and 24.6 are a good example of where the choice of which time variable to facet by is important. Both plots convey the information, but the second one does it better.

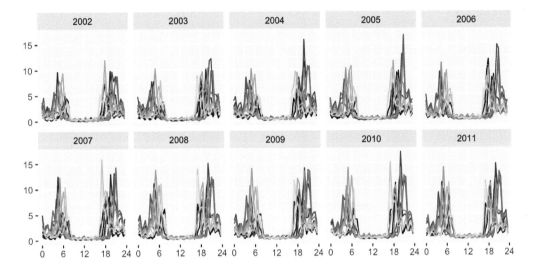

FIGURE 24.5: Average daily patterns in numbers of deer-vehicle accidents by month (the coloured lines) and year

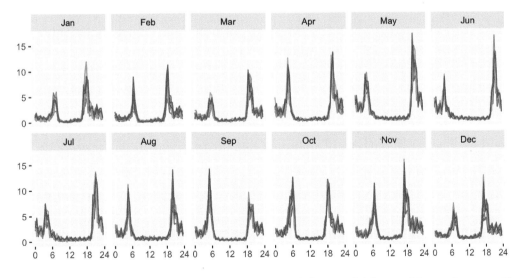

FIGURE 24.6: Daily patterns in numbers of deer-vehicle accidents by month across the years (the coloured lines)

24.2   What about vehicle accidents without deer?

Data are available over the same period for vehicle accidents not involving deer and these are useful for comparison purposes, in particular for studying what features of the deer-vehicle accident data are not found in the data for other accidents.

Figure 24.7 shows a smoothed version of the daily number of vehicle accidents not involving deer, together with the comparable graph for deer-vehicle accidents.

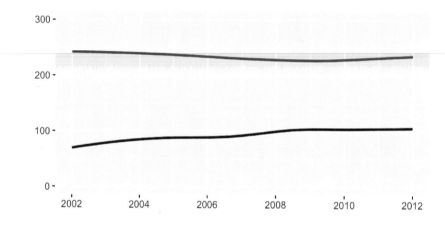

FIGURE 24.7: Smoothed number of non-deer-vehicle accidents (blue) and deer-vehicle accidents (brown) per day in Bavaria over ten years

There is little change over the ten years in non-deer vehicle accidents, with a decline of around 5%. The overall level is over twice the level of accidents involving deer. Graphics similar to Figures 24.2 and 24.3 can be drawn to show that there is a little seasonality in the data, but not nearly so much as in the deer-vehicle accident data. A graphic like Figure 24.4 would show that there is not much variation through the week either, apart from fewer accidents on a Sunday. The daily pattern of non-deer accidents is shown in Figure 24.8.

Instead of morning and evening peaks, there are higher levels through the day and lower levels in the middle of the night. Interestingly, the vertical scale is the same as that of Figure 24.6. In fact the half-hours with the highest average rates for deer accidents have slightly higher values than the half-hours with the highest average rates for accidents not involving deer, despite there being over twice as many non-deer accidents overall.

The daily plots have a sawtooth pattern that can also be seen in Figure 24.9 showing just the data for Tuesdays each year.

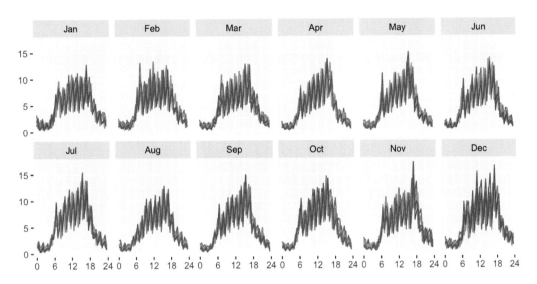

FIGURE 24.8: Daily patterns in numbers of non-deer-vehicle accidents by month across the years

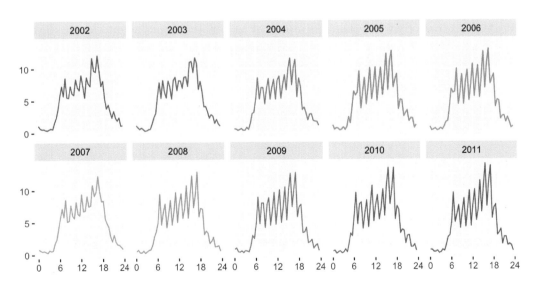

FIGURE 24.9: Daily patterns for Tuesdays in numbers of non-deer-vehicle accidents across the years

Overlaying the Tuesday data for the three years 2008, 2009, 2010 gives Figure 24.10.

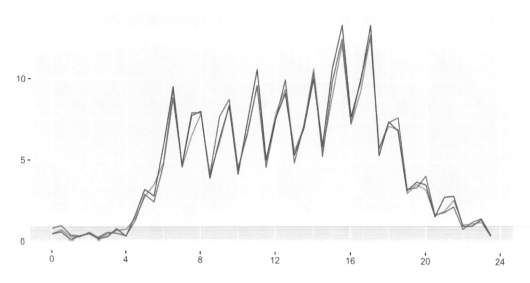

FIGURE 24.10: Daily patterns for Tuesdays in numbers of non-deer-vehicle accidents for the years 2008, 2009, 2010

The agreement across the three years is surprisingly close. Possibly it has something to do with how the data were collected and stored.

Answers The numbers of vehicle-deer accidents in Bavaria increased over the ten years covered, while the numbers of other accidents went down slightly. There are clear seasonal, weekly, and daily patterns in vehicle-deer accidents. Drivers should be particularly careful in the months of May, June, November around sunrise and sunset.

Further questions Can reasons for the daily patterns in non-deer vehicle accidents be found?

Graphical takeaways

- Axis labels for time series can be placed in different positions for the same data. Whatever is done should be stated. (Figure 24.1)
- Smoothing picks out trends in time series. (Figure 24.3)
- The choice of faceting variable is important. (Figures 24.5 and 24.6))
- Overlaying time series is effective for checking how similar they are. (Figure 24.10)

25

The Titanic Disaster

I cannot imagine any condition which would cause a ship to founder. I cannot conceive of any vital disaster happening to this vessel. Modern shipbuilding has gone beyond that.

Captain Smith of the *Titanic*, speaking of the *Adriatic* in 1907

Background The RMS Titanic sank in the North Atlantic on its maiden voyage in April 1912 with great loss of life, mainly because there were not enough lifeboats.

Questions Who travelled on the Titanic? Did women and children have better chances of surviving? What about the crew? Why did so many die?

Sources Encyclopedia Titanica ("Encyclopedia Titanica" (2021))

Structure 2208 cases with 16 variables

25.1 Who travelled on the Titanic?

The tragic event of the sinking of the Titanic has been remembered in innumerable books, films, and articles, and there has always been interest in who survived and who did not.

There are many datasets in circulation offering summary information on the Titanic, around fifteen or so in R and its packages. Some have more data, some less, some use different variable names—it can be confusing. Continuing effort by Titanic researchers has unearthed more detail and there are now lists of those on board available at Encyclopedia Titanica ("Encyclopedia Titanica" (2021)) giving full names and ages, as well as sex and passenger class or crew department. Information on fares is also given, but is incomplete. The dataset used here only includes passengers and crew who sailed for America.

Before looking at survival rates, it is interesting to look at who actually travelled. The ship started in Belfast, in the North of Ireland, where it had been built, sailed to Southampton, crossed the Channel to Cherbourg in France, stopped off at Queenstown (now Cobh), Cork's harbour in the South of Ireland, and then set off across the Atlantic.

FIGURE 25.1: Belfast to Southampton to Cherbourg to Queenstown Map:© OpenStreetMap contributors

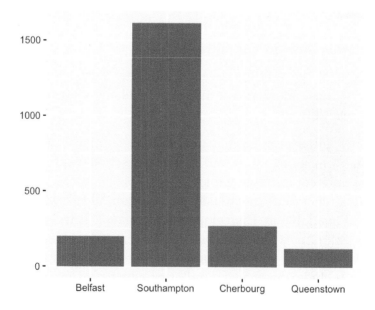

FIGURE 25.2: Numbers boarding the Titanic by port

The majority of passengers and crew joined the ship in Southampton and probably the people starting in Belfast were crew. Figure 25.3 shows where males and females boarded. No females joined the Titanic in Belfast and the numbers of males and females who joined in Cherbourg and Queenstown look about equal.

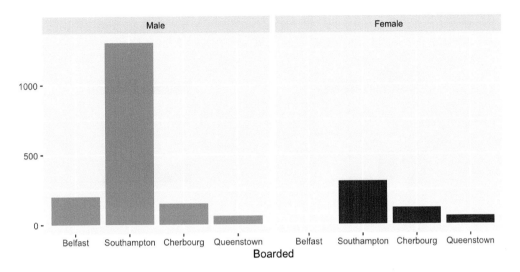

FIGURE 25.3: Numbers boarding the Titanic at each port by sex

Figure 25.4 shows the boarding patterns for passengers and crew by sex. The bulk of the crew joined in Southampton as did many more male passengers than female passengers, unlike at Cherbourg and Queenstown. There were even a very few passengers who boarded in Belfast, but, with one exception, these were employees of Harland & Wolff, the ship's builders.

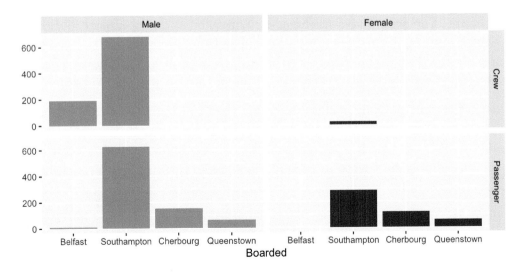

FIGURE 25.4: Numbers boarding the Titanic by sex and by passenger or crew

Figure 25.5 looks at differences in boarding patterns for passengers by sex and class. Almost all those who boarded in Ireland travelled third class. Of the first class passengers who boarded in France there were more females than males.

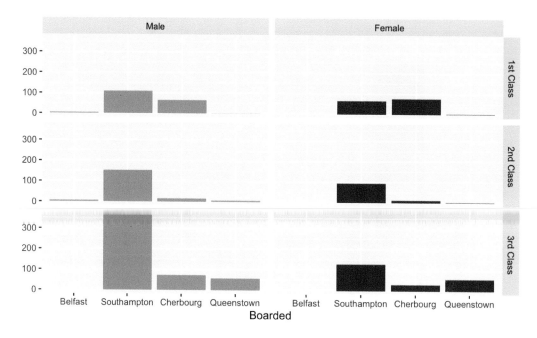

FIGURE 25.5: Numbers of passengers boarding the Titanic by sex and class

There is information on passenger nationality and this is shown by port of boarding in Figure 25.6. Any nationality with 25 or fewer passengers has been grouped together "Other". Most of the Irish (and almost only Irish) boarded in Queenstown. Americans boarded in Southampton and, to a lesser extent, in Cherbourg. The Scandinavians (Swedes, Norwegians, Finns) almost all boarded in Southampton. Most of the Syrian Lebanese group boarded in Cherbourg. The relatively few French boarded in either Southampton or Cherbourg. Possibly French people preferred to travel on a French liner across the Atlantic.

Nationality and passenger class are related. Figure 25.7 shows the patterns. North Americans from the US and Canada travelled mainly first class and made up the majority of passengers in first class. A few English travelled first class, but almost half were in second class. Apart from a few French people, the rest of first and second class were almost all from "Other" nationalities.

Some of the passengers are reported as being from two countries, some countries have changed borders over the last 110 years, some of the data may be inaccurate. Nevertheless the main conclusions remain.

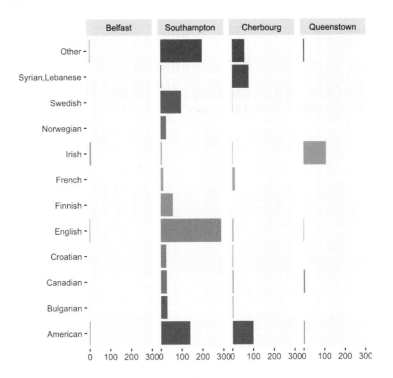

FIGURE 25.6: Nationality of passengers on the Titanic by port of boarding

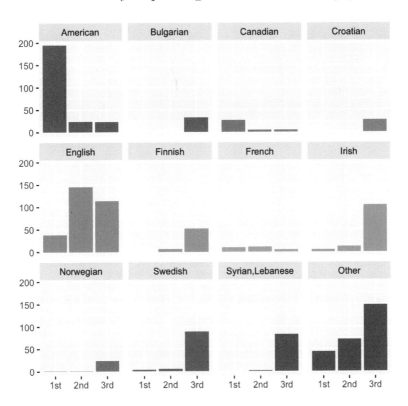

FIGURE 25.7: Nationality and class of passengers on the Titanic

25.2   Which groups had high survival rates?

Investigations of the earlier, less detailed datasets in R showed that survival
rates were higher for women than men, that first class passengers had higher
survival rates than second class, and that second class rates were higher than
third class rates. The survival rate for the crew was almost as high as the rate
for third class and this was assumed to be partly because crew members were
assigned to man the lifeboats. This can be confirmed by the more detailed
information now available. Figure 25.8 is a doubledecker plot of the survival
rates for the different groups on board. The width of each bar is proportional
to the number in that group.

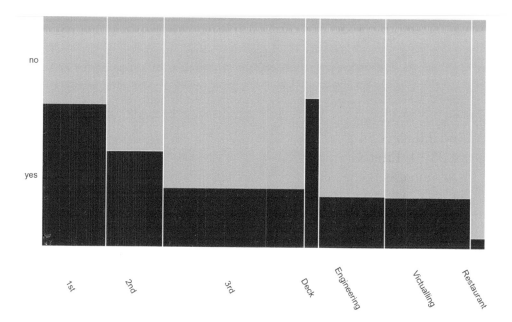

FIGURE 25.8: Titanic survival rates by passenger class and crew department

Deck crew members had a higher survival rate than even first class passengers.
They would have been the crew assigned to the lifeboats. Survival rates for
other crew members were lower than for third class passengers and those
working in the restaurant had a particularly low rate of survival.

Sex was an important factor as Figure 25.9 shows. All female passenger groups
had higher survival rates than all male groups. Second class males had the
worst survival rate of all passengers.

Additional information on the ages of those on board permits study of the

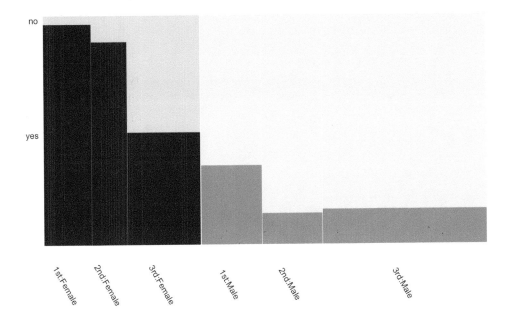

FIGURE 25.9: Survival rates by sex and class for the passengers

possible influence of age. Age distributions by class and crew are shown in Figure 25.10. First Class passengers tended to be older and there were few children amongst them. Most children travelled as Third Class passengers and the Third Class passengers were generally younger. There were a couple of fourteen year-old crew members, but most were aged between 20 and 50. A dotted line has been drawn at 14. This splits the ages into "young" and "old", close to the numbers in the older, less detailed dataset. Age information is not available for 4 adult passengers, three of whom did not survive.

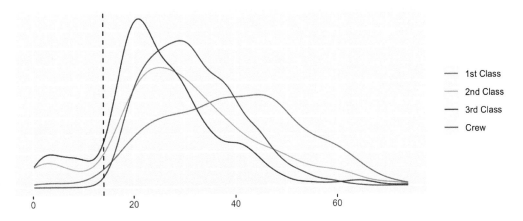

FIGURE 25.10: Density estimates of age by class on the Titanic

The survival rates by age are shown in Figure 25.11. The area of a point is proportional to the number of that age.

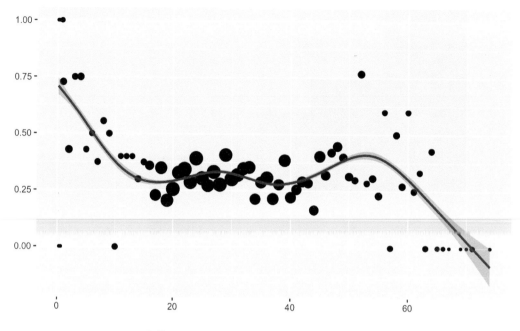

FIGURE 25.11: Survival rates by age

Survival rates vary little with age, although the few children have higher survival rates and the small number of the very oldest did not survive. Including the effects of sex and class or crew offers an in-depth view, Figure 25.12.

In all groups the females have higher survival rates across (almost) all ages. The smooths at lower ages are based on very little data. Differences are particularly large in the second class where few men survived. Overall, apart from the survival rates of children, there is little difference in the survival rates by age.

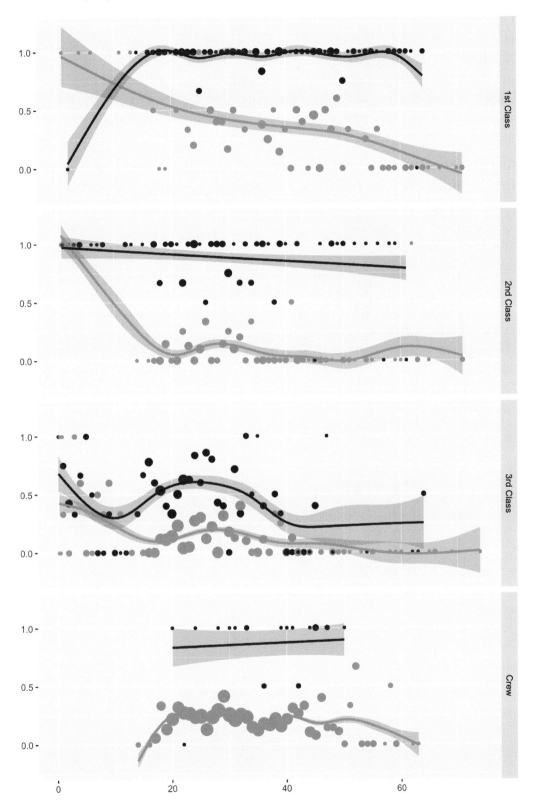

FIGURE 25.12: Survival rates by age, sex, and class or crew

Answers The majority of first class passengers were North Americans, probably returning home after a European trip. There were groups from smaller countries, travelling mainly in third class, who were presumably emigrating. Survival turned out to depend primarily on passenger class and sex, with almost all females travelling 1st class surviving. Amongst the crew, the deck crew who manned the lifeboats had the highest rate of survival by far. The fact that there were nowhere near enough lifeboats was crucial.

Further questions How full were the lifeboats? How many more could have survived if they had been full? Are there related datasets for other maritime disasters that this one might be compared with?

Graphical takeaways

- Drawing barcharts horizontally is essential when there are many categories, and for making sure labels are readable. (Figure 25.6)
- Doubledecker plots are excellent for comparing rates of groups of different sizes. (Figures 25.8 and 25.9)
- Density estimates work well for comparing distributions by group. (Figure 25.10)
- Smooths are valuable for summarising irregular scatterplot patterns. (Figures 25.11 and 25.12)

26

German Election 2021—what happened?

Just because you do not take an interest in politics doesn't mean politics won't take an interest in you. — Pericles

Background Angela Merkel was Chancellor of Germany from 2005 to 2021. The election in Autumn 2021 could be said to be the first of a new era in German politics.

Questions Which parties did well in the 2021 election? Are there geographical patterns in party support? What structural factors are linked to party support? Are Erststimmen (votes for candidates) and Zweitstimmen (votes for parties) closely related?

Sources The Bundeswahlleiter (Federal Returning Officer) has a website (Bundesamt (2021)) offering detailed election results in various forms, a dataset of demographic and structural data for each constituency, and maps of the constituencies. UK election data is available in the R package **parlitools**.

Structure There were 299 constituencies in 16 Bundesländer (states), just over 61 million registered voters, almost 200 smaller parties or groups standing in one or more constituencies, and 7 larger parties each getting over 2 million votes.

26.1 Who won the 2021 election?

The two big parties in the pre-election coalition, the conservative grouping of CDU/CSU and the social democratic SPD, were being challenged by the FDP (the traditional liberal party), die Linke (a party on the left), the Greens, and the AfD (a right-wing party).

Everyone has two votes in an election for the German parliament, a vote for a candidate (Erststimme or first vote) and a vote for a party (Zweitstimme or second vote). There is one seat for each constituency that goes to the candidate with the most Erststimmen. Additionally, about the same total number of seats are allocated to parties based on each party's share of the Zweitstimmen in the respective Bundesland. Needless to say, it is more complicated than that. Extra seats (Ueberhangmandate and Ausgleichsmandate) may be needed to satisfy the election rules. In the early years of the Bundesrepublik there were only Überhangmandate, designed to allow parties to win more individual seats than were due them according to their Zweitstimmen share. The system was declared unconstitutional and changed for the 2013 election. Since then Ausgleichsmandate have been included, additional seats to ensure that the Zweitstimmen shares of the parties are respected. There have been further attempts to amend the rules, not particularly successfully. In 2021 there were 138 extra seats, increasing the intended size of the parliament from 598 to 736. In 2017 there had been only 111 and in 2013 only 33. Figure 26.1 shows the numbers since the first postwar election in 1949, when the system was introduced. There is optimism that the government elected in 2021 will introduce a system in accordance with the constitution that will strictly limit the total number of seats in the Bundestag.

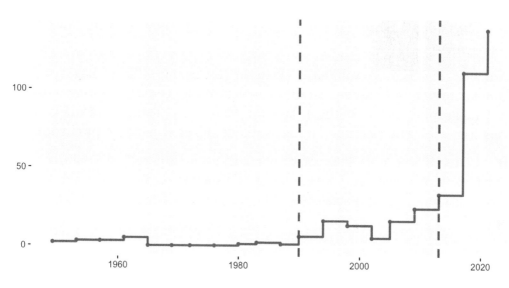

FIGURE 26.1: Extra seats in German elections since 1949. Each point marks the date of an election. The left dashed line marks the first election after reunification in October 1990. The right dashed line marks the first election with Ausgleichsmandate.

The support for the main parties in the elections of 2021 and 2017 is shown in Figure 26.2. Colours associated with the parties have been used. The CDU/CSU lost heavily, while the SPD and Greens gained. Changes in party performance are easier to see in a plot of the gains and losses in percentage points. It is now apparent that the Greens gained more than the SPD and the Linke lost heavily. The relatively big gain for 'Other' parties is also striking.

Absolute changes can be deceptive. The Greens gained more than the SPD,

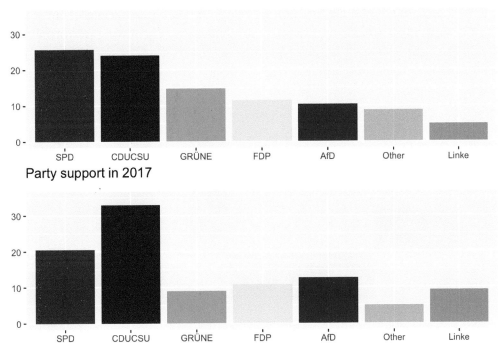

FIGURE 26.2: Party percentage support (in Zweitstimmen) for the last two elections

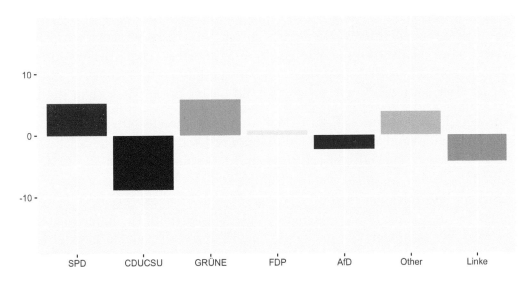

FIGURE 26.3: Changes in party percentage support between the last two elections

but from a much lower base. An UpAndDown plot (Unwin (2024)) shows the relative changes. The base of each bar is the party support in votes in 2017. The height of each bar is the change in party support as a percentage of their votes in 2017, so the bar areas equal the absolute changes. The strong performance of the Greens (and the even stronger performance of 'Other' parties in percentage terms) is more apparent, along with the poor performance of the Linke.

FIGURE 26.4: Relative changes in support between the last two elections

A key advantage of UpAndDown plots is that area is conserved when drilling down. Figure 26.5 shows the changes by region (West, East, Berlin) for each party. The SPD and FDP improved most in the East, albeit from low levels at the last election in 2017. 'Other' parties did better in the West than the East.

More detail can be seen in Figure 26.6 where the changes are shown for each party by Bundesland with the Bundesländer ordered by size. The SPD gained everywhere, but especially in the smaller Bundesländer. The CDU/CSU lost everywhere, but more in the smaller Bundesländer. The Greens did very well in Nordrhein-Westfalen and well everywhere else, with one exception. In Saarland, thanks to internal party disagreements, they did not fulfill the requirements for receiving Zweitstimmen and got none. The FDP mostly gained, but did badly where the Greens did best in Nordrhein-Westfalen. The AfD lost to different degrees everywhere except in Thüringen. 'Other' parties as a group had some big percentage gains (which is why the scale is different to that in Figure 26.4 and still does not include all values). The Linke lost roughly equally in all Bundesländer.

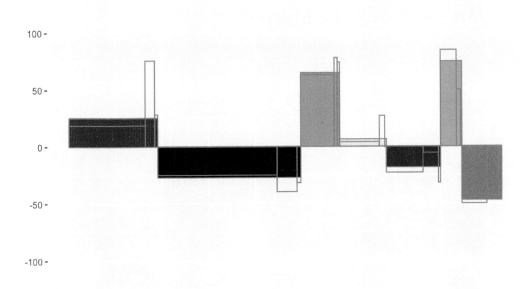

FIGURE 26.5: Relative changes in support by party and region.

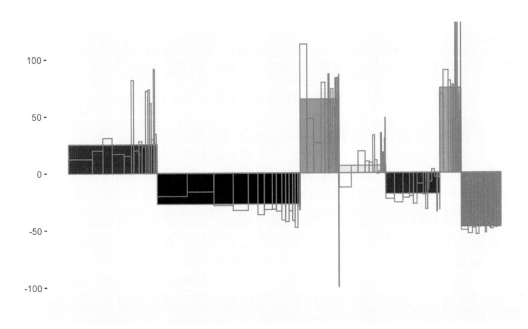

FIGURE 26.6: Relative changes in support by party and Bundesland.

26.2   Are there geographic patterns?

There are strong geographic patterns in party support across the constituencies.
Figure 26.7 shows support for the Greens in choropleth maps.

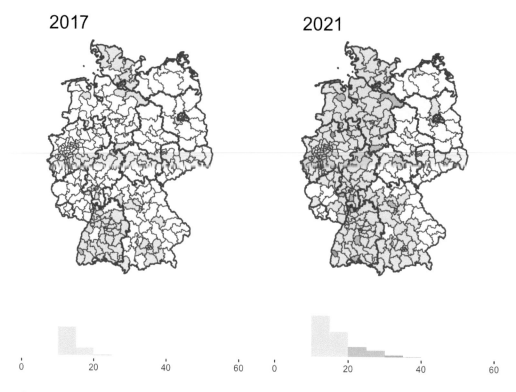

FIGURE 26.7: Percentage Green support across the constituencies in 2017
(left) and 2021 (right). Bundesland borders are drawn in thick black. The
colour scale goes from 0 to 60 in intervals of 10 (histograms below).

The Greens did much better in 2021, predominantly in the West of Germany.
They also did better in more densely populated areas, as Figure 26.8 shows
using the logarithm of population density as a measure.

Aside from the four constituencies of Saarland where the Greens got no party
votes, as already mentioned, there is a roughly linear relationship in the plot.
The Greens did worst in the rural East and best in big cities including parts of
Berlin. There is a little overplotting in Figure 26.8, so the points representing
West were drawn first and the smaller East and Berlin groups on top.

Associations with other variables can be explored using a parallel coordinate
plot (Figure 26.9). The Greens did well where there were more younger people
and where there were more qualified to go to university.

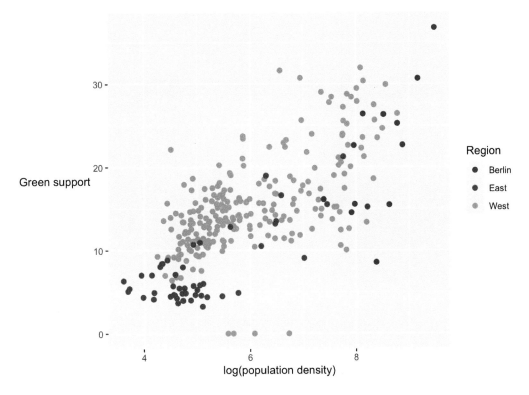

FIGURE 26.8: Green support plotted against log of population density

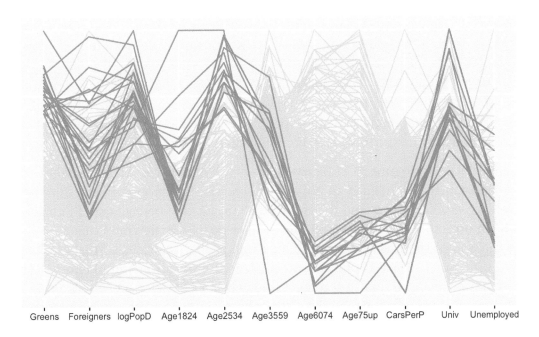

FIGURE 26.9: A parallel coordinate plot of Green support and some structural variables (constituencies with over 25% Green party votes are coloured green)

The AfD lost ground between the two elections and were weaker in the West.

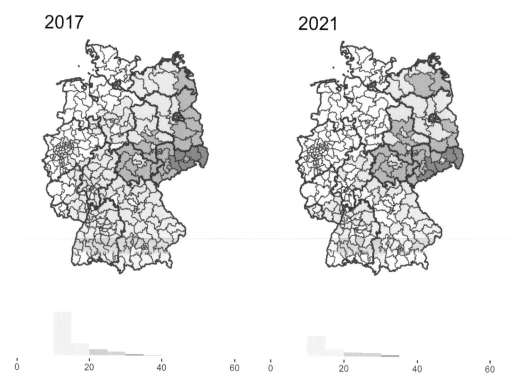

FIGURE 26.10: Percentage AfD support across the constituencies in 2017 (left) and 2021 (right). Bundesland borders are drawn in thick black. The colour scale goes from 0 to 60 in intervals of 10, as shown in the histograms below.

Figure 26.12 is a parallel coordinate plot of AfD support and the same structural variables as in Figure 26.9. The AfD were strong where there were more older people and low levels of foreigners (people without German nationality). They did not do well in cities, where the population density is higher.

The scatterplot, Figure 26.11, shows more detail of how the AfD vote related to the percentage of foreigners in the constituencies. AfD support is highest where there are few foreigners and relatively constant for any percentage of foreigners a little over 10%. They are generally weaker in the Berlin constituencies than in the rest of the Eastern part of Germany, probably because West Berlin is still different to East Berlin, even over thirty years after reunification. The association may be due to foreigners not voting for the AfD or more due to the party being stronger in the East where there are lower percentages of foreigners.

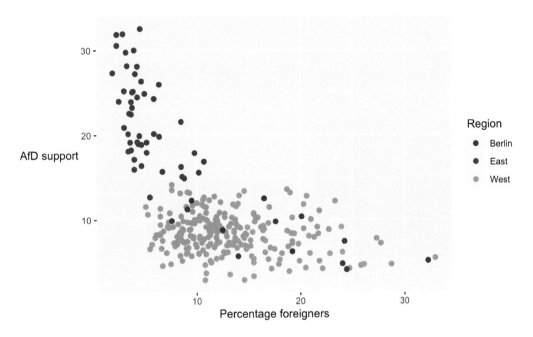

FIGURE 26.11: AfD support plotted against percentage of foreigners

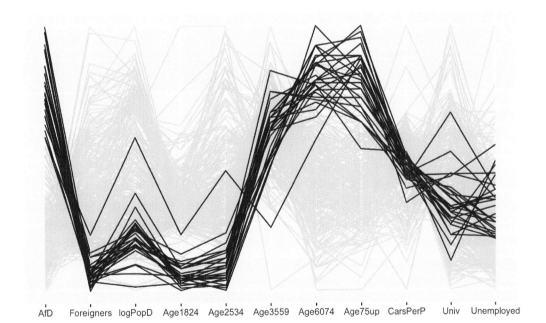

FIGURE 26.12: A parallel coordinate plot of AfD support and some structural variables (constituencies with over 20% AfD party votes are coloured blue)

The CDU/CSU have traditionally always been strong in Bavaria, the CSU's part of Germany.

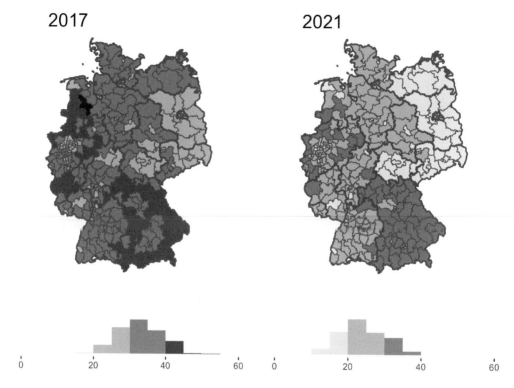

FIGURE 26.13: Percentage CDU and CSU support across the constituencies in 2017 (left) and 2021 (right). The colour scale goes from 0 to 60 in intervals of 10. Bundesland borders are drawn in thick black.

It is always possible with a large number of factors to find correlations that may or may not imply some causation. For the CDU/CSU one is car ownership, as Figure 26.14 illustrates.

As car density increases, so does support for the CDU and CSU. Car density tends to be lower in the East. The points to the far left are the 12 Berlin constituencies. For major cities car registration statistics are only available for the whole city and so all constituencies have the same (in this case, low) value. Cars are not so useful in large cities. The most outlying value to the right is Wolfsburg, Volkswagen's main base, and the other one is Main-Taunus, between Opel's base at Rüsselsheim and Frankfurt.

Drawing a parallel coordinate plot, as for the other two parties, shows that the CDU/CSU additionally did well in areas of lower population density where there were more middle-aged people and fewer unemployed.

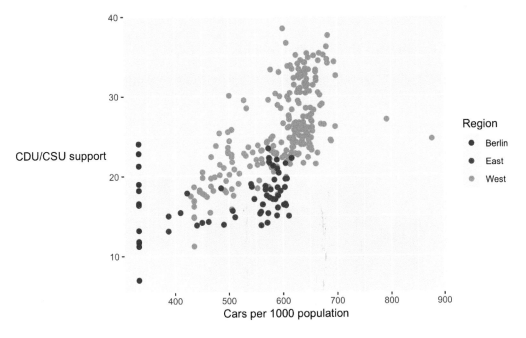

FIGURE 26.14: CDU and CSU support plotted against numbers of cars per thousand population.

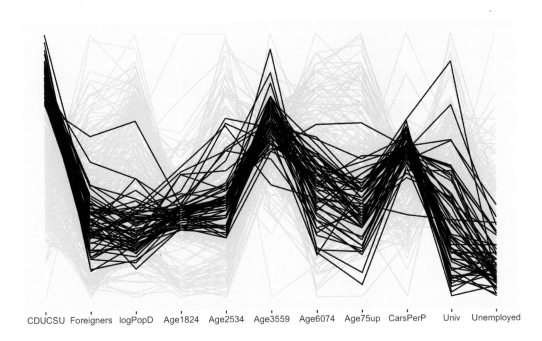

FIGURE 26.15: A parallel coordinate plot of CDU/CSU support and some structural variables (constituencies with over 30% party votes are coloured black)

26.3   Who won the first-past-the-post seats?

In each constituency there is a first-past-the-post system for the result of Erststimmen. In theory you might expect a few non-party winners, in practice there were none. Figure 26.16 shows a map coloured by the winning party.

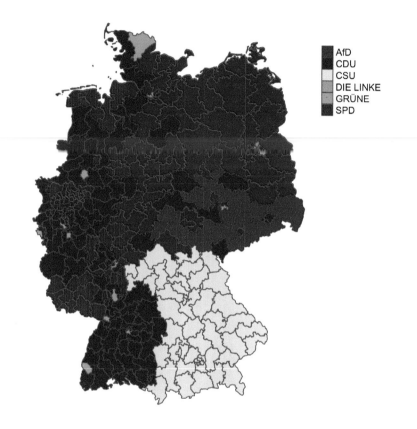

FIGURE 26.16: Winners of Erststimmen seats by political party

There are strong geographic patterns. The CSU in light blue won (almost) all the seats in Bavaria. The CDU did well in the West. The AfD did well in the South of the old East Germany. The SPD won seats in the North of the old East Germany and in former industrial heartlands like the Ruhrgebiet. The Greens won a sprinkling of seats across the country in mainly urban areas. On this map it is hard to see that they won the one seat in Munich that the CSU failed to win in Bavaria (but see the next maps). The Linke won two seats in Berlin and one in Leipzig (again, see the next maps), essential for them to be represented in the Bundestag. Otherwise their failing to achieve 5% of Zweitstimmen would have excluded them. The FDP won no seats with Erststimmen.

The following set of maps shows where each party won Erststimmen seats. Bundesländer borders have been included for orientation.

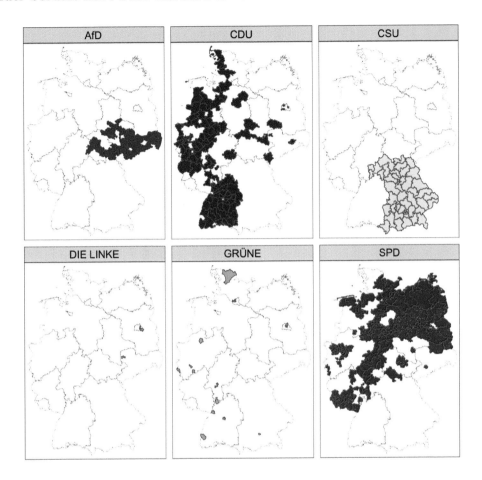

FIGURE 26.17: Where political parties won Erststimmen seats

The seats won by the Greens in cities and by Die Linke in Berlin and Leipzig are now just about visible.

With a first-past-the-post system it is possible to win a seat with a low percentage of the votes. Figure 26.18 displays dotplots of the winning percentages by party in the 2021 German election and in the 2019 UK election. For the UK the three dotplots to the right are for the 18 seats won by parties based in Northern Ireland, the 4 seats won by Plaid Cymru in Wales, and the 48 seats won by the SNP in Scotland. None of these parties put up candidates in other parts of the UK.

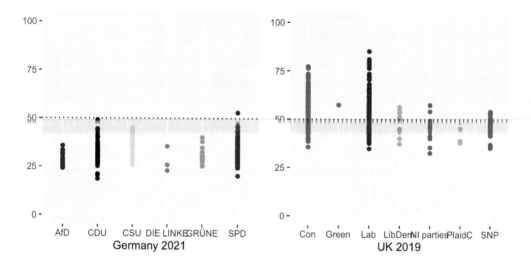

FIGURE 26.18: Seat-winning percentages by party in Germany 2021 and in the UK 2019

It is surprising to see that in Germany only one seat was won with more than 50% of votes cast (Aurich - Emden) and that one was actually won with less than 20% (Dresden II - Bautzen II). This is a consequence of having several competing parties. The UK uses a first-past-the-post election for every MP. In 2019, the most recent election, 425 of the 649 MPs elected won more than 50% of the votes cast in their constituency. The lowest percentage winner got 32.6% in South Down, Northern Ireland.

26.4 How do first-past-the-post and party votes compare?

Comparing the two votes for the six parties who got the most Zweitstimmen means dropping Die Linke and including the FDP.

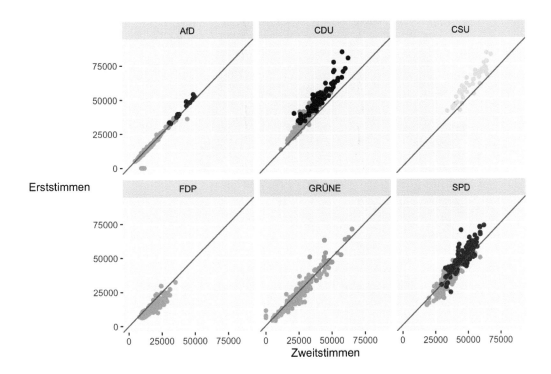

FIGURE 26.19: Erststimmen and Zweitstimmen by major parties (brown lines mark equality and seats that were won on Erststimmen are coloured by the party's colour)

There was more agreement than might have been expected. AfD voters stuck closely to their party, with the exception of six seats where they had no individual candidate and one seat in Thüringen, where the CDU ran a well-known right-wing candidate (although the SPD candidate still won). The CDU and CSU candidates generally got more votes than the party, possibly from the FDP and smaller parties who had no chances of winning individual seats. The Greens did not qualify for Zweitstimmen in Saarland, as previously discussed. Otherwise there were some seats where individual candidates did particularly well relative to their party. This happened with SPD and CDU candidates too.

Figure 26.16 was plotted using Erststimmen to show which parties won the individual seats. Replotting with Zweitstimmen and colouring by which party had the most votes in each constituency gives Figure 26.20.

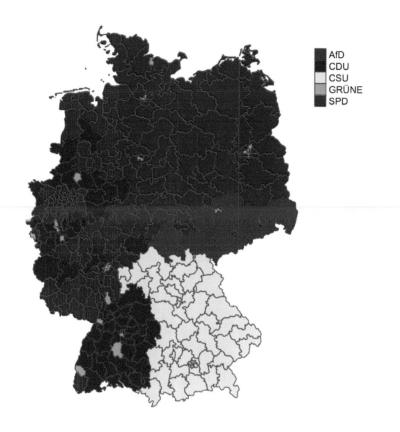

FIGURE 26.20: Which party got the most Zweitstimmen in each constituency

Figure 26.20 presents a more coherent pattern than Figure 26.16. As has been pointed out on Francois Valentin's Twitter feed (Valentin (2022)), the map's form is reminiscent of how voting in Germany looked over a hundred years ago. The SPD won most votes in the area that was Prussia, the AfD won most votes in Saxony, and the CSU most in Bavaria.

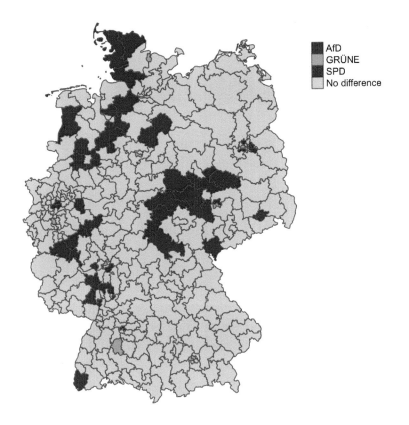

FIGURE 26.21: Consituencies where the party that got the most Zweitstimmen did not get the most Erststimmen, coloured by the party with the most Zweitstimmen

In many constituencies the party of the candidate that had the most Erststimmen also received the most Zweitstimmen. Restricting the map to the constituencies where one party had the most Erststimmen and another the most Zweitstimmen and colouring by the party with the most Zweitstimmen gives Figure 26.21. SPD candidates failed to win seats on Erststimmen relatively often, while Green and AfD candidates failed occasionally. Neither the CDU nor the CSU ever failed to win on Erststimmen when they won on Zweitstimmen.

Answers The Greens, the SPD, and "Other" parties did well in the 2021 election (compared with the 2017 election). There are strong geographical patterns of party support, for instance for the Greens and the AfD. The Greens did better in urban constituencies than in rural ones. Candidates winning individual seats with Erststimmen almost always won less than 50% of the votes in 2021.

Further questions Which structural factors were most important? Why did parties do much better in certain individual seats than in other similar ones?

Graphical takeaways

- UpAndDown plots show relative and absolute changes in the same plot. (Figure 26.4)
- Draw smaller groups last if colour is used and there is overplotting. (Figures 26.8, 26.11, and 26.14)
- Scatterplots reveal many kinds of information, e.g., points with equal values (Berlin in Figure 26.14), differences between groups (Berlin compared with the rest of the East of Germany in Figure 26.11), unusual cases within highly correlated variables (Figure 26.19).
- Highlighted parallel coordinate plots identify potential explanatory variables. (Figures 26.12, 26.9, and 26.15)

Part II

Advice on Graphics

27

Provenance and quality

Real evidence is usually vague and unsatisfactory. It has to be examined—sifted.

— Agatha Christie, 'The Mysterious Affair at Styles'

Graphics can be used to discover and display information in data. If the data are poor, then the information will be poor. If the source is unreliable, then the information will be unreliable. Data are often taken for granted in data visualisation. The elegance and technical aspects of the visualisations are discussed more than the quality and interpretation of the data. There is a telling remark of Peter Huber's: "Never underestimate the rawness of raw data." There should be a complementary aphorism along the lines of "Don't just look at the visualisation—look into the data."

27.1   What does provenance mean?

The word provenance has been used in the art world for a long time. The value of a work of art can depend on its origins and history having been fully authenticated—whether anyone likes it or not. Other subject areas have taken over the term and the provenance of datasets is talked about now too: their origin and source, the people and organisations involved, how the data were collected, their reliability and quality, and how they have been processed and used (cf. Meng (2021)). This has become more important as the ease with which data can be shared has increased. Lee Wilkinson told me that he included Anderson's iris dataset with his Systat software in the early 1980s by copying it in by hand. Forty years on, hugely larger datasets can be transferred across the web with a single click.

Provenance is about establishing a dataset's credibility and is an essential support for being able to reproduce results of others. Datasets do not emerge fully formed as they are collected. Checks are carried out, corrections made, various weightings and transformations are applied, some data and variables may be dropped and derived variables added. Huebner et al. (2020) describes a review of how Initial Data Analysis (IDA) was reported in 25 observational medical studies published by five medical journals in 2018. Their conclusion was that reporting of IDA was sparse and unsystematic. The PISA studies comparing the performance of school children in different countries are a different example. Complex weighting schemes are used to reflect the sampling methods for each country to make results comparable. Without detailed help explaining how the data were restructured it would be impossible to reproduce what has been done.

Data arise in many different ways, ranging from meticulously carried out scientific experiments to voluntary online surveys. At the latter extreme, all sorts of fanciful statistics are generated that have little or no meaning or value. At the former extreme it is still necessary to check how and under what conditions the experiments were carried out and whether results may be generalised beyond the bounds of that particular study. Testing a theory on a small group of students is at best an indication of more general validity, however conscientiously the research is carried out.

Stigler (2019) discusses the importance of investigating the source and processing of classical datasets. A classical dataset in his definition is one that "has been collected for some scientific or commercial purpose, and has been employed for instruction or exposition by several people". There are a few used in this book and the pre-checking carried out is described below. For around half the book's datasets users can download newer data and carry out fresh analyses themselves. Recent data are both more useful and more motivating than old data.

As an example of datasets collated and offered by public institutions, there is a valuable collection of demographic data by country available on the Human Mortality database (University of California and Demographic Research (2022)). Data are provided for many countries for many years, there are comments on the likely quality of the data for particular country-year combinations and corresponding advice to use with care. The Gapminder Foundation provides extensive data on many different countries over the years. For the life expectancy data used in Chapter 2 they provide accompanying information on how they estimated values for isolated calamitous years.

27.2   What problems arise with datasets?

Real datasets bring real problems. The original sources may be unknown. It may be unclear how the data were collected. The datasets may have unusual and awkward structures. They may be badly formatted. Variables may be ambiguously or just poorly defined. There may be duplicate variables and cases. There may be missing values, errors, inconsistencies, roundings, uncertainty.

Graphical displays can help identify many of these problems and sometimes, although not always, help to fix them. That is one important reason for using real datasets for all examples in this book, rather than invented or simulated datasets. Even if problems cannot be fixed, it is advantageous to be aware of them. Interpretations of results have to be qualified by how reliable and sound the underlying data are judged to be. Knowing the data and their possible weaknesses strengthens an analyst's position.

27.2.1 Data definitions

Sometimes the meaning of variables recorded is obvious, sometimes not. Sometimes the meaning seems obvious, but turns out not to be. In most countries the number of votes won by a party in an election is clear. In Germany everyone has two votes, the first for an individual, who is usually a member of a party, and the second for a party. There is a complicated system of determining how many seats each party then receives and there have been numerous attempts over the past few years to find a satisfactory solution that does not involve the total number of seats increasing after each election. Ireland has an electoral system based on proportional representation, so that you can talk about how many first preference votes a party receives, but this may not match the number of seats the party wins.

German car sales data does not include details for models with less than 5 sales in a year unless they are in the Luxury or Sportscar segments. Crime statistics cover reported crimes, but not all crimes. It is always advisable to have precise definitions for variables in a dataset.

During the Covid pandemic it was difficult to compare the rates of illness and death in different countries partly because of the difficulties in collecting the data and partly because of the different definitions used.

In any dataset collected over time, definitions change. Rules of sporting events change, conditions change, even countries change, as in the Olympics dataset.

27.2.2 Data collection

Even if definitions of variables are agreed upon and unproblematic, it may be impractical to collect the information accurately. Much height and weight information is self-reported, as are eating habits and exercising regimes.

A dataset that is designed for one purpose may not be suitable for another.

The number of tickets sold for a soccer game does not tell you how many people were there. Season ticket holders from far away may choose to only go to the top games. The number of cars registered may not be the same as the number of cars sold, as dealers may be encouraged to register more cars than they sell.

Data may have been collected at different times or by different people. Experimenters may improve their technique as they gain experience with a new method. Both these factors are relevant in considering Newcomb's data on the speed of light.

Car speedometers may or may not give accurate figures. To counteract possible complaints about the accuracy of the estimates of speed made by police cameras in Germany, a figure of 3 km/hr is subtracted from the actual estimate up to speeds of 100 km/hr and 3% is subtracted from higher speeds.

Results in clinical trials can be complicated by unexpected events (Sackett and Gent (1979)). If someone in the treatment arm of a trial for heart disease is run over by a bus, is that anything to do with the trial?

How questions are asked can influence answers to surveys (e.g., Thau et al. (2021) and several of the papers cited in it). In one of the episodes of the BBC comedy programme "Yes, Prime Minister", the civil servant, Sir Humphrey Appleby gave an example of how opinion poll questions and their order may affect results (and can be found on YouTube by searching for "yes prime minister opinion polls").

27.2.3   Data availability

Many datasets are available in R or one of its associated packages. Most have been polished or prepared before being published in R and while many were real datasets they were not as real as they might have been. Sometimes the documentation available for them is vague and incomplete.

Big datasets need preparatory work. The stages of checking, editing, and reorganising data—getting data ready for graphics and analysis—are discussed in more detail. The data wrangling code developed for these tasks is also included on the book's webpage. Several datasets are being continually publicly updated (e.g., Gapminder, movie ratings, fuel efficiency, the Comrades ultramarathon, chess ratings). Readers can download more recent versions and use the code on the book's webpage, possibly with minor amendments, to obtain new results. Estimates of how much of a project is spent in cleaning up data vary considerably, but everyone agrees it takes a lot of time and effort. Knowing which graphics to draw and how they can be drawn is not enough; the data must be prepared in an appropriate form. This involves data restructuring on top of data cleaning.

Although much work may be needed to clean datasets, it is essential to keep a copy of the dataset in its original form and keep all the coding used in cleaning. Auditors or others may have to be shown exactly what was done and analysts need to be able to remind themselves some time later of what they did. Rerunning cleaning code on the original dataset often takes little time, confirms that the original is being used, removing the need to store intermediate versions of the data. New information may arise, invalidating some of the data cleaning and requiring new approaches. Original datasets have be kept available in their original form.

Knowing why, how, and by whom datasets were collected is a key part of their value. Sources and contexts should be included in supporting information and reviewed. Standards have become better in general in this regard with Kevin Wright's R package **agridat** (Wright (2022)) and Jeremy Singer-Vine's Data is Plural collection (Singer-Vine (2020)) being positive examples. Yet there is always room for improvement.

27.3 The provenance of datasets used in the book

Datasets may be made available as part of a public service, as many governmental organisations now do. They may be provided as supplementary material to research publications, and some journals require that of authors, even if not all authors satisfy the requirements. They may be analysed as illustrations in articles or textbooks and made accessible on web pages. They may be included in software packages. Detailed background information may or may not be provided. Even with extensive details of how data were collected and how variables were defined, there may still be more to be found out. The following examples discuss datasets used in the book to illustrate the issues and to show that it can be helpful to dig deeper.

27.3.1 Gapminder (Chapter 2)

The Gapminder website (Rosling (2013)) provides substantial amounts of data on countries around the world and gives extensive information on the sources of the data and on what data cleaning has been carried out. Standards of data collection vary by country and over time and this has to be kept in mind in any comparison of countries.

27.3.2 Movies (Chapter 3)

The movies dataset was downloaded from the IMDb website (IMDb (2022)). Two of the files, one with runtimes and one with average viewer ratings, were merged. Only the categories "movie" and "short" were kept and only items which had over 100 ratings. As of the beginning of July 2022 these measures reduced the total number of items in the dataset from just over 9 million to just under 125,000. The database is continually updated with new films, more user ratings, and amended information.

IMDb report the genres classifying films using a maximum of three descriptors. The information is given in a single column with the descriptors in alphabetic order, separated by commas. There is no standard classification of films by genre, so other sources may use other classification schemes. (And you may personally disagree with some of the individual classifications too.)

Movie lengths show two uncommon features. There are a few extraordinarily long films that are not errors, but actual films, and there is heaping on rounded numbers of minutes, particularly at 90 minutes, the old standard length. Checking running times of the films on their imdb.com technical specs web pages also reveals that some films have been released in more than one version with different lengths.

Summary data on ratings of individual films by user age and sex are reported for the 70% or so of users who provide this information. How truthful those users are in their self-description is not known (and it is not known how truthful or reliable they are in their ratings either).

27.3.3 Democratic Convention 1912 (Chapter 4)

Initial analyses in Chapter 4 of the 46 ballots that took place at the 1912 Democratic Convention plotted results by ballot number. Checking the official report of the Convention more closely supplied opening and closing times for each session over the five days. These were used to produce estimates of when the ballots took place and to plot results over time. This showed that the crucial change took place in the first ballot after the last break, implying that the informal discussions that undoubtedly took place when the Convention was not in session had an important influence.

27.3.4 Speed of light (Chapter 5)

Elaborate experiments to determine the speed of light were carried out in the late nineteenth century. They generally involved timing the passage of light between mirrors a large distance apart. Individual readings were made a number of times over several days. One set of 100 readings reported by Michelson has frequently been used as an example in Statistics since Stigler included the data in his 1977 paper on robustness (Stigler (1977)). The data are usually assumed to have been collected under similar conditions and are described as being five sets of 20 readings. In fact, the splitting into five was an artefact introduced by Stigler for testing purposes, as his article clearly states. Michelson's original paper (Michelson (1880)) gives an exhaustive description of his procedures and lists a number of changes and alterations to the experiment that were made over the 100 experiments. Amongst other things he records when the readings were taken and by whom. Treating the data as i.i.d. is statistically attractive, but inappropriate in practice.

Newcomb also carried out experiments to determine the speed of light. Both Michelson and Newcomb provided precise descriptions in their publications of how they converted their results to estimates of the speed of light in a vacuum. This information is crucial for comparing results.

27.3.5 Olympic Games (Chapter 6)

The two datasets cover the modern Olympics from 1896 to 2016 and countries have changed over that period. Germany split for many years and was reunited. Imperial Russia became the Soviet Union and then Russia again. The same country name may refer to different areas at different times. It is not easy to be consistent and checks are needed. Defining the number of participants from Germany when the country was split as the sum of the participants from East and West suggests higher numbers than would have been the case if they had been a single competing country.

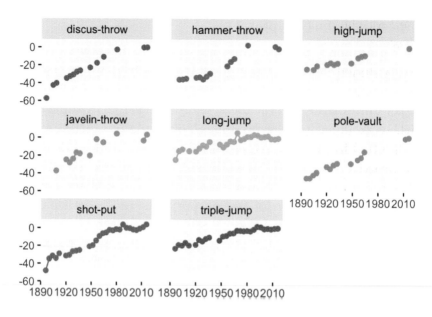

FIGURE 27.1: Athletics field events for men: percentage differences in gold medal performances compared with averages over the last six Games

The first dataset had been scraped from the web. Some issues arose concerning the consistency of the names used for events (cf. Figure 6.4) and there were some unexpected missing values. Figure 6.8, redrawn here as Figure 27.1, shows gaps (i.e. missing values) in the gold medal performances for some men's field events. The temporary decline in shot put performances at a time the results are missing for other events is suggestive.

27.3.6   Chess ratings (Chapter 8)

FIDE used to provide their annual datasets in the old fixed width format that has no separators between values. This required a bit of work to read (and care with format changes between datasets, often because more information had been added in later datasets). A line of variable names had to be added. Another issue with older datasets (and FIDE's oldest dataset in 2020 was one for 2001) can be encodings of accents in names. Names may have been anglicised or standardised in some way.

Using datasets from different time points may mean that some information is inconsistent, because different definitions are used. Comparing the ratings for 2015 and 2020, it turned out that the three-letter codings for Lebanon and Singapore had changed.

Large datasets may have issues of consistency because the data come from independent sources, in this case from different countries. More attention may be paid to some parts of the data than others. It is likely that the information about the best chess players is more reliable than information about some of the weakest.

The data included the year of birth of each player, but these data were incomplete. Sometimes they were recorded as missing (e.g., as NA), sometimes other codes were used. In the December 2015 dataset there were a few birth years with value 0, a lot with value 0000 (about 3.75% of the dataset), and a few with 1900. The latter may have been 00 during some phase of the data collection process and then inadvertently been converted to 1900. Using birth year rather than age means that that variable never has to be updated, but it is often more understandable to work with age as a variable and that is easy to calculate. It turned out that some supposedly old players had actually died a few years before and that leaving the list for any reason was not necessarily easy. This made clear how important the active/inactive classification used in the dataset could be.

Categorical variables may usefully be simplified or amended. The variable 'Flag' was described as an indicator of inactivity, but had 4 possible values, 'i' for inactive, 'wi' for female inactive, 'w' for female, and NA. It made sense to simplify this to a new variable that merely recorded whether a player was active or inactive as there was another variable recording sex.

Occasionally datasets have extra blanks at the beginning or end of inputs and these should be trimmed. Character variables with values for males ('M') and females ('F') may otherwise have additional categories such as 'M ' or ' F' (note the extra spaces). Numeric variables with extra blanks will not be recognised as numeric.

Country population data for 2019 was taken from the World Bank (Worldbank (2020)). Unfortunately, the three letter country codes used by FIDE and the World Bank are not always the same. After joining the datasets by code and then, for the rest, by name, little further editing was needed. For some sporting purposes, including chess, the United Kingdom splits into three countries (England, Scotland, Wales) and Northern Ireland is combined with Ireland. For others, such as soccer, Northern Ireland is treated as a separate country. Populations for these countries were taken from Wikipedia.

27.3.7 Attitudes to same-sex marriage (Chapter 9)

One of the datasets analysed in Gelman, Hill, and Vehtari (2020) concerns how people in the United States responded to questions on same-sex marriage. The book only looked at the issue of support for a law at state level, but a question was also asked in the survey on whether a constitutional ban at federal level should be introduced. The answers were different. One explanation could have been that the questions were asked in different ways. Getting the full raw data from Annenberg who carried out the poll in 2003-4 added more information. Only one third of the sample were asked the state question and there were slightly different versions of both questions asked at different periods during the survey. More relevantly, the state question was phrased so that "Strongly favour" meant for same-sex marriage, while the federal question was the other way round. This had a curious side effect. The authors of Gelman, Hill, and Vehtari (2020) simplified the responses to "yes" (in favour) or "no" (against), and classified those who responded otherwise as "no". This had different implications for the questions at federal and state levels. Fortunately, the overall effect was small, as respondents tended to have strong views one way or the other, so the difference in responses would have been mainly due to the difference between a state law and a constitutional change. A comparison of the responses of those who were asked and answered both questions is shown in Figure 27.2, a redrawing of Figure 9.11. The key feature is the bar lower right representing the group who strongly opposed a same-sex marriage law for their own state while also strongly opposing a Constitutional Amendment banning same-sex marriage.

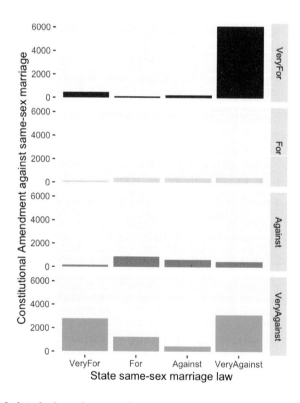

FIGURE 27.2: Multiple barcharts of the responses to supporting same-sex marriage at state level by the responses to supporting a Constitutional Amendment banning it

The handling of answers to surveys can be tricky. The precise wording of the questions and of the possible answers has to be checked. Political polls are often reported ignoring the responses of those who refused to answer or said they did not know. This can be deceptive.

27.3.8 Human spaceflights (Chapter 10)

This is an intriguing dataset with plenty of striking information. It was scraped from a number of sites on the web as part of a study of data available on the health of space travellers (Corlett, Stavnichuk, and Komarova (2020)). Others then made a version of it available on the Tidy Tuesday project (rfordatascience (2020a)). There are a number of inconsistencies and errors in this version and it is not obvious where they arose. There is plenty of interesting information, but careful checking is needed, as described in the chapter.

27.3.9 Diamonds (Chapter 11)

The diamonds dataset was scraped from a website selling diamonds. This makes it a convenience sample and so any conclusions drawn should be treated cautiously. It contains missing values, zero values that cannot be zero, a gap in the price data, some outliers that are obvious errors, and a likely upper limit on price. There is clear evidence of heaping on rounded carat values that also affects the distribution pattern of other variables. Some of these properties will affect analyses, some will not, they all contribute to a better understanding of the dataset. Figure 27.3, a reproduction of Figure 11.4, shows the heaping. Other examples of heaping can be seen in Figure 3.2 for movie runtimes and in Figure 21.9 for finishing times in the Comrades Marathon.

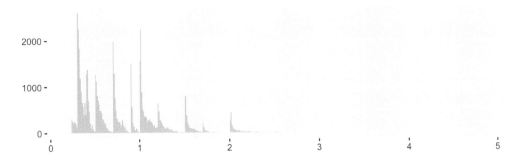

FIGURE 27.3: Histogram of diamond carats

27.3.10   Electric car charging (Chapter 13)

There is much interest in electric cars and how people use charging stations. The researchers wrote that they had an initial period of three months for testing before analysis (Asensio et al. (2021a)). This would be partly to let drivers acclimatise themselves to the new possibilities. However, as Figure 13.7 shows, redrawn as Figure 27.4 here, over half the locations had no charging stations in the test period and there had been little use of some of the others by then.

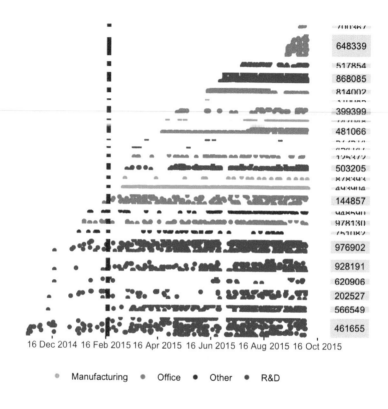

FIGURE 27.4: Use of charging stations, coloured by the type of facility, grouped by location, ordered by first installation at location and by first date of use, with the end of the testing period marked in red

The display provides an overall view of the study structure and suggests a number of questions on how it developed.

27.3.11   Darwin's finches (Chapter 14)

Darwin's visit to the Galápagos Islands as part of his voyage on the Beagle was short, but influential on his thinking. Other researchers have visited the islands since, and a number of datasets are in the public domain. The dataset used comes from the 1898-99 expedition and was chosen because it and the expedition report were readily available. Whether the selection of birds and measurement methods would match modern research standards is questionable. Nevertheless, the data still provide strong evidence for species differences as Figure 14.5 showed, redrawn here as Figure 27.5.

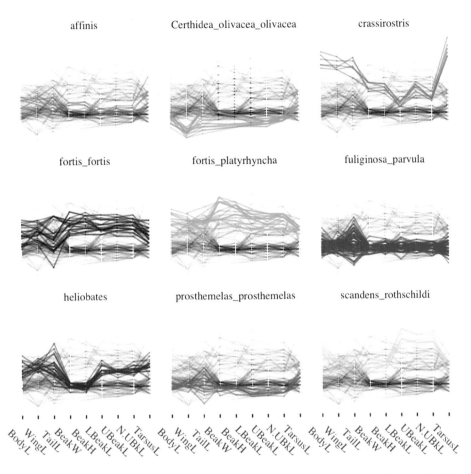

FIGURE 27.5: Parallel coordinate plot of nine measurements of nine Galápagos finch species from Isabela Island

27.3.12 Vehicle fuel consumption (Chapter 17)

The U.S. Department of Energy's dataset on fuel consumption revealed that some compact and subcompact cars performed very badly. The brands of cars involved were all from exclusive producers, such as Rolls Royce, Maserati, and Ferrari. Contacting website support brought the prompt reply that the definitions stemmed from the 1970s and were based on the total space for passengers and luggage. The Environmental Protection Agency were well aware of the unsuitability of their classification of some models. Definitions are not always quite what you think they ought to be and it is useful to check.

27.3.13 Comrades Marathon (Chapter 21)

The data for this race over the years make a good impression. A key feature is that the direction of the race generally alternates between "up" and "down". How much difference that makes can be seen in the righthand plot of Figure 21.12, shown again here as Figure 27.6. The difference in how much a runner would have to go "up" and "down" is striking.

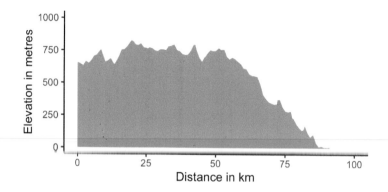

FIGURE 27.6: A profile plot for the planned down race starting at Pietermaritzburg to the left, finishing at Durban to the right, in 2020

27.3.14 Shearwaters (Chapter 23)

This dataset was used in Bouveyron et al. (2019) to illustrate model-based clustering. The description says it concerns two types of puffin, *Puffinus lherminieri* and *Puffinus subalaris*. However, these are both types of shearwater, a quite different bird from a puffin. The first is known as Audubon's shearwater and the second as the Galapagos shearwater. Surprisingly, Bouveyron et al. (2019) labelled the birds as *Borealis* and *Diomedea* in one of their graphics, i.e. Cory's shearwater and Scopoli's shearwater.

The dataset has also been used as an example in Giordani, Ferraro, and Martella (2020). It uses a version of the dataset called *birds*, published in the R package **Rmixmod**, in which all values of `collar` that are not equal to "none" are given the value "dotted". The class variable is missing but the authors assume, correctly as it turns out, that the *Puffinus lherminieri* cases all come first. There is a further version of the dataset in the R package **MixAll**. It differs from the **Rmixmod** version for two cases of `undertail` (which it calls `sub-caudal`). Finally, the dataset used in the book covers three species of shearwater, the two already mentioned plus Tropical shearwaters, and is available in the package **CoModes**.

It is confusing when the same data are offered in different ways in different datasets. Unfortunately, this is by no means an isolated example.

27.3.15   Titanic (Chapter 25)

Data on the survival of passengers and crew from the sinking of the Titanic in 1912 have been analysed and visualised very often. The dataset is included in many R packages under different names. Some of these datasets have more data, some less, and many provide insufficient information about the origin of their data, although most are probably based on the report of the British Board of Trade in 1912. The best modern source appears to be "Encyclopedia Titanica" (2021). It has coordinated the efforts of many individuals and has steadily added to the information available on the sad fate of the Titanic. In particular, the knowledge of which departments individual crew members belonged to has improved (leading to Figure 25.8), as has knowledge of the ages of the crew and passengers (leading to Figure 25.12).

Figure 27.7 shows doubledecker plots of the survival rates by class and crew for the dataset in R's **datasets** package and for the newer dataset used in Chapter 25. The total numbers are only slightly different and so the class bars are pretty much identical. The big difference is apparent from the detailed breakdown for the crew. Deck crew, who manned the lifeboats, had a high survival rate. Other crew groups had lower survival rates, especially the restaurant crew.

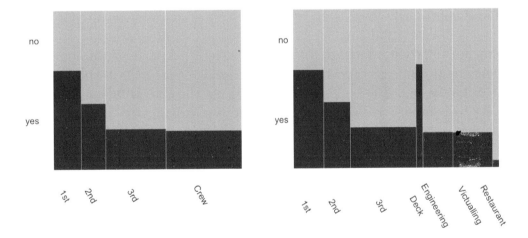

FIGURE 27.7: Titanic survival rates by class and crew, older dataset on the left, newer on the right

27.4   How do invented, simulated, and real datasets compare?

Datasets can be invented, simulated or real. Invented datasets were very common in older textbooks before many had access to computers. The datasets had to be small and the calculations simple, so that everything could be done by hand or perhaps with the help of a calculator. Some researchers claimed this was a good thing as students were closer to their data. Shayle Searle reminisced to me that in his Statistics course at Cambridge in the early 1950s this was the reason Dennis Lindley gave for not allowing students to use the old hand calculators that were then available. Times change.

Unfortunately, invented datasets are still found in some textbooks, sometimes with flippant background descriptions. Attempting to make statistics attractive to students by using superficial examples with supposedly amusing subjects will not necessarily encourage them to take actual statistics seriously.

Simulated datasets are often used in research to investigate the performance of methods on data with known structure. That can be informative. Using simulated data for exercises is not so helpful. Simulated datasets are just that—simulated—and rarely reflect the issues and problems that arise with real datasets, be they missing values, outliers, inconsistencies, errors or whatever. More importantly, there is no way to use context or additional data to check features discovered in simulated data. Simulated datasets are used in graphical inference to produce line-ups for checking whether a particular graphic display from a real dataset could reasonably be said to have the feature identified (Wickham et al. (2011)). This is an interesting theoretical approach, requiring users to compare groups of similar graphics looking for one that may be different.

Using real datasets means more work. You have to find out if you are permitted to use them, you have to check them, and you have to understand them. And, of course, you should cite the source properly to give credit where credit is due. It is a form of plagiarism to use data without acknowledgement. Many apparently simple datasets have only been put together with enormous effort. Think of the experiments on the speed of light by Newcomb and Michelson, think of the data on Darwin's finches collected by the Grants over many years, think of the researchers measuring penguins on the Palmer Archipelago on the North of Antarctica. Data collection may take a lot of time and effort, so may data preparation. This work should be acknowledged.

What is real about real datasets can be an issue. Many datasets that are publicly available have been cleaned, edited and filtered, even simplified. One example is the datasets on measurements of the speed of light. Another is the Titanic dataset where there are many versions and most are rehashes of early summaries. Modern research has provided more and better detail.

One of the most famous experiments in physics was Millikan's oil drop experiment to determine the charge on an electron. Millikan carried out his experiments before the First World War and according to his notebooks did not report all his results, excluding those where he believed the experiments to have been flawed in some way (Holton (1978)). At around the same time, Ehrenhaft carried out experiments with the same aim and, in contrast to Millikan, found a broad range of electron charges (Ehrenhaft (1910)). Ehrenhaft apparently reported all his experimental results, but scientific opinion sided with Millikan. Not all data are equal and you cannot treat all data equally.

Datasets are sometimes treated as objective truths and given too much respect. On the other hand, they are sometimes unjustifiably maligned as unreliable and worthless. The fact that the phrase "the camera doesn't lie" is not always true does not mean that all photographs are invalidated. It just means that you should take into account the choice of subject, the point of view, the weather, the lighting, the colouring, the lens and so on. A good dataset includes clearly defined variables, reliable data, and a verifiable provenance. No dataset may be perfect, but many are informative.

Main points

- It is essential to know the provenance of a dataset, its source, whether it has been edited and amended, and if so, how.
- Large, documented datasets are much more readily available now than in the past. They require extensive checking.
- Each dataset has its own issues. There is no uniform approach that will work for each one.
- Real datasets are better than invented or simulated ones.

28

Wrangling

He did not arrive at this conclusion by the decent process of quiet, logical deduction, nor yet by the blinding flash of glorious intuition, but by the shoddy, untidy process halfway between the two by which one usually gets to know things.

— Margery Allingham, 'Death of a Ghost'

28.1 Data wrangling: what and why

Data wrangling covers all the work put into cleaning, organising, and restructuring data. Few datasets arrive perfectly formed in an ideal shape—other than datasets found in textbooks. They have to be checked (correcting or excluding cases) and reorganised (reformatting, transforming, and restructuring them). A detailed example is described in Amaliah et al. (2022). In-depth studies require a range of analyses, involving grouping, subsetting, and aggregating datasets.

Data wrangling takes time and effort. Every dataset with problems has different problems. Sometimes they are immediately obvious, sometimes they only become apparent during analysis. There are many, many ways of restructuring datasets. Some will be better than others. It will depend on the particular dataset and the reasons for analysing it.

28.2 Data cleaning and transforming

28.2.1 Errors, typos, outliers, missing values

Some errors are obvious (e.g., impossible values like diamonds with zero dimensions in §11.2), some become visible thanks to graphics displays (such as the diamond outliers observed in Figure 11.6), some emerge after analyses. The Olympics dataset in Chapter 6 had different names for the same event at different Olympic Games, as uncovered by Figure 6.4. The human spaceflight dataset in Chapter 10 recorded different times for people on the same mission and had a few other data issues that are discussed in §10.3. Amongst the chess players with FIDE ratings in 2015 there were 15 supposedly born in 1900. These errors were doubtless due to a 00 coding used somewhere in the original data submission. The corresponding ages were marked as NA, a standard code for a missing value.

Often errors can be corrected. Sometimes they can be discarded as definitely wrong. Ideally there are not many of them. Whether whole cases should be excluded if some data are in error or missing depends on how the data are used. For small datasets it can be important to have exactly the same cases in each plot; for larger datasets this is less critical.

Missing values may be recorded with different codings. The Annenberg survey data in Chapter 9 used "998" for "Don't know" and "999" for "Refused". In the movie dataset in Chapter 3, some missing values were recorded as "\N".

28.2.2   Transforming and combining variables

Variable transformations can help to pick out individual data features. Standardising variables makes distributional comparisons across variables possible. Combining variables can reveal more complex structures.

Variables may be transformed onto alternative scales or combined with other variables to form new ones. The boxplot of movie runtimes, Figure 3.1, is scaled in weeks instead of minutes to help viewers make sense of the extreme values. Who remembers that 50,000 minutes is around 5 weeks?

Several transformations were used in Chapter 16 about football leagues. The main ones were needed to convert game scores into tables of results and league tables. The wrangling was complicated by a number of changes over time: three points for a win instead of two, using goal difference instead of goal average, changes in divisional structure, and, most recently, an incomplete season for two divisions due to Covid. Other transformations included a square root transformation used in Figure 16.7 to emphasise higher league positions over lower ones. In the wormcharts of team performances across seasons (Figures 16.8 to 16.10), cumulative team points were transformed by subtracting the league average at the time to make it easier to compare teams' performances.

The mission times of individuals on spaceflights were initially plotted on a linear scale in Figure 10.4, shown again on the left of Figure 28.1. Plotting mission times on a log scale in Figure 10.6, repeated on the right of Figure 28.1, provided a better view. It also led to adding a more informative vertical scale.

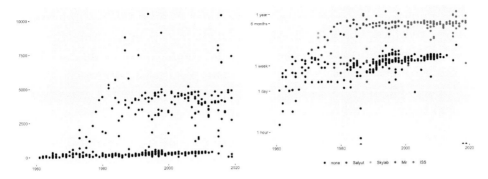

FIGURE 28.1: Individual spaceflight mission times over the years, plotted on a linear scale (left) and a logged scale (right)

Transformations can be used to standardise data to make distributions for different groups or variables comparable. In §6.2 performance improvements in athletics events at the Olympic were compared over the years. Figure 6.7, repeated in Figure 28.2, shows percentage changes for track and field events for men and women. Baselines were taken to be the average of gold medal performances at the Olympics from 1996 to 2016. For field events gold medal performances tended higher as winning distances became longer and winning heights became higher. For track events gold medal performances tended lower, as winning times got faster. An inverse transformation of the track events data could have been used to make their gold medal performances tend higher too.

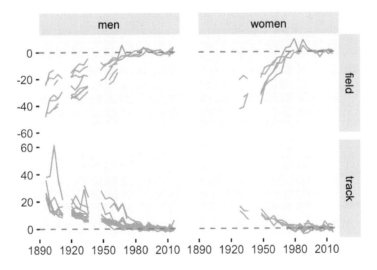

FIGURE 28.2: Percentage differences in gold medal performances in athletics events compared with averages over the last six Games

Variables in parallel coordinate plots almost always need to be standardised and there are several ways of doing it. Methods include putting variables individually onto [0,1] scales or normalising them by using the mean and standard deviation or by using robust statistics. There are examples in Chapter 14 for Darwin's finches and in Chapter 18 for the Palmer penguins, where the transformations of the continuous variables are to [0,1] scales.

The decathlon provides an example where special transformations are used. The current scoring system, introduced in 1984, converts performances in the ten events to points using a different three-parameter formula for each event (IAAF (2001)). As equal points are intended to reflect equal performances, no further standardisation is needed in principle. Figure 31.9 shows how that can work in practice.

Categorical variables may be reported as numbers instead of text and it is worth making the effort to convert them to meaningful labels. Transforming the order of levels of a categorical variable from a default such as alphabetic is always sensible (and is discussed in Chapter 31). Occasionally numeric variables are assumed by software to be character variables, usually because the data file has a text error, and they have to be converted to numeric after fixing the text error. Software can often make good guesses about data characteristics, but you need to check.

Date and time information need special handling in software and almost certainly have to be transformed first. Newcomb's estimates of the speed of light are displayed by experimental order in Figure 5.6 and by date in Figure 5.7. The differences are important for understanding the data. The two plots are shown again in Figure 28.3 below. The dates taken as text are from Newcomb's paper (Newcomb (1891)) and were transformed to a special date format so that the R software could scale them appropriately.

In Chapter 24 two datasets of half-hourly data over 10 years were analysed. Investigating patterns across days, months, and years required combining the textual date and time information and converting it into dates and times R could deal with.

Spatial datasets also require special treatment. They may be reported in any one of a large number of possible coordinate reference systems and it is essential in any study to convert all the spatial data to the same system. Much work has gone into transforming between these systems and the current state of play is summarised in Bivand (2020). One example here involved adding city locations to the maps of France in Figures 7.1 and 7.4. A further complication in Chapter 7 was converting a modern shape file of the departments of France to one matching the form in 1954. Finally cartograms may be used to take

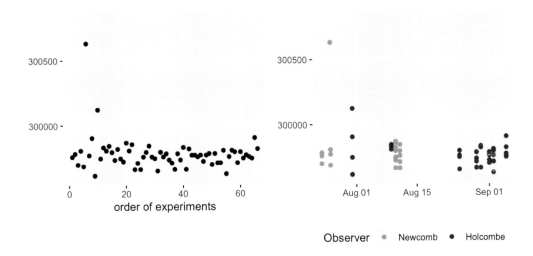

FIGURE 28.3: Newcomb's estimates of the speed of light, plotted in order (left) and by date (right)

account of differences between areas as in Figures 7.5 and 9.7. The spatial transformations applied require complex iterative methods.

28.3 Restructuring: subsetting, grouping, aggregating

Some subsets are investigated more than others. It depends on the aims of the study. Subsetting involves selecting the relevant variables and cases. Large datasets can be heterogeneous with cases being of many distinct kinds that should be analysed separately. Subsetting overlaps with excluding errors, outliers or other problematic cases.

In studying how gold medal performances had changed over the years at the Olympics, only the subset of athletics and swimming events were considered. Weightlifting events could have been studied too, but many Olympic disciplines—e.g., gymnastics, boxing, diving—are not readily comparable over time.

Subsetting selects part of a dataset to be analysed. Grouping splits a dataset or subset into groups to be compared. In Chapter 12 results for two groups, those getting a treatment for their psoriasis and those receiving a placebo, were compared. In Chapter 14 species of Darwin's finches were compared on one island, and one species was compared across different islands. In Chapter 18 three species of Penguins were compared. In Chapter 20 subsets of swimming performances were chosen and then compared by stroke, distance, and swimmer's sex. In the Comrades Marathon dataset the numbers running were grouped by sex and age and compared over time in Figure 21.2, shown here in reduced size as Figure 28.4.

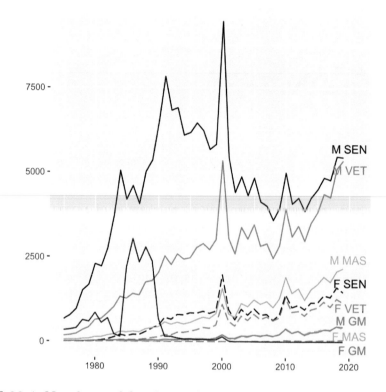

FIGURE 28.4: Numbers of finishers of the Comrades Ultramarathon by age group and sex from 1975 to 2019

Statistics are summaries based on aggregations. They depend on how data have been subset, grouped or aggregated. In the analysis of the 2021 German election in Chapter 26, results could be studied by individual constituency, by Bundesland, by groups of Bundesländer (such as the former East and West), or by the whole country. It is relatively easy to keep track of such hierarchical or nested structures. If there are several categorical variables with no hierarchical structure, as in the study of fuel efficiency of cars in the US in Chapter 17, there are many possible summarising levels. Just considering two of the classifying variables could lead to statistics for vehicle classes within manufacturer or for manufacturers within vehicle class or for vehicle classes and manufacturers.

Further flexibility arises when there are variables with many categories. Analyses may be simplified by combining smaller categories, as was done in Chapters 8, 15, 17, 25, and 26. Different analysts will have different opinions on how small small should be.

28.4 Naming, renaming and reclassifying

Datasets

Merging, subsetting, grouping, aggregating all create new versions of a dataset. Transforming variables and creating new ones do too. It is helpful to name and store these new datasets if they are going to be used more than once. This can lead to a large number of stored objects (Chapter 16 had over thirty), but provides structure for analyses—assuming supportive naming conventions are used.

Variables and categories

Variables may have abbreviated names when informative ones would be more helpful, for instance when software automatically uses names on plots and reports. Ideally, derived variables should be given names that reflect what they represent, so that it is easier to recognise what they measure. Software may classify numeric variables incorrectly if text is found amongst their values (perhaps notes or special codes like currency symbols). Exchanging data files between countries using decimal points and those using decimal commas also requires wrangling. It is common to have to reclassify variables as numeric after text has been replaced or removed.

Levels of categorical variables may be provided as numbers. It is better they be given meaningful names (which also ensures that the variables are not classified as numeric).

28.5 Wrangling for layered graphics

Wickham (2016) emphasised the advantages of thinking of data graphics as being built up of layers, one on top of the other, an idea that has been used in cartography for a long time. Sometimes the layers are all drawn using the same dataset, sometimes each layer is drawn with a different dataset. In the latter case, the datasets may be subsets, aggregations, or even models derived from one main dataset. Constructing them is part of data wrangling. A simple example plotting the distribution of bill lengths for the Adélie penguins shows the idea in Figure 28.5.

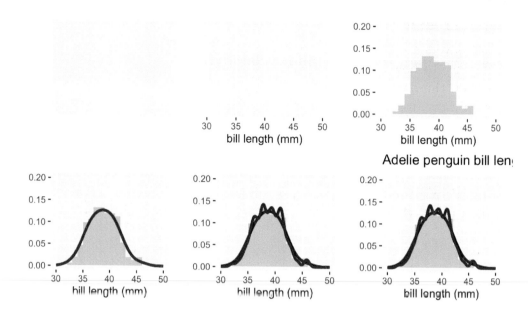

FIGURE 28.5: Layers building up to a histogram of the bill lengths of Adélie penguins with two superimposed density estimates.

The first layer top left is the background colour. The second adds a scale and x-axis label for the variable to be plotted. A histogram layer is added top right with the corresponding vertical axis scale (a density, not a count, so estimates can be overlaid). The first two plots of the lower row add a first and then a second density estimate. The final plot adds the plot title.

The advantages of a layered structure are that it is straightforward to add and remove layers to see what impact they have. It is clear where formatting options should be defined (such as binwidths for histograms or colours for points and lines). An additional advantage lies in being able to use different datasets in different layers. You might want to only use a subset in one layer, you might want to use data from a different year in another layer, you might want to use quite different, but related datasets. The only condition is that all fit in the scale limits of the plot. Layered structures offer flexible and explicit support.

Decoding graphics is easier when layers are clearly and separately defined. You can examine each in turn to study how it might be interpreted and what it contributes to the plot. It might emphasise information already present or add additional information. Reading code for plots made by others is simpler, as the code can be deciphered one layer at a time.

28.5.1 Types of layers

A plot's layers are of different types and the order the layers are drawn makes a difference to how a plot looks. Generally, the background layers are drawn first, then the data and summarising layers, and finally the guide and text layers. Filled areas, for instance with a histogram or a boxplot, should be drawn before points and lines to avoid hiding them. Using transparency can help. The effects of drawing colours on top of one another, when objects in one layer are directly above objects in another, has to be checked.

In Figure 28.5 the two density estimates cover up the histogram details in the final plot (which suggests that they are a fairly good fit). Similarly, the second, rougher estimate covers up the first, although the differences can still be seen. A bigger version of the plot would be better, as in Figure 28.6. Now all the details can be seen. Graphics need to be large enough to display the information in them.

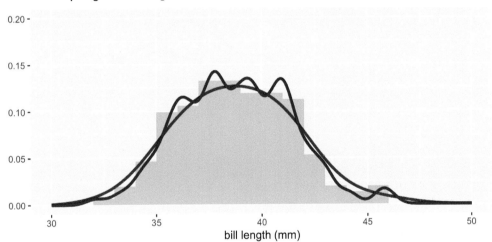

FIGURE 28.6: Histogram of the bill lengths of Adélie penguins with two superimposed density estimates

Background layers

The background colour of graphics in the past was usually white, as if they were drawn on a blank page. Nowadays, background shadings of your own choice can be used or even a mixture by drawing layers on top of one another. Combinations of colours, transparency, and shapes can produce distinctive and unique patterns—if that is what is wanted. One muted background layer may suffice.

Axes, scales and gridlines frame the data. Axes and scales are almost always needed for data graphics (the main exception being network displays). When variables are specified, axes and their scales are drawn on top of any background colours and may include major and minor gridlines.

Data layers

Data layers are drawn on top of the background layers. They may use points or symbols, lines, bars or other area shapes. There are many variants and any software should offer a wide range. Amongst other options there are horizontal lines, vertical lines, lines connecting points directly, using a step or in a path. There can be multiple layers of data types. Figure 4.7 and many others use separate layers of points and lines for the same data.

There can also be multiple layers of data using different datasets. Figure 16.2, repeated here as Figure 28.7, uses data from three different leagues over three overlapping but different time ranges. The scale limits must be set in the first data layer to ensure that all data are shown.

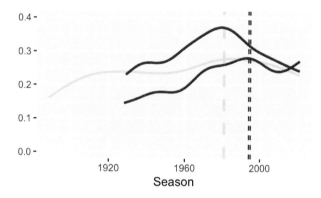

FIGURE 28.7: Rates of draws for the top tiers in Italy (dark blue) since 1934, England (light blue) since 1888, and Spain (red) since 1928

Summarising, modelling, and uncertainty layers

Data may be summarised using statistics or models. There could be several layers of such displays. On top of point data there might be a layer of group means and layers for linear fit and smoothed models. Data may be recorded as estimates with measures of variability. The corresponding uncertainty can be represented by error bars. Model uncertainty may be represented in a graphic by ribbons or bands around the model. Examples include chess ratings by age (Figure 8.21), age by year of mission of astronauts (Figure 10.2, redrawn here as Figure 28.8), and Titanic survival rates (Figure 25.12).

Data layers and summarising layers overlap to some extent. Histograms and boxplots summarise data, but are best thought of as data layers.

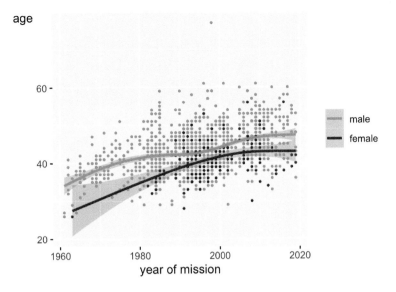

FIGURE 28.8: Scatterplot of age by year of space flight coloured by sex, with smooths and their confidence intervals

Guide and text layers

Guides can be added in additional layers: boundary lines, borders separating groups, plot areas coloured to differentiate them (Figure 4.7), arrows to point to particular features. Text layers can be drawn to add titles, legends, annotations, labels for points or lines.

Layering is effective for faceted data when the whole dataset is drawn in a muted colour in each facet first and each facet's subset is drawn on top in colour, ghostplotting. Figure 10.7 is an example, redrawn here as Figure 28.9:

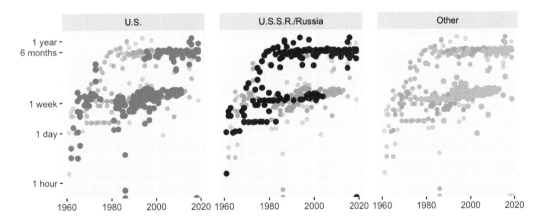

FIGURE 28.9: Logged spaceflight mission times of individuals by year of flight by nationality

28.5.2   The layers of a league wormchart

Figure 28.10 is a wormchart for the English League Championship of 1954-55, similar to the plots for other seasons in §16.6. There were 22 teams, each playing 42 games. There were just 2 points for a win and only two teams were relegated. Chelsea won with the low total of 54 points. At the half-way mark of 21 games, Chelsea were level on points with Cardiff City, who finished 20th. The bottom club, Sheffield Wednesday, had an appalling run in mid-season and would have finished much further adrift had they not surprisingly won three of their last four games.

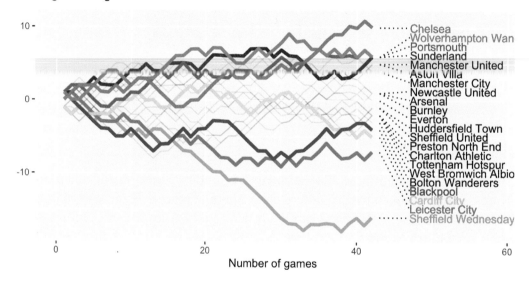

FIGURE 28.10: Wormchart for season 1954-55

Figure 28.10 has eight layers and uses four datasets. Figure 28.11 shows the build-up. There are background layers of colour and axes; a line layer of team performances drawn lightly (using a dataset of all teams); a layer of coloured, thicker lines for the top four and bottom four teams (using the subset of those eight teams); a text layer with the names of all teams (using a subset based on the last day of the season to get the order right); a segment layer connecting each team's name to the end of its line with dots; a coloured text layer for the top four and bottom four teams (using the relevant subset of the previous dataset); a title layer.

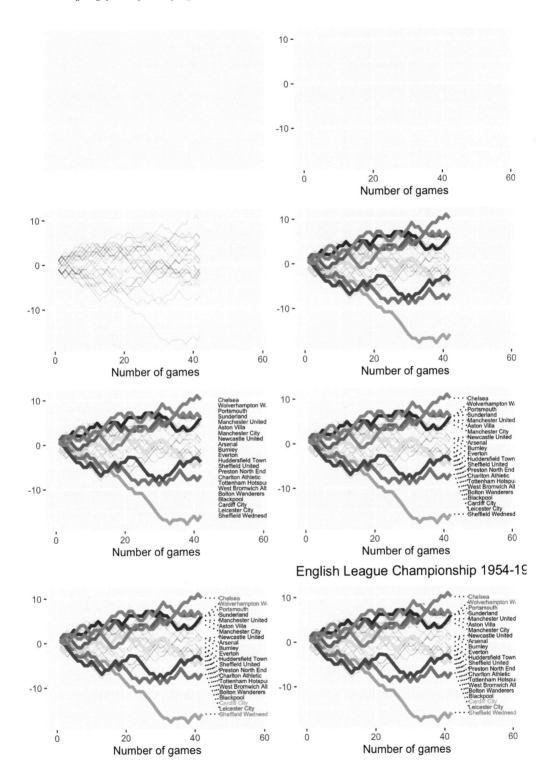

FIGURE 28.11: Layers building up to a wormchart for the 1954-55 English League Championship.

28.6   Putting datasets together and reproducibility

28.6.1   Reading in and merging datasets

Datasets come in different shapes, sizes, and formats. Modern software can usually read all of them, but some conversion may be necessary. Spreadsheets offer flexible structures with multiple sheets, and may include background information, annotations, and other non-standard structures. These need special treatment, as with the UN population dataset used in Chapter 8. Only the first and second sheets were required and the initial lines of the first had to be edited. Spreadsheets can be very useful for initial recording of data because of the notes and background information that can be included. Public organisations often distribute data in spreadsheet format. Journal authors sometimes make their data available in spreadsheets. There are disadvantages. Spreadsheets may include summary data along with case data. Additional text and multi-line headers may be employed. Different versions, subsets, aggregations of a dataset may be provided in individual sheets of a spreadsheet without being linked. In other words, if a data value were to be amended, it would have be be changed separately in each sheet in which it appeared (e.g., the spreadsheet used in Chapter 19).

If data are needed from more then one dataset, the datasets must usually be merged. Chapter 8 combined the chess ratings dataset with files for country populations, country codings, and regions. This increased the number of variables from 12 to 20, although many were unused and could have been dropped. The number of players included in this merged dataset dropped from 362502 to 191097, as only active players were considered. Finally the ratings data for two separate years were merged. The 2020 dataset had 362502 players and 12 variables, while the 2015 dataset had 227960 players and 12 variables. The merged dataset that included all players from both years had 364012 players.

In Chapter 4 the voting results file for the 1912 Democratic Primary was summarised by state and merged with files for the numbers of each state's electoral votes in 1912 and 2020, and with a file for state populations in 2018. The unsummarised data file was also separately merged with a file of estimated times at which the ballots took place.

Mapped data reveal spatial patterns. Shape files for areas can be merged with data files. This was done in Chapters 7 (Bertin's French workforce data), 9 (Gay Rights survey), 25 (Titanic), and 26 (German election 2021).

28.6.2 Reproducibility

For scientific publications it would be ideal to have authors provide code as well as data, both code for their data wrangling and for their analyses. Only base data would have to be made available, as other versions could be reconstructed with the code. This would improve the chances of being able to reproduce study results, providing a record of what had been done. Of course, that record would only be understandable to readers who could follow the coding language.

Reproducing published work is easier than it was, but is still not satisfactory, as various surveys in different fields have pointed out (e.g., Gabelica, Bojčić, and Puljak (2022)). Two examples arose in this book. In Chapter 22 numerous tables of percentage success rates of facial recognition software were reported, but the raw data were not made available. Making the reasonable assumption that the underlying results must have been integers, it was possible to reconstruct much of the data from the percentages reported. In the supplementary material to the article on tests for malaria discussed in Chapter 19, there was a multi-sheet Excel spreadsheet giving the raw data and the data used in the article's plots and tables. The sheets were not linked and formulae not reported. With a little work the connections could be reconstructed. With other datasets (that were not therefore not included in the book) insufficient information was provided or essential details were missing.

Main points

- Data cleaning is a continuing process through all of an investigation.
- Datasets may be subset, grouped or aggregated in many different ways, providing many different views.
- Layers of related data structures are a good way of building graphics.
- Wrangling is an essential support for graphical analysis.

29

Colour

I found I could say things with color and shapes that I couldn't say any other way - things I had no words for.

— Georgia O'Keeffe

29.1   Theory and implementation

Colour is a complex topic. There has been considerable progress made in our understanding of representing colour, even if that has led to a plethora of systems, be it HCL, HLS, HSV, LAB, LUV, RGB, XYZ or whatever. A valuable reference is Zeileis et al. (2020) and the accompanying R package **colorspace**.

R software has kept pace, and there are many packages offering colour palettes and ways of creating new ones. There are qualitative palettes for different groups or categories, sequential palettes for different values of the same variable, and diverging palettes for variables with a critical point such as zero between profit and loss. In addition, palettes have been designed to counteract colour blindness. There are R packages for generating colour palettes from images, and even a package with palettes inspired by Wes Anderson movies.

Many software defaults are effective and do not need to be changed. Colour defaults generally do need to be changed, as will be apparent from the examples. The illustrations used are smaller versions of graphics occurring elsewhere in the book.

29.2   Perception of colour

How colours are perceived depends on an individual's eyesight and experience and on the ambient lighting. Human perception varies. In 2015 a photograph of a dress became a big topic online as people disagreed whether it was blue and black or white and gold ("the dress"). Some people are better at discriminating between colours than others. There is some suggestion that women are able to identify more colours than men, seeing different shades where men see a single colour. Some people have strong associations with particular colours. The scene in "The Devil Wears Prada" where Meryl Streep takes Anne Hathaway to task for saying two belts look the same is a good example (and can be found on YouTube as the cerulean scene). A more academic reference is Mohammad (2011).

Colour perception changes depending on surrounding colours and can change over time. Solving a jigsaw puzzle is one example. At first the pieces may be sorted by major colours. Later on, various light blues of the sky may be almost as easily sorted, when these are the only pieces left.

The medium with which colours are viewed is also influential. A display on one computer screen may look different on another, and look different again in print. Ambient conditions, especially lighting, are important. All these factors can have unpredictable effects, yet there is still plenty of good advice to follow.

29.3   Value of colour

Colour can make images more effective, if you know what effect you want to achieve. There are several ways colour works, and colour schemes accentuate (or play down) particular features. There are many aspects to the use of colour and care must be exercised, default palettes may not work well. Sometimes graphics drawn in colour will be reproduced without colour, another factor to have to take into account.

29.3.1   Colours distinguish

The colour scheme in Figure 20.2, repeated here in a smaller form as Figure 29.1, emphasises the four different strokes in swimming. The colours work because there is no overlapping. If there was overlapping, facets with ghostplotting could be used.

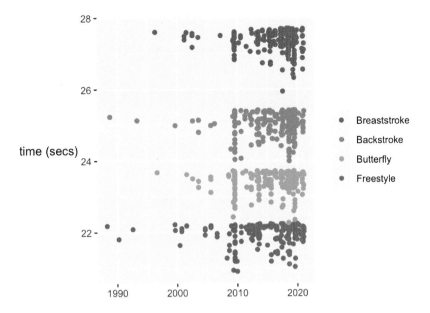

FIGURE 29.1: Male swimmer best times for four different strokes

In Chapter 5 there are three separate scatterplots using colour, each with different aims, each coloured differently. Figure 29.2 shows them: Stigler's division of Michelson's data into five groups (Figure 5.1); Michelson's grouping the data by three times of day (Figure 5.2); Newcomb's data including the responsible observers (Figure 5.7). In the first plot the colours show the arbitrariness of the division into groups. In the second plot the morning and afternoon cases are obvious, but the single night-time observation is not (the legend was ordered to help with this). Colour is effective in the third plot, because Holcombe and Newcomb observed on different days. Different colour schemes were used to discourage viewers assuming colours meant the same thing in all plots.

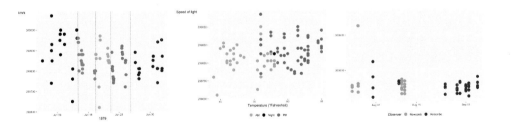

FIGURE 29.2: Three speed of light plots with three different colour schemes because they represent three different situations

29.3.2   Colours highlight

Colouring individual outlying points draws more attention to them, whether they are boxplot outliers or unusual values in scatterplots. The boxplot of Newcomb's measurements of the speed of light in §5.2 is one example of highlighting outliers (Figure 5.4).

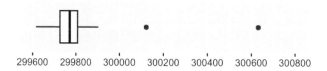

FIGURE 29.3: Speed of light measurements by Newcomb

The boxplots of chess players' ratings by age in §8.4 is another example, (Figure 8.19 repeated as Figure 29.4)

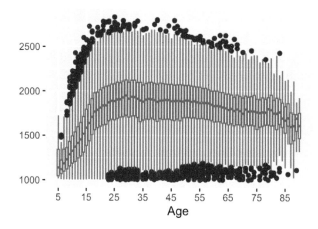

FIGURE 29.4: Boxplots of ratings for each age for active chess players in 2015

The scatterplot of chess ratings by age in Figure 8.17, repeated as Figure 29.5, uses red to pick out the players with the highest ratings and alpha transparency to downplay the others.

In Figure 16.4 colour is used to pick out English football teams with extreme proportions of points won at home in their leagues. Those 10 points are also drawn slightly bigger than the other 9545 points.

Highlighting some aspects can be achieved by playing down others. Some faceted plots have been drawn in the book with the complete dataset in the background of each facet drawn in a discreet grey rather than a default black, ghostplotting, to give context. Examples include Figures 10.7, 14.5, and 18.10.

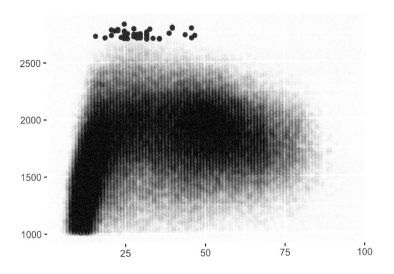

FIGURE 29.5: Rating by age for active players in 2015. Players with ratings over 2700 have been coloured red. An alpha value of 0.01 has been used for the other players.

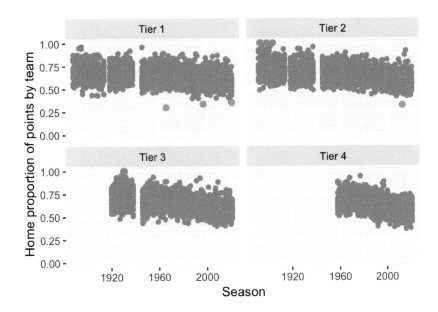

FIGURE 29.6: Individual home away points ratios for every English football team for every season

29.3.3 Colours connect

Using the same colours consistently for the same dataset underscores connections. If there are several displays involving the same data, then colouring by a grouping should be the same for all. In §14.1 five species of Darwin's finches are displayed in a barchart, two boxplots, a scatterplot, and a parallel coordinate plot. The first four plots are redrawn in miniature here (Figure 29.7).

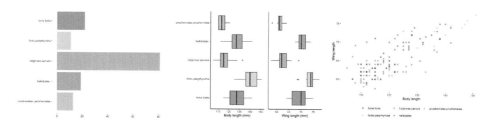

FIGURE 29.7: Plots of five species of Darwin's finches

Consistent use of colours in the same circumstances can be useful too. Throughout the book there are many datasets grouped by sex: Olympic sports, chess players, survey respondents, spaceflights, marathon runners, Titanic passengers. A purple colour has been used for females and a green for males.

29.3.4 Colours separate

Different groupings should use different colours. In §18.1 three plot ensembles have the same form, but with different subgroups selected, so different colours are employed (Figures 18.2, 18.3, and 18.4).

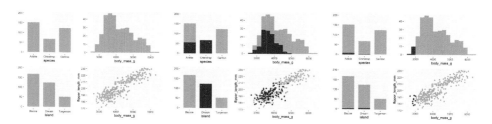

FIGURE 29.8: Plot ensembles for different groups of Penguins (using different colours for the selections)

With interactive graphics the same highlighting colour is always used for selected cases, because selection is temporary. The chosen colour defines the current interactive selection. Colours that separate are needed for static presentation graphics.

29.3.5 Colours signify

Colours should match known associations. If certain colours are associated with political parties, countries or international football teams, then consider using those colours in statistical displays.

In Chapter 26 the German political parties have been represented by their own colours, as in Figure 26.16, shown here as Figure 29.9.

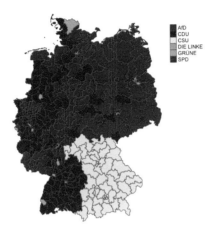

FIGURE 29.9: Winners of seats by political party in Germany

Whether this is effective or not may depend on the type of plot. The Gapminder dataset discussed in Chapter 2 splits the world into four regions and colours those regions consistently. Using that colour scheme for the time series in Figure 2.5 is not effective, although it is fine for the associated faceted plot and barcharts.

This may not always work as expected. In the 2022 FA Cup Final at Wembley, Chelsea played in yellow against Liverpool instead of their normal blue, possibly because they had lost the 2022 Carabao Cup Final against the same opponents wearing blue earlier in the year. It was striking to see their fans wearing blue when the team were wearing yellow (and did not need to). Chelsea lost again.

Different countries have different associations with different colours, as can be seen in the Colours in Culture poster that looks at colour associations for 84 concepts in 10 populations around the world (McCandless (2022)). It is too difficult to cope with all possible associations in an international context, but it is worth bearing in mind. There are many stories and traditions linked to colours, as is entertainingly described in St Clair (2016). Amongst other thought-provoking comments, she points out that the colours pink for a girl and blue for a boy are a mid twentieth-century development. Formerly, it was common to associate pink with boys and blue with girls.

29.3.6   Colours attract

Well chosen colours can turn a mundane, grey graphic into an attractive and pleasing picture that is a pleasure to work with. Studying a succession of similar, dry graphics can be disheartening and discouraging. A restrained use of colour is an advantage. Not all plots of the same type have to look the same. As Bertin writes of colour (Bertin (2010) Chapter II.C.2): "It captures and holds attention, multiplies the number of readers, assures better retention of the information, and, in short, increases the scope of the message."

29.4   Choice of colour

There is a huge range of colours and colour palettes to chose from, and plenty of advice on which to use. That does not make choosing any easier. Similarly, there is a great deal of advice on fashion and on what to wear, but not everyone is well dressed.

29.4.1   Colour blind palettes help

Colour blind people are more the exception than the rule, but that is no excuse for ignoring their needs, particularly as graphics are being increasingly used. Various sources offer colour palettes that are readable for the colour blind and using these or subsets of them is worthwhile. Free software is available that enables designers to check how their graphics would look to viewers with different kinds of colour blindness.

The same colour blind palette has been used in several figures in the book for datasets as diverse as a gay rights survey, electric car charging, penguin species, swimmers' nationalities, and groups of marathon runners. Three examples, Figures 9.11, 18.8, and 21.2, are shown together in Figure 29.10.

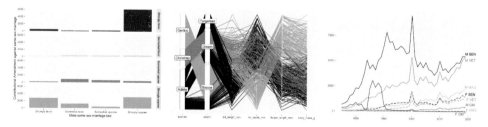

FIGURE 29.10: Three uses of a colour blind palette

29.4.2 Palette order counts

In §10.1 spaceflights are coloured by the space station program they joined, if any (Figure 10.5, redrawn as Figure 29.11). The default ordering of the colour blind palette from the R package **ggthemes** was changed to make the Skylab station that was only used briefly in 1973-4 more visible and to keep similar colours apart.

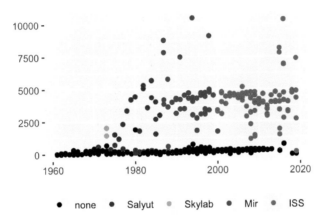

FIGURE 29.11: Spaceflight mission times coloured by space station programme

29.4.3 There may not be enough colours

Sometimes there are too many groups. Gapminder countries, football shirts of teams playing at Euro2020, nationalities of passengers on the Titanic are all too numerous to be assigned different, distinguishable colours.

Sometimes there are too many different groupings. In Chapter 2 colours are used for three Scandinavian countries, for four world regions, and for the six most populous countries. In Chapter 10 colours are used for sex, space station programmes, and nationalities.

29.4.4 Avoid using the same colours for different datasets

Colour schemes stand out. If the same palettes are used for different examples, readers may mistakenly assume they are looking at the same dataset. Figure 29.2 shows an example.

29.4.5   Avoid overlapping colours, use faceting

A display with several groups or time series may be hard to disentangle and decode. An alternative is to plot each subset individually in its own facet, together with the rest of the data underneath in a light grey (ghostplotting). At the end of §14.1 there is a faceted parallel coordinate plot, Figure 14.5, redrawn here as Figure 29.12. If it was drawn as a single plot with all 9 species, it would be much more difficult to read.

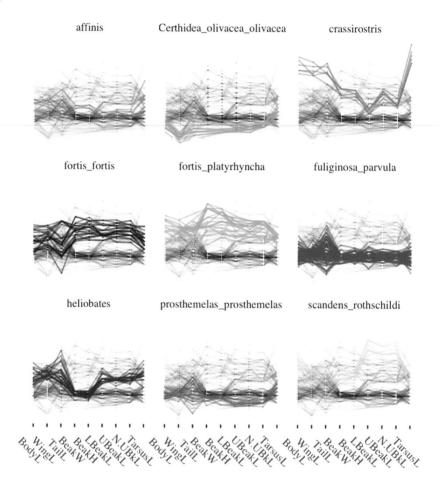

FIGURE 29.12: Nine measurements of 9 species on Isabela Island

29.4.6   Backgrounds matter

Finally, take the colour scheme of background and surroundings into account. Individual media outlets usually have a house style, as do firms and organisations. A particular display may be perceived quite differently, if presented otherwise unchanged.

In this book the default **ggplot2** background has often be used. This does not work well for maps, mosaicplots, and parallel coordinate plots, where scales and gridlines are not appropriate. Figures 7.1, 25.8, and 14.4 have been drawn with plain backgrounds. Other plots might benefit from a change of background too.

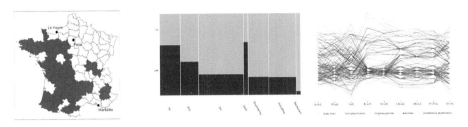

FIGURE 29.13: Graphics drawn with plain backgrounds

At art exhibitions in the past the walls were covered with paintings. There are etchings showing this by Pietro Antonio Martini of the French Academy's Salon exhibitions of 1785 and 1787 at the Louvre and of the English Royal Academy's exhibition of 1788. Reproductions can be found on the web. In the nineteenth century, Manet thought about how his pictures might stand out in such collections, if they were accepted by the annual Salon. Drawers of graphics should think about the likely surroundings of their plots too.

Main points

- There are many colours and many colour systems. Colour is not simple.
- Colours distinguish, highlight, connect, separate, signify. Think about why colour is used.
- Choosing effective colours is important and difficult. Others may perceive colours differently.
- Ghostplotting gives context.

30

Setting the scene

To find a form that accommodates the mess, that is the task of the artist now
— Samuel Beckett

Drawing graphics involves choosing the variables to look at, deciding what raw data and statistics to display, and selecting plot types. Initial plots may benefit from changing the scales or transforming the variables. It might be useful to exclude some of the cases. It could be helpful to add models. All of these actions are concerned with the content of the graphic.

With graphics for exploration, analysts should have background knowledge about the data and the main aim is to make structural features stand out. Exploratory graphics need little text of any kind, possibly just variable labels and simple scaling. With graphics for presentation, more information is needed. Few viewers will have enough background information, so context must be provided to make the graphic understandable. Guidelines of a journal or organisation may demand particular formatting standards. Ideally graphics should be polished as well as informative. Whether graphics are drawn for exploration or presentation, it is sensible to avoid overcrowding within a plot and to avoid overcrowding of plots together.

The content itself, the data objects like points and lines, can be reformatted. Sizes, colouring, shapes, and ordering can be changed, sometimes dependent on dataset variables. The framing of the content could be extended and amended: the axes, tickmarks, gridlines, background, text (title, caption, labels, legends, annotations), spacing, size, and aspect ratio. Colouring, size, width, typeface apply to many of these. Most of this kind of formatting is for refining graphics for presentation, but improving the look of graphics helps exploratory work too.

Exploratory graphics involves drawing large numbers of graphics (this cannot be said often enough). Software is not as supportive as it should be in handling many graphics. They need to be ordered, aligned, and arranged. Scales and colouring should be consistent. Graphics texts tend to give advice on drawing individual graphics, but much advice is also needed for drawing and organising sets of graphics.

Recognising information in data graphics is easier if the graphics are well displayed. It is best if they are carefully laid out with plenty of space, both within and around them, and that they are appropriately formatted. When actors prepare to put on a play, they rehearse the words first, the content, and then add actions, while the stage designer, light manager, costume manager, and other specialists organise how best to display the content and set the scene. It is all brought together for the performances.

There are two kinds of graphical scene setting, for exploration and for presentation. Although they are not distinct, it is helpful to think of them separately. Exploration benefits from flexible layouts and plenty of space, concentrating on overviews more than details. Scales and labels may be the only text needed. Formatting should be supportive and unobtrusive, ideally just using defaults, so that little, if anything, needs to be changed. Exploration is open and informal. Presentation requires precise layouts of specified sizes, using space efficiently, with detailed formatting and explanatory text including titles, captions, legends, annotations, accompanying comments and more. Presentation is closed and formal.

Exploration is at most a small group activity, involving only a few people who know the aims and background of the project. For presentation the audience is potentially huge and their interests, knowledge, and experience will vary. This chapter discusses four aspects of graphical scene setting to make the information in graphics stand out: scaling, formatting, space, and layout.

30.1   Scaling

Success is a science; if you have the conditions, you get the result.

— Oscar Wilde

Scaling is a mapping from a variable's values to how they are represented in a display. The variable to be scaled may be part of the dataset or a statistic calculated from the data, perhaps a count or subgroup means. The mapping is a function for converting the values to the visual properties of the plot, including the limits of the range of data that will be included. The resulting scale is annotated with breaks (tickmarks) and labels to make it more readable. A variable can be transformed and then plotted or the variable can be plotted on a transformed scale.

Scaling sets the limits of a display. Anything outside the limits is not shown. One example is Figure 3.2, which is a histogram of movie lengths of up to 3 hours that excludes the 682 films with longer runtimes. Or limits cover a wider range than the data to provide more space or to include particular standard values. Figure 9.5 is drawn with a scale from 0 to 100% although the maximum upper limit of the confidence intervals is only just over 75%. The reason is to emphasise the full range of possible values and to make clear that most states opposed the measure. It is sometimes suggested that 0 should always be included on count and other scales. This is generally sound advice and is followed, for instance, in the first plot of Figure 21.12. There the intention is to show that the down race is slightly longer than the upper race and that there is variation in the distances up and down over the years, but that these differences are small compared to the overall race length. Using 0 as a baseline would not be as sensible in many of the other plots in Chapter 21. Displays of race times (such as Figures 21.6 and 21.14) and of race speeds (Figure 21.11) are designed to point out the differences in times and speeds, not the overall levels. Figures 21.11 and the left plot of 21.12 are shown again in Figure 30.1.

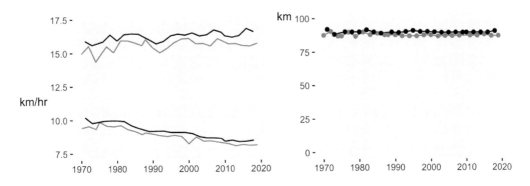

FIGURE 30.1: Average speed of the fastest runners (above) and median runners (below) in km/hr for the "up" (dark orange) and "down" (black) races, and distances in km for the "up" and "down" races, all since 1970

Outliers are a problem for scales. A single extreme outlier can stretch the limits and compress the rest of the data into a single, uninformative block (cf. the left plot in Figure 32.10). It will also affect boxplots, scatterplots, and parallel coordinate plots. This only applies to cases that are outliers on individual dimensions. Higher dimensional outliers (for instance, some of the cases revealed in Figure 11.6) do not affect graphics in this way.

Scales are for guidance not precision. Graphics are unsuitable for reading off individual values, although it is useful to know roughly what values apply. This is why the choice of units for scale labels is worth thinking about. The data displayed in Figure 3.1 are recorded in minutes up to 51420, not a number that makes sense to most readers. Converting the scale into weeks makes the plot more understandable with the maximum being just over 5 weeks. Similarly,

Figure 10.6 uses a log scale for mission times and adds labels for recognisable lengths of time (hour, day, week) rather than marks equally spaced on the log scale.

Labelled breaks in scales aid understanding and offer points of reference. Too many can lead to crowding or even overplotting and too few do not offer enough assistance. The overall size chosen for a graphic has an influence and it can be curious to see what happens to scale labels when graphics are shrunk.

There are several ways a variable can contribute to a display including horizontal position (x-axis), vertical position (y-axis), pointsize, linewidth, colour, and alpha transparency. Some are easier to assess than others. As Cleveland and McGill (1987) and other research since have pointed out, lengths along a common scale are best for comparison. Pointsize and linewidth are useful for showing large differences, as in Figures 9.12 and 25.12 (pointsize), and Figures 2.10 and 8.9 (linewidth), but not for finer differentiation

Some attributes have continuous scales, some are categorical, such as shape or linetype. Colour can be continuous (as in Figure 9.4) or discrete (Figure 26.7) or categorical (Figure 4.2). Alpha transparency is a valuable adjunct to colour for emphasising or de-emphasising particular features (e.g., Figure 8.17). The main use of colour is for categorical variables and is the subject of Chapter 29.

There were publications in the past suggesting methods for producing 'optimal' continuous scales. These usually produced exact numbers to several decimal places rather than interpretable round numbers. The term 'pretty' scales has emerged to describe the latter. There is no such research for categorical scales, although, as covered in Chapter 31, ordering of these scales makes a great deal of difference. When there are too many categories, some kind of aggregation is helpful. This was done in Figures 15.6 and 15.7 collecting the smallest groups into "Other". Something similar was done in Figure 9.1, combining the oldest age groups into one of over 80.

There can be several scales in the same plot. Figure 8.12 uses two transformed variables (active chess players and grandmasters per million population), a regional colour coding, and pointsize proportional to population.

Context is important for specifying limits and breaks. In Chapter 17 on fuel efficiency of car models sold in the US, the values are reported in miles per gallon, so those have been used. Most other countries use litres per 100 kilometres. 'Pretty' scales would differ for the different units with the same data.

Variables representing dates and times bring their own issues. Months are of different lengths (even years are not always the same length). Should scales include Saturdays and Sundays if no data is recorded on those days? Conversely, for Figure 6.3, redrawn as Figure 30.2, missing values were added to the dataset for the Olympic Games that did not take place because of the World Wars. This was to ensure that gaps appeared in the time series to signify what had happened.

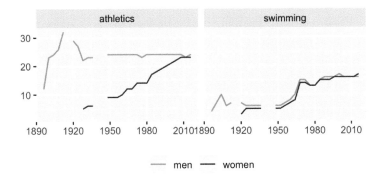

FIGURE 30.2: Numbers of athletics and swimming events for men and women at the Summer Olympics from 1896 to 2016

If scales are labelled by months, should the label be at the beginning of the month or the middle of the month? Again, much will depend on context. The level of detail of the labelling of time scales is problematic. The timing of the ballots at the Democratic Convention in 1912 was important, as can be seen in Figure 4.7. The times can be read from the dataset. Adding them to the graphic would overload the display and would add information that barely contributes more to what can be seen already.

Scales for spatial data are a quite separate matter. Maps can be drawn using any number of different projections. This does not affect most of Europe much, but has a big effect near the poles. Consider drawing a map of the Palmer Archipelago where the data used in Chapter 18 were studied.

Default scales drawn by software will usually be good for exploratory purposes for individual graphics. They will usually not be as good for comparing graphics. Then common scaling (i.e. using the same scale for comparable axes) will be more suitable. Figure 7.2 is an example where common scaling has been used for three histograms to emphasise the differences in the ranges of numbers of workers. In Figure 7.3 default scales have been used for studying the associations, if any, between the sectors. It is often useful to put vertical count axes on the same scale, as in Figure 23.1 where numbers may be compared across graphics as well as within since the graphics are all of the same dataset. Finally, if related variables are plotted together it makes sense to use a common scale (e.g., for the x and y axes of each plot in Figure 18.11). The default for drawing faceted graphics is common scaling, even if occasionally this is not what is wanted. Graphics are like that, there are always exceptions to any rule.

Common scaling has been used above to refer to using the same scale. It is better to think of it more generally as designing scales that support comparing variables. The transformations used to convert individual event performances in the Decathlon into points are an example (even if they do not work as well as desired, cf. Figure 31.5). Transformations for the axes of parallel coordinate plots are another, although it is more to do with treating variables equally than comparing them: variables can be transformed to [0,1], to z scores, to robust equivalents of z scores, to ranks.

Scales are needed immediately for drawing graphics. They may be amended after seeing the data. Reasons include making more space around the data, including special values, excluding outliers, and supporting comparisons. Overlaying graphical layers may require changes in limits if the range of the initial layer is not wide enough.

30.2   Formatting

Accuracy is a duty, not a virtue.   — A.E. Housman

There are many formatting tools. Some affect content directly, some indirectly by changing the scene. It is easy enough to find advice on how to achieve particular effects, it is more relevant to think about why they are wanted. As Wilson et al. (2014) recommend in "Best Practices for Scientific Computing": Document design and purpose, not mechanics.

Objects are made bigger to draw attention and made smaller to be less obvious. The overall effect depends on which objects are resized and by how much. Enlarging too much can lead to objects overlapping with loss of clarity. Shrinking too much can make some objects almost invisible. Space is increased between objects to make them more distinct.

Objects are coloured for several reasons (§29.3). Highlighting, colouring one group strongly, emphasises that group against the rest of the dataset. Alpha transparency plays down the impact of objects as in ghostplotting. It is also helpful for displaying point density in scatterplots of large datasets. Using colour and size consistently emphasises links and connections across displays. Common scaling, using the same scale for a variable in all plots in which it appears, ensures consistency of displays. Alignment of axes aids comparisons.

Text plays a major role in presentation graphics. There may be a caption, a title, a subtitle, variable labels, axis labels, legends, annotations (including case labels, line labels, numeric values). All these may be formatted, spaced, and positioned in a variety of ways. Few are needed for exploratory graphics and any formatting would be discreet and low-key.

There are so many formatting options for graphics that it can be difficult to see the wood for the trees. In 2006 the coffee chain Starbucks claimed that, including all variations, it offered 87,000 different drinks (this has not been independently verified (Bialik (2008))). Looking through long lists of graphics options that you have to decide on is not dissimilar. It is more important to know the effect you want to achieve and how the options are structured.

Objects representing the content of a graphic, like points or bars, and components that are part of the setting of a graphic, like axes or legends, can both be reformatted. Rather than content and setting, Wickham (2022) uses the terms data and non-data parts of a plot. Formatting can be structured in a number of ways. The approach described here works up from details of data to an overall view: Points, Plot, Position. Colour and ordering are especially important and are treated in detail in separate chapters.

30.2.1 Points, areas, lines, ...

There are different levels of data that can be displayed: values for individual cases (e.g., as in scatterplots), aggregates (e.g., by category as in barcharts or by value as in histograms) or statistics (e.g., as in rates with confidence intervals by group). As always, boxplots are a mixture. They show individual outlying cases (if there are any), an aggregate (if the boxwidth is drawn proportional to group size), and five statistics.

Representations of cases may be formatted by colour, transparency level, shape, and size, either dependent on a variable or by direct assignment (when they are all the same colour). Edges may be coloured differently to the areas they border (this may also apply to points if they are drawn large enough). Edges and lines may be drawn in different forms (solid, dashed, dotted, ...) and thicknesses. Multivariate glyphs may be defined as radar charts, rose diagrams, Chernoff faces or some other form.

The type of graphic chosen will determine how values are shown. Each case may be represented by a point in a scatterplot, by an area in a bar, by some other form of area, by a time series curve in a plot over time, by a polyline in a parallel coordinate plot, by a multivariate glyph. A variable may be weighted by another (numeric) variable. The regions in Figure 2.7 could be weighted by population, as in Figure 2.8. Both plots are shown again in Figure 30.3.

The rankings are quite different. Africa has the most countries, while Asia has the biggest population by far.

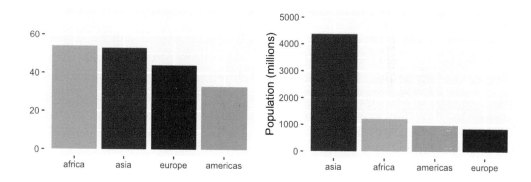

FIGURE 30.3: Barcharts of numbers of countries by region and populations in millions in 2016

The assignment of variables to axes will also affect a plot's appearance, especially in multivariate plots such as parallel coordinate plots and mosaicplots. This also applies to faceted plots where each faceting variable may work either horizontally or vertically and the order of the faceting within the horizontal and vertical groupings matters.

Variables may be represented as given or may be transformed. Logarithms of positive skewed variables and model residuals are both transformations of data, if of very different kinds. Others include cumulative versions of variables, first differences or ranking, and there are many more. It may be productive to create new variables that are combinations of more than one of the original variables, such as differences, ratios, and sums.

Figure 30.4 shows barcharts of the change in population of regions by amount on the left and by percentage on the right. The changes in population over the 60 years from 1956 to 2016 are striking. Asia had the biggest increase in numbers, but Africa by far the biggest in percentage terms. Europe's population increase is the lowest in absolute and percentage terms.

With point plots there can be multiple cases with the same values for the plot variables causing overplotting. This can occur with lines in a parallel coordinate plot or with multiple time series too. The order in which the cases (or lines) are plotted will affect how the display looks. Faceting can counteract overplotting, as in Figure 2.6.

The formatting alternatives in this section are predominantly about content and are relevant to both exploration and presentation.

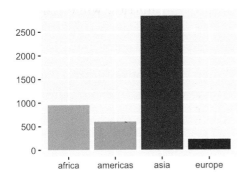 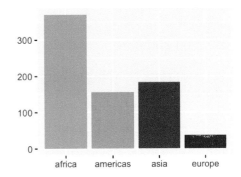

FIGURE 30.4: Barcharts of population changes by region between 1956 and 2016, absolute numbers in millions on the left, percentages on the right.

30.2.2 Plot

There may be frames around a plot to clearly delineate its borders. How the frames are drawn, how much space there is between the plot and the frame, how much space there is between the frame and the total area allotted, all influence the look of a graphic. Needless to say, all these areas can be coloured differently, although that is seldom advisable. A soft, light colour for the area within the frame including the plot background is best.

Plots require axes and are mostly better with axis labels giving names to what is being shown. The axes should have appropriate limits and generally meet at the origin. How many tickmarks are drawn on an axis, where they are drawn, and how they are labelled must also be considered. Major and minor gridlines can be helpful in making comparisons, if drawn lightly on the background.

If bars or rectangles are drawn for categorical variables as in barcharts and mosaicplots, then their width, their individual aspect ratios, and the space between them matter. For mosaicplots it is common practice to increase the space from the lowest level to the highest.

If a plot is composed of different layers, as described in §28.5, then the order in which the layers are drawn will affect how the graphic looks. Alternative views can be offered by including or not including particular layers.

Individual plots can be given titles and subtitles. If colours, shapes, or sizes vary, then legends are necessary to describe the options shown. Special features in a plot can be annotated. All these texts should be in the same typeface, but the font and size may differ to reflect the importance of the texts. Too much text may divert attention from the graphics themselves. Legends, labels, annotations can be like subtitles in a film: having them can be helpful, reading them may be distracting.

These choices are part of a graphic's setting, non-data formatting. They are incorporated in themes in the **ggplot2** R package. It is relatively easy to ensure a common standard across plots by specifying the same theme for all.

Four examples of well-known themes are shown in the next figure. They are distinctive and different, imitations of actual styles offered in the **ggthemes** R package. Corresponding default colour palettes from the same package have been used. Experts from the organisations whose themes have been imitated would produce better displays using their own software.

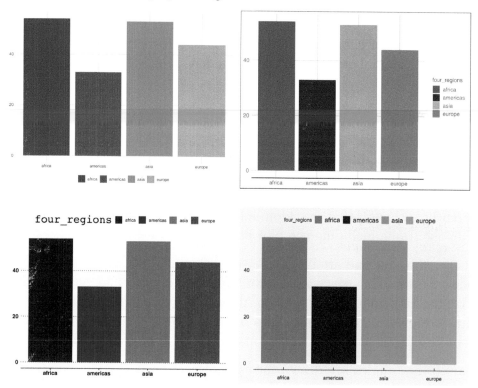

FIGURE 30.5: Barchart of population by region 2016 using four themes, Excel and Google docs (above), Wall Street Journal and Economist (below)

30.2.3   Position

A graphic or group of graphics can be placed at the top of a page, at the foot of a page, in the middle of text. A helpful rule for printed graphics is that the display is on the same page or on the facing page of the text accompanying it. Flicking between pages requires extra effort, increasing the cognitive load on readers (Ware (2020) and Munzner (2014)). They have to recall what was in the text when they look at the graphic, and remember what was in the graphic when they read the text.

HTML versions on electronic devices do not have an issue with paging. Instead the problem is more that different devices may have quite different screen sizes and shapes. Just because a plot looks good at one size says little about how good it may look at another size. Associated material, text or graphics, may or may not be visible.

When several graphics are drawn together in an ensemble it is necessary to arrange them and set the sizes of the individual graphics so that the information in them can be seen and the graphics fit together. This is automatically carried out for a group of graphics of the same size and shape by software offering faceting. Displaying a number of differently sized graphics is not unlike hanging paintings: horizontal and vertical axes should generally be aligned. Variables appearing in more than one graphic should have axes with identical scales (common scaling), as in Figures 18.1 to 18.4. This eases cognitive load when a viewer's gaze moves from one graphic to another.

30.3   Making space

The notes I handle no better than many pianists. But the pauses between the notes - ah, that is where the art resides.

— Artur Schnabel

It is easier to pick out features if a display is uncluttered, with plenty of space around so that there are few distractions. As mentioned at the end of Chapter 29, pictures in art galleries and exhibitions were often hung closely together in the past, so that as many as possible could be shown. That made it awkward to inspect individual pictures, depending on how high or low they were hung, while neighbouring pictures would distract and interfere with the artist's intentions. There is a story that Manet submitted pictures to the Salon, the premier art exhibition in Paris in the 19th century, that would stand out and be noticed under these conditions. Nowadays, pictures are usually hung individually in their own space in galleries. It is similar for graphics, unless they are part of a coordinated ensemble. It is better that there is space around them, not just space around the overall graphic but space within the graphic around the main content as well.

A scatterplot matrix gives an overview of associations between several variables. If one of the scatterplots looks interesting, it is useful to be able to zoom in and check. In Figure 11.7 of diamond measurements several of the plots could be worth more attention, for instance the scatterplot `table` and `carat` shown enlarged in Figure 30.6. Two features already noted in other plots are visible here. Most of the table values are integers, and there is heaping in the carat distribution that consequently has a slight sawtooth pattern (which is easier to see in the earlier histogram). Additionally, there are a few outliers that are probably errors, and there is no relationship between the two variables.

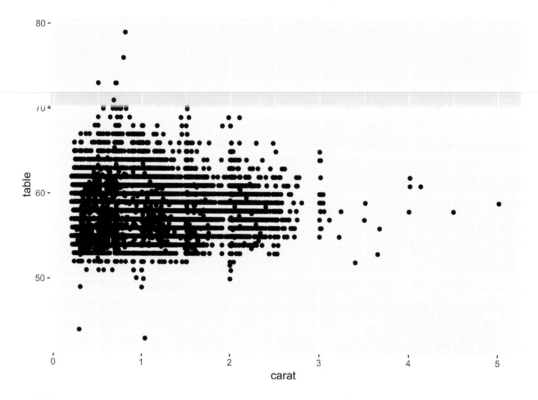

FIGURE 30.6: A scatterplot from the diamonds dataset of carat and table

Space is needed for distinguishing shapes and forms, and for studying features in combination. Empty space surrounding content is needed to discern what is there. There are trade-offs. The plot on the right of Figure 30.8 shrinks space around the point cloud to make more space between the points.

More space is needed for exploration than for presentation just as more space is needed for making a jigsaw than for displaying the finished picture. Jigsaw pieces need to be moved around, sorted, compared with others. Using graphics to explore data is similar (if without the certainty that a complete picture involving all the pieces will be possible).

Sometimes unrelated graphics are packed together. Sometimes axis limits are chosen that are too tight, so that a display seems cramped in its boundaries. Different text elements, whether titles, legends, labels, variables names or annotations, can be drawn too close to other display elements or even overlapping on top of them and affect perception detrimentally. Making a graphic bigger is a quick and simple way of counteracting or at least reducing any overlapping of points and labels.

Values drawn above bars can have the effect of artificially lengthening them, hindering proper comparisons. Borders may be drawn around graphics to separate them from text. This can also have the effect of appearing to constrain them. If a vertical axis is drawn at the left of a plot then a border to the right may be interpreted as a boundary of some kind.

An example of using internal spacing can be seen in doubledecker plots such as Figures 22.3 and 22.4 in Chapter 22 on checking Facial Recognition software. Another example from Chapter 9, Figure 9.3, is redrawn here as Figure 30.7.

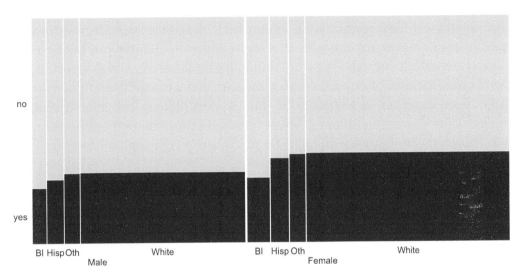

FIGURE 30.7: Support for same-sex marriage at state level by sex and race

Gaps between groups at the top level, in this case male and female, should be bigger than gaps between the individual groups at the next level down. If there is a further level down, then those gaps should be even smaller. The same goes for other forms of mosaicplots. The eye is good at picking out blocks of information when the separation between the blocks is supportive. It is similar for displays of small multiples or faceting. You need to be able to distinguish the individual plots while at the same time being able to make comparisons between them. This is a matter of fine judgement and experience, as with all effective displaying and interpreting of graphics.

30.4   Layout

Life is like a 10-speed bike. Most of us have gears we never use.

— Charles Schulz

Layout of graphics is essential for presentation and important for exploration. Drawing a graphic includes choosing the size and aspect ratio and deciding where to place it in text or in relation to other graphics. In Exploratory Data Analysis graphics need to be resized and moved around to get a better look at them. Varying graphics changes the point of view, giving fresh impressions and drawing attention to other features. Single, fixed points of view are limiting. There are sound recommendations for drawing graphics, but other views suggest additional insights.

If two variables are measured the same way with the same limits, then scatterplots should be square. Figure 9.12 comparing percentage support for two statements on Gay Rights is an example. If default scales are used and the plot is drawn wider but less tall, then more individual states can be picked out. One state, which turned out to be Maine, had a relatively low support at state level given its level of opposition to a constitutional amendment. The two plots are shown together in Figure 30.8. The square plot on the left with equally scaled axes shows the different levels of support for the two opinions and the close association between them. The plot on the right emphasises individual states more and the overall structure less.

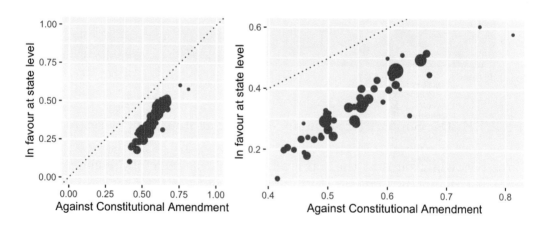

FIGURE 30.8: Scatterplot of responses to the two same-sex marriage questions by state with equal and default scales (point areas are proportional to the number of respondents in that state)

The plots in Figure 30.8 could be drawn with the variables switched and this would give another view of the data. When one of the two variables in a scatterplot is dependent on the other, then the convention is to put it on the vertical axis. Examples can be found in Figures 5.2, 8.17, and 26.8.

If two bars in a chart are close in height or if a bar is barely visible, then it helps to stretch the graphic to see which bar is bigger or how big the barely visible bar is (as in Figure 10.3). The same applies to histograms, particularly with possibly empty bins in the middle (as in Figure 11.5). Empty ranges near the extremes can be checked with boxplots (as in Figure 11.2 following Figure 11.1).

Barcharts are often better horizontally, making use of page width and allowing longer text labels for the bars. Figure 30.9 compares the horizontal version in Figure 8.11 with a vertical version. The left barchart emphasises the countries with most registered chess players. The right barchart emphasises how many players there are in countries not in the top thirty.

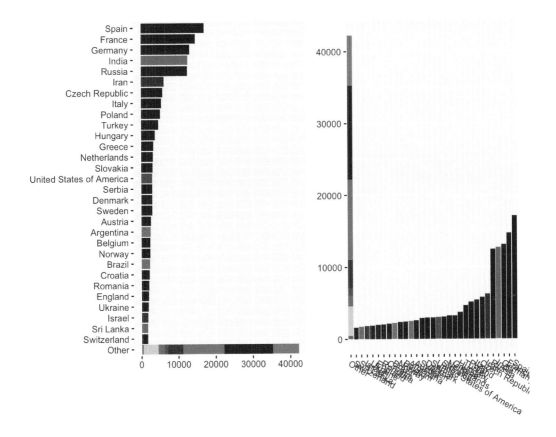

FIGURE 30.9: Barchart of numbers of chess players by country and region plotted horizontally and vertically

Boxplots and scatterplots can be transposed to give alternative views. Boxplot examples include Figures 3.1, 8.2, 8.6, 10.8, 17.3, and 20.4. In Figure 14.2, repeated here as Figure 30.10, the boxplots were rotated to make the labels more legible and to ensure only one set of labels was needed.

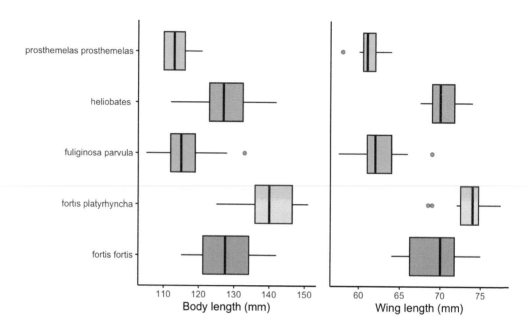

FIGURE 30.10: Body and wing lengths for the five species from Isabela Island

The scatterplots of associations between the numbers in the three sectors of the French workforce in Chapter 7 could be looked at the other way round. Figure 30.11 shows the first plot from Figure 7.3 on the left and a transposed version on the right. The first plot may emphasise the relatively low levels of the Industry numbers in most departments more, while the second may emphasise the two extreme Industry values more.

Another example can be seen in Figure 30.12 which shows Figure 9.12 on the left and a transposed version on the right. The greater support in all states for opposing a Constitutional Amendment looks more obvious in the plot on the right. Different people may respond to different shapes of features. There is no display that will be optimal for all. Best practice is to look at more than one.

Trying different layouts for single graphics is simple. Laying out several differently shaped graphics in an ensemble for presentation is harder (Unwin and Valero-Mora (2018)). Optimal sizes for individual plots may not be optimal for the ensemble as a whole. Other factors include aligning axes and using common scaling.

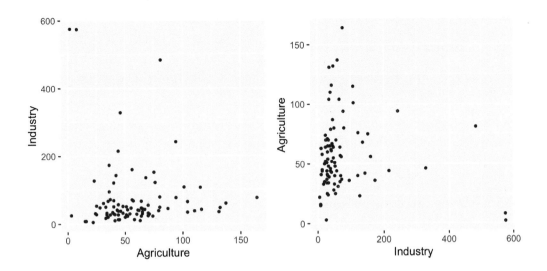

FIGURE 30.11: Scatterplot of numbers of Agriculture and Industry workers in France in 1954 plotted two ways

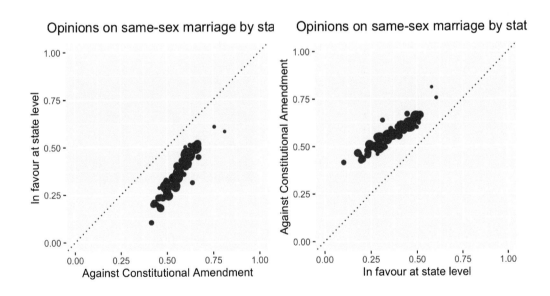

FIGURE 30.12: Scatterplot of responses to the two same-sex marriage questions by state plotted two ways (point areas are proportional to the number of respondents in that state)

30.5   Comparisons and graphics

Painting is easy when you don't know how, but very difficult when you do.
— Edgar Degas

Looking at graphics involves making comparisons—comparisons with expectations, comparisons within graphics, comparisons between graphics. A well-structured layout helps.

30.5.1   Types of comparison

Comparisons may be made between different variables for the same individual cases. They could be different measures (e.g., Figure 14.4 and the top plot of Figure 33.2) or the same measure taken at different times (e.g., top right of Figure 12.1). The comparisons may be improved by looking at differences or ratios as well as the measures themselves.

Comparisons can be made between different subsets or groups, between one selection and the rest of the dataset, between a selection and the whole dataset. These comparisons may be made by distributional forms (Figures 8.9 and 8.14), by features (Figure 10.7) or by statistics (e.g., Figures 11.11, and 25.8, shown again in Figure 30.13).

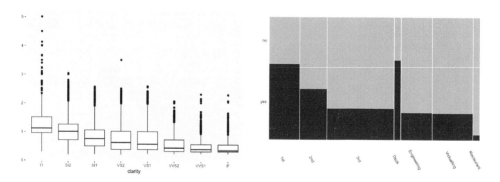

FIGURE 30.13: Diamond carats by clarity (left) and Titanic survival rates for passengers and crew (right)

In statistical analysis it is common to specify a particular comparison, for example whether two means can be taken to be equal or not. In exploratory analysis many comparisons are made, some explicit that are of interest in advance and some that arise because they stand out. There may be a large number of groups that could be compared in a large number of ways, as with the fuel efficiency data in Chapter 17.

Comparisons may be made with a variety of graphics, some perhaps more informative than others, but all contributing. In Chapter 26 the votes for parties in two German elections were initially compared by barcharts, then by a barchart of percentage changes between the elections, then by an UpAndDown plot of relative and absolute changes.

Comparisons must be made precise, both in the definitions of the groups being compared and in the features or statistics used to compare them, and they must be checked thoroughly (cf. §32.3).

30.5.2 Superposition, juxtaposition, and faceting

Graphics can be compared by putting them on top of one another (superposition) or by putting them beside or above one another (juxtaposition). Figure 8.3 juxtaposes histograms of chess ratings for active and inactive players picking out the peak at 2000 well. Figure 8.4 superposes density estimates of the same data showing the overall difference in distributions better, but the peak is harder to see. The plots are redrawn in Figure 30.14.

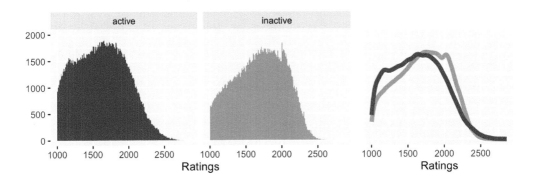

FIGURE 30.14: Juxtaposed histograms (left) and superposed density estimates (right) of ratings for active and inactive chess players

Colour (occasionally shape or form) can be used to distinguish the parts of superposed graphics. The order of drawing is crucial as the last group drawn will be on top (e.g., Figures 10.2 and 21.13). For comparisons of many groups, faceting by placing them on a grid is a practical alternative. Much depends on how separated the groups are.

Superposition is good for comparing time series that look similar (e.g., Figures 2.4 and 24.10), for comparing density estimates of different groups (e.g., Figure 8.15), and for scatterplots in which groups are separated (e.g., Figure 18.9). It is not effective when overlapping occurs, as with histograms or barcharts where juxtaposition is better (e.g., Figures 7.2 and 3.14).

Juxtaposition can be better for crowded scatterplots (e.g., Figure 4.4 rather than Figure 4.3, both shown again in Figure 30.15 with the slight change that the plot on the right now includes ghostplotting to provide context for the individual regions). The disadvantage of juxtaposition is the extra amount of space needed if all plots are full size.

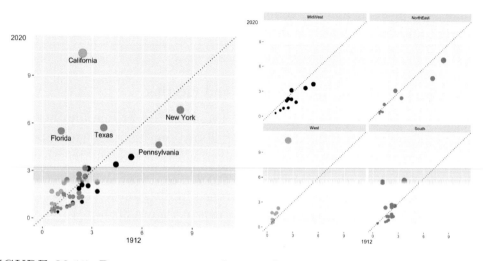

FIGURE 30.15: Percentage state shares of delegates at the 1912 and 2020 Democratic conventions (left) and by region (right)

Grids in faceting are constructed using conditioning. Order the conditioning variables and categories to place groups of interest together (Figure 23.4). Ghostplotting works well for faceted scatterplots by including comparisons of each individual group with the rest of the data.

These approaches are not mutually exclusive. Ghostplotting is often useful with faceting (e.g., Figure 18.10). Superposition and juxtaposition were used together in Figure 9.9. Figures 6.10 and 16.10 use superposition, ghostplotting, and juxtaposition.

30.5.3   Advice

Whichever objects are to be compared should generally be on the same scales, carefully aligned, and close together. Scales can be the same because they are measured in the same units, when differences in levels are emphasised (e.g., Figures 8.10 and 10.3, drawn again in Figure 30.16), or because they have been standardised to a common scale, when distributional shapes are compared (e.g., Figures 3.13 and 21.9). There are many possible standardisations (cf. §28.2.2).

Alignment of axes and placing objects together makes comparisons easier. The doubledecker plot of Titanic survival rates by passenger class and crew department in Figure 25.8 shows the higher survival rate of passengers over

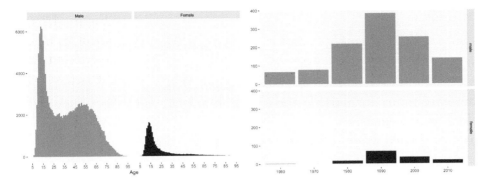

FIGURE 30.16: Age distribution of active players by sex (left) and numbers of spaceflight participants by decade and by sex (right)

crew, the decline in survival rate by passenger class, and the relatively high rate of survival of the deck crew (because they manned the lifeboats).

30.6   Defaults

Software packages always offer default ways of drawing. With graphics there will be default sizes and aspect ratios, default point sizes and shapes, default scales, default axis and line thicknesses, default typefaces and fontsizes, default colour schemes. There are defaults of all kinds, many of which are rarely thought about—and may not need to be thought about often.

Descriptions of how the graphics in this book were drawn refer to using the defaults offered by R or to changing them to achieve a particular effect. Different softwares have different defaults. Organisations define their own defaults to provide a consistent and uniform design. A newspaper looks different to other newspapers because it has its own standard layout and uses a specific typeface. Its graphics look different because they are drawn in a particular, consistent style.

The look of a graphic can be changed considerably by changing the defaults. What is ideal for some purposes may be not so good for others. Sophisticated packages offer complete control and, consequently, can be complex to use. If many graphics are drawn quickly to explore data, the defaults should be sensible, so that time does not have to be spent making adjustments. Analysts should be able to concentrate on content, not on details of presentation.

Main points

- Scaling, formatting, space, and layout all influence how information stands out.
- Scales should be readable and meaningful.
- There are many formatting tools. Think about what effect they will have before using them.
- Space is needed around features to see information.
- Comparisons benefit from common scales, appropriate alignment, and closeness.

31

Ordering, sorting, and arranging

When Laura was here I had the records arranged alphabetically; before that I had them filed in chronological order. . . Tonight, though I fancy something different, so I try to remember the order I bought them in:

— Rob in Nick Hornby's 'High Fidelity'

Ordering items means using a numeric or lexicographic criterion to rank them and having a rule for handling ties. Sorting items places them in groups and may include ordering. Arranging items includes ordering and sorting, but may involve using a subjective criterion. Flowers could be ordered by height or sorted by colour. They might be arranged in quite different ways, depending on how well they then look to the person arranging them.

31.1 What gets ordered, sorted, arranged?

31.1.1 Cases

Datasets can be sorted and ordered in many ways. The cases in the *astronauts* dataset on space travel (rfordatascience (2020a)) could be sorted into groups by nationality or sex. They could be ordered by year of mission or by year of birth. They could be sorted and ordered by combinations of these variables, for instance, by year of birth within nationality. Grouping and ordering datasets often reveals structures that default orders—whether lexicographic, temporal or random—may not. Ordering and sorting cases can be useful for checking extreme or special cases quickly. If some text has crept into a numeric variable, sorting can often identify which values are in error.

For sortings or orderings of the *astronauts* dataset there can be ties, cases that have the same values for the sorting variables, for example people born in the same year of the same nationality. These cases may be ordered randomly amongst themselves or in their original order (whatever that was) or in some other way. Ties would be much less likely if exact dates of birth and exact launch dates of missions were used, although even then pairs like the identical Kelly twins, two Americans, might cause difficulties. To ensure that a return to a particular ordering is always possible, it is essential to have a variable with a unique value for every case, possibly an ID variable constructed for just this reason. Being able to return to the initial order of a dataset is useful if something goes wrong (and something will).

The ordering of cases can affect printing if cases or lines overlap, as the dataset is printed in order. The lines for the three football teams in Figure 16.6 were drawn in alphabetic order, first Bournemouth, then Portsmouth, then Southampton, as can be seen by looking at where the lines cross. (The lines for the other teams in the leagues, drawn in light grey in the background, were drawn in a background layer first.) Figure 11.9 compares calculated values of diamond depth with the values given in the dataset. The data were ordered by the size of the absolute difference, so that the bigger differences, coloured red, were plotted last and hence on top.

Chapter 21 on the Comrades Marathon includes two plots of the performances of the Nurgalieva twins over the years, Figure 21.13, redrawn here as Figure 31.1. Elena ran every year from 2003 to 2015, while Olesya did not run in 2006 and 2012. In the plots, the line for Olesya is drawn on top. This works if it is remembered that Elena ran every year. If the line for Elena had been drawn on top, that would not have worked, even for the zoomed plot on the right.

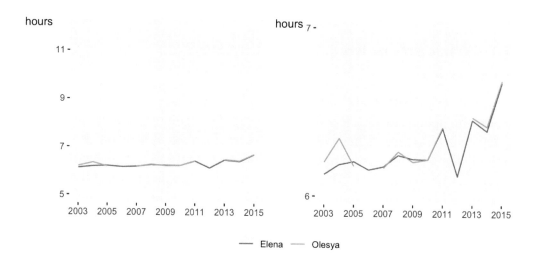

FIGURE 31.1: Performances of the Nurgalieva identical twins in the Comrades Marathon races (same data, different vertical scales)

31.1.2 Levels of categorical variables

Variables such as nationality and occupation each have two or more categories. If you draw up a summary table of counts or draw barcharts of them, the categories are likely to be ordered alphabetically by default. This has its advantages (it is easy to find a category in the table) and its disadvantages (categories with names early in the alphabet get more attention, categories you would like to compare may be far apart). Wainer calls this the "Alabama first" issue, as Alabama comes first alphabetically amongst the US States (Wainer (1997)). Categories may be ordered by counts, by weights, by proportions, by summary statistics on other variables. Comparisons for whatever statistic you order by become easier. Bars far apart must be different and you can tell which bars that are close together have higher or lower values by the order. More complex sortings, say countries within continents, are possible too.

One example is the barchart of the numbers of passengers and crew who boarded the Titanic at the four different ports. Figure 31.2 shows a plot with the default alphabetic ordering on the left and the plot used in §25.1 on the right, using the order the ship called at the ports. The great majority, including many crew, joined in Southampton.

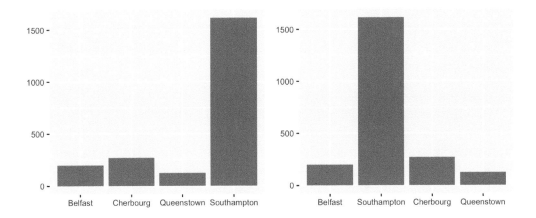

FIGURE 31.2: Barcharts using the default alphabetic ordering and the order in which the Titanic visited the ports

In the Gapminder analysis, §2.3, there are two barcharts of the four regions, one for the number of countries in each region (Figure 2.7) and one for the total population (Figure 2.8), both ordered by bar heights. The two are shown again here in Figure 31.3. The first shows that Africa and Asia have more countries than Europe or the Americas, while the second shows that Asia has more of the world's population than the other three regions put together.

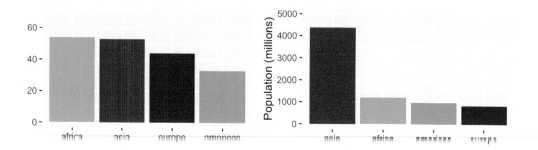

FIGURE 31.3: Numbers of countries and total populations in the four Gapminder regions

A common reason for reordering categories is to produce a recognisable and memorable pattern, for instance steadily increasing or decreasing. Figure 17.7 shows sales of station wagons and SUVs by year. The original plot is on the right of Figure 31.4 and a plot using a default lexicographic ordering of the vehicle types is on the left.

The ordering chosen put the station wagons first and then the SUVs. Within the station wagon group, the models were ordered by increasing size and earliest available production year. Within the SUV group, they were ordered by type using earliest available production year and within that by 2WD and 4WD (two-wheel and four-wheel drive). Multivariate ordering offers many different possibilities, especially when variables are not nested within one another.

31.1.3   Variables

Datasets come with a particular order of variables. There might be an ID variable, some demographic or structural variables, and then some measurements. All of these might be in a rational order, they might not. Datasets with large numbers of variables are easier to handle if the variables are grouped and ordered. The vehicles dataset made available by the US Department of Energy includes 83 pieces of information on 43516 vehicles. The first 65 variables are labelled alphabetically, so that three defining variables, `make`, `model`, and `year`, appear rather late and not together.

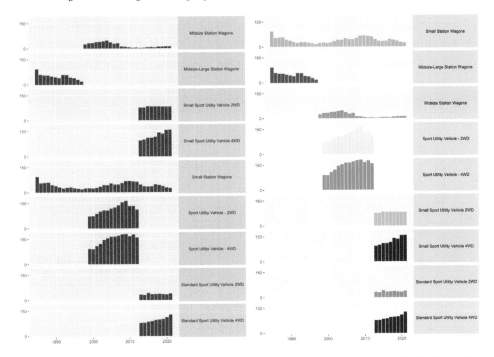

FIGURE 31.4: Annual sales of station wagons and SUVs in default ordering (left) and revised ordering (right)

31.2 Ordering and sorting within graphics

31.2.1 Boxplots

Boxplots by group are a space-efficient way of comparing distributions. The group ordering is sometimes given (e.g., in Figure 11.11 of carat by clarity from the *diamonds* dataset). If not, it is useful to look at different orderings, possibly by a statistic of the individual boxplots (e.g., median or maximum) or by using another dataset statistic associated with the group variable. In Figure 8.13 the rankings of chess players were displayed in boxplots for the countries with the most rated players, and the countries were ordered by their median player rating. As with bars in barcharts, the ordering of the boxplots will facilitate some paired comparisons more than others. The median ordering makes comparison of the medians easy by definition. An ordering by, say, maxima, would favour that comparison.

Boxplots are handy for summarising decathlon data. Each competitor competes in ten track and field events. The results are converted to a points system to make them comparable and the winner is the person with the most points. Figure 31.5 shows the points scores for the 116 top-ranked decathletes in April 2021 (Salmistu (2021)).

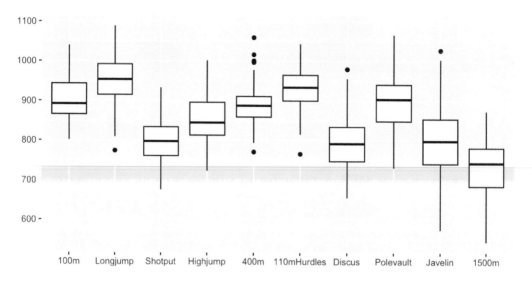

FIGURE 31.5: Boxplots for the points in the 10 decathlon events in the order they take place for the top 116 decathletes in April 2021

It is striking that, although the points are supposed to be comparable, more are awarded for some events than others. Long jump performances get the most points and performances in the 1500 metres the least. The javelin appears to have the most variability and the 400 metres stands out in including three high outliers. The 1500 metres is a special event for a number of reasons: it is a longer run than the other three running events, requiring different abilities; it is the last event at the end of the second day, so the athletes will be tired; the top decathletes in the competition after nine events run the 1500 metres together, so tactics may be more important than a fast time.

31.2.2   Sorting into groups and faceting plots

Faceting displays data subgroups in the same graphical form, e.g., Figures 3.6 and 6.4. The subgroups are defined by combinations of variables. If the graphical form can be internally ordered (e.g., the bars in a barchart, the boxplots in a group of boxplots or the dotplots in Figure 6.4) then you have what might be called zero order faceting.

Sorting cases into groups is often carried out to display statistics, as was done in Figure 9.5 grouping cases by states (and grouping the states by region), or to draw summary plots as in Figure 17.1 grouping cars by class, drive type, and petrol.

Sorting into groups was used in Chapter 2 to draw countries in the same region together (Figure 2.5), in Chapter 13 to keep charging stations at the same location together and to colour locations by type, in Chapter 17 to put what were thought to be similarly sized cars together, in Figure 20.7, shown again here as Figure 31.6, to place events for the same swimming stroke together, and in Chapter 26 to keep constituencies in the same Bundesland together and to display the spatial distributions of seat wins for the individual parties.

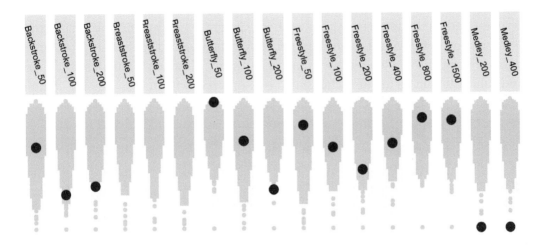

FIGURE 31.6: Katinka Hosszu's best times by event (in purple) compared with the 200 best in each event, with events sorted by stroke and distance

Figure 15.7 displays 24 barcharts, each with 17 bars. The facets are ordered by the percentage of squad players playing in their own country. The bars themselves are ordered by the numbers of players from a country's league playing in EURO2020, except for the 'Other' category, which has been placed last. The aims are to put countries close together that are similar in home percentage value and to put leagues close together that have similar numbers at the tournament.

Another example of arranging facets is shown in Figure 6.13 where the countries are put in order of the first time they hosted the Olympic Games. This matches the aim of the graphic better than a default alphabetic order.

Sorting into groups gets complicated when there are several grouping variables. Variables may be nested in a hierarchy, such as constituencies within regions or they may have no such structure, such as type of car, manufacturer, type of fuel. Groupings need to be found that reflect the aims of the study.

31.2.3   Mosaicplots

Mosaicplots offer a variety of ways of displaying multivariate categorical data. Both the order of the variables and the orders of the levels of the individual variables can have a big influence, as can the choice of mosaicplot form and whether variables are plotted horizontally or vertically (Hofmann (2008)).

There are two mosaicplots in Chapter 25 about the sinking of the Titanic, Figures 25.8 and 25.9, shown again in Figure 31.7. In the plot on the left the passenger classes have been drawn first in the natural order of first, second, third (alphabetic in English, but not in all languages), followed by the crew departments ordered by survival rates. This shows that survival rates declined by class and that the rates were lowest for the crew—excepting the small group of deck crew who would have manned the lifeboats. In the second plot on the right of only the passengers, sex has been drawn first with females to the left and males to the right, and class has been ordered within sex. Placing females first and then males means that there is a general decline in survival rate from left to right—apart from the low rate for males travelling second class.

In both plots the numbers in each group are shown by the widths of the bars. This information can be seen in many other plots. Here in the first plot it shows how small the two groups with differing survival rates amongst the crew are. In the second one it reminds readers that there were more male than female passengers and that the largest group was third class males.

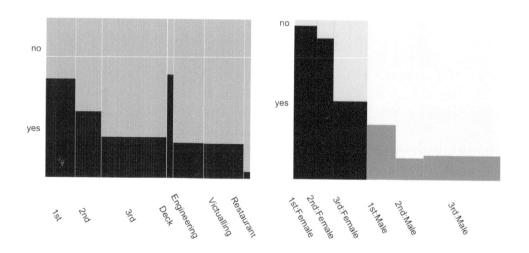

FIGURE 31.7: Mosaicplots of Titanic survival rates

In the analysis of software for facial recognition in Chapter 22 the plots are all drawn with males first and then females to emphasise the general error increase from left to right.

31.2.4 Parallel coordinate plots

Parallel coordinate plots are drawn with one horizontal axis and many vertical axes, one for each variable drawn. The ordering of the axes makes a major difference to what information can be seen. Orderings can be based on a variety of variable statistics.

Returning to the effect of decathlon events not being scored comparably, consider the differences in scores between competitors. Giving each competitor 50 points more in an event will not change overall rankings at all. Figure 31.8 is a parallel coordinate plot of points given to the top 79 ranked performances in the individual events with points for the 40th highest subtracted. Here the ranked values are joined by lines, not the individual competitors.

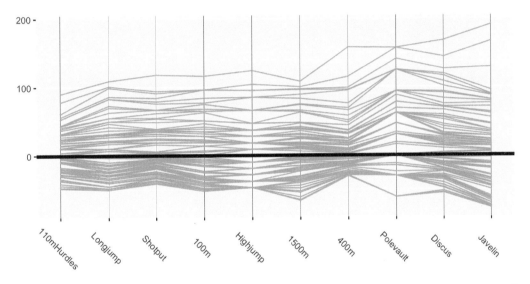

FIGURE 31.8: Parallel coordinate plot of the top 79 ranked scores for each decathlon event in April 2021

The nth highest polyline connects the nth best performance in each event. Subtracting the same statistic from the points score for each event makes the levels comparable while keeping the differences on the same scale. The zero line equivalent to the 40th best performance has been coloured brown. There is bigger variability above than below as the distributions are, of course, skewed. The events are not in the same order as in Figure 31.5. They have been ordered by increasing range. The lines are close to parallel for the first few events, implying similar distributions, including for the long jump and the 1500 metres, the two most different events in terms of points awarded. The javelin has greater variability, as observed already. The discrete nature of the high jump and pole vault points is because the bars are set at certain fixed heights that competitors either clear or fail to clear.

Parallel coordinates are excellent for studying the data from individual decathlon performances too. Now the polylines link performances of the same individual. The scales of the vertical axes are the same for each event and the same as in Figure 31.5. The difference in Figure 31.9 is that the events are ordered by increasing median event points.

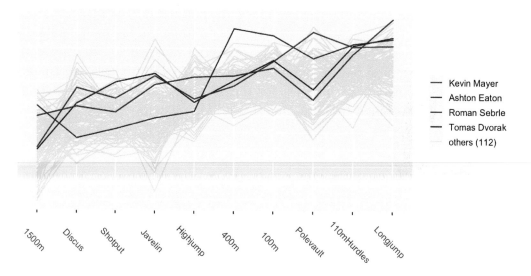

FIGURE 31.9: Parallel coordinate plot of the 10 decathlon events

The four best decathletes are listed in the legend in order of their total point scores. They have been highlighted in different colours and drawn last so that their lines appear on top. Mayer, the world record holder, is clearly better at the pole vault than the others highlighted. Eaton is strong in the four running events, particularly the 100 and 400 metres, where he is best of all the decathletes in the dataset. His weaknesses are the three throwing events.

So ordering is not only relevant for the variables in a parallel coordinate plot, it is advantageous for ordering the cases when they are coloured by groups (cf. Figure 31.9). The cases of most interest should always be drawn last, so that their polylines appear on top of the others. There are many other options influencing how parallel coordinate displays are drawn and all have to be considered together to get effective displays. Using more displays reveals more information.

At a more complex level, generalised parallel coordinate plots that can handle both numeric and categorical variables, are affected by several orderings: the order of the variable axes across the plot, the orders of the levels of categorical variables, the orders of the cases within category levels, and the order of the cases in the dataset (as this determines the order the lines are drawn). The **ggpcp** package offers tools for including categorical variables in parallel coordinate plots (Hofmann, VanderPlas, and Ge (2022)). Its key innovations are to draw each case individually and to order the cases within categories. These reduce the numbers of line crossings, make the display more readable, and make it possible to follow individual cases across the display.

Figure 31.10 shows Figures 18.7 and 18.8 from §18.2. The reordered version on the right is easier to decode.

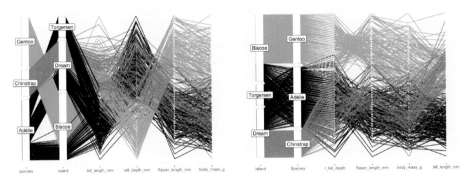

FIGURE 31.10: Parallel coordinate plots of the Palmer Penguin data (initial and reordered)

31.3 Numbers of orderings and sortings

Often there are surprisingly many possible orderings. The basic Titanic dataset has 4 variables. The `Survived` variable should doubtless always be the final variable, but the other three variables, `Class`, `Age`, and `Sex` could be ordered in 3!=6 ways. The categories of the three binary variables could each be ordered in 2 ways, making 8 in all. The four categories of `Class` have a natural order, but could be reversed giving another two possibilities. Altogether that makes 96 orderings of variables and categories that might be considered.

The letters of the word 'sorting' can be ordered themselves in 7! = 5040 ways, but only one other makes a common word, 'storing'. A random ordering would have little chance of making sense, although some subsets of the letters, for instance 'strong', 'ingots', 'string', or 'grist', would. Sortings and orderings in graphics have a better chance of conveying information, especially when guided by context and statistics. As always with graphics there is unlikely to be an 'optimal' solution, and so the task is more to find a set of informative sortings and orderings.

31.4   Arranging graphics

Ensembles of graphics are affected by how the individual graphics are arranged, as in Figure 13.1 and Figure 12.1. Other arrangements might not have fitted together as well or given a different impression. It is worth trying more than one, however informative a first arrangement appears.

Small multiples, named and popularised in Tufte (1983), are displays of many graphics of the same type and may have a natural order. The boxplots of chess rankings by age in Figure 8.19 are one example. Often there will be no such natural order, for instance in ordering variables in a scatterplot matrix. Grouping variables by type may be effective, as in §11.2, where two scatterplot matrices are drawn. The first one is for the three dimensions and carat and the second for carat and the remaining three continuous variables. Ordering by statistics of various kinds can be informative, the best strategy is to consider more than one ordering.

The arrangement of graphics in a faceted display is determined by the faceting variables chosen for the rows and columns, their ordering within rows and within columns, and the ordering of their category levels. This is apparent in Figure 23.4, drawn here as Figure 31.11, showing groups across four shearwater measurements. The rows are arranged first by `border` and then by `undertail`, the columns are ordered by `eyebrows`, and the order of each of those three variables has been specifically chosen. Other orderings would have made it more difficult to interpret the structure.

The 22 facets of Figure 3.13, showing numbers of films of different genres over the years, could have been drawn all with the same vertical scale or all with individual vertical scales. It seems more helpful to display them in rows with different vertical scales, but with the same scale across each row.

Main points

- Cases, categorical variable levels, variables can all be sorted and ordered.
- The impact of boxplots, faceted plots, mosaicplots, and parallel coordinate plots is strongly influenced by the orderings within the plots.
- Ordering categories is better than leaving them in a default alphabetic order.
- There are no best sortings and orderings: there are very many of them. Different alternatives may reveal different information.

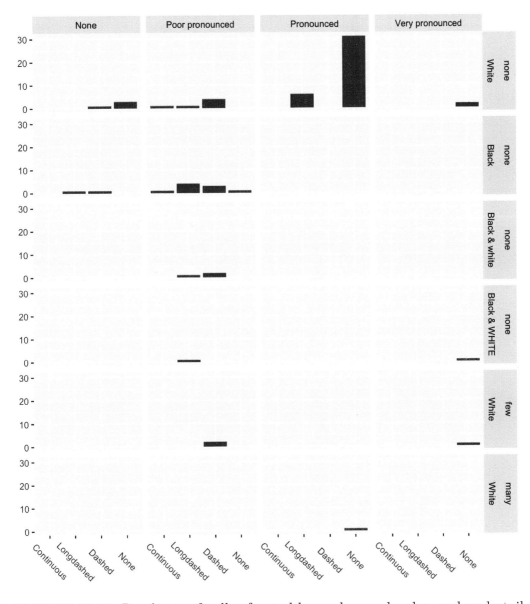

FIGURE 31.11: Barcharts of collar faceted by eyebrows, border, and undertail for the Audubon and Galápagos shearwaters

32

What affects interpretation?

As in most cases when the truth becomes clear you wonder how you could ever have seen things differently.

— Ruth Rendell, 'Not in the Flesh'

Interpreting graphics depends on paying attention to the graphics, understanding what is seen, and checking what is seen.

32.1 Attention

"Can you describe her?"

"It's a bit difficult. She was sort of middle-aged and ordinary."

"What was she wearing?"

"Tweeds, oatmeal flecked with brown, a three-quarter coat with patch pockets... a scarf, felt hat, brown shoes, a tussle shirt... and a small blue handkerchief in her breast pocket. I can't remember any more."

"You couldn't have been paying attention."

— Michael Redgrave questioning Margaret Lockwood in 'The Lady Vanishes'

Graphics texts generally consider perception and interpretation, including optical illusions, but do not pay as much attention to attention. There is an implicit assumption that viewers who look at a graphic are giving it their full attention. That seems as unrealistic as assuming that all the students attending a lecture are giving it their undivided attention.

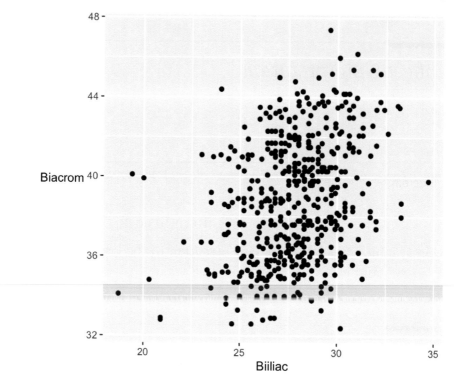

FIGURE 32.1: Scatterplot of Biacromial diameter against pelvic breadth (Biiliac) for 507 adults

Does Figure 32.1 demand attention? Someone might glance at it and decide the scatterplot did not look interesting. Perhaps the measurements did not mean anything to them or perhaps they did, but the topic did not attract them. They might have been distracted by the cup of coffee they had just made, by an email or by a noise in the street. They might have been tired or bored. Or, perhaps, they devoted sustained and concentrated attention to Figure 32.1. Graphics are often discussed objectively and yet there are many subjective factors affecting how they are viewed.

Biacromial diameter is a technical term for a measurement of the width between the shoulders and Biiliac may be described as "pelvic breadth". Knowing that might make someone look at the graphic more closely and think that is is surprising the two measurements are not more correlated. Many body measurements are. There are a few Biiliac values that appear lower than the rest. It is curious that the highest pelvic breadth value and two of the three lowest have about the same middling shoulder width.

A graphic without structure can be interesting because it was expected to have structure and did not or because there is more to it when additional information is included. Figure 32.2 colours the points of the plot by sex.

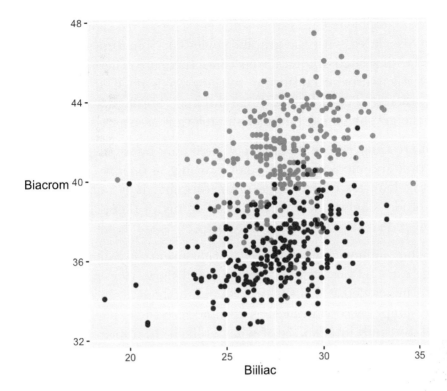

FIGURE 32.2: Scatterplot of Biacromial diameter (shoulder width) against Biiliac (pelvic breadth for 247 men (in green) and 260 women (in purple)

Generally, women have about the same pelvic breath as men but narrower shoulder widths. The displays in Figures 32.1 and 32.2 use data collected around twenty years ago (Heinz et al. (2003)). There are not many datasets of multivariate measurements of individuals and in working with this one, the authors' proviso should be remembered that "the sample is not a representative sample from a well-defined population". The R help file says it was men and women who were primarily in their twenties and thirties and who all exercised several hours a week, hardly typical of the general population.

If information is to be gained from a graphic, it has to be paid some attention. How much attention is paid and how that attention is paid are important. A quick scan of a display can suggest the type of graphic and what the overall structure could be. More focused and concentrated attention may be needed to confirm first impressions, to pick out additional features, and to consider what further information might be useful. Background knowledge of what the variables mean and of how the data were collected are needed, as is information about the quality of the data.

Inspecting a graphic once is rarely sufficient The source should be checked and any text associated with the graphic reviewed. Sometimes a graphic can be compared with related graphics, sometimes there are other questions that need to be investigated before returning to the graphic itself. If a graphic is worth drawing, then it should be worth careful and thorough study. This involves not just the graphic itself, but also any relevant associated information.

Initial impressions can be deceptive. There may be several features that can be seen in a graphic and rather than fixating on one, it is more effective to consciously look for others. Like brainstorming, it is helpful to generate a number of ideas before being too critical of any of them. As always, varying the shape and size of the display may help.

Expectations influence what is seen, either negatively or positively. If there are strong expectations of what a graphic will show, viewers may only look for corroborating evidence On the other hand, if there are no expectations then they may simply accept what they see and lose the capacity to be surprised. It is best to think in advance of what is likely to appear and to look more closely—even if expectations are met.

32.1.1   Types of attention

Before paying full attention, there is what is referred to as preattentive processing (although attention does play a role, Healey and Enns (2012)). People can pick out 2 red dots in a cloud of blue dots without even trying. They might then use focused attention to concentrate on those points and their neighbourhoods or they might distribute their attention over the whole display looking for other features.

Sometimes something may catch a viewer's eye when they are not looking directly at it, thanks to their peripheral vision. Potter et al. (2014) concludes that in certain circumstances people can see meaning in a photograph within 13 ms. Perhaps that ability encourages them to only glance at graphics, and not try to see more in them. Even if graphics are studied more closely, there is the effect that Barbara Tversky calls the fourth law of cognition (Tversky (2019)): The mind can override perception. She writes: "We don't always look, even when the answer is right in front of our eyes. Memory overrides perception." Both effects contribute to explaining why graphics are often poorly interpreted. The fourth law of cognition may also underlie why some graphics are poorly described by their own authors. They may be writing about what they wanted to present and not what can be seen in the graphic.

What attention is paid to may be goal-driven (top-down), stimulus-driven (bottom-up) or history-based (depending on the viewer's experience). The goal of drawing the map of German election results in Figure 26.16, repeated here in Figure 32.3, was to see if there were geographical patterns. The main ones for the CDU, CSU, SPD, and AfD stand out (goal-driven). The smaller constituencies where the Greens did well imply that they did well in urban areas and the fact that Die Linke party are in the legend means they must have won seats somewhere (stimulus-driven). Political maps give poor representations of party support because they display areas and not populations (history-based).

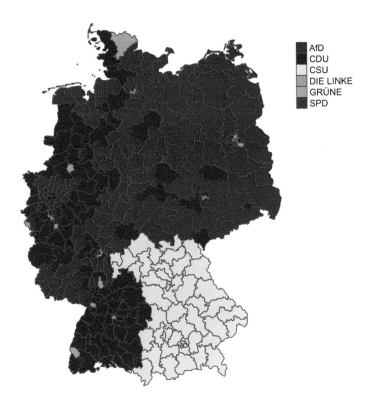

FIGURE 32.3: Winners of Erststimmen seats by political party in Germany 2021

Theeuwes (2018) claims that stimulus-driven and history-based attention selection are effortless, while goal-driven requires effort. His research is related to dynamic situations, such as driving, but is still relevant. It is easier to respond to a strong feature or recognise a familiar pattern than to identify a feature that may or may not be associated with a particular goal. Having experience of what types of feature a graphic can show is valuable.

Studying a graphic display closely may reveal a number of features, yet frequently a later inspection of the same graphic can reveal other features. It is useful to look at graphics afresh, to break the train of thought. A graphic you have drawn yourself or is on the web can be varied by changing the size, the aspect ratio or the position on screen. You can change the colours, the symbols and the scales in your own graphics. You could zoom out to see where the data lie on some grander scale or you could zoom in to investigate a small sector in detail. The more complex the plot, the more options there are. Multivariate displays like parallel coordinate plots and mosaicplots have a particularly large number of alternative options, especially the numbers of possible orderings. Different graphics can be used for the same data, e.g., boxplots or density estimates instead of histograms for single continuous variables. Graphics for related variables in the same dataset can be drawn. The essential principle is to regard graphics as doorways to information, not as static pictures.

Presentation graphics are sometimes designed to attract attention to make them memorable, sometimes to direct attention to a feature in them. It is easy to make a display memorable by adding an outlandish touch, overly dramatic colours or exotic background pictures. Whether the graphic's information is then also memorable is another question.

32.1.2   Cognitive load

Complex graphics can be difficult to study and understand. Sometimes graphics in scientific articles are complex and tightly packed with information because space is limited. Sometimes a complex graphic is just a good summary of complex data, as with Figure 13.7 or Figure 18.8, shown again in Figure 32.4.

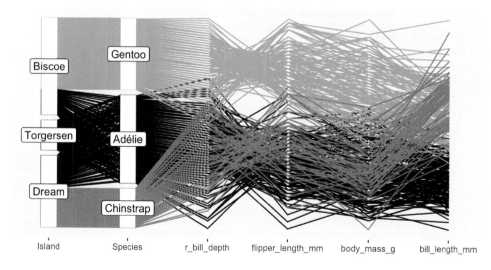

FIGURE 32.4: Reordered parallel coordinate plot of the Palmer Penguin data

Muddled graphics can be difficult to understand for other reasons. Anything that increases the cognitive load or mental effort required to look at a graphic should be avoided. Having graphics and accompanying text on different pages demands extra effort. Poor labelling and awkward scales make work. A poorly ordered and positioned legend does not help. Overlapping text and confusing colours need to be disentangled. Data points that are too close to axes or borders can be difficult to distinguish. Comparisons are made more difficult if scales that should be the same are not or if graphics to be compared are not aligned as they should be.

32.1.3 Rewards for paying attention

Paying close attention to graphics can reveal much more information. The Gapminder life expectancy graphic of Figure 2.1 and Figure 3.9 for movie ratings, both shown again in Figure 32.5, are striking examples. Figure 4.6 for the 1912 Democratic choice of candidate is another.

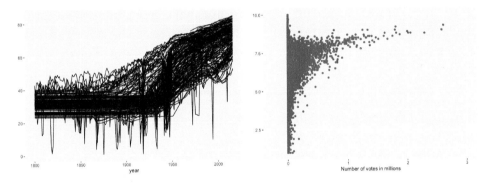

FIGURE 32.5: Gapminder life expectancy data (left) and movie ratings (right)

Accepting the title of a graphic or what other accompanying text says may not tell the full story. It is worth paying graphics detailed attention. However, relying on graphics alone will not be sufficient. Graphics have a background and context and need to be understood within that framework. A closer look at the data underlying a graphic is warranted too.

32.2   Understanding

The more I practise, the luckier I get.

— the golfer Gary Player

32.2.1   Knowledge

Knowledge of what graphic forms represent is necessary to understand what information features might convey. Individual graphics have a general structure with local details that suggest additional information. Combined with other graphics they provide an overall picture of the data whose interpretation will depend on the context and background. Familiarity with what features may arise, and why, makes it easier to understand what is being shown by the graphics for a new dataset.

Some of the graphics literature is concerned with new, innovative graphics, emphasising novelty over familiarity. The advantage is the novelty itself, the attraction to viewers of something unknown, possibly striking. The disadvantage is viewers' lack of experience with the form. While new developments are welcome, viewers will see more with graphics they are familiar with.

Background knowledge is also indispensable, whether your own or that of collaborating domain experts. With data by country over time it was necessary to know how countries have changed (e.g., Chapters 2, 8, Chapters 6, and 15). With swimming, information on the rules for different strokes, on full body swimsuits, and on the introduction of the butterfly was valuable (Chapter 20). Another swimming example, Figure 20.11, repeated here as Figure 32.6, concerned the reasons why the best 200 times for individuals and relay teams were so different.

Much can be found out about the Olympics on the web, such as stories surrounding particular events, how times were measured, when rules were changed (Chapter 6), but you have to look. The web is not always helpful. Going back to original documentation can be, as with the articles by Michelson and Newcomb on their attempts to measure the speed of light (Chapter 5), and with getting the full survey from Annenberg that included the gay rights questions (Chapter 9). Often dataset owners/maintainers are very helpful as happened with Chapters 17 and 21.

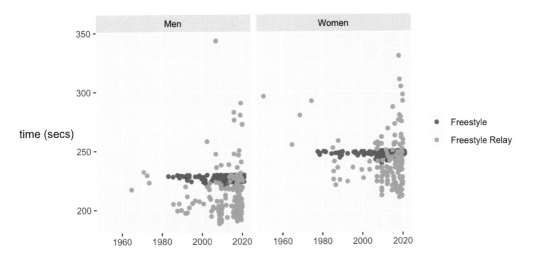

FIGURE 32.6: Best times for the 400 m freestyle events for men and women, individual (red) and relay (blue)

32.2.2 Experience

What do people pay attention to when they visit a famous building? Architects will study the building. Historians may study the symbolism, and locals will have their own ideas about what stands out. What can be seen happening during a sporting event? Coaches will view it differently than fans, and with team games, different sets of fans will see the same game very differently (Hastorf and Cantril (1954)). In these situations it comes down to motives, interest and background knowledge, education, and experience. The same goes for looking at graphics. Motives may vary between viewers, interest and background knowledge can hopefully be assumed, but education and experience can not. It is helpful to study how to look at graphics and to look at a lot of graphics to learn how to recognise what might be seen in them. Just looking is not enough. Or as Spear put it: "there is quite a difference between simply looking at a chart and seeing it." (Spear (1969)).

And what should be looked at in a graphic? If researchers have no experience, it is hard for them to know what to look for. De Groot showed that international master chess players chose better moves than club players because they recognised the structure of positions (Groot (1978), a second edition in English of his Dutch thesis from 1946). The same doubtless applies to viewers studying graphics. If they are familiar with data graphics and understanding and interpreting them, they will find it easier to understand and interpret graphics from a new dataset.

The peaks in the finishing times for the Comrades marathon in Figure 21.9, drawn again in Figure 32.7, are an example. Others have seen similar patterns in other marathon races (marastats (2019)).

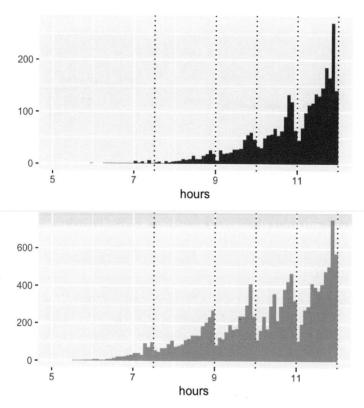

FIGURE 32.7: Finishing times in the 2019 race for females (above) and males (below), dotted lines mark limits for awarding medals other than gold

32.2.3   Possible cognitive biases

Even if you pay proper attention there may be influences hindering your making proper use of what you see. Examples of forms of cognitive bias include

- Confirmation bias: look for information supporting prior beliefs

- Hindsight bias: past events seem more likely than they were

- Recency bias: recent events are more important than historic ones

- Anchoring bias: overemphasise the effect of a reference point. It can mean anchoring thoughts about a graphic to what is seen first. It is always best to look at the data in different ways, developing alternative perspectives.

- Availability bias: rely too much on examples to hand. Data are available on the web for Olympic results that were missing in Figure 6.8, shown again here as Figure 32.8, but discussing the problems is more instructive (and less effort) than solving them in this case.

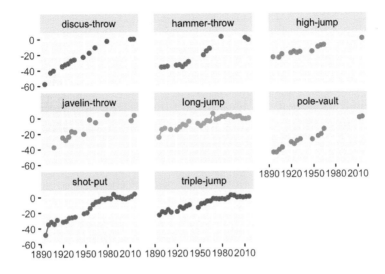

FIGURE 32.8: Athletics field events for men: percentage differences in gold medal performances compared with averages over the last six Games

- Representativeness bias: use particular examples without taking account of sample size and base rates. Avoid by using spineplots for comparing rates (e.g., in Figure 9.3) and UpAndDown plots for comparing changes, as in Figure 26.4, drawn again in Figure 32.9.

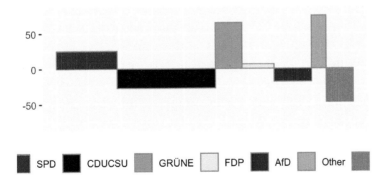

FIGURE 32.9: An UpAndDown plot showing absolute changes in party support between the last two German elections as area and relative changes as height

- Perceptual bias: we see what we want to see

32.3   Checking

Aristotle maintained that women have fewer teeth than men; although he was twice married, it never occurred to him to verify this statement by examining his wives' mouths.

— Bertrand Russell, The Impact of Science on Society

Published graphics may appear polished, attractive, and convincing. Photographs prepared by estate agents for houses they are selling may also be described that way. Many graphics were drawn first and discarded just as many more photographs were taken than are used. Scepticism and thorough checking are called for. Popper's concept of falsification suggests that it is better to search for evidence to refute your impressions than to look for supporting evidence. As xkcd has pointed out (xkcd (2012)), with enough options you have a good chance of finding something that looks significant that is not. Checking develops your own trust in your conclusions and should help to convince others. There are several independent ways of checking features detected in graphics.

32.3.1   Provenance

Are the data from a reliable source? Is it known how they were collected, edited, and summarised? Are they precise measurements or uncertain estimates? Do the variables mean what you think they do or have they been defined or collected differently? All this and more is discussed in Chapter 27.

32.3.2   Looking at the numbers

Do the scales look sensible? Perhaps the minima or maxima look too extreme (Figure 2.2 (left) or Figure 3.1). Do the data appear to be complete? Perhaps there are gaps in the data (Figures 3.6, 6.8, or 11.5) or missing categories (Figures 6.4 to 6.6). Categories that are missing altogether can be difficult to spot. Political opinion polls show party support, but not always how many who were asked did not respond. Maybe the data just look wrong, as in Figure 10.8 for differences in spaceflight mission times.

Sometimes there is heaping at particular values, usually due to rounding (Figure 3.2), sometimes particular values are never recorded (Figure 11.5). Sometimes all the data have been rounded, so that a continuous measurement appears to be discrete. If you ask people what their height is they will report a rounded, possibly inaccurate number. Better data would be obtained by measuring heights in a uniform way under identical conditions for all (Student (1931)).

32.3.3   Varying plots

Graphics redrawn in different ways leave different impressions, emphasising different information. Size, aspect ratio, and position can strongly influence what can be seen. Graphics can be resized, moved, and zoomed in or out. Plot options can be changed: maxima and minima of scales, origin location, histogram binwidths, point sizes, colours, ... Whether some variations are better than others is neither here nor there: the important principle is to check several. Figure 30.12 shows an example for the gay rights data. Figure 32.10 displays a default histogram for the movie runtimes and the one used in the chapter, Figure 3.2, including only films of 3 hours or under and using a binwidth of 1 minute. Far more graphics were drawn for each case study than are included in the book.

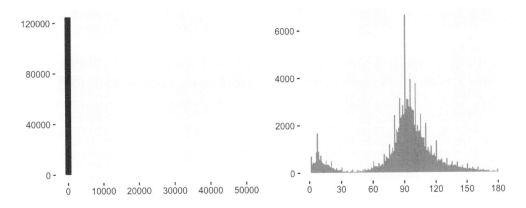

FIGURE 32.10: Histograms of movie runtimes, the default on the left and a varied one on the right (note the different scales)

32.3.4   Varying plot forms

Drawing different kinds of plots of the same variable(s) provides new insights: a boxplot or density estimate instead of a histogram (Figures 5.3 to 5.5 or Figures 8.1 and 8.2), scatterplots by group (faceting) instead of a single scatterplot (Figures 2.5 and 2.6), a doubledecker plot instead of stacked barcharts (Figure 9.3).

32.3.5   Statistical checks

Statistical models and graphics complement and augment one another, although it is an unbalanced relationship. There are almost always graphical ways of visually assessing the results of statistical models, but there are not always statistical models that can evaluate ideas derived from graphics. If there are, they should be used. If it looks as if there is a nonlinear relationship between two variables in a scatterplot, then a spline model could be fit. This was used for modelling trend in Figure 8.22 for ratings of Chess players and Figure 16.2 for proportions of draws in different football leagues. Both are drawn here again in Figure 32.11.

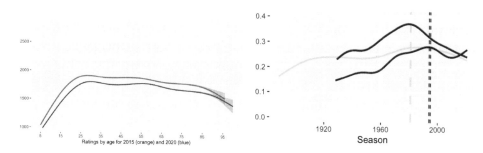

FIGURE 32.11: Smooths of chess ratings (left) and football league draws (right)

If a spineplot suggests two categorical variables are not independent, a chi-squared test could be used. More complicated data, such as the survival rates on the Titanic in Figure 31.7, could be examined using logistic regression.

Examples where statistical models are not so readily available include assessing possible outliers in a scatterplot and whether there are multiple modes in a histogram.

32.3.6 Checking consequences

- Internal checking
  Are patterns across the whole dataset also found in subgroups? The surprising peak in the chess ratings at 2000 shown in Figure 8.1 was explained by comparing ratings for active and inactive players in Figure 8.3, shown here again as Figure 32.12.

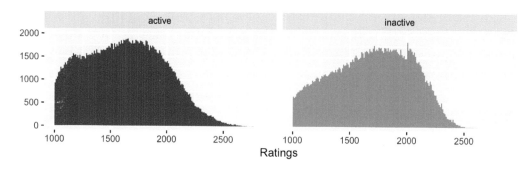

FIGURE 32.12: Ratings of active and inactive chess players in 2020

The decline in survival rate across the Titanic's three passenger classes applied to women, but not to men (Figures 25.8 and 25.9). Conclusions might have implications for other variables and it is useful to see if patterns are consistent across a dataset.

- External checking
  If relevant data can be found, compare results with other related datasets (§4.2, §8.4 or Figure 26.18, drawn again here as Figure 32.13).

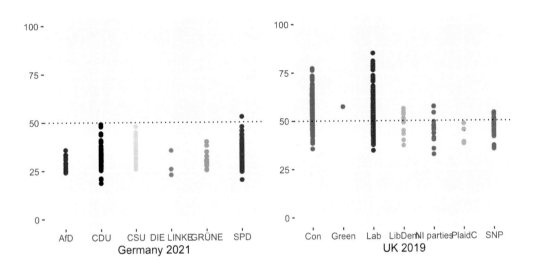

FIGURE 32.13: Seat-winning percentages by party in Germany 2021 and in the UK 2019

32.3.7   Context

Results have to make sense and be interpreted in context. A pattern of points in a scatterplot will be judged in different ways for different datasets or different variables (Figure 33.1). Errors like negative heights or zero dimensions (Figure 11.1) are obvious. Weekly patterns in sightings by birdwatchers or in disease reporting may need to be checked. More birdwatchers may be out and about at weekends and reporting of diseases may be influenced by media attention. Differences in mortality rates between countries or over time may be due to definitions, conditions or treatments as Covid pandemic statistics have illustrated.

In comparing opinions on same-sex marriage from Figure 9.9, redrawn here as Figure 32.14, it is well to remember that the questions were about different situations, that they were framed differently, and that only a third of the sample were asked the state question.

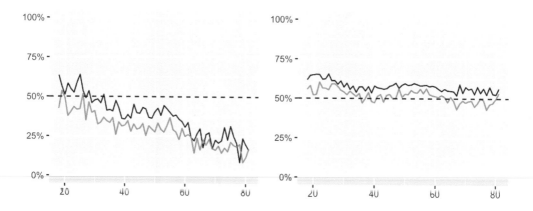

FIGURE 32.14: Line plots of support for same-sex marriage at federal level (left) and opposition to a Constitutional Amendment (right) by age of respondent by males (green) and females (purple)

32.3.8   Discussing with others, especially domain experts

What one person sees when they look at a graphic may not be what another person sees. Combining opinions is more effective than relying on one person's views—provided that the opinions are independent. Graphics analysts will not have the subject knowledge of experts in the field and they should be consulted. Amongst other topics expertise was sought on chess ratings (Chapter 8), ornithology (Chapters 14, 18, and 23), swimming (Chapter 20), and German elections (Chapter 26). The role of Ausgleichsmandate in making the German parliament much larger than intended was important information gained. This was shown in Figure 26.1, repeated in Figure 32.15.

32.3.9   Replicate

All of the checks listed so far can be carried out relatively quickly. The ideal would be to attempt to independently replicate results. Replication should be possible for scientific studies by having different researchers carry out fresh studies in different environments. This may be impractical for reasons of time, organisation, and finance, but is the ideal to aim for. Examples include estimating the speed of light (Chapter 5), evaluating treatment of psoriasis (Chapter 12), and distinguishing shearwaters (Chapter 23).

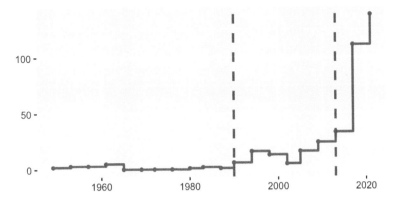

FIGURE 32.15: Extra seats in German elections since 1949. Each point marks the date of an election. The left dashed line marks the first election after reunification in October 1990. The right dashed line marks the first election with Ausgleichsmandate.

If datasets are large, a partial replication can be achieved by splitting the dataset into independent groups by sampling. This was suggested in connection with fitting a smooth to the chess ratings data in Figure 8.18.

Some datasets are regularly updated, e.g., movies (Chapter 3, fuel efficiency (Chapter 17, and elections (Chapter 26. Results can then be checked for consistency over time.

32.3.10   Example of checking

The best times for swimming events were studied in Chapter 20. The form observed in the first plot for the 100 m freestyle for men, Figure 20.1, was checked by looking at other strokes and other distances. The possibility of an overlap in times between female butterfly and freestyle swimmers in Figure 20.3 was checked by drawing a different display, multiple boxplots, in Figure 20.4. This display was also drawn horizontally rather than vertically, to make better use of space and to provide an alternative point of view. The data behind the outlier in Figure 20.5 was checked and a classification error was uncovered: it was a time for that swimmer at that competition, but in a different event.

The displays for 50 m races and 200 m for men and women, Figures 20.3 and 20.5, were different in one important respect: the backstroke swimmers caught up on the butterfly swimmers. Checking with swimming experts revealed the reason, the different rules on turning between lengths for the events. The figures are shown again in Figure 32.16. Note the different vertical scales of the left and right plots.

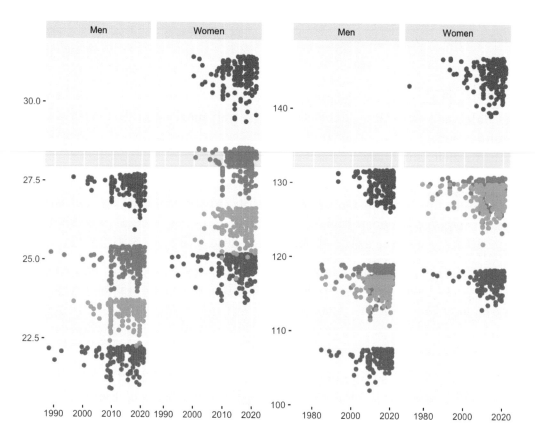

FIGURE 32.16: Best times in seconds for the four 50 m (left) and four 200 m (right) swimming events achieved by men and women in the order breaststroke, backstroke, butterfly, freestyle from the top

Main points

- Attention varies depending on goals and conditions. Excessive cognitive load should be avoided.
- Successful understanding depends on knowledge, experience, and avoiding biases.
- There are many ways to check ideas and all should be used.

33

Varieties of plots, developing plots

"I repeat, as long as you have studied the theory hard enough"

"And what good's theory going to be in the real world?" said Harry loudly, his fist in the air again.

— Professor Dolores Umbridge and Harry Potter in 'Harry Potter and the Order of the Phoenix'

33.1 Varying various plots

There is a wide variety of plot types available (e.g., see Holtz (2018) or Schwabish (2021)). Each plot type can also be drawn in many different ways: varying size, aspect ratio, scales, colour, symbols, styles, whatever. A key message of this book is that drawing a variety of plots, and varying the plots drawn, can provide more insights than searching for a single 'optimal' display. Just as taking many photographs of a complicated object can help people appreciate its structure, so can drawing many graphics help viewers grasp the structure of a dataset.

Approaches vary too. Some like to study individual graphics thoroughly before moving on to other ones. Some like to flick through lots of graphics and then return to particular ones for a closer look. Being swamped by too many graphics can be as unsatisfactory as not having enough. As yet there is little guidance available on how to explore large datasets effectively.

Not all graphics are the same. There are different types of graphics—histograms, barcharts, scatterplots, and so on, there are different types of data displayed in graphics—individual cases, aggregates, statistics, parameter estimates, residuals, and so on, and there are different uses for graphics—exploration, explanation, and exposition (or presentation). Accordingly, the same display may be interpreted in different ways depending on its context and on what kind of data it represents.

For illustration, consider the 100 m freestyle swimming event, one which has been swum by both men and women at all Olympics since 1912. Figure 33.1 shows four scatterplots of the data. Top left is a scatterplot of the times in seconds for the male and female gold and silver medal winners by Olympic year. Times improved relatively steadily after initial high values. It is likely that the females are the group of higher points and the males the group of lower ones (which could be confirmed by using colour). Differences in gold and silver performances at later Games can barely be seen. Top right is a scatterplot of gold medal times of women against those of men. The winning times are strongly correlated. Lower left is a Tukey mean-difference plot for the differences between gold and silver times for men. There are two extreme values, one to the right for the (relatively) slow times of 1896 and one up high in 1924 when Johnny Weissmuller won by a very large margin. Interestingly that hardly shows in the first plot. The most surprising point is the negative value—from 1960 at Rome. After much discussion Lance Larson was awarded the silver medal by the judges although the handtiming then used gave him a faster time than John Devitt to whom the judges awarded the gold medal. Lower right is a residual against fitted plot for a simple linear model of women's gold medal times as a function of men's gold medal times. The gold medal for women has been shared twice (in 1984 and 2016), so it was necessary to remove one gold medal record for each of those years. The plot shows that a curvilinear model would give a better fit.

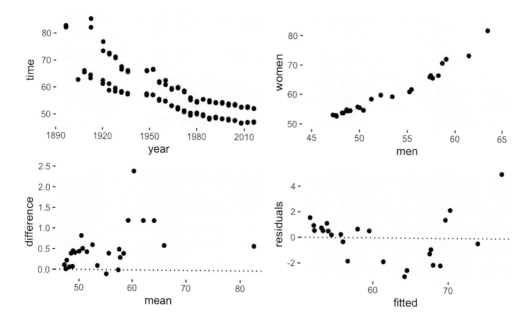

FIGURE 33.1: Four different kinds of scatterplot of data for gold and silver medal performances by men and women in the Olympic freestyle 100 m

A set of boxplots in parallel could be plots of individual variables or plots of one variable conditioned on another. Figure 33.2 displays two groups of boxplots. Above, there are boxplots of the five beak measurements for Darwin's finches in the Isabela Island dataset (Chapter 14). All are skewed to the right, especially beak height and width, doubtless due to the mix of species. Below, there are boxplots of beak height for the five species on Isabela Island. Two have clearly bigger beak heights than the other three. It is important to indicate what kind of plot each is. Titles and colour can help (intentionally left out here), as can using boxplot widths to show group sizes. Barring missing values (there are none here) the boxplots are based on equal numbers of cases in the first plot. In the second the numbers vary from 11 *fortis platyrhyncha* to 81 *fuliginosa parvula*.

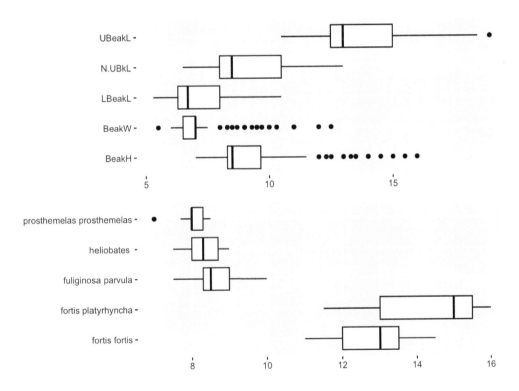

FIGURE 33.2: Boxplots of beak measurements (above) and beak height by species (below) on Isabela Island

The individual graphics of Figures 33.1 and 33.2 have purposely been drawn similarly. In practice groups of graphics like this would be drawn distinctly. For instance, whatever else one might think of them, the four graphics standardly produced by plotting a model in R are. The danger lies more in glancing quickly at isolated, individual graphics and not checking what they display.

33.2   Ensembles of plots

Thanks to trellis plots (Becker, Cleveland, and Shyu (1996)), lattice plots
(Sarkar (2008)), and faceting (Wilkinson (1999) and Wickham (2016)), displays
of small multiples are well understood. Each of the component plots is of
the same type and is conditioned on other dataset variables. By comparison,
ensembles made up of different types of plots have been less discussed. Unwin
and Valero-Mora (2018) suggest that the key element is coherence: having a
coherent theme, a coherent alignment, coherent look, consistent scales and formatting. Examples include Figures 3.4 and 15.1, and the set of four Figures 18.1
to 18.4. Another example is Figure 21.8, repeated here as Figure 33.3.

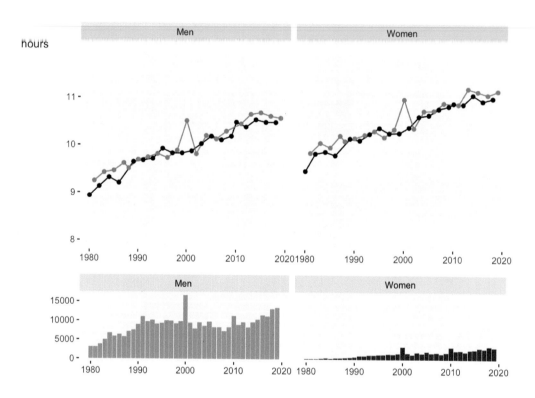

FIGURE 33.3: Median times for men and women for "up" (orange) and "down"
(black) races of the Comrades Marathon since 1980

The graphics are aligned horizontally and vertically, as are the scales. The
colours above refer to the "up" and "down" races, while the colours below refer
to the sex of the runners.

A more complex ensemble is shown in Figure 12.1 reproduced here as Figure 33.4. Three separate pieces of information are compared for the two groups with three different sets of graphics: proportions of dropouts in a barchart, two initial measurements in scatterplots, ten life quality index question means with line charts. There is no need for common scaling as the variable scales all differ. The groups are coloured alike in the scatterplots and the line charts, but not in the barchart, where the dropouts are coloured to emphasise how few there were and how similar the proportions were. The lines are drawn differently according to whether the responses were at the start or end of the study.

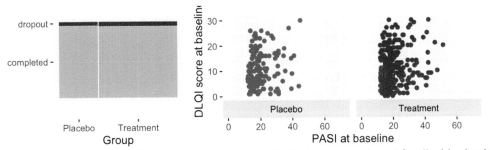

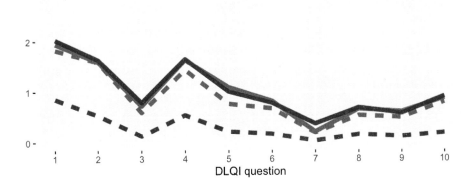

FIGURE 33.4: The spineplot top left shows that the treatment group was much bigger than the placebo group and that the dropout rate was small, about the same for both groups. The scatterplots of PASI scores and DLQI scores at the start of the study top right show that the two groups had similar initial distributions. The bottom plot shows that the average initial scores on each of the 10 questions were similar for the two groups (solid lines) and mostly slightly lower for the placebo group after 16 weeks (blue dashed line). For the treatment group the average scores were substantially less on all questions (dark orange dashed line)

33.3   Differences between early drafts and later graphics

Quickly drawn default graphics can reveal valuable information. Taking the time to improve them can make it easier to see this information by making it stand out and can uncover further information. It is instructive to compare pairs of initial and better graphics to study what changes might be made and how effective they are. Readers will have different opinions on what might be done and how. They are welcome to experiment with the data themselves.

The term "initial" here usually means that the graphic has been drawn after some data cleaning. Quite often the first graphics drawn indicate further data problems of one kind or another that require data wrangling to fix. So there can be many early graphics, just as there can be many later graphics that are amended in a range of ways. What there cannot be is a final graphic; there are always potential alternatives. And whatever improvements can be made to individual graphics, most information will be gathered by looking at more than one data display—however good an individual graphic is.

33.3.1   1912 Democratic Convention

Chapter 4 studied the selection of the Democratic candidate for President at the 1912 Convention. The voting was initially shown in Figure 4.1 and later, with changes, in Figure 4.6. The two plots are shown here in Figures 33.5 and 33.6. The changes made are listed below.

The main features seen in the first plot were that there were many candidates, but only a few serious ones; that Clark was ahead initially, particularly after the 10th ballot; that Wilson gained steadily and made the decisive breakthrough around the 43rd ballot. The second plot emphasises the key changes and shows that the breakthrough for Wilson took place on the ballot after the last adjournment.

Changes include:

1. The simple order of ballots on the horizontal scale has been replaced by estimated ballot times.

2. Only candidates who received over 35 votes in at least one ballot have been included. This was to concentrate on the main candidates and reduce the clutter due to minor candidates who never had much support. The legend in Figure 33.5 listed 13 candidates and the cate-

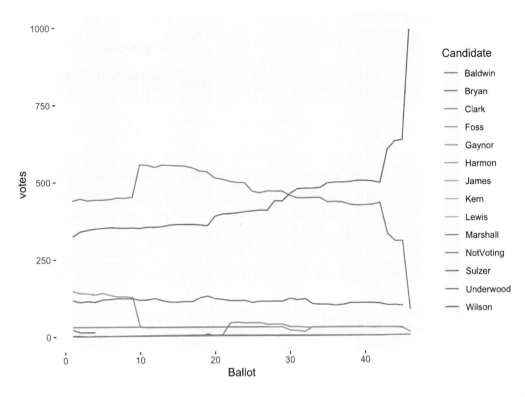

FIGURE 33.5: Voting at the 1912 Democratic convention shown in the initial plot

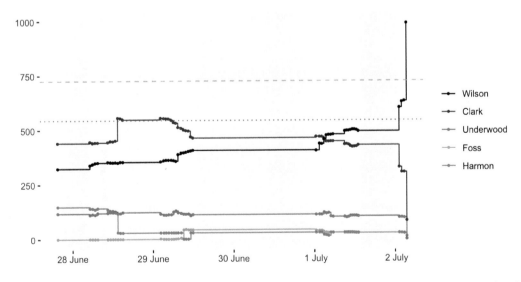

FIGURE 33.6: Voting at the 1912 Democratic convention shown in the final plot

gory "Notvoting". Figure 33.6 displays the voting for only 5 candidates.

3. The plot background has been coloured white when the convention was in session and grey when it was not.

4. The aspect ratio of the plot has been changed to 0.5. Time series are generally better wider than tall, not square or taller than wide.

5. The dataset has been expanded to include ballots in which the candidates got zero votes. Otherwise the lines for candidates who withdrew were left hanging and the connecting lines for candidates who had no support for some intermediate ballots were not correctly drawn (as happened in Figure 33.5 for Harmon).

6. Vote changes have been shown by vertical lines when the ballot occurred, not as a sloping line between consecutive ballots. This reflects what actually happened. A disadvantage is where lines are drawn on top of one another, as at the last ballot.

7. Points have been drawn for each ballot to emphasise when and how often they took place, especially when very little changed between ballots.

8. Horizontal lines have been added at two-thirds support (needed to win the nomination) and at 50% support. Both levels played important parts in the convention. (At the Republican convention a simple majority sufficed.)

9. A colour blind scale has been used instead of the default colour scale. Colour blind scales assist in distinguishing the candidates.

10. Candidates have been plotted in reverse order of their votes in the penultimate ballot so that if two candidates overlap the colour of the candidate with more votes is on top.

11. The legend order has been changed to match the order in the last few ballots. This makes it easier to identify the lines for each candidate.

12. The legend title and the vertical axis label have been removed. These texts are not necessary and take up space and attention.

33.3.2 Gapminder Life Expectancies

The first plot in Chapter 2, Figure 2.1 showed how life expectancy changed for many countries round the world over the past 200 years. Several insights could be derived, but the display was overcrowded and there might have been more information in the data. Figure 2.6 was an alternative version with the countries faceted and coloured by region. Figure 33.7 displays both figures.

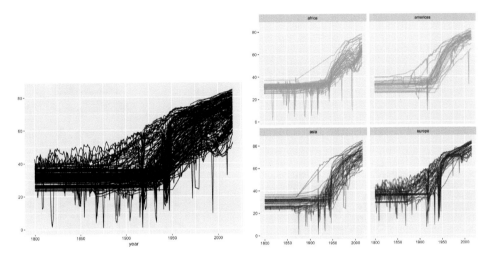

FIGURE 33.7: Gapminder life expectancy data drawn for all countries (left) and with countries grouped by region (right)

The initial plot shows the steady increase in life expectancy in the 20th century, the surprisingly constant values for many countries in the 19th century, and occasional sharp falls and rises for individual countries. The later plot shows that life expectancy was generally higher in Europe than elsewhere in the 19th century, that the overall patterns, if not the levels, were similar in all four regions, and that there were countries whose life expectancy graphs differed strikingly from others in their region.

Changes include:

1. The countries have been coloured by region to provide some information on geographic location.

2. Each region has been plotted separately so that regional differences and local outliers can be seen.

3. Some 13 small countries with incomplete data were excluded as they provided little information.

33.3.3 Electric car charging

Chapter 13 included two graphics of the use of charging stations over time, Figure 13.5 and Figure 13.7. They are drawn here as side by side in smaller form in Figure 33.8.

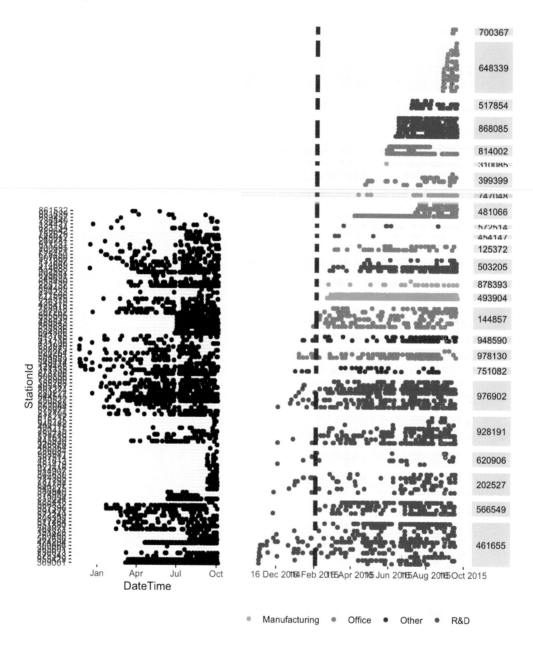

FIGURE 33.8: When charging stations were used

From the first plot it is apparent that a number of charging stations only started to be used late on in the study, and that some charging stations were used relatively little. The second plot highlights when the testing phase stopped. It shows that some charging locations were little used, that office locations came later than R&D locations, that there were differences worth investigating further in patterns of use of charging stations at the same location.

Changes include:

1. Using a high aspect ratio for the amended plot in Figure 13.7 to show the points for the individual charging stations better.

2. Sorting charging stations by location to be able to see how usage of neighbouring stations compares.

3. Ordering locations by first use to put them in an order matching the development of the study.

4. Ordering charging stations within location to show how the installations developed.

5. Colouring facility types to highlight group differences.

6. Drawing a dashed red line at the time the study switched from the test phase to the analysis phase. This emphasises how many locations were not used (not available?) during the test phase.

7. Dropping the vertical axis label and the individual Station IDs. The caption makes clear what is shown vertically and the Station IDs are just codes that provide little information.

8. Adding Location ID labels. Although the labels are uninterpretable codes, they do emphasise that the locations are different. Should someone have access to which locations those codes relate to, they could look up the details.

9. The date formatting in the default plot is does not include the year and does not explain where in a month the month's name is placed. Detailed dates provide better context. The horizontal axis label was dropped as the name was uninformative and it is obvious from the more detailed labelling that time is being plotted.

Additionally a much fuller caption was used in the amended plot in Chapter 13.

33.3.4   Gay rights

The choropleth map in Chapter 9, Figure 9.4 gave an overview of the geographic distribution of support for same-sex marriage at state level. Individual states have very different population sizes and the survey design reflected that. A default plot of confidence intervals for the state estimates is shown here with the amended plot drawn in the chapter, Figure 9.5, in Figure 33.9.

The first plot shows that states have different rates and different confidence interval lengths. Many pairs of confidence intervals do not overlap. The second plot shows that: the few states with over 50% support are in the North East; Washington DC and Delaware have rates more like the North East than the South; MidWest states have similar rates to each other; the Dakotas have broader intervals (i.e. smaller survey samples matching smaller populations).

Changes include:

1. The states have been sorted by Census Bureau region so that local comparisons are easier.

2. States have been ordered by estimate within region, again to facilitate comparisons.

3. Estimates have been coloured by region to differentiate the groups.

4. Points have been drawn bigger to make the estimates themselves stand out more.

5. Intervals have been drawn as straight lines without end bars to reduce clutter and give less emphasis to the smaller states.

6. Horizontal scaling has been changed to percentages instead of proportions to better match the data.

7. Horizontal limits have been set to [0,100%] to avoid false impressions of the amount of support.

8. Breakpoints on the horizontal axis have been chosen to include the critical 50% value, so that it is easy to see which intervals do not even reach majority support.

9. Axis name labels have been dropped to leave more space for the graphic.

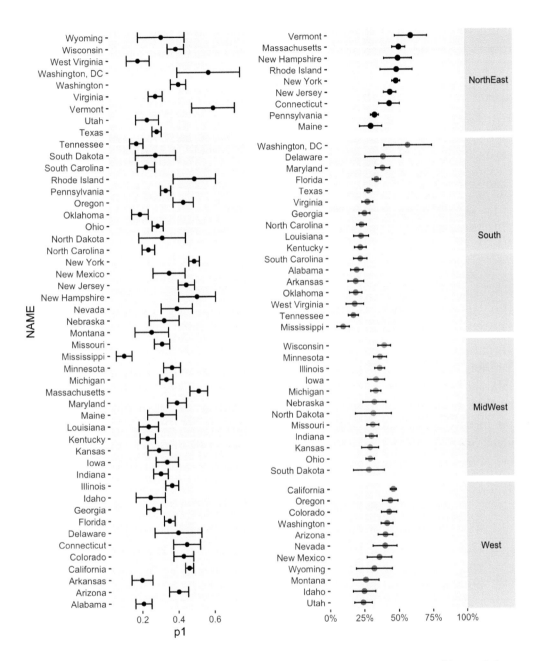

FIGURE 33.9: Support for same-sex marriage by state with 95% confidence intervals

33.3.5   Human space flight

Figure 10.4 in Chapter 10 shows the mission time of space flights by year of
flight. If the flights went to a space station, they were coloured accordingly in
Figure 10.5. The final version after taking logarithms was given in Figure 10.6.
Figures 10.4 and Figure 10.6 are redrawn here as Figure 33.10.

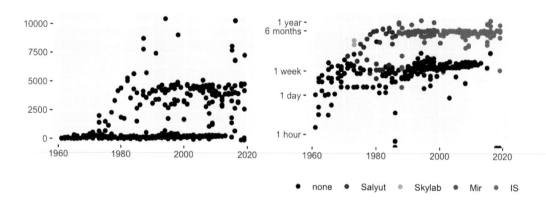

FIGURE 33.10: Mission times by year (left) and log mission times by year
coloured by space station programme (right)

The plot on the left shows that most mission times were short, especially before
1980, that there were a few very long missions, and that there was a group of
missions between about 4000 and 5000 minutes. The plot on the right show
that mostly the missions split into short ones of a week or so, that there were
longer ones of several months as part of space station programmes, that there
were some low mission times that required further investigation.

Changes include:

1. The logarithms of mission times have been used instead of the mission
   times as the plot then shows more structure. (Figure 10.5 revealed
   that it primarily splits the missions into whether they were to a space
   station or not.)

2. The breaks on the vertical axis scale were not set equally but chosen to
   reflect familiar time periods to make the times readily understandable.

3. The display was coloured by space station programme to explore the
   differences between the shorter and longer missions.

33.3.6 Euro 2020

For each team taking part in the Euro 2020 soccer competition, Figure 15.7 showed in which countries the players in the squad played. A default plot for this example is shown in Figure 33.11. The figure from Chapter 15 is replotted below.

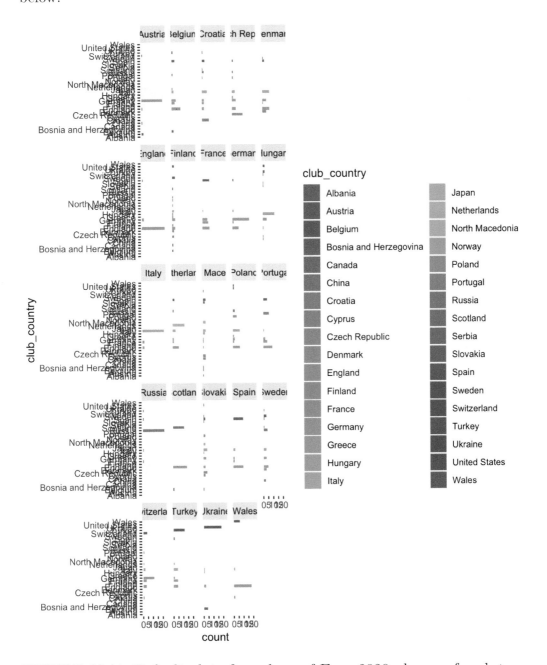

FIGURE 33.11: Default plot of numbers of Euro 2020 players of each team playing in other countries' leagues

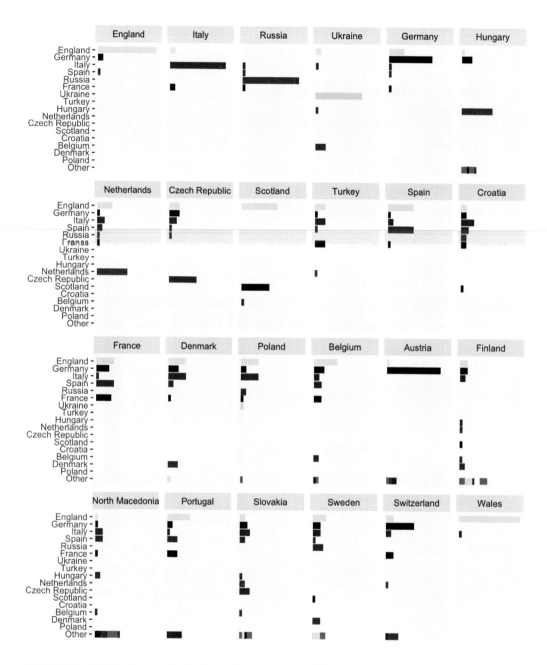

FIGURE 33.12: Amended plot of numbers of Euro 2020 players of each team playing in other countries' leagues

The first plot shows that some teams' players are from only a few countries' leagues and some from several. In the second plot the teams and leagues can be seen and individual patterns identified (e.g., England, Italy, Russia, Spain, Austria, Wales).

Changes include:

1. The teams have been ordered by the percentage of players playing in their own national league.

2. The bars have been ordered by the total number of players from that league playing in Euro 2020. Countries with less than 9 players have been grouped into "Other". This emphasises the more important leagues and makes the labels readable.

3. Colours close to country colours have been used instead of default colours.

4. The legend has been dropped as it takes up a lot of room (even with fewer countries) and the labels show what the colours mean.

5. The number of rows has been set to 4 to get a better balanced display and give more vertical space for the country labels of the leagues.

6. Axis title labels have been dropped leaving more space for the display.

7. The horizontal axis scale has been dropped as exact counts are not important. Extra space has been added to the ends of the scale to improve readability.

8. Gridlines have been removed to reduce clutter.

33.3.7   Characteristic changes

1. Grouping information supports understanding. It is easier to work with chunks of information than with all the individual components. Grouping may be achieved by spatial separation (Figure 33.8), by faceting (Figures 33.7 and 33.9), by colour (Figures 33.8 and 33.10).

2. Plot aspect ratios are important (Figures 33.6 and 33.8).

3. Ordering is an effective way of emphasising patterns (Figures 33.9 and 33.12).

4. Colour is a powerful tool and should be chosen with care (Figures 33.6, 33.7, and 33.10).

5. Reducing clutter and making space by reformatting or by excluding less important cases is always worth considering (Figure 33.7 and Figure 33.12).

6. Scaling and labelling should be sufficient but not excessive (Figures 33.9 and 33.12).

7. Time scaling and labelling should be chosen carefully (Figures 33.6 and 33.10).

8. Adding guidelines for critical values is useful (Figures 33.6 and 33.8).

33.4   Classifying graphics

Graphics may be classified in different ways and a number of terms are used. Data graphics generally refers to displays of raw data. Model graphics implies displays associated with models, such as plots of predictions or residuals, plots of parameter estimates or of statistics for comparing models. Multivariate graphics includes displays showing many variables such as parallel coordinate plots and mosaicplots, small multiples including facetings, and dimension reduction displays such as biplots and multidimensional scaling plots. Interactive graphics describes displays which can be directly manipulated: queried, sorted, reformatted, linked across multiple displays. Dynamic graphics means displays which can be set in motion, such as rotating plots and animated plots. There is some overlap between interactive and dynamic graphics, but the emphasis with the former is on interaction and the emphasis with the latter is on dynamics. And there are further terms mentioned in the literature.

It is not just the technical aspects and the data background that affect the use of graphics. The setting is important. This can range from a publication of a research project in a specialist field to an item on the television news about the progress of an epidemic. In some circumstances a graphic may be paid close attention, in others the graphic may be competing for attention. Sometimes much must be explained, sometimes it is safe to assume substantive knowledge on the part of the graphic's viewers. Graphics are not an easy matter.

Main points

- Not all graphics that look the same are the same. Context matters.
- Ensembles of plots require coherence of look, theme, alignment, scales, and formatting.
- Graphics can be changed in many ways and describing why a change has been made is more enlightening than describing how it has been made.

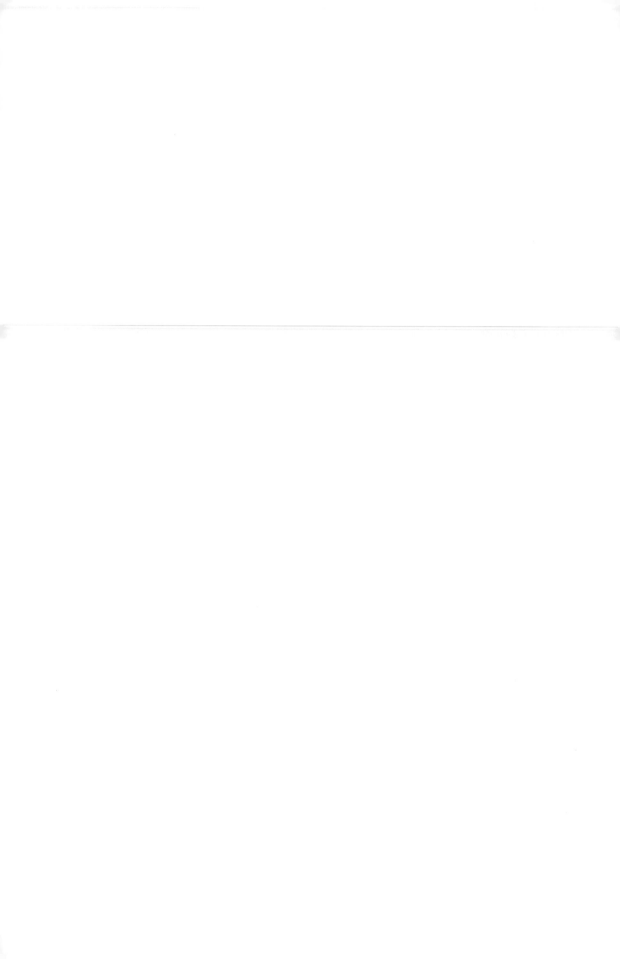

34

Conclusions and recommendations

Knowledge is knowing that a tomato is a fruit; wisdom is not putting it in a fruit salad.

— Miles Kington

Studying and thinking with graphics is different. It is about staying flexible, being open to new ideas, drawing many graphics—varying, amending, and adjusting them. Text is read in a given order, a graphic may be viewed in any order. Sometimes the information in a graphic is obvious, sometimes it takes more time and effort to see what is there. The graphic has to be "grounded", based on a firm foundation of background knowledge. You need time to think and space to view.

This book has concentrated on exploratory graphics rather than presentation graphics. The difference is not a simple dichotomy. There are raw exploratory graphics, drawn quickly for content and relying on good defaults. There are amended exploratory graphics with adjustments and improvements to emphasise features. Finally there are polished presentation graphics to attract attention and to impress. Some of the graphics in the examples have been adjusted and amended more than others, often because studying graphics stimulates you to modify them and improving them supports your thinking about the graphics. Some exploratory graphics can be much improved with a few adjustments and amendments. Some default graphics can look fairly bad unless something is done about them.

Where there is a difference between exploratory and presentation graphics is in the workflow. Exploratory graphics are studied to discover information, to look for content, and there may be many different graphics. To get the most value from them, you have to have expectations of what you might see. Presentation graphics are drawn to present information, to improve their look, and, while there may be many drafts of related ones, at most a few are shown. To draw an effective presentation graphic, you have to have a picture of what you want others to see.

There are no piecharts, waffle charts, pictograms or examples of the many other chart types there are in this book. This is no reflection on them. Everyone can use the charts they find most informative. The general advice on layout, colour, ordering, formatting, and so on applies just as well to these chart types as to those in the book. Varying graphics, using many of them, and checking insights is good practice whichever graphic forms are used.

Several interesting and important topics for graphics deserve more attention. Some like perception, design, and displaying uncertainty are more relevant for presentation graphics. Some like graphics for spatial data are more specialist. Interactive graphics really deserves a book of its own—once there is suitable software that is sufficiently fast, flexible, effective, and integrated with other systems.

The datasets in the book have been chosen because they were interesting and because they were available. There was no attempt to pick datasets to illustrate or show off particular graphical tools. Graphics reveal more information in some datasets than in others. For every statistical method of whatever kind, whether a graphic or a model, there is doubtless an Achilles heel dataset that it just cannot cope with. Suggestions of such datasets would be welcome.

Some claim that 10,000 hours of deliberate practice is enough to turn a person into an expert. The key word is the undefined 'deliberate'. Reading the case studies, evaluating the graphics, and trying out alternatives might well be a good step in the right direction. Check the results produced using your own graphics. Look for other results by questioning the book's datasets and by studying datasets of your own.

References

28East. 2022. "Comrades Marathon 2020 Interactive Map." https://comrades
.28east.co.za/.

Abbott, Karen. 2012. "The 1904 Olympic Marathon May Have Been the
Strangest Ever." https://www.smithsonianmag.com/history/the-1904-
olympic-marathon-may-have-been-the-strangest-ever-14910747/.

Abel, Guy. 2021. "uefa-Ec." https://github.com/guyabel/uefa-ec/.

Amaliah, Dewi, Dianne Cook, Emi Tanaka, Kate Hyde, and Nicholas Tierney.
2022. "A Journey from Wild to Textbook Data to Reproducibly Refresh
the Wages Data from the National Longitudinal Survey of Youth Database."
https://arxiv.org/abs/2205.06417; arXiv.

Andrews, R. 2019. *Info We Trust*. Wiley.

Arndt, L., T. Koleala, and Á. Orbán. 2021. "Magneto-Optical Diagnosis of
Symptomatic Malaria in Papua New Guinea." *Nature Communications* 12,
969: 1–10.

Asensio, Omar, Camila Apablaza, M. Cade Lawson, and Sarah Walsh. 2021a.
"A Field Experiment on Workplace Norms and Electric Vehicle Charging
Etiquette." *Journal of Industrial Ecology.* https://onlinelibrary.wiley.com/
doi/abs/10.1111/jiec.13116.

Asensio, Omar, C. Apablaza, M. Cade Lawson, and S. Walsh. 2021b. "Replication Data for: A Field Experiment on Workplace Norms and Electric
Vehicle Charging Etiquette." https://doi.org/10.7910/DVN/NFPQLW.

Becker, Richard A., William S. Cleveland, and M. J. Shyu. 1996. "The Visual
Design and Control of Trellis Display." *Journal of Computational and
Graphical Statistics* 5 (2): 123–55.

Bertin, Jacques. 1973. *Semiologie Graphique*. 2nd ed. The Hague: Mouton-
Gautier.

———. 2010. *Semiology of Graphics*. Redlands, California: Esri Press.

Bialik, Carl. 2008. "Starbucks Stays Mum on Drink Math." https://www.wsj.
com/articles/BL-NB-309.

Bilalic, M., K. Smallbone, P. McLeod, and F. Gobet. 2009. "Why Are (the Best)
Women so Good at Chess? Participation Rates and Gender Differences in
Intellectual Domains." *Proc. R. Soc. B* 276: 1161–65.

Bivand, Roger. 2020. "Why Have CRS, Projections and Transformations
Changed?" https://rgdal.r-forge.r-project.org/articles/CRS_projections_t
ransformations.html.

Blonder, B. 2019. *Hypervolume.* https://CRAN.R-project.org/package=hype rvolume.

Bouveyron, Charles, Gilles Celeux, Brendan Murphy, and Adrian Raftery. 2019. *Model-Based Clustering and Classification for Data Science: With Applications in R.* Cambridge University Press.

Bremer, Nadieh, and Shirley Wu. 2021. *Data Sketches.* Boca Raton, Florida: Chapman & Hall/CRC.

Bundesamt, Statistisches. 2021. "Der Bundeswahlleiter." https://www.bundes wahlleiter.de.

Buolamwini, Joy, and Timnit Gebru. 2018. "Gender Shades: Intersectional Accuracy Disparities in Commercial Gender Classification." *Proceedings of Machine Learning Research* 81: 1–15.

Cairo, Alberto. 2012. *The Functional Art.* San Francisco: New Riders.

———. 2016. *The Truthful Art.* San Francisco: New Riders.

———. 2019. *How Charts Lie: Getting Smarter about Visual Information.* W. W. Norton.

Carr, Dan, Richard J. Littlefield, Wesley L. Nicholson, and J. S. Littlefield. 1987. "Scatterplot Matrix Techniques for Large n." *JASA* 82 (398): 424–36.

Chang, Winston. 2018. *R Graphics Cookbook.* 2nd ed. Beijing: O'Reilly Media.

Cleveland, William S. 1993. *Visualizing Data.* Summit, New Jersey: Hobart Press.

———. 1994. *The Elements of Graphing Data.* Revised. Summit, New Jersey: Hobart Press.

Cleveland, William S., and Robert McGill. 1987. "Graphical Perception: The Visual Decoding of Quantitative Information on Graphical Displays of Data." *Journal of the Royal Statistical Society A* 150 (3): 192–229.

Collier, Andrew. 2019. "Datawookie." https://datawookie.dev/.

Comrades Marathon Association. 2022. "Comrades Marathon." https://www. comrades.com.

Corlett, Tatsuya, Mariya Stavnichuk, and Svetlana Komarova. 2020. "Population Analysis of Space Travelers." *Life Sciences in Space Research* 27: 1–5.

Coulmont, Baptiste. 2010. "Cartographie Avec R." http://coulmont.com/carte s/rcarto.pdf.

Curley, James. 2016. "EnglishSoccer." http://fivethirtyeight.com/contributors/ james-curley/.

———. 2022. *engsoccerdata.* https://github.com/jalapic/engsoccerdata.

Ehrenhaft, Felix. 1910. "Über Eine Neue Methode Zur Messung von Elektrizitätsmengen, Die Kleiner Zu Sein Scheinen Als Die Ladung Des Einwertigen Wasserstoff-Ions Oder Elektrons Und von Dessen Vielfachen Abweichen." *Physik. Zeitschr.* XI: 940–52.

Elo, Arpad. 1978. *The Rating of Chess Players, Past and Present.* 1st ed. New York: Arco.

"Encyclopedia Titanica." 2021. https://www.encyclopedia-titanica.org/.

English, Colleen. 2015. ""Not a Very Edifying Spectacle": The Controversial Women's 800-Meter Race in the 1928 Olympics." https://ussporthistory.com/2015/10/08/not-a-very-edifying-spectacle-the-controversial-womens-800-meter-race-in-the-1928-olympics/.

Environmental Protection Agency. 2021. "Fuel Economy." https://www.fueleconomy.gov.

FIDE. 2020. "International Chess Federation Ratings." https://ratings.fide.com.

FINA. 2021. "Fédération Internationale de Natation." https://www.fina.org.

Fountain, Henry. 2022. "Where the Ice Is Still Abundant, These Penguins Are, Too." https://www.nytimes.com/2022/04/12/climate/antarctica-penguins.html.

Friendly, Michael. 2007. "A.-M. Guerry's Moral Statistics of France: Challenges for Multivariable Spatial Analysis." *Statistical Science* 22 (3): 368–99.

———. 2008. "A Brief History of Data Visualization." In *Handbook of Data Visualization*, edited by C. H. Chen, W. Haerdle, and A. Unwin, 15–56. New York: Springer.

Friendly, Michael, and Howard Wainer. 2021. *A History of Data Visualization and Graphic Communication.* Cambridge, Massachusetts: Harvard University Press.

Gabelica, Mirko, Ružica Bojčić, and Livia Puljak. 2022. "Many Researchers Were Not Compliant with Their Published Data Sharing Statement: Mixed-Methods Study." *Journal of Clinical Epidemiology.* https://doi.org/10.1016/j.jclinepi.2022.05.019.

Gelman, Andrew, Jennifer Hill, and Aki Vehtari. 2020. *Regression and Other Stories.* Cambridge: Cambridge University Press.

Giordani, P., M. Ferraro, and F. Martella. 2020. *An Introduction to Clustering with R.* Singapore: Springer.

Gómez-Ruano, Miguel, Richard Pollard, and Carlos Lago-Peñas. 2022. *Home Advantage in Sport.* Routledge.

Gorman, K., A. Williams, and W. Fraser. 2014. "Ecological Sexual Dimorphism and Environmental Variability Within a Community of Antarctic Penguins (Genus Pygoscelis)." *PLoS ONE* 9 (3). https://doi.org/10.1371/journal.pone.0090081.

Grant, Peter, and Rosemary Grant. 2014. *40 Years of Evolution: Darwin's Finches on Daphne Major Island.* Princeton University Press.

Griffin, Randi. 2019. "Olympics." https://www.kaggle.com/datasets/heesoo37/120-years-of-olympic-history-athletes-and-results.

Groot, Adriaan de. 1978. *Thought and Choice in Chess*. 2nd ed. The Hague: Mouton.

Hastorf, Albert, and Hadley Cantril. 1954. "They Saw a Game." *Journal of Abnormal and Social Psychology* 49: 129–34.

Healey, Christopher, and James Enns. 2012. "Attention and Visual Memory in Visualization and Computer Graphics." *IEEE Transactions on Visualization and Computer Graphics* 18 (7): 1170–88.

Healy, Kieran. 2018. *Data Visualization: A Practical Introduction*. Princeton University Press. https://books.google.de/books?id=o6BYtgEACAAJ.

Heinz, G., L. Peterson, R. Johnson, and C. Kerk. 2003. "Exploring Relationships in Body Dimensions." *Journal of Statistics Education* 11 (2).

Hoare, C. A. R. 1981. "The Emperor's Old Clothes." *Communications of the ACM* 24 (2): 75–83.

Hofmann, Heike. 2008. "Mosaic Plots and Their Variants." In *Handbook of Data Visualization*, edited by C. H. Chen, W. Haerdle, and A. Unwin, 617–42. Springer.

Hofmann, Heike, Susan VanderPlas, and Yawei Ge. 2022. *ggpcp: Parallel Coordinate Plots in the Ggplot2 Framework*. https://github.com/heike/ggpcp.

Hofmann, Heike, Hadley Wickham, and Karen Kafadar. 2017. "Letter-Value Plots: Boxplots for Large Data." *Journal of Computational and Graphical Statistics* 26 (3): 469–77.

Holton, Gerald. 1978. "Subelectrons, Presuppositions, and the Millikan-Ehrenhaft Dispute." *Historical Studies in the Physical Sciences* 9: 161–224.

Holtz, Yan. 2018. "R Graph Gallery." https://r-graph-gallery.com.

Horst, Allison, Alison Hill, and Kristen Gorman. 2020. *palmerpenguins*. https://allisonhorst.github.io/palmerpenguins/.

Hothorn, Torsten. 2020. "Most Likely Transformations: The Mlt Package." *Journal of Statistical Software* 92 (1): 1–68. https://www.jstatsoft.org/article/view/v092i01.

Hothorn, Torsten, J. Müller, L. Held, L. Möst, and A. Mysterud. 2015. "Temporal Patterns of Deer–Vehicle Collisions Consistent with Deer Activity Pattern and Density Increase but Not General Accident Risk." *Accident Analysis & Prevention* 81: 143–52.

Huebner, Marianne, Werner Vach, Saskia le Cessie, Carsten Oliver Schmidt, and Lara Lusa. 2020. "Hidden Analyses: A Review of Reporting Practice and Recommendations for More Transparent Reporting of Initial Data Analyses." *BMC Medical Research Methodology*, 1–10. https://doi.org/10.1186/s12874-020-00942-y.

Humphries, G. R. W., R. Naveen, M. Schwaller, C. Che-Castaldo, P. McDowall, M. Schrimpf, and H. J. Lynch. 2017. "Mapping Application for Penguin

Populations and Projected Dynamics (MAPPPD): Data and Tools for Dynamic Management and Decision Support." *Polar Record* 53 (2): 160–66.

IAAF. 2001. *Scoring Tables for Combined Events.* Monaco: IAAF.

IMDb. 2022. "Internet Movie Database." https://datasets.imdbws.com.

IOC. 2022. "Olympic Games." https://olympics.com/en/.

Kandogan, E., and H. Lee. 2016. "A Grounded Theory Study on the Language of Data Visualization Principles and Guidelines." *Electronic Imaging*, no. 16: 1–9.

Kirk, Andy. 2016. *Data Visualisation—a Handbook for Data Driven Design.* Los Angeles: Sage.

———. 2023. "Visualising Data." https://www.visualisingdata.com.

Lebret, Rémi, Serge Iovleff, Florent Langrognet, Christophe Biernacki, Gilles Celeux, and Gérard Govaert. 2015. "Rmixmod: The R Package of the Model-Based Unsupervised, Supervised, and Semi-Supervised Classification Mixmod Library." *Journal of Statistical Software* 67 (6): 1–29.

Lindgren, M. 2014. "Guesstimating Life Expectancy for Disasters." https://www.gapminder.org/data/documentation/gd004/.

Link, Arthur. 1947. *Wilson, Vol i: The Road to the White House.* Princeton, New Jersey: Princeton University Press.

MacKay, R. Jock, and Wayne Oldford. 2000. "Scientific Method, Statistical Method and the Speed of Light." *Statistical Science* 15 (3): 254–78.

marastats. 2019. "General Marathon Stats." https://marastats.com/marathon/.

Marbac, Matthieu, Christophe Biernacki, and Vincent Vandewalle. 2016. *Co-Modes.* https://rdrr.io/rforge/CoModes/man/.

McCandless, David. 2022. "Colours in Culture." https://www.informationisbeautiful.net/visualizations/colours-in-cultures/.

Meirelles, Isabel. 2013. *Design for Information.* Rockport Publishers.

Meng, Xiao-Li. 2021. "Enhancing (Publications on) Data Quality: Deeper Data Minding and Fuller Data Confession." *JRSS A* 184: 1161–75.

Michelson, Albert. 1880. "Experimental Determination of the Velocity of Light Made at the U.S. Naval Academy, Annapolis." *Astronomical Papers* 1: 109–45. https://books.google.de/books?id=343nAAAAMAAJ.

———. 1927. "Measurement of the Velocity of Light Between Mount Wilson and Mount San Antonio." *Astrophysical Journal* LXV: 1–22.

Mohammad, Saif. 2011. "Colourful Language: Measuring Word-Colour Associations." In *CMCL@ACL*. https://api.semanticscholar.org/CorpusID:3924081.

Munzner, Tamara. 2014. *Visualization Analysis & Design.* CRC Press.

Murrell, Paul. 2018. *R Graphics.* 3rd ed. London: Chapman & Hall.

National Science Foundation. 2022. "Long Term Ecological Research Network." https://lternet.edu.

Newcomb, Simon. 1891. "Measures of the Velocity of Light Made Under the Direction of the Secretary of the Navy During the Years 1880-1882." *Astronomical Papers* 2: 107–230.

Nicault, Christophe. 2021. "History of National Olympic Committees Participating in the Olympic Summer Games." https://www.christophenicault.com/pages/visualizations/.

Oppenheim, F. 1970. *The History of Swimming*. North Hollywood, California: Swimming World.

Ornithology, Cornell Lab of. 2022. "EBird." https://ebird.org.

Playfair, William. 2005. *Playfair's Commercial and Political Atlas and Statistical Breviary*. Cambridge: Cambridge University Press.

Posavec, Stefanie, and Giorgia Lupi. 2016. *Dear Data*. Particular Books.

Potter, Mary, Brad Wyble, Carl Erick Hagmann, and Emily McCourt. 2014. "Detecting Meaning in RSVP at 13 ms per picture." *Attention, Perception, and Psychophysics* 76: 270–79.

PSI. 2021a. "DLQI." https://github.com/VIS-SIG/Wonderful-Wednesdays/tree/master/data/2021/2021-01-13.

———. 2021b. "Wonderful Wednesdays." https://www.psiweb.org/sigs-special-interest-groups/visualisation/welcome-to-wonderful-wednesdays.

R Core Team. 2023. *R: A Language and Environment for Statistical Computing*. Vienna, Austria: R Foundation for Statistical Computing. http://www.R-project.org/.

Rahlf, Thomas. 2017. *Data Visualisation with r — 100 Examples*. Cham, Switzerland: Springer.

Rendgen, Sandra. 2019. *The Minard System*. Princeton Architectural Press.

rfordatascience. 2020a. "Astronaut Database." https://github.com/rfordatascience/tidytuesday/tree/master/data/2020/2020-07-14.

———. 2020b. "Tidy Tuesday." https://github.com/rfordatascience/tidytuesday.

Robinson, Roger. 2012. ""Eleven Wretched Women"." https://www.runnersworld.com/advanced/a20802639/eleven-wretched-women/.

Rosling, Hans. 2009. "The Best Stats You've Ever Seen." https://www.ted.com/talks/hans_rosling_the_best_stats_you_ve_ever_seen?

———. 2013. "Gapminder." http://www.gapminder.org.

Sackett, David, and Michael Gent. 1979. "Controversy in Counting and Attributing Events in Clinical Trials." *New England Journal of Medicine* 301: 1410–12.

Salmistu, J. 2021. "Decathlon2000." http://www.decathlon2000.com/eng/.

Sarkar, Deepayan. 2008. *Lattice: Multivariate Data Visualization with R*. useR. New York: Springer.

Schwabish, Jon. 2021. *Better Data Visualizations*. New York: Columbia University Press.

Singer-Vine, Jeremy. 2020. "Data Is Plural." https://tinyletter.com/data-is-plural.

Smith, Alan. 2022. *Bookdown: Authoring Books and Technical Documents with R Markdown.* Harlow, England: Pearson.

Snodgrass, Robert, and Edmund Heller. 1904. "Papers from the Hopkins-Stanford Galapagos Expedition, 1898-99. XVI. Birds." *Proceedings of the Washington Academy of Sciences* V: 231–372.

———. 2008. "Data from: Papers from the Hopkins-Stanford Galapagos Expedition, 1898-99. XVI. Birds." http://datadryad.org/resource/doi:10.5061/dryad.152; The Dryad Digital Repository.

Spear, Mary E. 1969. *Practical Charting Techniques.* New York: McGraw Hill.

Spearing, Harry, Jonathan Tawn, David Irons, Tim Paulden, and Grace Bennett. 2021. "Ranking, and Other Properties, of Elite Swimmers Using Extreme Value Theory." *JRSS A* 184: 368–95.

St Clair, Kassia. 2016. *The Secret Lives of Colour.* London: John Murray.

Stigler, Stephen. 1977. "Do Robust Estimators Work with Real Data?" *Annals of Statistics* 5 (6): 1055–98.

———. 2019. "Data Have a Limited Shelf Life." *Harvard Data Science Review* 1 (2).

Stratton, K. 2019. "Comrades Marathon." https://www.kaggle.com/suugaku/comrades-marathon-results/.

Student. 1931. "The Lanarkshire Milk Experiment." *Biometrika* 23 (3/4): 398–406.

Thau, Mads, Maria Falk Mikkelsen, Morten Hjortskov, and Mogens Jin Pedersen. 2021. "Question Order Bias Revisited: A Split-Ballot Experiment on Satisfaction with Public Services Among Experienced and Professional Users." *Public Administration* 99 (1): 189–204.

Theeuwes, Jan. 2018. "Visual Selection: Usually Fast and Automatic; Seldom Slow and Volitional." *Journal of Cognition* 1 (1): 1–15.

Tonnessen, E. 2020. "What Is Visual-Numeric Literacy, and How Does It Work?" In *Data Visualization in Society,* edited by M. Engebretsen and H. Kennedy, 189–206. Amsterdam University Press. http://www.jstor.org/stable/j.ctvzgb8c7.18.

Tufte, Edward. 1983. *The Visual Display of Quantitative Information.* Cheshire, Connecticut: Graphics Press.

———. 1990. *Envisioning Information.* Cheshire, Connecticut: Graphics Press.

———. 1997. *Visual Explanations.* Cheshire, Connecticut: Graphics Press.

———. 2001. *The Visual Display of Quantitative Information.* 2nd ed. Cheshire, Connecticut: Graphics Press.

Tversky, Barbara. 2019. *Mind in Motion.* New York: Basic Books.

University of California, Berkeley, and Max Planck Institute for Demographic Research. 2022. "Human Mortality Database." https://www.mortality.org.

Unwin, Antony. 2015. *Graphical Data Analysis with R*. Boca Raton, Florida: Chapman & Hall/CRC.

———. 2024. *UpAndDownPlots: Displays Percentage and Absolute Changes*. https://CRAN.R-project.org/package=UpAndDownPlots.

Unwin, Antony, and Pedro Valero-Mora. 2018. "Ensemble Graphics." *Journal of Computational and Graphical Statistics* 27 (1): 157–65.

Valentin, Francois. 2022. "Valentin Twitter." https://twitter.com/Valen10Francois/.

Wainer, Howard. 1997. *Visual Revelations*. New York: Springer.

———. 2004. *Graphic Discovery: A Trout in the Milk and Other Visual Adventures*. Princeton, New Jersey: Princeton University Press.

Ware, Colin. 2020. *Information Visualization: Perception for Design*. 4th ed. San Francisco, California: Morgan Kaufmann.

Wehrli, Urs. 2004. *Tidying up Art*. Zürich: Prestel.

Weiner, Jonathan. 1994. *The Beak of the Finch*. Jonathan Cape.

Wickham, Hadley. 2007. "Diamonds in the Rough." http://www.diamondse.info/.

———. 2016. *ggplot2: Elegant Graphics for Data Analysis*. 2nd ed. Springer-Verlag New York. https://ggplot2.tidyverse.org.

———. 2019. *Tidyverse: Easily Install and Load the 'Tidyverse'*. https://CRAN.R-project.org/package=tidyr.

———. 2022. "ggplot2." https://ggplot2-book.org.

———. 2023. *ggplot2: Create Elegant Data Visualisations Using the Grammar of Graphics*. https://CRAN.R-project.org/package=ggplot2.

Wickham, Hadley, Di Cook, Heike Hofmann, and Andreas Buja. 2011. "Graphical Inference for Infovis." *IEEE Transactions on Visualization and Computer Graphics* 16: 973–79.

Wikipedia. 2020a. "Bill Nelson." https://en.wikipedia.org/wiki/Bill_Nelson.

———. 2020b. "List of Human Spaceflights." https://en.wikipedia.org/wiki/List_of_human_spaceflights.

———. 2020c. "The Blue Banana." https://en.wikipedia.org/wiki/Blue_Banana.

———. 2021. "Positive and Negative Predicted Values." https://en.wikipedia.org/wiki/Positive_and_negative_predictive_values.

———. 2022. "Comrades Marathon." https://en.wikipedia.org/wiki/Comrades_Marathon.

Wilke, Claus. 2019. *Fundamentals of Data Visualization: A Primer on Making Informative and Compelling Figures*. O'Reilly Media. https://books.google.de/books?id=L3ajtgEACAAJ.

Wilkinson, Leland. 1999. *The Grammar of Graphics*. 1st ed. New York: Springer.

———. 2005. *The Grammar of Graphics*. 2nd ed. New York: Springer.

Wilson, Greg, D. A. Aruliah, C. Titus Brown, Neil Chue Hong, Matt Davis, Richard Guy, et al. 2014. "Best Practices for Scientific Computing." *PLoS Biol* 12. https://doi.org/10.1371/journal.pbio.1001745.

Wood, Jo, A. Kachkaev, and Jason Dykes. 2018. "Design Exposition with Literate Visualization." *IEEE Transactions on Visualization and Computer Graphics* 25 (1).

Woodson, Urey. 1912. *Official Report of the Proceedings of the Democratic National Convention*. Chicago: Peterson linotyping Company.

Worldbank. 2020. "World Bank Open Data." https://data.worldbank.org.

Wright, Kevin. 2022. *Agridat*. https://CRAN.R-project.org/package=agridat.

xkcd. 2012. "Significant." https://xkcd.com/882/.

Youden, William. 1972. "Enduring Values." *Technometrics* 14 (1): 1–11.

Zeileis, Achim, Jason Fisher, Kurt Hornik, Ross Ihaka, Claire McWhite, Paul Murrell, Reto Stauffer, and Claus Wilke. 2020. "Colorspace: A Toolbox for Manipulating and Assessing Colors and Palettes." *Journal of Statistical Software* 96 (1): 1–49.

Index

For Product Safety Concerns and Information please contact our
EU representative GPSR@taylorandfrancis.com Taylor & Francis
Verlag GmbH, Kaufingerstraße 24, 80331 München, Germany